ANIMALS, GODS AND HUMANS

Ingvild Sælid Gilhus explores the transition from traditional Greek and Roman religion to Christianity in the Roman Empire and the effect of this change on how animals were regarded, illustrating the main factors in the creation of a Christian conception of animals. One of the underlying assumptions of the book is that changes in the way animal motifs are used and the way human–animal relations are conceptualized serve as indicators of more general cultural shifts. Gilhus attests that in late antiquity, animals were used as symbols in a general redefinition of cultural values and assumptions.

A wide range of key texts are consulted, ranging from philosophical treatises to novels and poems on metamorphoses; from biographies of holy men such as Apollonius of Tyana and Antony, the Christian desert ascetic, to natural history; from the New Testament via Gnostic texts to the Church fathers; from pagan and Christian criticism of animal sacrifice to the acts of the martyrs. Both the pagan and the Christian conception of animals remained rich and multi-layered through the centuries, and this book presents the dominant themes and developments in the conception of animals without losing that complexity.

Ingvild Sælid Gilhus is professor of the History of Religions at the University of Bergen. Her publications include *Laughing Gods, Weeping Virgins* (Routledge 1997).

ANIMALS, GODS AND HUMANS

Changing Attitudes to Animals in Greek, Roman and Early Christian Ideas

Ingvild Sælid Gilhus

Routledge
Taylor & Francis Group

LONDON AND NEW YORK

First published 2006
by Routledge
2 Park Square, Milton Park, Abingdon, Oxon OX14 4RN

Simultaneously published in the USA and Canada
by Routledge
711 Third Ave, New York, NY 10017

*Routledge is an imprint of the Taylor & Francis Group, an
informa business*

© 2006 Ingvild Sælid Gilhus

Typeset in Garamond by Taylor & Francis Books

British Library Cataloguing in Publication Data
A catalogue record for this book is available from the British Library

Library of Congress Cataloging in Publication Data
A catalog record for this book has been requested

ISBN10: 0-415-38649-7 (hbk)
ISBN10: 0-415-38650-0 (pbk)

ISBN13: 978-0-415-38649-4 (hbk)
ISBN13: 978-0-415-38650-0 (pbk)

CONTENTS

CONTENTS

ACKNOWLEDGEMENTS

This study of animals in ancient religion started as part of a cross-disciplinary research project, "The construction of Christian identity in antiquity," funded by the Norwegian Research Council. By means of this project our research group established Christian antiquity as a distinct and interdisciplinary field of study in Norway. The stimulating environment created in this group has been a great inspiration for this study of animals. I am deeply indebted to those involved, especially to Halvor Moxness who was instrumental in getting the idea of a joint project on Christian antiquity to materialize.

I will like to thank all my colleagues of the interdisciplinary milieu of the Institute of Classic Philology, Russian and the History of Religions at the University of Bergen for inspiring seminaries, interesting discussions and constructiv criticism.

During the last three years the study of animals has been continued in a small research group focusing on life-processes and body in antiquity, funded by the Norwegian Research Council. I want to thank Dag Øistein Endsjø, Hugo Lundhaug, Turid Karlsen Seim and Gunhild Vidén for critical reading, fruitful discussions and inspiration.

My thanks are also due to Siv Ellen Kraft and Richard H. Pierce for helpful comments on parts of the manuscript. My friend and colleague Lisbeth Mikaelsson has been a great support during all the ups and downs of the project. Troels Engberg-Pedersen generously offered to read the whole manuscript, I am grateful for his careful reading.

I extend my thanks to the anonymous reviewers of Routledge who provided many valuable suggestions. I further want to thank the librarians at the University Library, Bergen, especially Kari Nordmo, who have always provided me with the books I needed. I offer my sincere thanks to Marite Sapiets for improving my English.

I would like to thank Walter de Gruyter and the Swedish Institute in Rome for permission to reprint revised versions of previously published papers. Chapter 11 contains part of my article "... you have dreamt that our God is an ass's head": Animals and Christians in Antiquity", published in

Michael Stausberg (ed), *Kontinuitäten und Brüche in der Religionsgeschichte*, Berlin/New York: Walter de Gruyter, 2001, pp. 210–221. Chapter 7 contains revised portions of my article "The animal sacrifice and its critics", published in Barbro Santillo Frizell (ed), *PECUS. Man and Animal in Antiquity*, Rome 2004, pp. 116–120.

As for institutional support, I am grateful to the University of Bergen for excellent working conditions and to the Norwegian Research Council for grants.

Finally, with all my heart I thank my husband Nils Erik Gilhus for his unfaltering encouragement and never failing support.

Ingvild Sælid Gilhus
July 2005

INTRODUCTION

Animals, gods and humans

Animals are beings with which we may have social relations. We feel sympathy and affection for them, but we also exploit them for our own benefit, for company, sport or nourishment. They are persons and things, friends and food. We communicate with animals, but we also kill, cook and eat them. Animals are similar to us as well as different from us, which encourages us to imagine ourselves as them to conceptualize our own being and to use them as symbols to make sense of our world.

Our thinking about animals is not simple, any more than our feelings for them are straightforward. There is a conflict between our friendliness for some animals and our fear of others, also between our economic interest in them and a natural empathy for living beings when we have the imagination to think of ourselves in their place. By arousing contradictory thoughts and a multitude of emotions, animals become natural symbols and such stuff as myths are made of.

The relationship between animals and humans is a relationship between one species and a tremendous variety of others. Even if we feel that there is an unbridgeable gap between our species and all others, this gap is viewed differently with regard to different species, which contributes to making the relationship between humans and animals extremely complex (Midgley 1988). How kinship and otherness, closeness and distance between humans and animals are experienced and expressed varies in different types of discourse, and different cultural interpretations may be made of the same animal.

In religions, animals appear as the third party in the interaction between gods and human beings, often as mediators. In this trinity, animals and humans share a flesh-and-blood reality, while gods are creatures of human imagination and tradition. This does not necessarily mean that gods are seen as less real than humans and animals – usually they are thought of as more real. Rituals function above all to establish and confirm the reality of the gods. Killing animals in honour of them and offering them part of the meat from the sacrifice was one way in which their reality was established.

1

Historical changes and outdated answers

At some points in history, major changes occur in the religious meaning and functions of animals. This was so in India nearly three thousand years ago, when the sacrificing of animals was replaced by bloodless offerings, eating meat was deemed less pure than a vegetarian diet, and doing no injury to any living being became a universal ethical command in Brahmanical lawbooks (Jacobsen 1994). In England, attitudes to the natural world changed in the early modern period. Animals were viewed with increasing sympathy, and even writers in the Christian tradition no longer saw animals as made solely for human sustenance (Thomas 1984: 166). In late antiquity, a major change appeared, when the main religious institution, the animal sacrifice, was replaced by Christian rituals, which no longer included any offering of animal flesh. At the same time, Christians continued to employ a sacrificial terminology. They regarded the death of Christ as fulfilling the sacrificial rites of the Old Testament and used the sacrificial lamb as a symbol for Christ (Snyder 1991: 14–15). With Christianity, the human body became the key symbol in a religion that focused on the death and resurrection of Christ, and the ultimate hope of believers was their own bodily resurrection.

This change from a sacrificial cult, where the animal body had been a key symbol, to the Christian cult, where the human body became the new key symbol, is one of the dramatic changes in the history of religions. What this change implied for the way human beings, through symbols, myths and rituals, imagined their relationship with the rest of the living world has been remarkably little investigated.

Few have found it strange that the bloodless cults of Christianity replaced the sacrificial cults of the Roman Empire. The reason why the worship of gods by means of animal sacrifices gave way to the cult of Christ has not been discussed very much. This curious lack of research may be due to a combination of assumptions based on evolutionism and implicit Christian beliefs.[1]

That the religious significance of animals was discussed for so long in the context of cultural evolutionism has associated the problem with an outdated way of thinking. The religious significance of animals is still mainly associated with earlier stages of cultural development, even if the evolutionistic paradigm on which these ideas were originally based has been rejected. Therefore, one reason why few have seriously asked why the bloodless cults of Christianity replaced the sacrificial cults of the Roman Empire is simply that this problem was regarded as solved. The solution was enlightenment and civilization. The slaughter of sacrificial victims is more primitive than bloodless cults, the worship of gods in animal form is a less advanced type of religion than the worship of gods in human forms, and polytheism is more primitive than monotheism. Seen from this perspective,

Christianity stands for cultural progress. In the case of animal sacrifice, furthermore, there has been a tendency to give universal answers to phenomena that in reality are extremely varied and perhaps have only a superficial resemblance (Bloch 1992).[2]

In the present study, we are dealing with a limited period in human history, the first to the fourth century CE, and a limited geographical area, the Mediterranean. Animal sacrifice did not originate in this period; on the contrary, it was brought to an end – at least in its traditional form. After it had been banned, people managed very well without killing their animals in a sacrificial and religious setting. The end of sacrifice did not mean that people stopped killing animals or that they declined to eat meat, only that they no longer did these things in religious settings. One difference between the earlier and later periods was that the butchering of animals, which had been a religious activity, was now secularized. However, the end of animal sacrifice did not mean the end of sacrificial ideology, which was continued in Christianity.

The transition from paganism to Christianity offers us an opportunity to look at the much debated question of the origin of sacrifice in a different way and ask other questions instead. We will not ask why people started to sacrifice animals (about which, when all is said and done, we can know very little) but rather why they stopped doing so. Why did the bloodless Christian cults replace animal sacrifice? We are better equipped to suggest reasons why sacrifice came to an end in late antiquity than to give a reason for its origin in prehistory.

If it is strange that the sacrificial cult came to an end, it is likewise strange that the change from a sacrificial non-Christian cult to a Christian cult was not accompanied by essential changes in diet, for instance by a turn to vegetarianism similar to the one we witness in India in the last millennium BCE – even more strange since the question of purity of food was an issue among the different religious factions and sects in the empire. Representatives of various religious elites, for instance the Stoic Seneca (1–65 CE), the Neopythagorean Apollonius of Tyana (*c.* 40–120 CE) and the Neoplatonist Porphyry (234–305 CE), abstained from eating flesh. Why was the sacrifice of animals discontinued apparently with no other dietary consequences for mainstream Christianity than that meat was desacralized?

Sacrifice is only one element in Graeco-Roman human–animal relations. As animal sacrifice lost its significance, the religious and moral value of animals was reduced in general. The lowering of the status of animals is reflected in philosophical debates between Aristotelians, Epicureans, Platonists, Neopythagoreans and Stoics in which the Stoic position gradually became dominant. According to the Stoics, *logos* is the categorical boundary marker between humans and animals, animals are *aloga* – creatures without reason. The degradation of animals is also to be seen when animal worship was used as an example of barbarism and regarded as a primitive form of religion. The growing importance of the arena with its massacres of animals could also reflect a devaluation of animals.

Two complementary religious processes that concerned the relationship between animals and humans were at work in the Graeco-Roman world. One was a sacralization of the human form, seen in several of the new cults, among them Christianity. The other was a desacralization of animals, a process that can be observed when the traditional sacrificial cult came to an end. The desacralization of animals is also to be seen in the criticism of people who were suspected of animal worship. It is as if animals and humans had been placed on two scales, and the scales had started to move apart. The humans were given greater religious value, the animals less. But even if the process of sacralization of humans and desacralization of animals was not Christian in origin, Christianity developed these processes further. They were given a final form and incorporated into the continuous cultural work of building a new Christian identity.

The study of animals

The present study owes much to several branches of cultural research. One includes the classic studies of animals in religions. In the heyday of evolutionism, totemism and the religion of hunters and gatherers were the main contexts for the discussion of the religious function of animals (Willis 1994: 1–24). This discussion focused on totemism as a social system, but it sometimes also stressed the nutritional value of the animals involved in this system. However, the debate about totemism took a new course in 1962, when Claude Lévi-Strauss said that natural species are chosen, not because they are "good to eat" but because they are "good to think" (Lévi-Strauss 1962: 127–8). From that point on, totemism has mainly been regarded as a system of symbols where animals appear as "chiffres" and as illustrations of human thought processes. However, it must be pointed out that the structuralist turn initiated by Lévi-Strauss, although it offered a fruitful new perspective, also implied a reduction in the broader significance of animals. One point was that economic factors in the relations between animals and humans were downplayed; another was that emotional factors were overlooked. Animals are not only good to think, they are also good to "feel", and they give emotional value and impetus to anything they are linked with. That at least is one of the reasons why they are so effectively used as symbols and metaphors.

Like totemism, sacrifice has been treated in recent research as a system of signs and as an institution that links and divides elements in the social fabric (Detienne and Vernant 1989). Animal sacrifice has further been linked with economic factors and, above all, the distribution of power (Gordon 1990; Jay 1993; Stowers 1995).

Research on animals in antiquity is the second branch of research that has been of value to this study. This is a wide field that includes ancient debates on the status of animals as well as veterinary medicine; studies of animals in art as well as the analysis of ancient physiognomics; and studies of animals in the Roman arena as well as ecological treatises. Three books have been a special inspiration to the present study. These are J.M.C. Toynbee's survey of the Roman use of animals, *Animals in Roman Life and Art*; Urs Dierauer, *Tier und Mensch im Denken der Antike. Studien zur Tierpsychologie, Anthropologie und Ethik* and Richard Sorabji, *Animal Minds and Human Morals: The Origins of the Western Debate*. Toynbee's book takes its point of departure from the study of Roman art, while the books by Dierauer and Sorabji are based on close readings of Greek and Latin texts and investigations of the ancient debate on the status and value of animals.

The flourishing field of research on religion/Christianity in late antiquity has been vital for the present study. This research is characterized by a willingness to see Christianity and paganism synoptically, which implies taking Christianity out of Church history and into the wider ancient world of which it was part.[3] It also implies looking at the different branches of Christianity without automatically applying an orthodoxy/heterodoxy perspective. Some of these more recent studies are characterized by a certain subversive perspective: the texts are not only to be read with the elite that produced them but also against it (Burrus 2000).

Antiquity and late modernity have in common an increased interest in the status and value of animals. Contemporary studies of the cultural and moral value of animals is the fourth branch of research from which this study has profited. The modern debate has focused on ethical issues surrounding the treatment of animals by humans. Peter Singer argues for a radical change in the treatment of animals and bases his arguments on the principle of equality and the idea that we should minimize suffering. Singer compares "speciesism" to racism and equates human and animal suffering (Singer 1975, cf. also Regan 1983). A more moderate stand on "speciesism" is taken by Mary Midgley in her *Beast and Man: The Roots of Human Nature* (1995), where she persuasively attempts to set humans within their animal context. These authors are alike in their call for respect for non-human animals, their claim that suffering of sentient beings matters and their extension of the principle of equality across species barriers.

Complementary to these "pro-animal" authors are Mary Douglas' critical perspective and searching questions about why compassion towards animals has become an issue in late modernity. She points out that it is simplistic to stop at identifying some people as being more compassionate towards animals than others. One must ask what sort of ideology and social structure generally produces such attitudes in the first place. How we think about the relations between animals is based on our own relationships (Douglas 1990, 2001). Concepts of animals reflect human concerns, and animal categories are moulded on principles of how humans interact with each other, which means that human social categories are extended to the animal world.

According to Douglas, "animal categories come up in the same pattern of relations as those of humans because the said humans understand the animal kinds to be acting according to the same principles as themselves" (Douglas 1990: 33). And, she asks, "how could we think about how animals relate to one another except on the basis of our own relationships?" (*ibid.*).

Douglas is certainly right in pointing to a fundamental connection between how humans think of themselves and the ways they think of animals. But it must be added that the animal world does not consist of non-intentional objects on which human relations can be projected as on a blank slate. Animals have their specific ways of behaviour and own interests to pursue that contribute to determining how they are conceived of. Animals also interact with humans, at least some animals do, and their societies are not only parallels to human ones but extensions of them as well. All the same, a cultural analysis of animal categories must include the references of these categories to the world of humans.

Steve Baker, who has written about late modern depictions of animals, has attempted to show the meanings that animal metaphors give to humans; at the same time, he is attentive to the views of animals that are conveyed by means of these metaphors (Baker 2001). The idea that animal representations, which may be literary or social constructions, reveal something about the way living animals are perceived and treated is not uncontroversial. Baker recalls that when he spoke at a conference in Oxford in the mid-1980s, called "Animal Images of Sex, Race, and Class", and at the end of the paper suggested "that animal representations may indirectly reveal something about how a culture regards and thus treats living animals, the suggestion was considered, to be frank, bizarre" (cf. *ibid.*: xvii). At a conference fifteen years later, "many speakers took for granted that the 'real' and the representational can no longer be regarded as conveniently distinct realms" (*ibid.*).

Baker makes several interesting points. I will especially mention his warning against drawing a sharp distinction between representations and reality – the representational, symbolic and rhetorical use of animals deserves, according to him, as much conceptual weight as any idea about "real" animals (*ibid.*, 10). In *The Treason of Images*, the famous picture by René Magritte of a pipe accompanied by the words "Ceci n'est pas une pipe", the difference between an object and its representation is visualized. A picture of a lion is not a lion, but a picture of a lion may help us to recognize a lion when we see one. The challenge is to understand when and to what extent representations of animals make comments on animals, and what they say about them.

In relation to animals and cultural expressions of contempt in relation to animals, Baker points out that "it *may* be that the practice somehow accounts for the rhetoric; it *may* be that the rhetoric sustains and substantiates and consolidates the practice, leading us to continue to hold animals in contempt; I contend only that they run in parallel, and that it is rash to assume that the parallel is without significance" (*ibid*.: 90). In this cautious observation, there lies an appeal not to see the different contexts where animals appear totally in separation from each other but to see them and the conception of animals that they generate as somehow connected.

Finally, I will mention Baker's point that we have a tendency to deny animals. Animals in fairytales and cartoons are read as humans. They are not animals in any meaningful way, only a medium for messages that concern humans (*ibid*.: 136–8). In other words, their animality is denied. Something similar may be at work in Christian antiquity, when texts about animals are explained as if they did not concern animals.

The present study

One challenge is to track the relations between a society's metaphorical systems based on animals and that society's treatment of them. I do not mean that animal metaphors are related to a society's evaluations and practices towards animals as a one-to-one relationship, and not in each and every case. But as an overall "mechanism" I will suggest that metaphors are dependent on how animals are evaluated, and further that the evaluation of them is interconnected with practices towards them. When, for instance, Achilles is spoken of as a lion, the metaphor will say something not only about the object it is used to describe (Achilles) but also about its original referent (the lion).[4]

Furthermore, it is important to stress that a representation of an animal does not mirror the actual animal; nor is it a "true" description of that animal but reflects popular conceptions of it. Mary Midgley has pointed out that "Actual wolves, then, are not much like the folk-figure of the wolf, and the same is true for apes and other creatures. But it is the folk-figure that has been popular with philosophers" (Midgley 1995: 27). Midgley has also poignantly revealed how the folk figure of the wolf has influenced the actual treatment of wolves.

However, there is a danger in confusing representations of real animals with animal symbols and metaphors. This problem is not new but was realized in antiquity. In his refutation of the Ophites, a gnostic sect, Epiphanius, archbishop of Salamis on Cyprus, struggles with a saying in Matthew: "Be ye wise as the serpents and harmless as the dove" (Matthew 10:16; *Panarion* I, 37.1–9). It is well known that serpents have a problematic standing in Christian religion, but neither do doves escape Epiphanius' criticism, as he says that

> in many ways doves are not admirable. They are incontinent and ceaselessly promiscuous, lecherous and devoted to the pleasures of the moment, and weak and small besides. But because of the

harmlessness, patience and forbearance of doves – and even more, because the Holy Spirit has appeared in the form of a dove – the divine Word could have us imitate the will of the Holy Ghost and the harmlessness of the harmless dove, and be wise in good but innocent in evil.

(*Panarion* I, 37.8–9)

The dove is here depicted in anthropomorphic language as a disgusting animal, which clearly makes the bird unsuitable as a Christian ideal. In Epiphanius' enumeration, the bird's bad qualities far outdo its good ones. Epiphanius contrasts one positive folk figure of the dove with what he takes to be real doves and shows that the connection between "real" doves and symbolic ones is slight and selective indeed. The common properties of a dove and the Holy Spirit do not cover the totality of the dove but consist of only a few characteristics.

The selection of animals that are used as metaphors is governed by certain interests in the first place. It is also true that different characteristics of an animal are used in different contexts – an animal may be mapped in several ways, as Epiphanius (who does not especially like allegorical readings) shows in his characteristics of ordinary doves in relation to the dove that is used as a symbol for the Holy Spirit. When Christ is described as a lion, his wrath, manliness and rulership appear in the context of his saving power, while in relation to Satan the lion describes his wrath and rulership in the context of evil. Different animals can be used as metaphors for the same entity: Christ is both a lion and a lamb, and Satan is described as a wild boar, a serpent, or a lion. Some animals tend, to a higher degree than others, to have a fixed range of metaphorical meanings in Christian discourse, for instance the lamb and the dove.

Thinking about animals, experiencing them and interacting with them is done in certain cultural contexts. A context may be mental as well as physical. The point is that an animal – be it a real one or a metaphorical one – is never a transparent object and accordingly can never be grasped in isolation; animals are always woven into specific contexts. There are pagan contexts for animal concepts, such as arenas, sacrifices and philosophical debates; Jewish contexts, such as the Genesis account of creation and the dietary laws based on purity and impurity; and Christian contexts, for instance, martyrdom, asceticism and the Christian interpretations of paganism and heresies – contexts in which animals appear as symbols and metaphors. One aim is to show how animals were contextualized during the Roman Empire, what meanings they were given and what changes Christianity made.

In the Graeco-Roman world, animals were described in an anthropomorphic language and often in moralizing ways. Similarities and differences were always emphasized in this language: animals were similar to humans but at the same time radically different from them. How, in what ways, and by what means the interplay between similarities and differences between animals and humans was construed varied with context and purpose.

Such variations are closely connected to the fact that when texts mention animals they are often referring to humans in a sort of code. However, this code is only comprehensible if the evaluation of animals that it is dependent upon is known and shared. When texts are talking about humans by means of animals, what is the specific issue? On what conditions are animals present? What do these texts say about animals?

The theme of this book is the transition from traditional Greek and Roman religion to Christianity in the Roman Empire and the effect of this transition on the conception of animals. The changes in the religious evaluation of animals, the effects of these changes and the cultural processes that these involved will be investigated. The disappearance of animal sacrifice is the most visible sign of more general changes in the relationship between animals and humans. However, the use of animals in symbols, myths and rituals and the value they were given also changed profoundly in these centuries.

One of the underlying assumptions of the book is that changes in the way animal motifs are used and the way human–animal relations are conceptualized serve as indicators of more general cultural shifts. In late antiquity, animals were used as symbols in a general redefinition of cultural values and assumptions. Cultural issues were focused through them. We will trace the changes in the religious significance of animals in the centuries when Christianity grew from a minority sect to a world religion and look into the significance of these changes, to understand not only the conception of animals but also its functions in the development of a new Christian identity.

The present study of animals and religious changes in the first to fourth centuries CE is intended as a contribution to research on religion in late antiquity. I will investigate changes in the concept of animals during the transition from a non-Christian to a Christian culture. The aim is to see how people in the Graeco-Roman world imagined, interpreted and dramatized animals and how they related to them. Key texts consulted range from philosophical treatises to novels and poems on metamorphoses; from biographies of holy persons such as Apollonius of Tyana and Antony, the Christian desert ascetic, to natural history; from the New Testament via gnostic texts to the Church fathers; from pagan and Christian criticism of animal sacrifice to the acts of the martyrs.

The texts consulted will be treated as equally valuable. They reflect parallel or interlocking discourses on animals that all have an equal right to be heard. One of the project's aims has been to bring these various texts together and confront them with each other. A second has been to present the dominant themes and developments in people's conception of animals without losing their complexity. Both the pagan and the Christian conception of animals remained rich and multilayered through the centuries. Furthermore, it has been an ambition to give an outline of the main factors in the creation of a Christian conception of animals.

The book is intended as a macro-investigation based on selected texts, aiming at an understanding of the dominant religious and cultural processes relating to animals in the first to fourth century CE and at creating an overall picture. The selection of texts has been made on the basis of which texts were estimated to be most helpful. Geographical differences and variations due to social strata will be commented upon only to some degree.[5] As for the relationship between non-Christian religions and Christianity, Christianity will be viewed as both a continuation of general religious developments in these centuries and a religious innovation in itself.

In the first part of the book, the concept of animals will be described in relation to public institutions, thought, imagination and religion. Chapter 1 is a broad survey of the various contexts in which living animals appeared in the cultural and religious landscape of the early Roman Empire. Three of these are singled out as being especially significant. These are sacrifice, divination and the arena. In Chapters 2–4, the role and function of animals in philosophy and literature will be discussed. Considering how much time was spent, how much cultural work was done to keep up the categorical boundaries between humans and animals, a number of interesting questions arise: when, in what way, in which media and for what purposes were these boundaries overstepped, as they most certainly were.

The theme of Chapter 5 is the religious value of animals. While animals and humans share a flesh-and-blood reality, gods and animals have in common the fact that they are not human. They also have it in common that humans relate to them and define themselves in relation to them. Furthermore, both gods and animals are usually described as if they were human, with human attributes and consciousness. The mysteries of Mithras, Cybele and Attis, Isis and Osiris are examples of cults in which animals appeared. Alexander of Abonouteichos had his sacred serpent, and in the temples of Asclepius serpents and dogs were present. Animals appeared in magic, and in several other systems of expertise such as divination and astrology. How and in what ways were animals associated with the divine world in antiquity?

In Chapters 6 and 7, animal sacrifice as the old religious key symbol will be analysed and compared with the appearance of the human body as the new Christian key symbol. In the change from a pagan to a Christian culture, a great symbolic burden was lifted from sacrificial animals and laid upon Christian bodies. What does this shift of key symbols imply? Why did it come about?

The second part of the book will be a more systematic investigation of how animals appear in Christian texts. Its point of departure is the New Testament. From these biblical texts we will proceed to the discourse that took place on martyrs and then on ascetics. Next to the animal sacrifice, the arena was the most significant context in which animals appeared in the empire. In the arenas, Rome played out its superiority and might. Rome had conquered the world and continued symbolically to conquer it in the spectacular hunting of wild animals in the arenas. In Chapter 9, we will look into the acts of the martyrs and the Christian narratives about the arena and see what meaning animals were given in relation to Christian martyrs.

In addition to their discourse on martyrs, ascetic discourse was one of the main Christian contexts for talk about animals. In Chapter 10, this subject will be investigated through Egyptian sources – the Nag Hammadi texts and the *Life of Antony*. In Chapter 11, the use of animals to characterize other beings will be discussed, while in Chapter 12, we will proceed from bestial humans to humanlike animals. Here the anomalies within the neat Christian hierarchical system, the lack of winged humans and the presence of speaking animals will be scrutinized.

1

ANIMALS IN THE ROMAN EMPIRE

The presence of animals

In the Roman Empire, humans exploited animals on their farms, hunted them in the wilderness and at sea, trained and tamed them, used them to transport people and goods, utilized them in magic and medicine, kept them as pets, cheered them on the racetrack, killed them in the arenas, and sacrificed them to the gods. Generally speaking, the type of society contributes to determining conceptions of animals – an agricultural society will have other perspectives than a society of hunters and gatherers, an industrial society or a late modern society. Conceptions of animals in the Roman Empire were among other things influenced by these societies being agricultural and dependent on organic power and the productivity of animal muscles.

The presence of animals was not the same everywhere. Some people, such as farmers, hunters and fishermen, were dependent on animals for their living. On small farms and in villages, people lived closer to the animal population than they did in Rome, for instance. However, the difference between the countryside and the cities was only one of degree – Egyptian cities had an extensive animal population (Bagnall 1996: 50, 81). The empire with all its provinces was held together by animals trotting through mountainous areas, forests and deserts, transporting food over land to the cities. Export articles were carried on their backs or on wagons to the docks, and animals were used for personal travel. Everywhere, the Mediterranean economy was totally dependent on and involved with animal life.

How human animals and non-human animals relate to each other depends on the moral, material and technological developments in a particular human society. It further depends on how the distinctions between humans and animals are drawn and on which sort of animal species we are talking about. The relationship between humans and sheep, for instance, will always be different from the way humans relate to lions or locusts. The cultural value of animals is strongly influenced by their usefulness to man, whether they are conceived of as useful, destructive or neither. A hierarchy of animals is normally based on the affinity that animals have with humans. Often an animal represents conflicting values. While a tame snake could be a benevolent protector of the house and a pet, and snakes generally were regarded as guardians, some were dangerous. While the Christians usually conceived of the serpent as evil and a symbol of Satan, in Christian texts too, the serpent sometimes appears as a wise animal and even as a symbol of the saviour.

Out of the conglomeration of contexts in which animals appeared, the emotions and thoughts they awakened, the ways they were used and the dangers some of them were taken to represent, a tangle of different discourses about them emerges. Animals were treated as subjects of philosophical debates and of natural histories, they were part of the cultural imagination and were used in descriptions of people as well as in images of the divine. The first part of this book aims at surveying the interaction between humans and animals in the Roman Empire: what people did to animals, how they thought about animals, what they felt in relation to animals, what images they made of them and how they included them in their religion.

This first chapter will start from a description of real animals, animals of flesh and blood. It will give an overview of their function and use in the Roman Empire. We will proceed from surveying types of relation between animals and humans and the different uses of animals for food, clothes and hauling power to describing specific institutional ceremonies using animals, ceremonies that were typical of the Graeco-Roman world in the first to the fourth century CE. Such ceremonies were connected with entertainment and religion. They included hunting spectacles as well as sacrifice and divination. In these ceremonies, animals were given a central role, cultural issues were focused on, and animals contributed to defining the limits and norms of Graeco-Roman culture. We are interested in what these animals were defining but even more in the views on animals that these established customs reflect. How was the role of animals interpreted by the establishment that exploited them?

End — Animals and humans

The relationship between humans and animals depends on which animal species we are talking about but also on which human group is involved – whether it consists of Romans or foreigners, men or women, free or slaves, old people or children, rich or poor. Some of these groups viewed the link between animals and humans as being closer than others did. Animals and humans in some instances have similar functions and roles. One example is that of animals and children, who are often associated with each other. Hellenist artists made statues of children with pets, and Hellenist epigrammatists wrote epitaphs for little animals in which these animals were described in connection with childhood and simplicity (Fowler 1989). These pet animals were bemoaned when they died – dolphins, cockerels, locusts, cicadas and ants have their own epitaphs as well as dogs and horses. Some pets were played with and attended to in ways similar to human children.

The inhabitants of the Roman Empire were completely dependent on an animal labour force. For instance, animals worked in the fields, they pulled carts and chariots, and served as mounts and beasts of burden. Oxen were used for ploughing, donkeys worked the millstones and the wheels that were used to draw water from wells, mules and oxen pulled wagons, and horses served in war. The functional division between humans and animals was not absolute. As the roles of animals and children sometimes overlapped, so did the roles of working animals and poor people and slaves, who often engaged in the same sort of work. If people were poor and could not afford to buy animals to help in the work, they carried, pulled and laboured themselves – like beasts. Millstones were pulled by slaves as well as by donkeys. The similarities between animals and slaves in their physical work were noted by Aristotle: "And also the usefulness of slaves diverges little from that of animals; bodily service for the necessities of life is forthcoming from both, from slaves and from domestic animals alike" (*Politics*, 1254b).

In Roman law, animals and slaves were sometimes treated together, as in the *Lex Aquilia*: "If anyone kills unlawfully a slave or a servant-girl belonging to someone else or a four-footed beast of the class of cattle, let him be condemned to pay the owner the highest value that the property had attained in the preceding year" (*Lex Aquilia*, in *The Digest of Justinian*, 9.2.2; cf. also 9.2.5.22). The jurist Gaius, commenting on the law, stresses that this statute "treats equally our slaves and our four-footed cattle which are kept in herds" (9.2.2.2). A discussion follows as to whether pigs should be included among cattle. Dogs do not fall within this class, and neither do wild beasts such as bears, lions, and panthers, while elephants and camels do (*ibid.*). Authors on agriculture such as the elder Cato (234–149 BCE), Columella (fl. 50 CE) and Varro (116–27 BCE) associate slaves and cattle with each other and sometimes treat them alike (Cato, *On Agriculture*, 2.7; Columella, *On Agriculture*, 1.6.8; Varro, *On Agriculture*, 1.17.1). Cato exhorts us: "Sell worn-out oxen, blemished cattle, blemished sheep, wool, hides, an old wagon, old tools, an old slave, a sickly slave, and whatever else is superfluous. The master should have the selling habit, not the buying habit" (*On Agriculture*, 2.3). In Greece, the terminology used stressed the functional similarities between slaves and certain animals. A slave was designated *andrapodon*, "man-footed creature", a term invented as an analogue to *tetrapodon*, "four-footed creature" (Bradley 2000: 110).

Between humans and animals there are similarities and dissimilarities, functions that overlap as well as restrictions on the sort of contact that is permitted between them. Differences between humans and other species tend to be stressed in the continual work to maintain the categorical boundary. Meat eating is especially significant. It marks the boundary showing the difference between humans and animals. Humans cooked and roasted meat and did not, like other meat-eating species, eat it raw, a point made by Lévi-Strauss and refined in relation to Greek religion by M. Detienne and J.-P. Vernant (Detienne and Vernant 1989).

Which animals are eaten depends on which species are – for religious or other reasons – regarded as permitted and edible. Judaism is the classic example of a religion with strict rules for food that is permissible. In contrast, the Romans had few religious dietary regulations and seem not to have been squeamish in their tastes. According to Galen's (c. 129–199 CE) directions, restrictions on the Roman kitchen seem to have stopped only at cannibalism (Garnsey 1999: 84). Although carefully chosen diets based on physiological knowledge appealed to the Graeco-Roman world (Rousselle 1988), the goal of these diets was to keep the balance between the humours in the body and thus keep it vigorous and healthy. Diets clearly emphasized class and elite status but did not contribute to maintaining a clean/unclean distinction based on religious taboos, as was the case with the Jews (see Chapter 8).

While humans were allowed to eat the meat of animals as well as turning their wool and skin into clothing, they were not permitted to eat human flesh. This prohibition was a strong cultural taboo. An underlying presupposition is that humans are not animals, and therefore human meat must not be eaten. The prohibition is a boundary marker that was also transferred to animals, which were likewise kept from eating humans. But even if the right order in the food relationship was that animals are food for men, not men food for animals, this hierarchy of correct diet was sometimes reversed. In the Roman Empire, animals were sometimes allowed and urged to taste human flesh. The wild beasts destined for the arena were perhaps trained to eat humans (Auguet 1994: 94). According to Suetonius (b. c. 70 CE), who is in the main hostile to Caligula and depicts the emperor as a bloodthirsty monster, Caligula showed his brutality (sauitia) by feeding the wild animals with criminals instead of feeding them with small animals, because small animals were more expensive than convicts (Caligula, 27.1).[1] The Church fathers were especially concerned about the bodily resurrection of humans whose bodies had been devoured by beasts, which in their turn were devoured by other beasts (see Chapter 9).

When animals were allowed to eat humans, it was an extreme degradation of the human form – "in all his body was nowhere a body's shape", writes Martial (c. 38/41–101/104 CE) about a crucified robber after he had been attacked by a bear in the arena (On the Spectacles, 7). Sometimes what was eventually eaten had never been recognized as being really human in the first place. Not only criminals who were thrown to the beasts but also newborn babies who were exposed and sometimes killed by animals were thus denied their humanity. In the case of infant exposure, where the abandoned child risked being eaten by stray dogs or other animals (Harris 1994: 6, 8), such children had not been recognized by their father, the *pater familias*, and were therefore not classified as proper human beings. It is also worth noting that there were open pits on the Esquiline where all sorts of refuse – as well as the bodies of the poor and animal carcasses – were thrown (Robinson 1994: 122; Kyle 1995: 185). They were called *puticuli*, a word that is associated with *putescere*, "to rot" (see Potter 2002: 169, note 2). In death, the similarities in the material and physiological equipment of animals and people were underlined as they were united through the stench that engulfed the area of these pits.

Another important restriction between animals and humans is that they are usually not permitted to have sexual contact with each other. Thus the categorical distinction between the species is maintained. But even if this relationship is forbidden, it tends to exist all the same, both as a phantasm and in reality. Apuleius' (*c.* 125–170 CE) novel *Metamorphoses* tells about a woman who especially hired the ass as her partner. In this novel, sexual intercourse with an ass is further thought of as a special punishment for a female transgressor, reflecting something that also seems to have been actual punitive practice (cf. Martial *On the Spectacles*, 5; Coleman 1990: 63–64; Barton 1996: 68).

Necessities of life

Meat

The usefulness to man of animals had three main aspects, one pertaining to the necessities of life, another to religion and the third to entertainment, all of which overlapped.

Animal husbandry was the basis of Mediterranean economics. From domesticated animals people obtained meat, milk, eggs, honey and material for clothing. Columella describes the care of animals on a Roman farm. The management of oxen, bulls and cows, horses, mules and asses, sheep, goats, pigs, dogs, as well as different types of farm bird and fish in the fish ponds is explained. Columella also includes lengthy instructions for the management of bees (*On Agriculture*, 6–9). His description shows the variety of animal life on a farm and the diversity in food production, in which different types of animal husbandry were combined with other kinds of food production. Animals that are not domesticated in the Western world today were also kept by the Romans. One example is dormice (*glires*), which were fattened in small pottery vessels with holes and served as delicacies (Zeuner 1963: 415–16).

The daily diet of common people did not necessarily consist of meat. Animal husbandry in the Graeco-Roman world was not primarily for the production of meat but for producing hides, wool and milk. Meat and food from animals have often been regarded as being of minor importance in the

Graeco-Roman diet, especially red meat (Garnsey 1999: 122–3). At the same time, meat was highly valued, eaten on special occasions and viewed as a prestige food, with pork as the favourite. The eminence and status of meat as a foodstuff is seen, above all, in the significance of the animal sacrifice, where the commonest species were pigs, sheep, goats and cattle.

Classification of animals based on the taste and wholesomeness of their meat represents their demotion to the status of objects. They were made into things to be eaten (*The Hippocratic Collection, Regimen*, 2. 46–9). At the same time, sacrifice involved domestic animals in a process of religious elevation before they were reduced to meat. As well as turning animals into meat, the sacrificial process transformed parts of the bodies of the animals into food for the gods on the altar and made it possible for the priests to read the future in their intestines. Imperfect animals or working cattle were prohibited as sacrifices (Jameson 1988).

In Greece, most of the slaughtering was ritual, and the meat that was eaten came from animals that had been sacrificed. In Rome, sacrificial meat was eaten by the upper classes, and the leftovers were sold on the market. Sausages and other products made of low-quality meat, mixed with spices and cereals, could easily be obtained as snacks from street sellers (Garnsey 1999: 122–7).

In addition to farming and pastoralism, animals that ended up on the table had also been hunted. Game played a part in Roman cookery. The capture and killing of wild animals included the hunting, fishing and catching of birds. Hares were driven into nets, and deer, boars and bears were speared. The antlers of stags and fangs of wild boars were nailed on the walls of temples (Balsdon 1969: 219–20). This sort of meat was not classified as sacrificial (Wilkins 1995: 104). Meat from animals killed in the arenas was probably also distributed among the people (Kyle 1995).

As a supplement to what could be obtained in Italy, Roman elites had access to a wide variety of foodstuffs, and their exotic, elaborate and costly cuisine is well known. Thus their *haute cuisine* reflected the width and breadth of the empire and the way the representatives of this empire related to its complexities by virtually eating their way through its exotica. Seneca comments on the subject: "Look at Nomentanus and Appicius, digesting, as they say, the blessing of land and sea, and reviewing the creations of every nation arrayed upon their board!" (*On the Happy Life*, 11.4). In another work, Seneca describes the variety of animals eaten by the Roman elite in a more malicious way: "From every quarter they gather together every known and unknown thing to tickle a fastidious palate . . . they vomit that they may eat, they eat that they may vomit, and they do not deign even to digest the feast for which they ransack the whole world" (*Consolation*, 10.3). According to Suetonius, Emperor Vitellius mingled on a big platter ingredients from various birds and fish brought to him from the whole empire (*Vitellius*, 13). Plutarch (*c.* 50–120 CE) maintains that "nothing that flies or swims or moves on land has escaped your so-called civilized and hospitable tables" (*Gryllus*, 991D). Rather than keeping up distinctions between themselves and their neighbours by avoiding certain types of food, as did the Jews, the Romans ate meat and other foodstuffs from all over the empire.

There were different patterns of consumption. One was that more meat was consumed by people of the upper classes than those of the lower ones. Another was that vegetarian ways of life also existed. So even if meat was the sacrificial food and thus obligatory, there were those who rejected meat eating. This rejection could be partial or total. Vegetarianism was motivated by religious reasons, compassion for animals, or by reasons concerning diet and health. Thus vegetarianism could be based on concern for animals as well as on the idea that the slaughter of living creatures had a corrupting effect on human beings (see Chapter 3). In any case, vegetarianism reveals that meat was not neutral but had great symbolic value.

Fish

More important than meat in the daily diet was food from the sea. The Mediterranean consists of diverse and shifting micro-regions, and fishermen had to be flexible. But even if the fish population is less abundant than in the oceans, the Mediterranean was a treasury of animal life with more than 500 species living in the sea. Especially in the lagoons, many fish were caught, as the lagoons were probably twice as productive as the open sea (Horden and Purcell 2000: 190–7).

Fish was consumed fresh, made into sauces, dried, or pickled in salt for sale and export. Salt fish was exported from Egypt, the Black Sea and Spain. Fish were also kept in artificial ponds (*piscinae*) (Varro, *On Agriculture*, 3.17), which seem to have become fashionable among the elite in the first century BCE (Zeuner 1963: 479). When it was sold far from the sea, fish was expensive, even more expensive than meat (McGowan 1999: 42), but at least for those who lived close to the sea, fish and other types of seafood were important elements in the diet, even if the daily diet was mainly based on cereals, vegetables, wine, and oil.

The Romans were interested in the richness and variety of the life of the sea. Mosaics, for instance from Pompeii, show fish, shells, crayfish and octopuses, realistically modelled (House of the Faun and House VIII). Although these mosaics were reproduced in workshops, they were apparently based on original precise zoographical observations (Dunbabin 1999: 47–8). It is not unexpected that a fishing population knew a great deal about the varied life in the sea, but the care with which these artists made the animals look realistic is worth noting. The sensitive and accurate depiction of these sea creatures reveals a precise understanding of the distinctive qualities of the species in question.

Ancient authors wrote extensively on aquatic species and the food that these creatures provided. The famous interpreter of dreams, Artemidorus of

Daldis (mid/late second century CE), mentions more than fifty species of fish and marine life that have specific meanings in dreams (*The Interpretation of Dreams*, 2.14). In his didactic epic *Halieutica*, a hexameter work in five books devoted to fishing, Oppian from Cilicia (late second century CE) mentions more than 120 different varieties of sea creature.[2] He describes the life of sea creatures and the characteristics of different species, where they live, what they feed on and how they mate:

> all that inhabit the watery flood and where each dwells, their
> mating in the waters and their birth, the life of fishes, their hates,
> their loves, their wiles, and the crafty devices of the cunning fisher's
> art – even all that men have devised against the baffling fishes.
> (*Halieutica*, 1.4–9)

Oppian points out that the sea "is infinite and of unmeasured depth" and that no fewer types of animal dwell there than on earth (1.80–92). He stresses the dangers of the sea and the uncertainty of the fishermen's labours. In particular, "the sea monsters" (*ketea*), a term that denotes the great creatures of the sea – whales, dolphins, seals, sharks and tunny – can be terrible (1.35–55). The society of the sea creatures is not an attractive one: "Among fishes neither justice is of any account, nor is there any mercy nor love; for all the fish that swim are bitter foes to one another" (2.43–45). Oppian's description of the inhabitants of the sea conveys an image of a different world, foreign to men, a society in its own right. At the same time, men do business with this world in their efforts to catch its inhabitants.

Halieutica gives the impression that the battle between humans and sea creatures is a battle of wits and skill. Oppian sees fish both as cunning and with specialized skills. Fish not only use "cunning wit and deceitful craft" against each other, they also deceive wise fishermen (3.92–97). To catch them, fishermen have to be artful, strong and intelligent. And although Oppian claims that "nothing is impossible for men to do" and sees men as a race similar to the gods, albeit with inferior strength (5.1–4), the sea creatures often get the better of men. *Halieutica*, which is a vivid illustration of the dangers of the sea, ends with a sponge diver who is cut in two by "a huge and hideous beast" (5.667) and his shipmates, returning to the shore, weeping for their friend. Ovid (43 BCE – 17 CE), in the rest of his *Halieuticon*, also describes the cunning of the different types of fish and how they manage to escape the traps of their hunters (1–48).

The Graeco-Roman view of sea creatures is markedly different from the way we regard fish and other sea creatures today. The natural historians Pliny (23/4–79 CE), Aelian (165/70–230/35 CE) and Oppian (late second century CE), who all describe sea animals extensively, suggest that these creatures were regarded as intelligent and as having societies that in some ways were rather similar to human societies. Pliny, for instance, in his *Natural History*, in thirty-one books, which was completed in 77 CE, describes able leader shells among the pearl oysters, which fishermen had to capture to make their hunt easier (*Natural History*, 9.55). Pliny is also surprised that some people hold that sea animals have no sense (*Natural History*, 9.67) and gives his readers proof of their cunning (*sollertia*). Plutarch discusses which group is the cleverer, sea animals or land animals, and ends by leaving the competition undecided (*On the Cleverness of Animals*), which, from a post-Darwinian point of view, is rather a tribute to fish (see Chapter 2). Iamblichus (*c.* 245–325 CE) tells of Pythagoras that he once paid some fishermen for their catch so that they should release all the fish alive (*On the Pythagorean Way of Life*, 36).[3] This episode shows that sometimes the life of fish was also conceived of as being valuable – at least for some Pythagoreans and Neoplatonists.

Magic and medicine

Several expert systems, wholly or partly based on animals, flourished during the empire. In these systems, animals were in one way or another used as instruments. The most important was animal sacrifice (see Chapters 6 and 7) including the divination based on the entrails of the sacrificial animals (see below). But divination based on live animals and magical and medical practices that included animals were also common.

Unlike the Graeco-Roman *cuisine de sacrifice*, but like the Roman *haute cuisine*, Roman magico-medical cookery was based on ingredients from all over the empire, taken from wild animals as well as from domestic ones. In his *Natural History*, Pliny describes Roman medical recipes in detail.

All sorts of elements – fat, blood, internal organs and body wastes – were used in the *materia medica*. For example, the blood of an elephant, especially that of the male, was thought to heal catarrh (*Natural History*, 28.24); camel's brain, dried and taken in vinegar, was a remedy against epilepsy (*Natural History*, 28.26); the urine of a lynx was used for pain in the throat (*Natural History*, 28.32); and bladder stones were relieved by the urine of a wild boar or by eating its bladder as food (*Natural History*, 28.60).

The rationale for these procedures described by Pliny was an imagined relationship between diseases and remedies that was based on the idea of a general system of sympathies (*concordia*) and antipathies (*discordia*) in the world. The natural world was criss-crossed by multiple interaction between its disparate parts. Pliny argues for the attraction and repulsion that exist between things by describing how water puts out fire and magnetic stones attract iron, but also how a diamond, which is "unbreakable and invincible by any other force", is broken by goat's blood (*Natural History*, 20.1). This system of implied relationships involved either the principle that like cures like (*similia similibus*) or its opposite, that remedies were found in contrasts, opposites cure opposites (*alia aliis*). Bites and diseases caused by one animal could be healed by ingredients taken from a similar animal. But the remedy could also be taken from an animal that was the opposite of the first. Harm done by the crawling creatures of the earth was cured by ingredients taken from the flying fauna of the air. Protection against serpents and their bites was taken from either vulture, chicken, dove, swallow or owl (*Natural History*, 29.24–6). The principle of curing by opposites was based on the humour system and on the need to keep the humours in the body in balance, while the like-to-like principle is dependent on a simpler and older system of sympathetic magic (cf. Hanson 1998: 72–3).

In addition to medicine and magical potions based on animal ingredients, animals were also used as intermediaries in cures. A disease could be transferred to an animal and taken away by that animal. A person with a cough spat into the mouth of a frog and got rid of the cough (*Natural History*, 32.29). Often in these cases, the animal in question died, and the disease then also "died". Another way to turn an animal into an intermediary is described in a Greek magical papyrus in which the drowning of a cat as part of a magical ritual was intended to make the cat into a demonic helper (*PGM* III, 1–164, in Betz 1996). The flourishing magical practice of the empire had a rich source in Egyptian magic. Magical techniques applied animal ingredients, and small animals were often sacrificed to empower the magical formula and make it work in a proper way.

Animals were further regarded as able to predict weather and dangers. A special case of animal wisdom was the way in which animals themselves were thought to be using natural medicine. Thus wise use of natural medicine on the part of animals was taken as an example of how clever animals were (Aelian, 2.18; 15.17). In some cases, the accident that originally happened to the animal was sometimes more strange than the cure, as when an elephant swallows a chameleon and the remedy is the wild olive (*Natural History*, 8.41).

In the case of domesticated animals, one did not rely too heavily on the ability of animals to cure themselves. In works on agriculture, the diseases of farm animals and remedies against these diseases were thoroughly discussed (Cato, 70–3; Columella, 6.5–38; Varro, 2.1.21–4; 2.2.20; 2.3.8–10; 2.4.21–2; 2.7.16). The economic value of horses created a special market for veterinary medicine, for instance, as reflected in Publicus Vegetius Renatus' work *Mulomedicina*, on the diseases of horses and mules, written between 330 and 450 CE (Walker 1996). The importance of this branch of veterinary medicine was also reflected in the Greek term for a veterinarian, *hippiatros*. Barbro Santillo Frizell has pointed out that sanctuaries in Italy that were associated with mineral water also played a role in animal husbandry and clearly were a resource in ancient veterinary medicine.[4]

Religion

What has been said so far has suggested the importance of animals in the Mediterranean economy. Animals were providing people with useful products such as food and clothes, hauling power, and a means of transportation, and they were also instrumental in medicine and magic. In addition to such daily use of animals, there were also special ceremonies where animals were in focus in more significant ways. These ceremonies pertained to religion and entertainment.

Different societies have different contexts in which they encounter and relate to animals and interpret their behaviour. In modern cultures, the pet industry, the abattoir and laboratories are examples of significant social institutions in which animals are involved. In the Roman Empire, there were also defined spaces in which animals were contained – geographical spaces as well as mental and social ones. We will call special attention to three types of animal space that were especially significant in the Graeco-Roman world. These spaces were required by sacrifice, divination and hunting spectacles. Here the relationships between humans and animals were explored within the framework of public ceremonies, and people participated on a collective basis. These ceremonies are essential in gaining an impression of the value and meanings of animals in the empire. Pet keeping must also be mentioned, but this was of less importance than the other institutions in defining what animals meant to the Romans.

Sacrifice and the contract with animals

Over the millennia, hunting and later domestication has completely altered the zoological picture in the Mediterranean. After the agricultural revolution, domestication of animals had become the most important context for human–animal relationships. Agricultural animals were animals that in exchange for their services were given food, shelter and safety. Aristotle had stressed that "tame animals are superior in their nature to wild animals, yet for all the former it is advantageous to be ruled by man, since this gives them security" (*Politics*, 1254b). This saying indicated a sort of agreement between domestic animals and humans that the former give up their freedom for protection, and the latter give protection in exchange for meat, skins and labour.

In Graeco-Roman culture, the idea of a contract between animals and humans was discussed as part of law and philosophy, but the existence of such a contract was usually denied. Roman law explicitly says that animals could not be part of contract making and adds that "an animal is incapable of committing a legal wrong because it is devoid of reasoning" (*The Digest of Justinian*, 9.1.3). Damage done by animals "without any legal wrong on the part of the doer" (*ibid.*, 9.1.1,3) was labelled "pauperies" and was to be paid for by the owner or not to be paid for at all, depending on the situation and the circumstances. An animal was not a legal subject. In earlier times, however, it was said that either the animal that had done damage could be handed over or compensation had to be paid for the damage it had done (*aut noxiam sarcire aut in noxiam dedere*). The animal was regarded as being capable of guilt in committing a crime (cf. the discussions in Haymann 1921; Düll 1941).

The question of whether humans and animals were covered by a common form of justice had been discussed in philosophy. While Aristotle's successor, Theophrastus (*c.* 370–287 BCE), seems to have held that animals and humans were related to each other, and for that reason animals had a claim on justice, this was contested by Stoics and Epicureans. Cicero writes that *homini nihil iuris esse cum bestiis* – animals have no rights in relation to humans (*About the Ends of Good and Evil*, 3.67). He quotes Chrysippus, who said that all things were created for the sake of men and gods, and therefore "men can make use of beasts for their own purposes without injustice" (*ibid.*). This teleological argument was standard for the Stoics (see Chapter 2), but had ancient precedents. In Greece, Hesiod had maintained in the sixth century BCE that Zeus had "ordained this law [*nomos*] for men, that fishes and beasts and winged birds should devour one another, for right [*dike*] is not in them; but to mankind he gave right [*dike*] which proves far the best" (*Works and Days*, 276–80).

Like the Stoics, the Epicureans denied justice to animals on the grounds that they were not rational. Accordingly, they could not make contracts:

> Those animals which are incapable of making covenants with one another, to the end that they may neither inflict nor suffer harm, are without either justice or injustice. And those tribes which either could not or would not form mutual covenants to the same end are in like case.
>
> (Diogenes Laertius, *Epicurus*, 32)

However, the first part of this quotation is clearly ambiguous: "Those animals which are incapable" may allow for the possibility that there are in fact animals that are capable of making contracts (Sorabji 1993: 162; Clark 2000: 128, note 52). The successor of Epicurus, Hermarchus, whose opinion is discussed by Porphyry, is unwilling to allow for such a possibility (*On Abstinence*, 1.12.5–6). According to Hermarchus, it would have been fine if it had been possible to make a contract "with other animals, as with human beings". But it is impossible "for animals that are not receptive of reason to share in law" (1.12.5–6).

A different attitude is found in the Roman poet Lucretius (*c.* 99–55 BCE). In his poem about the history of civilization, *On the Nature of Things*, he contrasts wild animals with domestic ones such as dogs, beasts of burden, sheep and oxen:

> Firstly, the fierce brood of lions, that savage tribe, has been protected by courage, the wolf by cunning, by swiftness the stag. But the intelligent dog, so light of sleep and so true of heart, beasts

of burden of all kinds, woolly sheep also, and horned breeds of oxen, all these are entrusted to men's protection, Memmius. For these have eagerly fled from the wild beasts, they have sought peace and the generous provision gained by no labour of theirs, which we give them as the reward of their usefulness.

(On the Nature of Things, 5.864–70)

In Lucretius' view, men's protection or guardianship (tutela) is given to the animals that are useful to men (utilitas), while animals of prey are described as enemies of domestic animals as well as of humans. Lucretius apparently supported the idea of a mutual agreement between domestic animals and humans – meat, clothes and other services in exchange for food and protection (see also 5.860–1). Thus the agreement implied that animals should not be maltreated. Animals that were not useful to men were not covered by this agreement. Primitive man, who lived a life similar to the beasts, and those animals who were later domesticated had a mutual interest in making a pact with each other.

The question about Lucretius and animal contract has recently been discussed by Jo-Ann Shelton, who argues convincingly that the contract formation between animals and humans indicated by Lucretius resembles on some points human–human contracts as described by Epicurus (Shelton 1996: 51–2). She concludes that for Lucretius security and peace of mind are in part achieved "by a natural co-operating (contract formation) with some species and a separation from other (non-contract) species" (ibid.: 64).

However, it could be argued that Lucretius presents a vaguer idea than a contract. A mutual agreement is weaker than a contract, which, in contemporary philosophical parlance, was something more specific. Richard Sorabji makes the distinction when he discusses animal contracts (suntheke) (Sorabji 1993: 161–6). He distinguishes between an artificial contract on the one hand and parties having a natural agreement with each other on the other. Ancient authors sometimes implied that a sort of vague resemblance to contracts existed in the animal world, either between animals and animals or between animals and humans (cf. Sorabji 1993: 121, 165). One example is the act of ransom among ants, described as displaying the seeds (spermata) of justice (Plutarch, On the Cleverness of Animals, 967D–967E; Aelian, 6.50).

Similar examples are put forward by Pliny, Oppian and Dio. Pliny mentions that small snakes at Tiryns and serpents in Syria were said not to harm those who lived in the country, only foreigners (Natural History, 8.84). Apparently, the original inhabitants were believed to have a sort of tacit agreement with the snakes. Oppian calls special attention to the grey mullet, which "nurses the gentlest and most righteous mind" and does not touch fleshly food (2.642–3). According to Oppian, the mild nature of the mullet is the reason why no other fish harm it. Their behaviour is an expression of justice (dike), although, as Oppian remarks, justice usually dwells apart from the sea (2.664–5). When Pompey held a spectacle in 79 BCE, the elephants brought in to be killed by hunters throwing javelins at them were said by later commentators to have raised their trunks in the air and to have called upon heaven to avenge them. The reason was that before they left Africa, the elephants had received a pledge under oath from their drivers that they would not suffer any harm (Dio 39.38.2–5; cf. Pliny, *Natural History*, 8.7). In other words, an agreement had been made with these animals. Cicero thought that the crowd felt the elephants had "a fellowship with the human race" (*Letters to his Friends*, 7.1.3).

From these examples, it should be clear that even if one did not have to take into account an explicit contract (*suntheke*) between animals and humans in the same way as humans made contracts with each other, there was in some cases a notion of the existence of a natural agreement between animals and animals and between humans and animals.

The idea that such agreements existed between useful animals and humans is seen most clearly in the institution of animal sacrifice. Animal sacrifice, which originated in prehistory and continued through the first centuries CE, was the most significant symbolic context for domestication. In the sacrifice, the contract between humans and sacrificial animals was given a visible expression in the way the animal was led by a slack rope, not dragged by force, because any show of resistance was a bad omen (*Natural History*, 8.123), and by its being expected to nod in assent to its own slaughter. Consent was obviously an ideal in the institution of animal sacrifice (see Chapter 6).

One could make the objection that the animal did not know or expect that it was to be killed. Animals have no mental equipment for anticipating what is going to happen to them at the altar, so there is obviously a discrepancy in how animals and humans interpreted the implied agreement. It must also be added that the voluntary cooperation of the animal – its assent to its own slaughter – was not taken for granted. On the Parthenon frieze, some of the animals in the sacrificial procession are obviously unwilling. Iron rings bolted to the altars, where reluctant animals could be tied, bear further witness to a routine where lack of consent on the part of the animal in question was expected. But even if the voluntary consent of the animal was a fiction, a formality and a pious comedy (van Straten 1995: 100–3), the idea that the sacrifice was ideally based on an agreement between animals and humans was still intact.

When sacrificial animals are described as contract animals, the description covers the idea of a tacit understanding shared by humans and domestic animals that mutual cooperation would be beneficial to both.[5] Animal services towards humans are exchanged for food and shelter, and domestication rests on mutual benefits between humans and animals. "Contract animal" covers Graeco-Roman ideas about natural agreements between humans and animals, sometimes made explicit in relation to specific animals or groups of animals.

The idea of the existence of an agreement between humans and domesticated animals is reflected in the animal sacrifice.

Divination by means of animals

Divination by means of the inspection of the internal parts of the victim was part of animal sacrifice. Divinatory specialists took care of the dead animal. The *haruspices* interpreted the entrails, and others inspected the liver (*hepatoscopy*) or sometimes also their shoulder blades (*omoplatoscopy*).

In addition to divinatory practices connected with sacrificed animals, the Romans based part of their divinatory techniques on systematic observation of the movement and behaviour of living animals, especially birds. *Auspicia* means "bird watching". It implies that signs were taken on the basis of the flight of birds, their singing or their manner of eating, while *alektryonomancy* consisted of observing the behaviour of sacred chickens (see van der Horst 1998).

An example of how divinatory birds were viewed is the well-known story about the consul Publius Claudius Pulcher, who consulted the sacred chickens during the first Punic War (264–241 BCE) (Cicero, *On the Nature of the Gods*, 2.3.7; *On Divination*, 1.29, 2.71). These chickens were kept in a cage, and omens were taken from the way they ate. When the chickens were released, they declined to eat. This was a bad omen, indeed, and Claudius Pulcher "ordered them to be thrown into the water, so that as they would not eat, they might drink" (*On the Nature of the Gods*, 2.3.7). The moral of the story is that because Claudius Pulcher disobeyed the auspices, he lost a fleet. Obviously, his lack of respect for chickens is not the point. This is not a story about the evil of maltreating animals but about the stupidity of not listening to the messages of the gods and not acknowledging their divine power. The chickens appeared neither as persons nor as the confidants of the gods but were vehicles of meanings and conceived of as signs.[6]

Some thought that birds actually spoke and that chosen people knew their language and understood what they foretold (Porphyry, *On Abstinence*, 3.4). The idea that some animals have a conception of the divine and that prophetic animals – for instance birds – are in close communication with God was defended, for instance by Celsus (second century CE) (Origen, *Against Celsus*, 4.88).

Observations based on spontaneous occurrences in the natural world were also interpreted as signs about the future (*prodigia*). A considerable part of such observations was based on animals. Often the unsolicited signs were abnormal, or rather supranormal occurrences, as is clearly seen when Livy (59 BCE–17 CE) and Obsequens (fourth or early fifth century CE) report talking cows and oxen.[7] Prodigies were usually forebodings of evil, and countermeasures had to be taken.

Consulting and interpreting omens was a necessary part of Roman decision-making processes. The point has recently been stressed by historian

Jorgen Christian Meyer, who describes how, through divination, decisions were given legitimacy and invested with persuasive power (Meyer 2002). Cicero, for instance, thought that augury was established for reasons of state (*On Divination*, 2.70, 2.75). The importance of divination as an element in political as well as private decisions must not be underestimated. From a Roman perspective, gods existed. They ruled the universe, sometimes revealed their will and advised men through signs about the future. In addition, historical examples proved the validity of augury – even if the sources agree that the augurs did not always manage to interpret the signs correctly at the time these signs were given. When, just before his own death, Emperor Julian was presented with a lion that had been slain, he thought it a good omen. As was later revealed, this traditionally royal animal did not herald the death of the emperor's enemies but the death of the emperor himself (Ammianus Marcellinus, *The History*, 25.5.8–9).[8] It was obviously important to take control of the interpretation and lines of communication between gods and men and not allow rivals to promote their own agendas through competing interpretations (Linderski 1982).

Different types of divination were frequently combined, as is clear from a remark by Suetonius about Augustus: "Again, as he was taking the auspices in his first consulship, twelve vultures appeared to him, as to Romulus, and when he slew the victims, the liver within all of them was found to be doubled inward at the lower end, which all those who were skilled in such matters unanimously declared to be an omen of a great and happy future" (95). Such combinations of omens based on living animals with omens based on dead animals suggest that the living animals had a similar status to those that had been sacrificed. Both categories were normally regarded as ignorant of the message they were transmitting. However, according to Pliny, one exception is ravens, which "are the only birds who in the auspices understand the message that they convey" (*Natural History*, 10.33). When Porphyry (234–305 CE) mentions the possibility that it is the souls of dead animals that respond to the divinator's questions by means of signs in the entrails, it is not the animals as such that are responding, but their liberated souls (*On Abstinence*, 2.51.3). However, Porphyry states that birds understand the gods more quickly than humans and pass the message on to humans as best they can (*On Abstinence*, 3.5.5). Similarly, Iamblichus (245–325 CE) thinks that factors that are external to the animals set them in motion. According to him, the gods are transmitting impulses but themselves remain above creation (*On the Egyptian Mysteries*, 3.16). Iamblichus even mentions that birds sometimes destroy themselves, an act that is highly unnatural for any creature. This clearly shows that the birds did not act according to their own will, power or personality but that something else accomplished the signs through the birds (*On the Egyptian Mysteries*, 3.16).

Not everybody believed in divination. Cicero, himself an augur, wrote a treatise about divination with the purpose of showing that it was a superstition. One of his many examples is of cocks, which by their crowing were said to have signalled victory for the Thebans. Cicero asked if it really was believable that "Jupiter would have employed chickens to convey such a message to so great a state?" He pursued the point, saying ironically that it is natural for cocks to crow, and therefore it would have been more of a portent if a fish and not a cock had done the crowing (*On Divination*, 2.56). Cicero's point is that animals can only do what is natural to them.

Christian authors were opposed to divination and wrote against it. Origen (184/5–254/5 CE) wrote that if birds really had prophetic power and wisdom, they would not have been caught in traps by men (*Against Celsus*, 4.90–1). These animals are not in any way close to the divine, wrote Origen. The true God uses neither irrational animals nor ordinary men to reveal knowledge about the future but only the most holy human beings, who are the biblical prophets (4.95.1–4). Man is God's instrument, not irrational animals. On the contrary, evil demons creep into wild animals so that they in reality become instruments for the demons (4.92). Their prophetic power is thus the work of the Devil. In a similar way to non-Christian authors, Origen regarded it as possible that spiritual beings could talk through animals, but because he identifies these voices as demonic, some demonic quality also seems to infect the animals in question. Divinity is connected with the human, while the demonic is connected with the beasts. All the same, Origen is no more willing than pagan authors to regard these animals as free-acting agents.

Consequently, when living animals were used as oracles, they were not conceived of as acting freely – at least by the text-producing elite – but as media for the messages they were transmitting. Forces that were external to the animals were thought to be moving them when these animals were rein-vented as divinatory signs. They were natural texts written on by others. In this way, the divinatory animals did not receive a superior status in relation to other animals. Although like sacrificial animals they probably received the best treatment so that they were kept in good shape, they appeared as little more than vehicles of meaning and thus functioned as instruments of superior powers. So while a faint notion of the animal as a free-acting agent that gave its consent to be slaughtered clung to the sacrificial beast, animals used in divination seem to have been seen as acting freely to a lesser degree than the sacrificial animals.

Entertainment

Personal animals

On the Graeco-Roman entertainment scene, animals appeared as pets, competed on the racetrack and fought with each other or were hunted in the arenas. In general, when animals are kept as pets, relationships based on intimacy and mutual understanding between animals and humans are established. Pet keeping probably appeared very early in the history of man (Zeuner 1963: 39). In his description of attitudes to animals in England (1500–1800), Keith Thomas stresses three particular features that distinguished pets from other animals: the pet was allowed into the house; it was given an individual personal name; and it was never eaten (Thomas 1984: 112–16).

However, Graeco-Roman society was not a pet-keeping society in a similar way to early modern English society and even less so than advanced capitalist societies today. No general compassion or sympathy for oppressed groups, human or animal, existed, and no industry catered specifically for pets and their needs. It is probably better not to call the animals in question pets but rather to label them "personal animals" to avoid identifying these human–animal relationships too closely with modern pet culture. On mosaics, for instance, children are shown killing small animals such as rabbits and ducks in what seems to be an imitation of *venationes*, hunting games. These mosaics reveal a playful attitude, and the artist seems to have found the scene rather cute (Brown 1992: 200ff; Dunbabin 1999: 116, 133, 140–1).

The personal animals described in our sources mostly belonged to the elite. They are examples of how animals were individualized on a one-to-one basis. Creating a personal relationship with an animal represented humanization of it, although different species were made personal animals in different ways. A relationship with a dog was different from a relationship with a snake or, for that matter, with an eel. In some occupations, there was daily contact between humans and animals. In some cases, this contact also created mutual bonding and a personal relationship. The love and pride displayed by representatives of the emperor's horse guard towards their horses and the way they identified with them are to be seen in the fact that nearly all the tombstones from their cemetery in Rome portray horses (Speidel 1994: 109).

In some cases of human–animal relationships, one could ask if they were more a product of Roman misanthropy than of love for fellow creatures. An often-told tale is about Vedius Pollio, a friend of Augustus, who is said to have fed his lampreys on slaves who had been sentenced to death (Seneca, *On Anger*, 3.40.2; *Natural History*, 9.39; Dio Cassius, 54.23). Pliny says that the lampreys were the only creatures through whom Vedius Pollio was able "to have the spectacle of a man being torn entirely to pieces in one moment". The Christian author Origen describes how the lampreys' owner cooked these pets and ate them together with the contents of their entrails.

Such stories are gruesome comments on the status of one human group (slaves) in relation to animals, and, in the case of Origen, on pagans in relation to Christians (no better than man-eating lampreys). Also, when Elagabalus made his lions roam loose in the palace during the night, terrifying his guests (the animals had had their teeth and claws extracted, a fact that the guests did not know), the lions' behaviour was a comment on the status of animals in relation to humans and not least on Elagabalus' status in relation to his guests.

What was special in Rome was the way "unapproachable" animals were kept as pets. Lions were kept by some of the emperors, for instance Elagabalus and Caracalla. Bears could also be held inside houses, and stags appeared in private gardens. These expensive wild animals may reasonably be interpreted as status symbols. However, most peculiar is the way in which chosen fish were elevated to the status of personal animals. Kept in artificial ponds, they were said to recognize the voice of their owner, to come when they were called, to take food from their owner's hands and to let themselves be cuddled. Crassus (d. 53 BCE), triumvir with Caesar and Pompey, mourned his moray eel (*muraena*), which had beautifully marbled skin, when it died and had it buried (*Natural History*, 8.4). Crassus' fish is also said to have been adorned with jewels, to have obeyed the call of its master and to have fed from his hand.

Less strange were caged birds and mice appearing as children's pets. Although cats are seen on mosaics and tombstones and played roles in fables and folklore, their value seems primarily to have been as destroyers of vermin (Engels 1999: 83–137). Monkeys were not uncommon, and some people, for instance Emperor Tiberius, had tame snakes.

As in Western societies today, the Greeks and Romans kept dogs. Poems and grave monuments show how affectionately they were treated by their owners. A rather touching example is a tomb from the recent excavations for the Metropolitan Railway of Athens, which contained the buried remains of a dog (tomb 82, Syntagma station). The tomb was constructed of brick walls and had paved floors. Buried with the animal were two perfume bottles made of glass dating from the first–second century CE. The relics of the dog's collar – a number of bronze roundels – were also *in situ* near the animal's neck. A further dog burial, as well as one of a horse together with a dog, were found on the same site (*The City beneath the City, Exhibition in the Museum of Cycladic Art*, 2000).

But Greeks and Romans did not in principle recoil from the thought of eating dogs, which is a warning against identifying modern pets too closely with Graeco-Roman personal animals. In the Hippocratic collection, the quality of their meat is discussed: "Dogs' flesh dries fevers and gives strength, but does not pass through as stool" (*Regimen*, 2.46). This discussion is also taken up by Galen (Garnsey 1999: 83–4).

Like dogs, horses had a reputation for fidelity towards humans (*Natural History*, 8.61). Pliny regarded horses as intelligent (*ibid.*, 8.64–5). Generally, the horse was a status symbol – social rank could be defined in relation to owning a horse, as the Roman *equites*, "horse owners", show (McK. Camp 1998: 10). To be able to afford a horse conferred social dignity. There was a passion for chariot racing. All over the empire it was the most popular sport, with the best horses coming from North Africa and Spain (Balsdon 1969:

315). The horses had personal names. There is the famous story about Caligula, who, according to Suetonius, threatened to make his horse Incitatus a senator, built it a palace and slept in its stable (*Caligula*, 55.3). The emotional climate surrounding racehorses and their achievements on the race-track is reflected in curse tablets. There are numerous examples of curse tablets naming drivers and steeds and willing the horses to fall or break their legs (Gager 1992: 15, 21). The opposite are spells to force the horses to run even when they are tired (*ibid.*: 59, 62, 69). Horse-demons – hybrids between men and animals – are sometimes used as illustrations on magical spells.

Although there never was a great zoo in the city (Balsdon 1969: 303), animals were sometimes exhibited in the theatre, the arena and the circus. Augustus, for instance, displayed animals sent to him from the provinces in the Forum (Auguet 1994: 83). At the end of a hunting spectacle (*venatio*) in the arena, animals that had been trained to perform tricks were sometimes shown (*ibid.*: 84). Romans were also fond of the type of entertainment in which animals appeared without being killed, and they were thrilled by the thought that some animals could learn to speak. Plutarch says that "fair Rome has provided us a reservoir [of examples of the cleverness of animals] from which to draw in pails and buckets as it were, from the imperial spectacles" (*Moralia*, 963c).

Personal relations with animals were not institutionalized on a common social basis in the Graeco-Roman world. These relations were individual ventures into the animal world. All the same, they are examples of a general aspect of human–animal relations in which the categorical boundaries between humans and animals are partly dissolved.

Animals as enemies

More characteristic of the entertainment business of the empire than personal animals and animals performing tricks were animals that took part in hunting spectacles in the arenas (*venationes*), where they were normally killed in great numbers. The hunting spectacle implicitly showed animals as enemies to each other and to humans.

In contrast to animal sacrifice, which was an age-old institution, the arena was a relatively new institution. Its roots were older than the empire, but it developed in parallel with the growth of the empire. The first hunting spectacle with exotic animals – lions and panthers – was put on by Marcus Fulvius Nobilior in 186 BCE (Livy, 39.5.7–10; 39.22.2). These hunting "games" enjoyed growing popularity during the last century of the Roman republic. The construction of permanent stone amphitheatres in the first century CE made it easier to control the animals, and more spectators could be seated with a higher degree of safety (Balsdon 1969: 252–61; Coleman 1990: 50–1). In the Flavian Amphitheatre (Colosseum), one of the precautions was to install nets between the animals and the spectators.

The killing of animals in the arena presupposed an imperialistic state and a system that made it possible to catch, preserve and deliver the animals in Rome or to arenas in the provinces. Wild beast fighting, especially in North Africa, was extremely popular. In his *Natural History*, Pliny recalls the occasions when the different species of animal were first introduced to the Roman people. His account reflects a consciousness of the arena as a relatively new institution and of some of the animal species as recent innovations. One of the origins of the arena, and one of its models, was the hunt, which is one of the oldest institutional contexts of human–animal relations. The arena can be regarded as the end-product of a long process in which people gradually established control over, and in some places eliminated, the threat from wild beasts.

To early man, carnivores were a real threat to his life and society, and he may have seen himself as subordinate to animals (Lorblanchet 1989: 137–9). All the same – or precisely because animals were a real threat – Palaeolithic and Neolithic societies seem to have admired animals, to judge from their art. Animals were also admired by the high cultures around the Mediterranean. In Mesopotamia and Egypt, conquering lions was a sport for kings, and the aristocratic elites hunted big game. A zoo with exotic animals had been a proof of Pharaoh's claim to rule the ordered world (Hornung 1999: 68–9).

While wild beast fights had been popular in the late republic, under the empire they developed into large-scale animal massacres (Pliny, *Natural History*, 8.20.53; 8.24.64). They took place in the morning and were called *venationes*. A *venatio* involved the display and slaughter of animals, which could include big cats, bears, rhinoceroses, elephants, hippopotamuses, hyenas, seals, aurochs, crocodiles, ostriches and even pythons. Probably from the time of Augustus, the *venatio* was followed by the execution of criminals in the middle of the day, and by gladiator fights (*munera*) in the evening. The animals used in *venationes* were attended by *bestiarii*, professional hunters, schooled in their art. The animals were both imported and indigenous. They included wild animals (*ferae, bestiae*) and carnivores (*dentatae* – "toothed"), but domesticated ones (*pecudes*) were also used.

The hunt really consisted of two stages. The first was the initial capture of the animals in the wild. They were trapped, captured in pits or with nets, and were transported roped, chained or in cages in ox carts and in ships. From all parts of the empire, from Mesopotamia and Egypt, England and the Rhine valley, animals were brought to Rome. Many of them were unloaded at Rome's docks (Pliny, *Natural History*, 36.4.40). From there, the animals were assembled at menageries (*vivaria*) in the city or nearby. In the arenas, the animals were kept in cages in the lower levels of the Colosseum and in special areas outside the city. An edict issued by those who were responsible for shows and spectacles, the *curule aediles*, pointed out that the keepers of dogs and wild animals were responsible for eventual damage caused by these animals. Wild and dangerous animals were not to be kept in a place where people could be hurt (Robinson 1994: 207). There were also collections of animals in several cities, private menageries or public exhibitions of animals; for instance, a *vivarium* existed outside the Porta Praenestina in Rome (Toynbee 1996: 20).

The second and final stage of the hunt did not take place in the natural habitat of the animal but when it had been transported to the heart of the empire, to Rome or to arenas in other cities. In the fights, bulls were set against panthers, rhinoceroses against bears and lions against tigers, as well as all types of animal against humans. The hunt had become a spectacular show over which the emperor presided as its patron and all classes of people participated as spectators.

What eventually happened in the arenas presupposed both an infrastructure and a huge organization – people who hunted, preserved and transported the animals from the place where they were originally caught to their final destination. For instance, the soldiers of the Roman imperial army were used to capture and transport exotic animals from the places where they were situated (Epplett 2001). Some of these soldiers had specific hunting duties as bear hunters (*ursarii*) or were assigned to capture lions (*ad leones*). The *venationes* would also have involved a large number of people who took care of the animals in the menageries and in the arena. Obviously, the trade in wild animals was a thriving business.

The number of slaughtered animals was continually being increased. The largest reliably proven number was 11,000 animals, both wild and tame, over 123 days in 108–9 CE during Trajan's triumph (Dio, 68.15.1). An alternative, and a supplement to increasing the number of animals, was to introduce new species, to set up new combinations of animals to fight against each other or to introduce new and more spectacular settings for their fights.

Besides fighting each other, animals were also used as executioners. One of the ways in which low-status offenders (*humiliores*) were punished was to be condemned to the beasts – *damnatio ad bestias* – and to be torn to death by the animals, a punishment introduced for deserters in the middle of the second century BCE by Scipio the Younger (see Chapter 9). Alternative types of punishment were burning or crucifixion, but there was an increasing tendency to condemn people to the beasts (Robinson 1994: 195). This sort of punishment was used for what were regarded as severe crimes such as murder of one's relatives or one's master, sacrilege, and arson. These executions could also be set in a mythological frame, an invention that flourished especially in the first two centuries of the empire. K.M. Coleman has labelled these mythological enactments of executions "fatal charades" (Coleman 1990). Martial describes how a criminal disguised as Orpheus was killed at the dedication of the Flavian Amphitheatre in 80 CE: "Every kind of wild beast [*genus omne ferarum*] was there, mixed with the flock and above the minstrel hovered many birds, but the minstrel fell, torn apart by an ungrateful bear [*ab urso ingrato*]" (*On the Spectacles*, 21).

The arenas implied human superiority over a new type of animal. Domesticated animals are by definition controlled animals, because humans have taken control of their lives, their reproduction and their death. With the introduction of the arenas, wild animals too were now put under human domination. This "domestication" of wild animals is to be seen for instance in their collective pet names. Roman wit labelled elephants "Lucanian oxen", ostriches were "sea sparrows", and leopards were "African mice" (Balsdon 1969: 303). Like racehorses, some of the animals that fought in the arena could be given their own personal names and thereby individual identities. Names of leopards and bears are recorded on mosaics. On a mosaic showing a *venatio* with leopards from Smirat in Tunisia, the four leopards are called Victor, Crispinus, Luxurius and Romanus (Potter and Mattingly 1999: 310). However, these beasts could never be controlled completely; sometimes they did not attack when they should, while at other times they maimed or killed the *bestiarii* or even some of the spectators. These traits were reminders of their wildness and hostility but did not radically change the fact that the animals had now been put firmly under human control.

Animals sometimes appeared in unusual contexts. Even a lion in the arena, presented as a foe, could turn into a personal animal. The story about Androcles, the slave who was condemned to the beasts but not killed because he had once taken a thorn out of the paw of the very lion that was sent against him, is perhaps the most famous. In this case, a human–animal friendship existed in spite of the human–animal division on which the spectacles of the arena were based. Such stories were greatly loved. Animals in unusual contexts created special effects, which were sometimes specially required.

The *venationes*, as well as the gladiator contests, contributed to demonstrating the authority of the emperor as well as the extent of the empire and the wealth of those who paid for the shows. The hunt was still a royal enterprise, and several of the emperors were ardent hunters, but in the arenas, the hunt had at the same time been democratized and made less dangerous. Although there were emperors who shot the animals themselves (Commodus is probably the best-known example), animals in the arenas were usually killed by professional hunters (Suetonius, *Tiberius*, 72.2; Balsdon 1969: 432, note 341).

Roland Auguet mentions how "the slaughter of a lion in the very centre of Rome" amounted to a considerable expense and "was considered by the Romans to be the symbol of their complete power over the universe" (Auguet 1994: 112–13). In a similar vein, Thomas Wiedemann has stressed that these games dramatized human domination over animals but also symbolized social domination. Cruel and destructive animals were got rid of, and the process showed both how man controlled nature and how Rome controlled the world (Wiedemann 1995: 62–7).[9] The rich variety of animals really illustrated the geographical expansion of Rome's influence. Like the obelisks from Egypt, the fragments from Eastern temples that adorned the city of Rome (Edwards 1996: 100) and the miscellaneous population that roamed its streets, the animal shows were one of the ways in which the extent of the empire and the might of Rome were demonstrated explicitly to the city's inhabitants.

In the shows, the animals were turned into each other's antagonists and the antagonists of Rome. All classes of people were thus cast as different from animals, except those criminals and barbarians who were exposed to the animals and killed by them. The spectacle consisted of parading the ferocity and wildness of the animals, at the same time as the beasts were controlled and did what they were staged to do. Displayed in agonistic contexts as foes to one another and to humans, the animals had at the same time lost their independence and become tools of human will and purpose.

Because of their courage in fighting and killing wild beasts, gladiators were linked with Hercules. When they retired, they dedicated their weapons to him. The emperors were also compared to and identified with Hercules, as witnessed on coins (Wiedemann 1995: 178). As Hercules fought mythological beasts and the gladiators conquered the animals of the arenas, the emperors fought the foes of Rome. Commodus, for instance, who showed himself to the Roman people as a gladiator, identified himself with Hercules and wanted to make the divine hero a symbol of his rule. Many statues of Commodus appear with the emperor wearing the skin of the Nemean lion and holding a club (Grant 1996: 75–6).

The arena outlived animal sacrifices, even if the fact that the Vandals held North Africa made supplies from this important area for export of wild animals difficult. The last time that *venationes* were organized in Rome was in 523 CE, after which they were outlawed. After that, there is no record of that type of spectacle in Rome, while in the Eastern provinces, *venationes* seem to have survived for much of the sixth century (Roueché 1993: 76–9).

Conclusion

In the Roman Empire, the use of animals was fundamental and absolutely necessary. Not only the consumption of food and clothes made out of animal products but also the use of power based on animals' bodies was essential for the management of the empire. Compared with the way in which other agricultural populations conducted themselves in relation to animals, it is also striking how actively the Romans used exotic animals. They were used as food, in medicine, as pets and in the arenas. This varied use of exotic animals visually demonstrated the extent of the empire and contributed to the integration of Rome as the centre of that empire and its different parts.

Institutional ceremonies showing animal–human relations were sacrifice, divination and the arenas. Animal sacrifices were among other things a ritualization of the agricultural relations between animals and humans and an illustration of the idea — if only a vague one — that the relations between humans and domesticated animals were based on a mutual contract. The prototype of the contract animal is the domestic animal, mostly the herbivore. And even if animal sacrifice adapted itself to the great empire with its new imperial ideology and emperor cult and eventually sometimes also included more exotic animals, its ancient origin and predominant use of indigenous animals made it different from the more recent introduction of the arena. Live animals that were used in divination were more like objects or media upon which the gods had inscribed their will.

The animal games in the arenas were a ritualization of hunting, and the arenas basically showed animals as foes that had to be conquered. The prototype of the animal as foe is the carnivore, although domesticated animals were also used. It is significant that the ritualized hunts in the arenas continued with the blessing of the government for more than a hundred years, in some places for nearly two centuries, after animal sacrifice had been banned.[10]

The fact that a ban was laid on sacrifice while the institution of the arena continued is a direct consequence of the victory of Christianity, but it probably also reflects a change in the evaluation of animals. While animal sacrifice had been an institution that showed the differences but also the mutual relationship between humans and animals, the arenas served to brutalize and radicalize the divisions between humans and non-humans. And while the sacrifice served as a focus for the relationship between humans and domestic animals, which was basically a contract relationship, the arena focused in principle on the domination, hunting and killing of wild animals. Since the hunting spectacles continued after animal sacrifices were stopped, the meanings linked with them must still have been culturally important. It probably also shows that the reciprocity and interdependence of humans and animals, which was an inherent meaning of animal sacrifice, had gradually changed to a more domineering view on animals. The different fate of the institution of animal sacrifice and the institution of the arena in the fourth to fifth century could be the result of a general change in the conception of animals in these centuries.

In the first centuries CE, there was continuous cultural work to establish new categorical boundaries between humans and animals. How these boundaries were set up varied according to different genres, as for instance in philosophy, in natural history and in literary works. It is also clear that the processes of keeping animal and human categories apart were matched with attempts to fuse them. The intertwining of these processes — making distinctions between animals and humans as well as investigating and developing the overlapping areas between them — can be traced in thought and science as well as in fantasy and imagination. These processes and their interplay will be the subject of the following chapters.

2

UNITED BY SOUL OR DIVIDED BY REASON?

Thinking about animals

In the Roman Empire, there was increased interest in animals and their status in relation to humans.[1] This interest was dependent on a general expansion of knowledge during the empire and was closely linked to imperial expansion, which led to the development of encyclopaedic knowledge in many fields, for instance in zoology. But more important for the present purpose, this interest in animals was also nourished by the growing interest in man and his personality and characteristics. Animals were used to describe humans and, not least, to be a contrast to them so that humans were set apart as something special and close to the gods.

What characterizes an animal? What are the differences between animals and humans? These questions were implied in natural histories and in the physiognomic tradition as well as in different types of vegetarian practice. And above all, they were the focus of philosophical debate (cf. especially Dierauer 1977, 1997; Sorabji 1993). The development of the conception of animals in philosophy, vegetarianism, natural histories and physiognomy is the theme of this chapter and the next.

How animals were thought of in the first to the fourth century CE depended on the imagination and thought of previous centuries. There were different layers in the tradition concerning animals. In the background of the debate, and frequently referred to, loomed the enigmatic and partly mythical figures of Pythagoras from the sixth century BCE and Empedocles from the fifth century BCE. From the fourth century BCE come the influential texts of Plato and Aristotle. However, it is striking that much of what we know about the thoughts of Pythagoras and Empedocles stems from the first centuries CE as part of a Pythagorean revival at this time. Their ideas about reincarnation and vegetarianism were transmitted by authors such as Ovid (43 BCE–17 CE), Seneca (4 BCE–65 CE) Plutarch (c. 50–120 CE), Philostratus (d. c. 250 CE), Porphyry (c. 232–305 CE) and Iamblichus (245–325 CE). What Pythagoras and Empedocles really thought about these subjects is difficult to know, as only fragments of their teachings have been preserved.

However, later generations of philosophers clearly looked to them for inspiration, and Pythagoras' and Empedocles' ideas about animals acquired a new relevance during the empire.

In the traditions of these past masters, as well as in the Orphic tradition, there was a belief in transmigration of souls according to which humans could be reborn as animals and animals as humans (Haussleiter 1935: 79–163). Orpheus felt that humans and animals were basically the same and that killing animals was murder. These traditions, and especially references to Pythagoras, were used to justify vegetarian practice during the empire (cf. Riedweg 2002: 162). Plato too spoke about reincarnation involving both humans and animals. Animals and humans were united by the same soul and participated in the same cycle of reincarnation. Although this cycle implied a hierarchy among living beings – it was better to be born a man than a beast – it also implied that humans and animals were interconnected and that the psychic space between them was reduced.

If the soul united man and beast, it was something else that had gradually started to divide them. That was reason. The discussion of the mental equipment of animals was a by-product of the more extensive age-old debate about the human mind and about perception and sensation, memory and knowledge. What was the status of animals in relation to humans? Did animals have speech? Were they equipped with reason?

In the debate about animals, there had been some key positions. There was an increasing tendency to see reason as a categorical boundary between animals and humans. While some of the older philosophers, such as Parmenides (540–480 BCE), Anaxagoras (500–428 BCE) and Archelaos (fifth century BCE) (Haussleiter 1935: 207ff; Lovejoy and Boas 1935: 390), were more positive towards animals' mental equipment, the Stoics and also the Epicureans in the main denied them reason and saw it as a special human characteristic. However, it was Aristotle who represented the real watershed in the conception of animals. Philosopher Richard Sorabji maintains "that a single decision in Aristotle, the denial to animals of reason and belief, led in Aristotle and the Stoics to a massive re-analysis of psychological capacities" (Sorabji 1993: 103). Sorabji quite clearly confirms that Aristotle represented a turning-point in thinking about animals and also that his influence on the subject was considerable.

Natural scientific descriptions of animals had as their main sources Aristotle's *History of Animals* (nine books), *Parts of Animals* (four books), *On the Generation of Animals* (five books) and *On the Locomotion of Animals* (one book). Basic to these descriptions is a comparison between men and animals according to which animals are naturally imperfect in relation to man. And while animals are imperfect in relation to man, man has, even if he is far from being perfect, something in common with the highest category of beings, namely the gods. According to Aristotle, "Man is the only animal that stands upright, and this is because his nature and essence is divine" (*Parts of Animals*,

686a). Although it must be stressed that Aristotle's texts about animals are nuanced and multilayered and do not represent a simple rejection of the abilities of animals (*History of Animals*, 588a, b) – for instance, many things that are fully developed in man exist as rudiments in animals – all the same, to Aristotle man is indisputably the high point of nature (French 1994: 59–62). It is also important to remember that even if Aristotle saw a continuity in nature, he did not see an evolution. This implies that the different species had always been separate from each other: there was no point in prehistory when their lines of development converged. Actually, the different species had no lines of development. A lion had always been a lion, and a pig had always been a pig. So even if animals and humans were in some aspects seen as close to each other and as sharing some properties, man was divided from animals by reason and the power of speech and held a unique position, because his mind (*nous*) was regarded as close to the divine.

In the centuries that followed, the Stoics especially developed a philosophy concerning animals. The theme that unifies the different Stoic texts on this subject is that animals and humans are categorically different. Human beings are related to gods: they have reason, language and freedom to act. Beasts are irrational. The standard term for animals (*ta aloga* – "the irrational ones") contrasts with the way a human being is described as a *zoon logikon*, a rational animal. According to the Stoics, animals acted according to nature (*apo physeos*) and not according to reason. Therefore, animals of the same species would always act in a similar way, even if they were isolated from other examples of their species. This explained for the Stoics why animals, which were not rational, still had an innate natural cleverness. Nature cares for them, and thus animals know things without learning them. This "natural cleverness" was also thought to explain why these irrational creatures did not simply perish. As Seneca put it laconically: "Dumb beasts, sluggish in other respects, are clever at living" (*Epistle*, 121.24).

Reason and speech were closely connected, and in Greek the same term, *logos*, could be used for both, although the Stoics distinguished between internal reason, which was thought (*logos endiathetos*), and external reason, which was expressed in speech (*logos prophorikos*). The distinction had been created in the debate between the Academicians and the Stoics. The Stoics regarded the human voice to be a reflection of thought, while the animal voice was essentially different (Pohlenz 1948: 39–40, 185).[2]

Lack of reason is a categorical boundary that is more absolute than prohibitions on how to interact with animals. That people may eat animals, but animals are not allowed to eat people; that animals eat raw meat, while humans must boil it; that humans and animals are not allowed to have sexual intercourse; these are all rules governing the relations between the species that do not necessarily imply that humans and animals have different mental equipment. When animals are characterized as being fundamentally different from humans by a lack of what was now seen as the basic human characteristic, *logos* (reason), this classification conveys a greater sense of difference between animals and humans than external controls on the relations between them. At least in a society where intellectual education and rhetorical power – the virtuoso use of words – were highly esteemed and marked out the elite in contrast to common people and barbarians, lack of reason was a flaw indeed. This categorical distinction placed animals and humans in a kind of binary opposition that lacked a middle ground. The principle of excluding the middle ground was common in antiquity, as seen in categorical opposites such as male/female, free/slave and Greek/barbarian (Malina and Neyrey 1996: 102–3). These opposites were basic elements in natural hierarchies of being. The distinction man/animal belonged to this type.

Stoics used teleological arguments in support of such natural hierarchies (cf. Aristotle, *Politics*, 1256b): plants exist for the sake of animals, animals for the sake of men. The idea that animals were created for the sake of man is seldom found in Greece before the Stoics, but it appears frequently in the Hellenist period as a result of Stoic influence. The purpose of animal existence was their usefulness to humans. Cicero has already been quoted as restricting the usefulness of sheep to their furnishing men with material for clothes (*The Nature of the Gods*, 2.63). About the pig he says that "it can only furnish food" (2.64) and adds, as the view of Chrysippus, that the pig's soul serves as salt to keep it from putrefaction (*ibid.*). The Stoic view that animals were made for the use of men was later taken over by Jews and Christians and applied in the interpretation of the biblical tradition (see below).

One might have thought that since, according to the Stoics, nature encompasses everything, and animals and humans are subject to the same processes and thus in the same boat, so to speak, the Stoics would have been more interested in the treatment of animals. But even if ethics was one of their major themes, the Stoics do not, according to Richard Sorabji, seem to have devoted any of their many handbooks to the need to treat animals well (Sorabji 1993: 125). It has been suggested that the price the Stoics paid for establishing a universal human community was that this community was simultaneously sharply divided from the animal world. The aim of the Stoics was in the words of Max Pohlenz "überall die Grenze zwischen Mensch und Tier scharf zu ziehen" (Pohlenz 1948: 40). The result of this division was that the complex philosophical tradition of Stoicism, with its great sophistication in describing psychological processes, offered a relatively simple and pragmatic solution to the "animal problem". The purpose of animals is to serve, and each animal has its specific purpose in the service of man. We have already quoted Cicero, Seneca and Chrysippus on this point, but similar views are also found among other leading Stoics, for instance Epictetus (55–135 CE):

> Each of the animals God constitutes, one to be eaten, another to serve in farming, another to produce cheese, and yet another for

some other similar use; to perform these functions what need have they to understand external impressions and to be able to differentiate between them? But God had brought man into the world to be a spectator of Himself and of His works, and not merely a spectator, but also an interpreter. Wherefore it is shameful for man to begin and end just where the irrational animals do; he should rather begin where they do, but end where nature has ended in dealing with us.

(Arrian's *Discourses of Epictetus, 1.6.18–20*)

But just as soldiers appear before their general, all ready for service, shod, clothed and armed, and it would be shocking if the colonel had to go around and equip his regiment with shoes or uniforms; so also nature has made animals, which are born for service, ready for use, equipped, and in need of no further attention. Consequently one small child with a rod can drive a flock of sheep.

(*ibid.*, 1.16.4–5)

In these passages, divine providence and the laws of nature legitimate man's elevation as well as the duty and purpose of animals to serve him. There is an overlap between animals and humans, but humans should not remain on the animal side but rather concentrate on developing what is specifically human.

More nuanced and complex approaches to animal roles and functions were offered by some of the Platonists. The Pythagorean revival and its influence on middle Platonism may also have contributed to making animals an issue in these centuries. It is also worth noting that both Philo's and Plutarch's writings on animals indicate that the status of animals was sometimes made a topic for staged debates. The status of animals was a controversial point between Platonists and Stoics – besides being an entertaining topic to discuss. This type of contextualization – a public debate – may have contributed to making sharp polarizations, rich exemplifications, a vivid discourse and entertaining reading.

The efforts of Aristotelians, Epicureans, Stoics, Jews and Christians did not close the debate on the status of animals. Some of the followers of Plato, especially Celsus, Plutarch and Porphyry, opposed them and were more nuanced in their views. There seems to have been a new impetus to the debate about animals in the first centuries of the Christian era. According to Robert Lamberton, "In Plutarch's time, the debate was broadening (as it has conspicuously in our own times) into a widespread concern with the proper relations between humans and animals" (Lamberton 2001: 9).

Some highly profiled texts about animals and their status and value have been transmitted from the last pagan centuries. Some of them also raised the question of whether reason was the only relevant categorical boundary mark. Even if animals were denied reason, they could still have sensations and feelings and therefore should be treated with compassion. Perhaps humans might even owe them justice?

Plutarch and Porphyry reacted against a one-sided devaluation of animals. From them we have the most extensive defences of animals from the first centuries CE. Their works, like those of Philo the Jew (first century CE) and the middle Platonic philosopher Celsus, are polemical.[3] The tone of these treatises is probably a reflection of the fact that they were written in a period when the position of animals in relation to humans and the position of humans in relation to the divine were being debated and were in a process of change. However, most of those who spoke in defence of animals – as did, for instance, Philostratus through the figure of Apollonius of Tyana – did so from a clearly anthropocentric perspective (around 220 CE).

Philo of Alexandria, Plutarch and Celsus are examples of philosophers who in the first and second century CE are writing about animals in the context of discussion and debate.

Philo: "animals have no share in reasoning ability"

In *On Whether Dumb Animals Possess Reason,* written in the early part of the first century CE (*c.* 45 CE), Philo takes up the gauntlet thrown down by the followers of Plato, namely their claims that animals have intelligence and should be given justice. The speakers in this dialogue are Philo and Alexander. Like Philo, Alexander is both a literary device and a real person: the real Alexander – Tiberius Julius Alexander – was a highly assimilated Jew. The Church historian Eusebius (260–339 CE) says that he was an apostate who had a high position in the state bureaucracy. The views that Philo makes his nephew present in the treatise could very well have been views that this fictitious Alexander shared with his namesake of flesh and blood.[4]

Actually, Alexander's presentation covers about 75 percent of Philo's text. The presentation is striking not because it is original but rather because its style of argument seems to be typical. It owes much to the arguments presented by the New Academy and is painstakingly composed, presenting the traditional stories about animals that illustrate the traditional arguments of the Platonists (Haussleiter 1935; Terian 1981: 50). Thus Alexander meticulously goes through the motions. He starts by comparing women and animals. They are both weaker groups that need protection from men. He argues that animals have both external reason and innate reason, albeit imperfectly. As examples of external reason he mentions different varieties of speaking and singing birds. Spiders, bees and swallows are characterized by an innate reason that is self-taught and expressed in their different skills. Innate reason is also seen in performing animals – they can be taught to perform, and they can serve humans. Both tame and wild animals may be trained, according to Alexander. The longest part of Alexander's exposition is about the virtues and vices of animals. His purpose is to show that animals can act morally. For instance, some animals show modesty in their sexual life, and some abstain from eating flesh. Because animals are capable of morals, they should be treated with justice.

Philo does not agree. In spite of his efforts, Alexander is no match for his uncle, not because Philo really counters all of Alexander's arguments but because Philo argues uncompromisingly from the axiom that animals lack reason and therefore are inferior to humans. If animals seem to act by reason, it must simply be a wrong impression, because animals always act according to nature. This point is hammered home by Philo who even compares animals to plants. He wants to show that plants also behave according to nature (78–80) and that animals thus have more in common with plants than with humans.

If we compare Alexander's and Philo's arguments, it is obvious that they are not having a discussion but arguing from *a priori* positions. Alexander praises animals:

> Is not the spider very proficient in making various designs? Have you not observed how it works and what an amazing thing it fashions? (17) . . . Its [the bee's] intelligence is hardly distinguishable from the contemplative ability of the human mind (20). . . . Not only do some of them (the animals) acquire self-heard and self-taught knowledge but many are very keen on learning to listen to and to comply with what their trainers command (23). This nature has placed a sovereign mind in every soul (29). . . . In addition to what has been said, it could be stated without disparagement, that many other animals have wisdom, knowledge, excellent discerning, superior foresight, and all that is related to the intellect – those things which are called "virtues of the rational soul" (30). . . . Animals, no less than men, show great – if not better – demonstrations of equality and justice (64).

Philo devalues animals:

> Each of the above mentioned creatures does it by its nature (78). . . . It is difficult to think that animals behave with great fraudulence and substantial wisdom. Certainly those who attest to such a wisdom do not realize that they themselves are utterly ignorant (82). . . . But surely animals have no share of reasoning ability, for reasoning ability extends itself to a multiplicity of abstract concepts in the mind's perception of God, the universe, laws, provincial practices, the state, state affairs, and numerous other things, none of which animals understand (85). . . . Animals do nothing with foresight as a result of deliberate choice. Although some of their deeds are similar to man's, they are done without thought (97).

Throughout, Philo defends his anthropocentric view of the world, according to which all things are made for the sake of man, a point the Christians later adopted. Rather pompously, Philo ends the dispute:

> Let us now stop criticizing nature and committing sacrilege. To elevate animals to the level of the human race and to grant equality to unequals is the height of injustice. To ascribe serious self-restraint to indifferent and almost invisible creatures is to insult those whom nature has endowed with the best part.
>
> (*On Animals*, 100)

Uncle and nephew are talking at cross-purposes. According to the literary framework, the texts Alexander is supposed to be the author of were read aloud and his views were criticized by Philo.

While in his other works Philo is strongly influenced by Platonism, on the subject of animals he leans heavily on the Stoics and brings up their standard arguments: that animals lack reason, do things according to nature, have much in common with plants and are made for the sake of men. However, what is really interesting is how Philo the Jew, the champion of allegorical exegesis of biblical texts, defends man's sovereignty over animals without making any explicit references to Genesis or the Bible at all. In fact, Philo does not once quote the Bible or use biblical traditions but relies throughout on a Stoic form of argument (Terian 1981: 47; Borgen 1995: 376–7).[5] This does not mean that Philo's position was indefensible from a biblical point of view. On the contrary, Philo interprets the Bible on the subject of man's domination over animals in other works, especially in *The Exposition of the Laws of Moses*, where man's god-given rule over animals is supported by Genesis 1:26–8 (see Borgen 1995).[6]

In principle, Philo reaches similar results whether he bases his argumentation strictly on Greek categories and the Greek philosophical debate or on traditional Jewish views and an exegesis of the Bible. Both procedures are found in Philo, but in different works. Both elevate man and debase animals. Apparently, one could as well argue for man's superiority from a Stoic position as from a Jewish position. Philo himself does both, and he is the best witness of how the message of the inferiority of animals was transmitted through several religious channels at the same time.

Plutarch: "the frogs don't die for 'fun' but in sober earnest"

In four works, Plutarch defends animals and their inherent merits and abilities. These works include a dialogue between Odysseus and the pig Gryllus (*Beasts are Rational*); *On the Cleverness of Animals*; and two treatises on the eating of flesh. In the later treatises, Plutarch forcefully defends a vegetarian lifestyle (see Chapter 3). These works were probably written around 70 CE, one generation after Philo, and at the same time as Pliny was compiling his *Natural History*. These four works are usually seen as evidence of Plutarch's Pythagorean background and belonging to his youth (Dillon 1977: 186–7).

On the cleverness of animals

The treatise *On the Cleverness of Animals* is the one that has most in common with Philo's work. Philo and Plutarch use common sources, and their works are presented as a competition between two parties. In Plutarch's case, it is a staged debate between two friends and a competition between those who think that either sea animals or land animals are the more clever.[7]

On the Cleverness of Animals consists of a mixture of natural history and marvellous stories about animals.[8] The point of this competition, which in the end has no winner, is to see all animals as winners. Terrestrial animals as well as those living in water possess rational intelligence and must therefore be treated well (985C). Thus the treatise is clearly intended as a contribution to the general discussion of the rationality of animals. Its premise is that animals do in fact possess intelligence: "For by combining what you have said against each other, you will together put up a good fight against those who would deprive animals of reason [*logos*] and understanding [*synesis*]", says Autobolus, one of the judges of this staged debate (985C) – probably Plutarch's own father (cf. Lamberton 2001: 7–10). Plutarch claims that the differences between animals and humans are only those of degree and not those of total contrast: "let us not say of beasts that they are completely lacking in intellect and understanding and do not possess reason even though their understanding is less acute and their intelligence inferior to ours" (963 B). A similar position was defended by Philo's nephew Alexander.

This work can be divided into four parts: an introduction, which is a dialogue between Autobolus and Soclarus (a person who appears frequently in Plutarch's *Moralia*); a defence of land animals; a defence of sea animals; and a short conclusion.

In the introductory discussion between Autobolus and Soclarus, the positions are not as polarized as in Philo's work (where a fictional Philo is set against his fictional nephew), and Autobolus seems gradually to get his Neopythagorean views on animals through at the cost of Soclarus' views, which are represented as less consistent and less clearly thought out. Opposition to the Stoic concept of animals is implied throughout the work – one of Plutarch's points is that the Stoics contradict themselves.

Soclarus describes hunting as "an innocent spectacle of skill and intelligent courage pitted against witless force and violence" (959C). Autobolus on his side describes hunting as a source of insensibility and savagery among men "accustomed to feel no repugnance for the wounds and gore of beasts, but to take pleasure in their violent death" (959D). He argues that the killing and eating of animals led to an increasing brutalization of man (959F). The Pythagoreans made a practice of kindness to animals, to inculcate humanity (*philanthropia*) and compassion (*philoiktirmon*) (960A).[9]

Autobolus and Soclarus discuss whether animals have reason and sensation. Soclarus launches the Stoic argument of oppositions: just as the immortal is opposed to the mortal, the imperishable to the perishable, and the incorporeal to the corporeal, so, if there is rationality, irrationality must also exist. However, Autobolus counters this argument by stressing that soulless things are irrational and continues by saying that all living beings have reason, sensation and imagination. It is a question of degrees and nuances between different types of living being, not of sharp oppositions.[10] He also challenges the "as it were" thinking so common among the Stoics and comments upon it in an ironic way:

> As for those who foolishly affirm that animals do not feel pleasure or anger or fear or make preparations or remember, but that the bee "as it were" remembers and the swallow "as it were" prepares her nest and the lion "as it were" grows angry and the deer "as it were" is frightened – I don't know what they will do about those who say that beasts do not see or hear, but "as it were" hear and see; that they have no cry but "as it were"; nor do they live at all but "as it were". For these last statements (or so I believe) are no more contrary to plain evidence than those that they have made.
>
> (*On the Cleverness of Animals*, 961E–F)

Autobolus distinguishes between mere reason, which is implanted by nature, and real and perfect reason, which is the result of education. So even if animals have reason, their intellect is inferior to that of humans. He argues further that a defect in a faculty reveals that the faculty is normally present, and he uses the example of a mad dog to show that dogs are regarded as having reason (963D). The crucial point is the question of justice, which Soclarus formulates in this way:

> For either we are necessarily unjust if we do not spare them; or, if we do not take them for food, life becomes impracticable or impossible; in a sense we shall be living the life of beasts once we give up the use of beasts.
>
> (*On the Cleverness of Animals*, 964A)

The question of justice towards animals raises a cultural dilemma in a society that is totally dependent on animals and based on animal muscle power. If man does not use beasts, his life becomes bestial (964A; cf. *Moralia*, 86E). However, Autobolus suggests a way out of this dilemma of either depriving animals of reason or denying them justice. He launches his solution as a principle that had been introduced by ancient sages and then reintroduced by Pythagoras (964E):

> There is no injustice, surely, in punishing and slaying animals that are anti-social and merely injurious, while taming those that are gentle and friendly to man and making them our helpers in the tasks for which they are severally fitted by nature.
>
> (*On the Cleverness of Animals*, 964F)

Autobolus' solution implies that it is equally just to kill harmful animals and make tame ones help humans.

In addition to the argument that there is a gradual transition between animals and humans and no absolute division, Plutarch also argues for the need to show compassion towards animals. He quotes Bion of Borysthenes (*c.* 335–245 BCE): "Boys throw stones at frogs for fun, but the frogs don't die for 'fun' but in sober earnest." And he stresses that "it is not those who make use of animals who do them wrong, but those who use them harmfully and heedlessly and in cruel ways" (965B).

When we turn from the introduction to the contest between the two parties, philosophical arguments about animal capabilities are exchanged for stories about animal wits and skills. The contenders are Aristotimus from Delphi for the land animals and Phaedimus for the sea animals. They are flanked by those who are fond of hunting on the one side and the sea folk or island dwellers on the other. This fight is accordingly not only about animals but also about the position of hunters in relation to fishermen.

When Aristotimus starts by abusing fishermen – fish are "more honourable to buy than to catch oneself" (966A; cf. 970B) – he implies that hunting is a sport for the aristocracy while fishing is a means of earning one's living. A similar social statement is made when Aristotimus at the end of his speech points out that when people are stupid, they may be called "fish", and that the gods never let their will be known through fish – fish are simply not used in divination or as portents (countered by 976B–C).[11]

As part of his introductory criticism of the mental capacities of fish, Aristotimus describes characteristics that he suggests will be difficult to find in marine creatures but easy to find proof of in "terrestrial and earth-born animals":

> In general, then, the evidence by which the philosophers demonstrate that beasts have their share of reason is their possession of purpose and preparation and memory and emotions and care for their young and gratitude for benefits and hostility to what has hurt them; to which may be added their ability to find what they need and their manifestations of good qualities, such as courage and sociability and continence and magnanimity.
>
> (*On the Cleverness of Animals*, 966B)

This is a catalogue of what it takes to be an ideal animal. An ideal animal – be it a marine creature or a land animal – is clever and has specific virtues. But when it comes to both intelligence and virtues, the model for this ideal animal is human. Plutarch uses the stories of the different animals to show that animals possess the characteristics that have been listed above.[12]

The defender of marine animals, Phaedimus, starts by arguing that land animals have profited from their close relationship with humans and have learned from humans by imitating them (975F). Since sea animals did not have that advantage, the development of their skills is presented as more meritorious. Characteristic of marine creatures are their skills in avoiding the nets and hooks of fishermen and the skilful techniques that they use to catch their prey. To further stress their superior qualities, Phaedimus emphasizes that some sea animals live in symbiosis with others and also that some marine creatures are affectionate towards their spouses and offspring. Finally, the dolphin helps man and gives its affection to men freely, and for that reason it is much loved by the gods.

Plutarch works his way through a wide range of animals – thirty-six different types of mammal, twenty-five birds, five reptiles or amphibians, thirty types of fish, seven molluscs, five crustaceans, four insects/spiders and two echinoderms – and also a swamp (Andrews 1957). There are a few more species of land animals than water animals – birds that are "earthborn" (*gegenesin*) go together with land animals. A combination of cleverness and helpfulness towards humans is clearly an ideal. One example is the fox, which the Thracians used to test the solidity of the ice before crossing a frozen river. This animal develops a logical reasoning from the evidence of perception: "What makes noise must be in motion; what is in motion is not frozen; what is not frozen is liquid; what is liquid gives way" (969A). Accordingly, the fox gets double marks in this text. It both helps humans and is clearly intelligent.

Some species of animal are described in more detail than others. These are animals that are either seen as in some ways similar to humans (for instance the society of ants) or which interact with humans in a constructive and affectionate way. Clever animals that are faithful and work together with humans, like dogs and elephants, or those that out of their kindness have done favours to humans, like dolphins, are at the top of Plutarch's hierarchy of animals.

Domestic animals like sheep, cows and pigs are included only to a small degree. It seems as if Plutarch, and probably the sources that he used, took little interest in them.[13] When they are introduced, it is briefly, and not in relation to meat production but in relation to other types of produce, as when Plutarch refers to "herds of goats and sheep that are milked and shorn" (965A). The reason for this limited interest in farm animals could simply be that the work is about hunters and fishermen, not about farmers. In addition, because sheep, goats, cattle and swine were tended by farmers and slaves, they were given few opportunities to show their intelligence to highly educated males. Perhaps these animals were regarded like slaves and looked down upon. It could also be that because farm animals were actually sacrificed and eaten they did not fit so easily into the dominant pattern in Plutarch's work, according to which harmless animals should be considered as helpmates to humans and should not be harmed. When the story about four elephants that were sacrificed is referred to, the point is that the god was angry because such clever animals had been killed. It is thus implied that the animals that were usually sacrificed were lower in a hierarchy based on wits and skills than these elephants.

The transformation from animal to meat is not really an issue in this text. When it is mentioned, it is in a historical context of falling standards in the human–animal relationship (959E, 964E): The first man to kill a bear or wolf won praise; then some cow or pig was condemned as suitable to slay because it had tasted the sacred meat placed before it; afterwards men ate the flesh of deer and hares and antelopes; sheep were consumed; in some places men ate dogs and horses; and as the end-product of this historical development from bad to worse, animals were killed for pleasure and eaten as appetizers.

The combative context in *On the Cleverness of Animals* is important (959C). The frame is a staged debate, a contest between two parties of humans about two parties of animals. It is in principle a contest of wits and skills between hunters and fishermen, between land animals and sea animals, but also between fish and fishermen, and between land animals and hunters (965F–966B, 975D, 976D–E). However, there is a discrepancy between the context and the content. Even if several of the land animals belong to species that were actually hunted (bears, hind and hares), they are not described in a hunting context (exceptions are three examples that involve dogs: 970F–971A). There is a contrast in this text between the combative setting, which is concerned with killing animals (hunting and fishing), and the fact that the text contains few comments on killing land animals and even fewer on eating them. Instead, animals are described in relation to medicine and cures, spectacles, divination, natural habitat and historical events. One might have expected that the defender of the land animals might have offered hunting stories to his audience. But he does not. And killing animals and eating meat are deliberately separated from each other in the story about a hare that has expired from being chased by hounds but is not eaten by them, because they "do not strive for food, but for victory and the honour of winning" (971A).

There are discrepancies in the views on hunting as well. Autobolus had been a hunter in his youth, and an alleged reading of a poem, *Praise of Hunting*, made him long to experience the hunt again.[14] At the same time, he is critical of the theatre, where animals are compelled to fight against their will, and he raises a basic criticism of hunting: "sport should be joyful and between playmates who are merry on both sides" (965A). He expands on his views:

> Just so, in hunting and fishing, men amuse themselves with the suffering and death of animals, even tearing some of them piteously from their cubs and nestlings. The fact is that it is not those who make use of animals who do them wrong, but those who use them harmfully and heedlessly and in cruel ways.
>
> (*On the Cleverness of Animals*, 965B)

It is not quite clear if all types of hunting are seen as using animals in cruel ways, but it seems as if Plutarch has made Autobolus present another view here than in the introduction, where he fondly looked back on the hunting of his youth.

If we move from the world of humans and animals to Plutarch's references to the divine world, we find that he mainly describes the function of gods in relation to animals in consonance with his ideal of a harmonious world, a peaceful coexistence between humans and animals, and his belief in the existence of a providential God.[15] Elephants are religious and for that reason the animals most loved by the gods. The deity becomes angry when these animals are sacrificed (972B–C). Animals have mantic powers and serve as instruments of the gods (975A–B). Practically all sea creatures are regarded by Aphrodite as sacred and related to her, and she does not want them to be slaughtered. The priest of Poseidon does not eat seafood, and the priestess of Hera at Argos abstains from surmullet (983E–F). Apollo's animal is the dolphin (984A). Dolphins show affection towards men and are therefore dear to the gods (984C).

In hunting and fishing, the relationship between humans and animals is one of predator and prey. But in spite of this framework, the issue in *On the Cleverness of Animals* is the friendly and mutually beneficent interaction between animals and humans. It is not the animal as enemy but rather the contract animal that Plutarch concentrates upon in this work. So while Plutarch solves the dilemma of both equipping animals with intelligence and handling them in a just way, he does not in this treatise consider the problematic questions of sacrificing and slaughtering animals and eating their meat. However, he does discuss the eating of meat in two other works (see Chapter 3). And a pig, the animal whose only function is to produce meat, is Plutarch's hero in the dialogue *Gryllus*.

Gryllus

The high-spirited work about Gryllus is probably the most delightful work on animals from the ancient world, at least the one with the greatest impact in later times. In this work, Plutarch has created a story on the basis of the myth from the Odyssey (10.237ff) where Circe turned Odysseus' men into pigs – although with human minds (*nous*). When Odysseus forces Circe to turn his comrades back into men, they are very happy to regain their human shape. However, Plutarch gives this story a new twist.

Its hero, Gryllus ("The Grunter") is one of the men whom Circe has transformed into a pig. When Odysseus asks Circe to let his men go free, Circe objects and says that Odysseus must first ask if they are willing, and if not, he must try to convince them. When Circe has transformed one of the men back into human shape, Odysseus asks who the pig was before. Odysseus not only wants humanity, he wants identity. However, Circe refuses to answer: "What's that to do with the issue? Call him Gryllus, if you like" (986B). Obviously, it is the generally human that has been transformed into the generally swinish – and that has temporarily been transformed back again. This has been considered a Cynic element in Plutarch. The Cynics also regarded the animal life that was lived *kata physin*, in accordance with nature, as an ideal compared with human life, which was lived *kata nomon*, according to the law. Gryllus proves to be a good Cynic: he wants to go on being a pig. And he chides Odysseus for not wanting to change *his* shape. A little piqued, Odysseus insinuates that it was probably Gryllus' inherent "swinishness" that conjured him into his shape as a pig in the first place.

Gryllus wants to show that animals far surpass humans in virtues and illustrates his point with examples of courage (*andreia*) in animals. The contrast with humans is shown, for instance, in how "a lion is never slave to a lion, or horse to horse through cowardice, as man is to man when he unprotestingly accepts the name whose root is cowardice" (here *douleia* – "slavery" – is seen as deriving from *deilia* – "cowardice") (987D–E).

Another of Gryllus' points is that in beasts courage is naturally equal in both sexes. He chides Odysseus because his wife "sits at home by the fire and troubles herself less than a swallow to ward off those who come against herself and her home" (988B). Gryllus also makes terminological points – for instance, that brave fighters are called "lion-hearted" (*thymoleontas*), while a lion is never called "man-hearted" (*anthropothymon*). It shows that when it comes to courage, the lion is a higher ideal than the human in a comparison between the two.

The self-restraint of beasts (*sophrosyne*) is illustrated by their not wanting to consort with "their betters" but "pursuing love with mates of like species" (989A). In contrast to animals, men have, in fact, attempted to consort sexually with various animals – unlike animals, they also take part in homosexual relations. Animals have simple pleasures in food and drink – men "alone of all creatures are omnivorous [*pamphagon*]" (991C).

The pig asserts that animals are good physicians and have a natural gift for all their skills. His conclusion is that if nature (*physis*) is their teacher, and if their intelligence is not to be called either "reason" (*logos*) or "intelligence" (*phronesis*), then it ought to be called by an even better and more honourable term. In short, Gryllus wonders why the Sophists consider all creatures, except man, "irrational" (*aloga*) and "senseless" (*anoeta*). When asked whether Gryllus attributes reason even to sheep and asses, which were usually regarded as notoriously stupid animals, the pig answers that all animals possess reason and intellect, although to a different degree (992D).

To Odysseus' last question, whether it is not terrible to grant reason to creatures that have no knowledge of God, Gryllus points out that Odysseus had Sisyphos for a father, implying the well-known fact that Sisyphos was an atheist. It is unclear if this was the real end or whether something is missing, but we can probably agree that the pig made its point. Beasts are rational!

In this text, Plutarch uses the pig to illustrate a simple and virtuous life, a life that is set up as a model for humans. Thus he employs the story about Circe to an opposite purpose than Horace, who connects the men's piggish form with their folly and greed (Horace, *Epistle*, 1.2.23–6): When Odysseus' men drank from Circe's cups, they behaved like beasts and became beasts. Plutarch on his side describes the virtues of the pig and makes it into a human ideal.

Like most ancient literature about animals, Plutarch has taken human virtues and applied them to an animal. On the other hand, one of his main points is that the pig is an ideal because it lives a natural life. It implies that all living beings are ends in themselves, and accordingly the purpose of the pig is to live like a pig. From this perspective, one could have thought that an animal life was the opposite of a human life and not worth being imitated by humans. Above all, among the Stoics, the goal of humans was to develop especially those characteristics that they did not have in common with the animal world. Remember Epictetus, who said that it was "shameful for man to begin and end just where the irrational animals do; he should rather begin where they do, but end where nature has ended in dealing with us" (*Arrian's Discourses on Epictetus*, 1.6.19). However, Plutarch wants to show that humans and animals share the same characteristics, including intelligence, although to varying degrees and with varying nuances. He does not say that humans should not develop their mental faculties, rather that they should develop other virtues as well, virtues that according to *Gryllus* are more naturally present in animals than in humans. He thus applies the pig in a reflection over similar views about animals as he did in *On the Cleverness of Animals*.

Although this is a playful piece, meant to throw an ironic perspective on human life and behaviour, its comments on animals and use of a pig as its mouthpiece at the same time create a liberal and complex view of animals. It also reflects a preoccupation with animals and reveals a certain fondness towards them as well.

Apollonius of Tyana: "and I do not like to bother the poor animals"

In the *Life of Apollonius of Tyana*, written about 220 CE, Philostratus describes a Pythagorean philosopher who lived in the first century CE.[16] This biographical novel shows "the way in which a knowledgeable Greek of the third century envisaged the condition of a philosopher in the first" (Jones 1971: 37). James Francis emphasizes that "Philostratus rehabilitates an ascetic philosopher with a reputation of a *goes*, in this case a Pythagorean, into a model of classical ideals and a defender of social order" (Francis 1995: 83). Animals are not a main topic in this work, but they appear so frequently that it is possible to say something about their functions and values. The views on animals that are proposed in this work may have been held by the historical Apollonius but are probably more in line with second- and early third-century pagan asceticism.

According to the biography, Apollonius was a wandering ascetic and Pythagorean philosopher who travelled widely and visited Persia, India and Egypt. He gave lectures, cured the sick, performed miracles and was presented as a holy man with supernatural abilities. In the long biography, written over a hundred years after his death, several narratives about animals and his meetings with them appear. This is to be expected in such a colourful description. Animals were an integral part of Mediterranean life, and many good stories were based upon their behaviour. Animals seem, in addition, to be natural ingredients in a description of the life of a Pythagorean sage and ascetic, because they are instrumental in showing both sagacity and asceticism. It is of special interest that the treatment of animals in Philostratus' biography indicates some of the dilemmas in the ancient conception of them. It also shows the relevance of animals in building up identity as they are clearly used in Philostratus' biography to create a social identity for Apollonius.

Apollonius' relationship to the animal world is typical of one religious faction of the empire. As a follower of Pythagoras and a new Pythagoras of his own time (1.2), Apollonius declined to make blood offerings, offered only hymns and prayers, ate no meat and wore no clothes made of animal products (1.8). When, for instance, the king of Babylon is about to make a sacrifice of a white horse to the sun, Apollonius leaves the scene of sacrifice in order not to be present at the shedding of blood (1.31–2). The Pythagorean tradition taught that meat pollutes the stomach and that the body must be kept pure (*katharos*). Therefore, Apollonius is clad in linen. Even wool is impure, because it is plucked from the back of living beings.

His behaviour is motivated by concern for the purity of his body and soul – but not solely: Apollonius also demonstrates concern for animals for their own sake. He declines to participate in a royal hunt and says that "it is no pleasure to me to attack animals that have been ill-treated and enslaved in violation of their nature" (1.37). When he is imprisoned and Emperor

Domitian asks him why he is dressed as he is, Apollonius replies that the earth clothes him, "and I do not like to bother the poor animals" (8.5). Thus he is a far cry from the Stoics, whose attitude to animals can be illustrated by this quotation from Cicero's (106–43 BCE) *The Nature of the Gods*: "What other use have sheep save that their fleeces are dressed and woven into clothing for men?" (2.63). Cicero also refers to Chrysippus (*c.* 280–207 BCE), who thought that the purpose of the pig's soul was to keep its flesh from decaying (*ibid.*, 2.64).

Apollonius' concern for animals is shown even more poignantly in a story about a healing in Tarsus. Here he heals a boy bitten by a mad dog and afterwards goes on to cure the dog:

> Nor did the sage neglect the dog either, but after offering a prayer to the river he sent the dog across it; and when the dog had crossed the river, he took his stand on the opposite bank and began to bark, a thing which mad dogs rarely do, and he folded back his ears and wagged his tail, because he knew that he was all right again, for a draught of water cures a mad dog, if he has only the courage to take it.
>
> (*Life of Apollonius*, 6.43)

Apollonius seems to have liked animals and respected their abilities. One example is the way he ascribes wisdom (*sophia*) and intelligence (*nous*) to elephants (2.15). On his travels, he demonstrated a keen interest in natural history, for instance in the wildlife in Ethiopia (6.24) (Anderson 1994: 58–60). This wildlife prompts Apollonius and his company to discuss the animals and "talk learnedly about the food which nature supplies in their different cases" (6.26).

However, while Apollonius has a positive conception of animals' abilities, he denies them any supernatural faculties. Apollonius wants real-life animals to remain animals. A youth who trained birds to talk is criticized by Apollonius, both because he spoils the birds' own natural notes, "which are so sweet that not even the best musical instruments could rival or imitate them", and because he teaches the birds "the vilest Greek dialects" (6.36). Because animals cannot learn and understand human languages, the youth is advised to leave the birds alone and get himself a proper education (advice that he followed).

In Apollonius' eyes, animals clearly had their limitations. Humans did not necessarily have the same limitations. Exceptional humans, such as Apollonius himself, are even able to understand animals. It is mentioned in passing that Apollonius had learned their language in Arabia, where he had also learned to understand prophesying birds (1.20).

In Philostratus' biography, one exceptional animal even seems to transcend the human–animal barrier. This is a tame lion that Apollonius met in

Egypt. This lion is "pure", which implies that it is a very atypical lion. It does not touch blood but lives upon honey cakes, bread, dried fruit and boiled meat, "and you also came on it drinking wine without losing its character" (5.42). Apollonius communicates with the lion, and he explains that it has a human soul, the soul of a former king of Egypt. So the lion is sent to Leontopolis and dedicated to the temple. In other words, it turns out that the lion is not a real animal but a human being reincarnated.

A transformation from the human to the animal form is also seen in the gruesome story of the stoning of a beggar. There is a plague at Ephesus, and as a remedy Apollonius persuades the Ephesians to stone a beggar. The Ephesians reluctantly do as he bids them. When they inspect the remains, it turns out that the beggar was not a man after all but a huge dog foaming at the mouth, in reality a demon of pestilence (4.10).

But even if a human soul can inhabit an animal body, and a demon can take on the guise of an animal as well as a man, Apollonius opposes those who imagine gods in the shape of animals. In a dispute with the gymnosophists, the naked sages of Egypt (6.19), Apollonius states that he does not find the Egyptian images god-like, for, he says, "the mass of your shrines seem to have been erected in honour rather of irrational and ignoble animals than of gods". In his view, the animal form makes gods ridiculous. Apollonius' protagonist, Thespesion, asks ironically if the Greek artists really went up to heaven and took a copy of the forms of the gods and then reproduced them. In answer to that question, Apollonius makes a distinction between imagination (*phantasia*) and imitation (*mimesis*). The Greek statues are made through the imagination of the mind, while the Egyptian ones are imitations, mere likenesses of animals, which by being animals lower the dignity of the gods. Thespesion protests that the Egyptian way of representing their gods reflects deep respect and reverence and that they are "symbols of a profound inner meaning, so as to enhance their solemnity and august character". Apollonius just laughs at this and says that it would have been better if the Egyptians had made no images at all of their gods, so that those who frequent the temples could instead imagine the gods for themselves. The conclusion we must draw from this discussion is that according to Apollonius/Philostratus, the human form is acceptable as a manifestation of a god, while the bestial form is not acceptable as a vehicle for the divine.

However, there is one function that is open to animals in which they clearly transcend their natural limitations. While the Pythagoreans did not eat animals, they could still use them as food for thought. Like many of his contemporaries, Apollonius uses animals metaphorically, and he is especially fond of birds, which he used abundantly to illustrate his lectures (4.3).

Birds are instrumental for instance in describing Apollonius' spiritual progress in his youth (1.7). The inhabitants of the city of Tarsus, who were fonder of luxury than philosophy and used to sit on the bank of the river, are likened to water fowl, while Apollonius' teacher, Euxenus, is compared to a bird that is trained to repeat what its master says without understanding it. In contrast, Apollonius is likened to the young eagles that eventually rise higher in the air than their parents. According to Philostratus, Apollonius was "fledged and winged" for the Pythagorean life "by some higher power" (1.7).

When Philostratus allows his hero Apollonius to use animals as substitutes for men to teach humans a lesson, he is participating in a well-known tradition with Aesop as one of its ancestors. Apollonius admired Aesop. This is made explicit in a discussion where he asked his opponents their opinion on Aesop: "Frogs", one of them, Menippus, answered, "and donkeys and nonsense only fit to be swallowed by old women and children" (5.14). Apollonius, for his part, preferred Aesop to the poets who wrote stories about the gods, because, unlike them, Aesop does not pretend his stories are true. He makes use of falsehood and adds a good moral to it. But Apollonius also mentioned another charming aspect of Aesop: "that he puts animals in a pleasing light and makes them interesting to mankind" (5.14).

The example of Apollonius shows the complexity of the ancient concept of animals and clearly reveals the ambiguous relationship between animals and humans. It reflects the main problems and some general tendencies in the overall picture.

The background to the *Life of Apollonius* is the tripartite hierarchy of gods, humans and animals. One function of the animal sacrifice was to divide these categories. Animals were the sacrificial matter, while gods and human beings received fixed parts of the meat and were thus kept separate from each other. But when Philostratus wrote about Apollonius, the place of humans in the hierarchy of being was in the process of change. There was a tendency to transcend the natural limitations of the human category and approach the divine. One step in this strategy was to establish a clear link between the human and the divine. Another step was to make the distinction between humans and animals visible and significant. Accordingly, a presupposition behind the author's understanding of animals in the *Life of Apollonius* is that a special link exists between humans and gods. Human beings must not be caught up in the animal world, as their purpose is to lift themselves above it. In Philostratus' words, "there is between man and God a certain kinship which enables him alone of the animal creation to recognize the Gods, and to speculate both about his own nature and the manner in which it participates in the divine substance" (8.7.7). A goal in life was to rise above the limitations of an earthly existence and the trivialities of material life, to be more like a divine being than a beast, and finally ascend to the divine.

The link between the divine and the human on the one hand, and the distinction between the human and the animal on the other, were made in spite of the fact that the similarities between some animals and humans are easy for everyone to see – they lie in the structure of the body and the basic facts of life such as birth, sexuality and death. However, these facts obviously made it even more urgent to determine the differences between animals and humans and to establish them convincingly. This categorical boundary could be set in a theoretical way, by introducing reason (*logos*) as that which divides humans and animals. Like those who wanted to ascend the caste hierarchy in India and therefore started to eat a diet without meat because it was purer, the Pythagoreans as well as the late Neoplatonists established themselves as a religious elite purer than most people by not eating meat or using clothes made from animals. The categorical boundaries were set by means of religious practice relating to animals.

Origen versus Celsus: "no noble or good man is a worm"

So far, two Alexandrian Jews – Philo and Alexander – have argued about the status of animals from a Stoic and a Platonist point of view, respectively; a pagan author – Plutarch – has argued from a Platonist/Cynic/Neopythagorean point of view; while Philostratus' Apollonius of Tyana defended Neopythagorean asceticism and reflected dilemmas in the human–animal relationship. There is also a Christian author with Stoic views, Origen, arguing against a pagan philosopher who held Platonic views – Celsus. Like Alexander and Plutarch, Celsus used arguments from the Academic tradition.

In the second century CE, probably about 180, Celsus had written a treatise against the Christians, *The True Doctrine* (*logos alethes*). This treatise included a criticism of Jews and Christians, although Celsus' criticism of the Christians was based on Jewish polemic against Christians. The treatise of Celsus is lost, but nearly a century after it was composed, it became the butt of an attack by Origen (*Against Celsus*, c. 248 CE). In his work, Origen defends Christianity, and also Judaism, because he wanted to give Christianity a historical basis in its continuity with Judaism.

Celsus' criticism of Christianity was informed and thoroughgoing as he was apparently very well versed in Christian texts, acquainted with how Christians appeared in the social world of his time and aware of the internal divisions of the Church.[17] The main targets of his attack were the Christian beliefs in the incarnation and the divinity of Christ and in the resurrection of the body. Among his minor targets were the Christian views on animals. Celsus saw these views as closely connected to the anthropocentric Christian world view. These views had been under discussion in the second century and were still an issue a century later, when Origen brought up the question of animals in the last part of Book 4 (74–99). As we will see, these views are deeply connected with Origen's Christian position.[18]

The kernel of the discussion about animals between Celsus and contemporary Christians in the second century, and of Origen's attack on Celsus in the third century on the subject of animals, was whether God had made all things for man or whether they were made just as much for animals (4.74.1–5). According to Celsus, all things had been made as part of the universe as a whole, and God cares for the totality. Origen disagrees and claims that God takes particular care of rational beings (4.99:5–6, 22–5). Origen also mentions that Celsus had asserted that irrational animals were not only wiser (*sophotera*) than men but even dearer to God (*theophilestera*).

The question of the rationality of animals and why they had been created were well-known topics of the Stoic/Platonic debates, as has already become clear in the dispute between Philo and Alexander. Origen identified his own position with that of the Stoics when he attacked Celsus for bestowing intelligence on ants and bees (4.81–6). He even criticized Celsus for being "confused" because Celsus, according to Origen, did not see that when he attacked the Christians because of their views on animals, he was also attacking the Stoic school of philosophers. Could it be that Celsus had not made an identification between Christians and Stoics because Celsus regarded Christian views on animals as in some ways different from those of the Stoics – for instance as more extreme? For in spite of Origen's wish to identify himself with the Stoic perspective on animals, his attitude to animals is not Stoic but part of his Christian agenda.

The real issue in the pagan/Christian debate about animals as it is reflected by Origen was not animal nature but rather God's election of the Christians, and, to a certain extent, his election of the Jews. This alleged election by God, which was claimed by Christians and Jews alike, was one of the things that Celsus had especially mocked. Book 4 is permeated by opposites:

> Christians/pagans
> humans/animals
> divine beings/animals
> rational beings/irrational beings
> worshippers of God/worshippers of irrational animals, images or created things
> righteous/unrighteous
> philosophers/common people
> reason/non-reason
> mastery over desire/sexual pleasure
> virtue/vice
> eternal life/damnation

These opposites are, to a certain extent, homologous, and the entities on each side participate in each other's values and meanings. Christians are associated with divine beings, humans, worshippers of God, righteous people, virtue, etc., while pagans are associated with animals, irrational beings, the unrighteous, vice, etc. If we interpret the subtext in Book 4 of Origen's *Against Celsus*, the answer to the question "For whom is the world made?" is primarily for Christians and humans, second for pagans and animals. It is a hierarchy based on polarities and excluded "middles". The underlying

Christian point was that humans are to animals as Christians to pagans. Celsus, writing in the second century, seems to have turned this point upside down in a highly ironic way: Christians are to humans as worms (and bats, frogs and ants) are to other types of animal.

According to Origen, Celsus is "laughing at the race of Jews and Christians, comparing them all to a cluster of bats and ants coming out of a nest, or frogs holding council around a marsh, or worms assembling in some filthy corner, disagreeing with one another about which of them are the worse sinners" (4.23.1–6). Behind this passage lies the famous simile in Plato's *Phaedo* in which Plato likened the inhabitants of the Mediterranean area to "ants or frogs around a pond" (109.B). Plato's point is that many similar hollows exist on the large earth, but their inhabitants do not realize that they live in hollows but think they are unique and live on the upper surface of the earth (109–10).

This simile sets the tone for Celsus' ironic comments in the passage 4.23–31. Celsus' preferred designation for Christians in this passage is "worms" (*skolex*), animals that are blind, and, unlike the frogs and ants of Plato, are living *in* the earth. *Skolex* may be read as "rain-worm". But worms are not necessarily innocent creatures living in the earth; they may invade people in the most fatal way. In the Acts of the Apostles, it is said of Herod that he was "eaten by worms [*skolekobrotos*]" (12:23), and when Alexander of Abonouteichos, the famous pagan prophet, died, it was from being "consumed by worms [*skolex*]" (*Alexander of Abonouteichos*, 59; cf. Victor 1997: 170).

Origen does not want to understand Celsus when Celsus compares Christians to worms. He ponders whether Celsus meant that all men are worms, because they are so small in relation to God, or if he meant only the Christians? And if Celsus meant all men, it was probably not because of their small bodies, but because the souls of humans were inferior compared to God. Origen admits that all evil men could be likened to worms, but not virtuous men, for rational beings cannot entirely be alienated from God. In Origen's opinion, "the people who really are worms and ants and frogs" are those who instead of worshipping God worship "either irrational animals, or images, or created things" (26.9–10).

Furthermore, those who master the most violent desire for sexual pleasures are not worms, "but those who live with licentious women and harlots" (4.26.23–33). If anyone among the Christians had said that "there is God first and we are next after Him in rank" (4.29.1–2), they are not representative, for Christians know that between them and God are angels, thrones, principalities and the authorities and powers. But if "we are next after Him in rank" (4.29.31) meant "the rational beings" (*hoi logikoi*), and especially "the good rational beings", then Origen accepts it as true.

Origen says, with reference to the philosophers, "do not compare with the wriggles of worms, or anything else of that sort, the profound intelligence of men . . . who are engaged not in the vulgar affairs of the common people, but with the search for the truth" (4.30.56–9).

Why *did* Celsus compare the Christians especially to worms? It is probably also their connection with corpses, which Celsus hints at when he mentions the resurrection, when those also long dead "will rise up from the earth possessing the same bodies as before". Celsus characterizes this hope as "simply the hope of worms". He asks what "sort of human soul would have any further desire of a body that has rotted?" (5.14). And he characterizes the idea as repulsive and impossible. Celsus probably also had in mind Aristotle's idea that worms were born from decomposed corpses.

Furthermore, when Celsus compares Christians to worms and bats and ants and frogs it is because when the Christians regarded themselves as the chosen ones among all people, they were regarded by Celsus as even more ignorant than the ants and frogs to whom Plato compared the Greeks. According to Celsus, the Christians (whom he characterizes as "worms") used to say: "There is God first, and we next after Him in rank since He has made us entirely like God, and all things have been put under us, earth, water, air, and stars; and all things exist for our benefit, and have been appointed to serve us" (4.24.12–15). Celsus wishes, according to Origen, "to argue that Jews and Christians are no better than the animals which he mentioned above" (4.31.1–3). This wish may be seen in connection with Celsus' claim that the Christians want to "convince only the foolish, dishonourable, and stupid, and only slaves, women, and little children" (3.49.1–3) or, as Celsus also said: "wool-workers, cobblers, laundry-workers, and the most illiterate and bucolic yokels" (3.55). According to Celsus, the uneducated and baser elements of human society are the equivalents of the baser elements of animal society. So Celsus clearly uses animal metaphors to get at the Christians, and so does Origen to get at the pagans.

In Book 4, Origen repeatedly returns to Celsus' claim that "the soul is God's work, but the nature of the body is different. And a man's body will be no different from the body of a bat or a worm or a frog. For they are made of the same matter, and they are equally liable to corruption" (54.4–7; cf. 56.1–4, 56.27–30, 58.1–2). Also, Celsus' claim that "no product of matter is immortal" (61.1, 61.8) is commented upon by Origen. With these claims, Celsus implied that humans and animals had similar corruptible bodies, a claim that was opposed by the Christians. According to them, humans had potentially incorruptible bodies. Consequently, humans were divided from animals not only by their rational souls but also by their flesh, which was of another kind than the corruptible flesh of animals. Human flesh was ultimately designed for immortality.

Against Celsus is a text in which the discussion about the relations between humans and animals can be interpreted as statements about categorical boundaries and tolerance and intolerance towards other people. On the one hand, Celsus criticizes the Christians for their anthropocentrism, which was among other things revealed in their views of animals as being created solely for the sake of humans. Celsus' point is that in the same way as Christians had set themselves apart from other people, they had made an absolute division between themselves and animals. On the other hand, Celsus uses animal metaphors of worms and frogs, animals that were perceived as low in the animal hierarchy, to characterize the Christians.

James Francis regards the *True Doctrine* as "an expression of the attempt to reunify higher and lower religion and culture, philosophical and popular belief, into one embracing system" (Francis 1995: 178). Celsus' approach is one of integration and inclusion, and he severely criticizes Christianity as an opposite type of approach, aiming at exclusivity and setting themselves apart and higher than all others. In the *True Doctrine*, Celsus highlighted and attacked Christian views by means of the Platonic/Stoic debate about animals. But his inclusive attitude does not embrace Christians. Celsus' view is that pagans are to Christians as humans to small insignificant or disgusting animals.

Conclusion

The main positions in the ancient philosophical debate about animals were those of the Stoics and the Platonists. Stoics and Platonists agreed that humans potentially had a more elevated position in the universe than animals. But while the Stoics saw a sharp distinction between humans and animals, the Platonists saw more subtlety and nuances. According to them, the different species of animals had virtues and intelligence in varying degrees. The dominant message of the Platonists, as reflected in these texts, is that animals are intelligent and have a claim on justice. Justice between animals and humans consists of protecting oneself against dangerous animals and having a mutually useful relationship with the harmless ones. The world is made for humans as well as animals, and animals are ends in themselves and not, as the Stoics taught, made solely for the sake of humans. According to Plutarch, humans are allowed to make use of animals in so far as it does not hurt them, but they are not allowed to harm anything harmless, a principle he shared with the Pythagoreans.[19]

Plutarch did not argue on behalf of harmless animals only by appealing to justice. In *On the Cleverness of Animals*, he refers to a more intimate understanding of other creatures – "frogs do not die for fun but in sober earnest" – and he does not approve of those who make a complete study of anthills and inspect them, as it were, anatomically (968A), probably out of compassion and respect for the ants. In the *Life of Marcus Cato*, Plutarch argues for showing compassion towards animals and refers to a more general need to develop mildness and gentleness in dealings with living beings (5.1–6). He says that law and justice are restricted to dealings between humans, but compares old slaves and old beasts of burden and speaks against treating creatures "like shoes or pots and pans, casting them aside when they are bruised and worn out with service" (5.5). In this treatise, he leaves open whether the main reason for treating animals better is that humans will improve or that one should show compassion towards animals for their own sake.

Divergent views of animals did not merely concern animals but were sometimes used to highlight social, cultural, religious and philosophical differences. Statements about animals contribute to placing people and groups in a shared social, cultural and religious landscape. When Philo illustrates Stoic and Platonist views of animals by means of a fictional debate between himself and his nephew Alexander, this debate probably also comments on the relations between Jews and their surroundings. In accordance with this interpretation, it is perhaps not really astonishing that the highly assimilated Jew Tiberius Julius Alexander, Philo's nephew, defended the Platonic position that there were degrees of difference between animals and humans, but no absolute division. However, Philo belonged to those Jews "who had significant social ties with the non-Jewish world but who were also careful to preserve their distinct Jewish identity" (Barclay 1996: 112–14). In Philo's view, Jews and Jewish culture were superior to other peoples and cultures. Consequently, Philo also spoke in favour of absolute categorical boundaries between animals and humans.

Plutarch attacked the Stoics and defended Platonic and Pythagorean principles in a work that is framed as a staged debate on behalf of hunters and fishermen and which may have had contemporary references. In *The True Doctrine*, Celsus highlights and attacks Christian views by means of the Platonic/Stoic conflict about animals. The subtext is that Christians are to pagans as humans are to animals. However, at the same time as Celsus defends animal intelligence, he uses animals metaphorically to debase Christians.

Both in the Stoic and the Platonist positions there were some loose ends and unsolved problems. In the case of the Stoics, they had few problems in justifying their use of animals for human purposes, but they were not always able to maintain a sharp distinction between animals and humans without introducing an "as it were" principle to explain how animals, who seemed to act according to principles similar to those of humans, did not really do so.

Plutarch and the Academicians regarded animals as clever, wanted to treat them justly, and needed them for the maintenance of society. Their problems did not arise with regard to harmful animals, which according to their views could rightfully be killed, or with regard to animals that worked for humans, because such relationships were seen as mutually beneficial, but with regard to sacrificing, killing and eating harmless animals. These problems were not new. Theophrastus, the successor of Aristotle, had considered it an injustice to kill and sacrifice harmless animals (Porphyry, *On Abstinence*, 2.22–4). Some of these issues, but not all, are discussed by Plutarch in his two works on vegetarianism; other problems, for instance the relationship between sacrifice and meat eating, are commented upon later by Porphyry and Iamblichus.

Several characteristic dilemmas in the human–animal relationship, typical of late antiquity, are reflected in Apollonius of Tyana as this figure is presented in Philostratus' text. Are animals moral agents or mere objects for human use? May animals be sacrificed, or must sacrifices of living beings be condemned? If sacrifice of animals is condemned, is this because of sympathy with animals leading to ethical considerations about how animals ought to be treated, or does it rather express a wish to improve the human condition through a higher purity? A related point is whether cruelty towards animals is condemned because of concern and sympathy for the animals involved or because it has a brutalizing effect on humans, making men cruel towards each other. Meat eating was an object of similar considerations, since vegetarianism was sometimes rooted in sympathy for the animals in question but more often in a concern for pureness of diet, as humans should not pollute themselves by eating animal food.

We will now turn to vegetarianism, natural history and physiognomics and to ambiguous views on the relationship between animals and humans.

3

VEGETARIANISM, NATURAL HISTORY AND PHYSIOGNOMICS

Vegetarianism

It seems to be the case, from the limited material at our disposal, that the "animal question" was pursued across the boundaries of religions and philosophical schools and was seen as an entertaining subject to disagree on. Sometimes, though, this subject had more serious subtexts. When animals were discussed in relation to diet, things became more serious, since eating is not a thing to be taken lightly.

The question of vegetarianism – abstention from eating flesh (*to sarkofagein*) – is closely connected to the definition of animals and humans in relation to each other. How one thought about animals and their status and value clearly had consequences for how they were treated. Could animals be eaten? Could they be sacrificed? The question of animal sacrifice in particular goes to the heart of ancient religion.

One of the main subjects of Porphyry's treatise *On Abstinence* is the question of a vegetarian diet. Together with Plutarch's two works against eating flesh, *On Abstinence* is the most vigorous defence of vegetarianism from the ancient world. Porphyry's solution to the problem of the relationship between animal sacrifice and eating flesh is to say that even if animals are sacrificed, it does not necessarily follow that they should be eaten (2.2). This is a point to which Porphyry repeatedly returns (2.42, 2.53, 2.57; see also Chapter 7).

A revival of Pythagoreanism in these centuries once again called attention to a vegetarian lifestyle, as seen in Philostratus' biographical novel about Apollonius of Tyana. And while a vegetarian diet is especially associated with Pythagoreanism, it also became, after Plato, part of the Academy (Haussleiter 1935: 204ff; Tsekourakis 1987).

Vegetarianism often had a religious dimension and could be a mark of religious affiliation. Seneca, for instance, put an end to his vegetarian lifestyle because his father did not want him to be regarded as one who participated in foreign cults (*Epistle*, 108). In several of the religions of the empire, only certain animals, parts of animals or certain plants could be eaten, and only at certain times (Haussleiter 1935: 128). In general, periodic fasting and prohibition against eating some types of food were found much more widely in ancient times. The Pythagorean prohibition against eating beans is well known.

Generally, vegetarianism may be built on two different attitudes to animals – or on a combination of these attitudes. Either humans should abstain from eating animals because animals and humans are part of the same community, or they should abstain from eating animals because humans are on a higher level than animals, and animals are a source of pollution for humans (see Dierauer 1977: 286–90). Thus a vegetarian diet was not only based on the idea of a unity of soul between humans and animals but could just as well be a means of showing the difference between them and making humans distance themselves from animals and move closer to the gods.

The classical defenders of vegetarianism had identified themselves with the first position. Both Pythagoras and Empedocles had connected vegetarianism with a belief in the transmigration of souls. If souls were passing from human to animal bodies and vice versa, would it not be just as bad to eat animals as it was to eat humans? The swine or the lamb that was slaughtered and eaten could have been one's dead father or mother. Beliefs in reincarnation and a vegetarian lifestyle are often found together. India is a case in point. The idea of reincarnation across species establishes a world in which all creatures have a life in common and makes it possible that relatives could be reborn as animals.

Even if Plutarch does not support the idea of a transmigration of souls wholeheartedly, he refers repeatedly to Empedocles and Pythagoras as well as to the Orphics in an argument about the eating of animal flesh, cannibalism and reincarnation in his two small vegetarian texts (993A, 996B–C), which are the two surviving ones of a whole series of discourses on the subject. Plutarch's position is rather one of modified support for the idea of reincarnation.[1] Perhaps the idea is true, and if it is, would anybody really take the chance of eating meat if it could be their mother, brother or son reborn as an animal (997D–E, 998D)? Thus Plutarch keeps open the possibility of such a close connection between animals and humans as the idea of reincarnation implies, but without wholeheartedly supporting it.

Reincarnation was not the only argument against slaughtering animals and eating food made from their dead bodies. Seneca mentions that Pythagoreans could have different reasons for abstaining from meat, but he hastens to add that "it was in each case a noble reason" (*Epistle*, 108). One reason for vegetarianism was that animals, like humans, had the capacity for suffering. Therefore, out of compassion towards their fellow beings, humans ought to treat animals well. In this case, a relationship between animals and humans was clearly recognized. According to Plutarch, eating flesh may take place because of hunger but never as a luxury (996F). The killing must be done "in pity and sorrow", not by degrading and torturing the animal. Plutarch also criticizes the fact that beasts are slain to fill the tables of the rich, who seldom eat what has been put on the table: "more is left than has been eaten. So the beasts died for nothing!" (994F).

This ethical vegetarianism often included an element of concern for humans. "Who could wrong a human being when he found himself so gently and humanely disposed towards other non-human creatures?" (*Moralia*, 996A) asks Plutarch. He argues that the killing of animals is part of a process that eventually leads to further moral debasement of humans. Slaughtering of animals may, for instance, lead to the slaughtering of humans (998A ff).

However, vegetarianism did not only imply a realization of the closeness between animals and humans. It could also be based on a wish to create a distance between man and beast. A means of attaining a pure soul was to keep up a vegetarian diet. One of Philostratus' issues was how man – the high point of nature – should think and act. As we have seen, his answer was the ideal of the gentle philosopher Apollonius of Tyana, who did not want to contaminate his body with such poisonous food as meat or sully his soul with bloody offerings or with unkindness towards other living beings. Compassion towards animals was, in the case of Apollonius, a by-product of his concern for humans and subordinate to Philostratus' wish to launch Apollonius as the ideal human being. This text signals not only that animals are on a lower level in the hierarchy of being but also that they are a source of pollution. Some of the Stoics led vegetarian lives and based their abstention from meat on rules about purity (Haussleiter 1935: 20–4). According to Plutarch, eating meat was not only disgusting, it was also polluting (*molysmos*, 993B).

Plutarch opens his defence of a fleshless diet vigorously in one of the two treatises that have been labelled *On the Eating of Flesh*:

> Can you really ask what reason Pythagoras had for abstaining from flesh? For my part I rather wonder by what accident and in what state of soul or mind the first man who did so, touched his mouth to the gore and brought his lips to the flesh of a dead creature, he who set forth tables of dead, stale bodies and ventured to call food and nourishment the parts that had a little before bellowed and cried, moved and lived. How could his eyes endure the slaughter when throats were slit and hides flayed and limbs torn from limb? How could his nose endure the stench? How was it that the pollution did not turn away his taste, which made contact with the sores of others and sucked juices and serums from mortal wounds?
>
> (*On the Eating of Flesh*, 993A–B)

This treatise has been characterized as a work of his youth and "on the whole, rather immature beside the *Gryllus* and the *De Sollertia Animalium*," and its rhetoric has been described as "exaggerated and calculated" (Helmbold 1968: 537). Be that as it may, these treatises are interesting because of their vigorous and varied arguments against eating meat.

Plutarch's point of departure is the question of what reason Pythagoras had for abstaining from flesh. Plutarch's answer is that the man one should seek out is not the one who abstains but the one who starts to eat animal flesh. Plutarch's point is that eating flesh is unnatural. Man is not a carnivorous animal, and accordingly eating flesh is not appropriate for him. Another of his points is that people are eating harmless tame creatures, not lions and wolves (994B). Implicit is the argument that it is unjust to harm those who do not harm humans. Plutarch compares the gain to men, a little flesh, with the fact that animals are deprived of the life to which they are entitled.

However, the pollution of animal flesh is also evoked in the battle against eating meat. It was conceived of as making humans spiritually gross, although it made their bodies strong: "It is a fact that the Athenians used to call us Boeotians beef-witted and insensitive and foolish precisely because we stuffed ourselves" (995E) says Plutarch. To cultivate the brilliance of the human soul, one must not burden the body with improper food:

> When we examine the sun through dank atmosphere and a fog of gross vapours, we do not see it clear and bright, but submerged and misty, with elusive rays. In just the same way, then, when the body is turbulent and surfeited and burdened with improper food, the lustre and light of the soul inevitably come through it blurred and confused, aberrant and inconstant, since the soul lacks the brilliance and intensity to penetrate to the minute and obscure issues of active life.
>
> (*Moralia*, 995F)

Plutarch supports the view that a fleshless diet is beneficial for health (cf. Porphyry, *On Abstinence*, 1.52). Seneca points out that he was more active when he abstained from animal food, which implies still another aspect of eating meat, namely that the human soul is weighed down by it (*Epistle*, 108).

When Porphyry in *On Abstinence* is defending a fleshless diet, he excepts those who are doing manual work, as well as soldiers, sailors and rhetoricians. The vegetarian life is especially designed for the man who considers what he is, where he came from and where he ought to go (1.27; cf. 2.3). Abstention from animal food is for the man who will stay spiritually awake (1.27) and who wants to withdraw himself from the senses and imagination, irrationality and passions (1.31). In short, an animal diet nourishes the body, while a vegetable diet nourishes the rational soul (1.47, 1.53, 4.20; cf. Philo, *On the Contemplative Life*, 74).

Vegetarianism could further be an expression of an even more acute aversion to incorporating anything from animals into human bodies. Sometimes a demonic presence was thought to linger in the dead bodies of animals. This thought is also seen in some Christian authors, especially in connection with meat that had been sacrificed to pagan gods. Porphyry mentions that the souls of animals that have been slaughtered and have died by violence used to lurk around their dead bodies. The animal soul, which no longer has its former abode, is attracted to a body of a kindred nature. Therefore, eating meat from these animals could include an incorporation of an alien soul – that of the dead animal – into the human body (2.43, 2.47). Such a soul is impure and is a disturbing presence within a human being.

A similar mechanism is at work in some types of prophecy. According to Porphyry, the souls of prophetic animals can be received into a person who eats the heart of the animal (2.48). A prohibition against eating the heart and brain of animals because they are ladders and seats of wisdom and life is found among the Neoplatonists. It expresses a link between humans and animals in terms of their mental capacities, even if it does not necessarily mean a belief in transmigration. It also implies that it is undesirable to develop this connection, because the animal soul is inferior. In other types of prophecy, purity of soul and a vegetarian diet are explicitly required. According to J. Haussleiter, the mantic motif was predominant in the vegetarian diet of Apollonius of Tyana and in his opposition to bloody sacrifices (Haussleiter 1935: 308).

As we have seen, both a belief in a close relationship between animals and humans and a wish to create a distance between them could lead to vegetarianism and abstention from eating meat. In both cases, abstinence from animal food shows a concern for the categorical boundary between the species. Both attitudes are often present in the same author – arguments supporting the human-like qualities of animals as well as arguments against the pollution inherent in their dead bodies. Plutarch, for instance, combines a mixture of respect and compassion towards living beings with an abhorrence of eating flesh because it is disgusting and polluting (993B). According to Plutarch, the eating of animal flesh is unnatural for man – it is not according to nature (*kata physin*) (994F) but contrary to nature (*para physin*) (993E, 996B).

All the same, and in spite of his highly rhetorical arguments against eating meat, Plutarch does not oppose meat eating under all circumstances. However, it is only permitted out of hunger and on the condition that the animal has been killed in a humane way (996F).

The question of vegetarianism was mainly a question of how to relate to *tame* animals. Greek authors made a clear distinction between tame animals (*hemeros*) and wild animals (*agrios*). Latin authors made a similar distinction between *pecus*, "cattle", and wild animals, which were designated *agrestis*, *ferus*, *bestia* or *belua*.[2] What pertains to the one category does not necessarily pertain to the other. Humans were said to wage a just war (*dikaios polemos*) against some animals. In consonance with his views in *On the Cleverness of*

Animals, where he distinguishes between what is just treatment of harmful and harmless animals, Plutarch says explicitly that it is the tame animals that people kill for food that he is concerned about: "harmless, tame creatures without stings or teeth to harm us, creatures that, I swear, Nature appears to have produced for the sake of their beauty and grace" (*On the Eating of Flesh*, 994B).[3]

A special case is the question of why "the Pythagoreans used to abstain from fish more than from any other living creature", a question that Plutarch discusses in Table Talk 8 (*Moralia*, 728C–730F). Several reasons are mentioned. One possible reason is that it was because the early Pythagoreans considered silence a god-like thing and fish are silent creatures (728E); another is that Pythagoras was influenced by Egyptian sages, who regarded the sea as unrelated, alien and hostile to humans and its creatures as being impure (729A–C); and a third possible reason is that Pythagoreans usually tasted flesh only from sacrificed animals, and these animals did not include fish. When Plutarch speaks in the text, he stresses that Pythagoras was friendly towards fish because these creatures gave humans no excuse to treat them badly: they "do us no harm, no matter how capable they are of doing so" (729D). At the end of the work, one of the participants mentions as yet another argument for not eating fish the belief that man originally developed from the moist element and was related to fish (730D–F).

Abstaining from fish, like abstaining from all types of meat, may have several reasons and may in a similar way be based on the belief in a close relationship between these creatures and humans, as well as in an experience of distance and impurity. Plutarch also stresses here his general argument against harming animals – never to harm those animals that do not harm humans.

Like Plutarch, Porphyry finds that "those irrational animals that are unjust and evil by nature" can be destroyed, but as for those animals that do not naturally harm humans, it is unjust (*adikos*) to destroy and murder them (2.22.2). Justice towards animals meant on this point treating them as they treat us.

Putting a distance between humans and beasts of prey, like lions and wolves, which themselves had a diet based on meat, was an issue. When Seneca supports vegetarianism, he quotes his teacher Sotion, a Pythagorean, who kept the question of transmigration open, saying: "I am merely depriving you of food which sustains lions and vultures" (*Epistle*, 108). Plutarch points out that if humans were meant to eat animals, their bodies would have been equipped for killing them, with fangs and claws (995A–B).

The human relationship with animals that is reflected in vegetarian practices mainly encompasses tame animals and is more complicated than Graeco-Roman attitudes towards wild animals. In vegetarianism, there is a mingling of different attitudes towards animals – empathy as well as distance, a naturalization of similarities as well as a wish to underline differences. This ambiguity was rather typical of several of the genres that in the ancient world had animals as their subject. Natural history is a case in point.

Natural histories

The relations between animals and humans were not only a subject of philosophical debate and vegetarian practice but also the focus of natural histories. Just as animals were assembled from all parts of the empire, so ethnographical and zoological information about them was collected as well. This collecting activity presupposed ample means of producing, circulating and storing books and texts, which is to be seen, for instance, in the fact that in the fourth century CE twenty-nine libraries existed in Rome (Balsdon 1969: 148; Casson 2001: 92). These collections of information belonged mainly to the literary elite, but the natural histories did not present observations on animals that were elitist or radically new. In comparison with modern science, Roman natural histories reflected a mixture of genuine knowledge about different species combined with animal lore and hearsay; often, the blend was quite fantastic.

This blend represented a change in comparison with earlier descriptions of animals. Even if many of Aristotle's commentaries on animals are obviously wrong and several of his views could have been rectified by observation, it is still a long way from Aristotle's dissections and direct observation of animals to the natural histories of Pliny, Oppian and Aelian, for instance. These Roman authors based their works more on knowledge compiled from texts and compendia than on direct observation of animals; they had little interest in the logical and philosophical problems of animal classification and had a tendency to mix fact and fancy (Wallace-Hadrill 1968: 34).

In these centuries, there is also a tendency to blur the concepts of real animals with fictional ones. Animals are food for thought, as well as for fantasy and imagination. Not only live animals but also imaginary ones are important to humans, and no absolute division exists between the two types. Since representations of animals, real or fictional, are always based on mental images, a sort of inner vision of the animal in question, and since this mental image is never identical with any "real" animal, the borderline between the real and fictional animals is not clear-cut.

Graeco-Roman authors of natural histories wrote about animals they had seen as well as those they had never seen but believed they existed. Among the many various animals that Pliny describes, he mentions camelopards (giraffes) (*Natural History*, 8.27), first seen at games held by Julius Caesar, but he also refers to the Scandinavian *achlis*, probably an elk or a reindeer, an animal that had never appeared in Rome (*Natural History*, 8.16, 8.39; cf. Zeuner 1963: 428). However, in parallel with these animals, Pliny also describes fantastic and non-existent creatures such as Ethiopian sphinxes and pegasi (*Natural History*, 8.30), as well as the Indian unicorn and the basilisk serpent of Cyrenaica (*Natural History*, 8.33), as if these animals were just as real as the camelopard and the *achlis*.

A similar phenomenon is reflected in art. In the upper part of the Palestrina mosaic from the second century BCE, which presents in a vivid and detailed way a general view of life in Egypt, forty kinds of animal are depicted. Some of them do not live in Egypt, which may suggest that the mosaic shows a contemporary zoological garden in Alexandria, as has recently been suggested by archaeologist Gyözö Vörös (2001: 114). The animals are labelled with Greek names, and although most of them can be identified as real animals, such as the giraffe, lion and rhinoceros, at least one of them seems to be a fabulous creature, the *onokentaura*, a female human-headed ass. But even if the depiction of the *onokentaura* may be an attempt to depict a gnu, as has been suggested (Meyboom 1995: 111–14), its human head shows a confusion of categories that makes this animal rather peculiar. In any case, the Palestrina mosaic is a picturesque illustration of the combination of well-known animals with lesser-known ones, some of which are on the verge of being fabulous. Thus this mosaic illustrates in a way similar to the natural histories the blurring of the borderline between real and more fanciful creatures.

However, to label this genre of natural history "natural history of nonsense", as one modern critic has done (Evans 1946), overlooks the fact that these natural histories also had other types of "cultural work" in view than modern natural science has.

Some of the content of this "cultural work" has recently been illuminated by Roger French, who has stressed how the authors and compilers of natural histories were interested in the material resources that existed in nature and how they eventually could be of use and interest to the Romans. According to French, the educated Roman was at the centre of Pliny's natural history, as Pliny was at the centre of the civilized world. A presupposition in these natural histories was the originally Stoic doctrine, which seems to have been more and more accepted, that all things had been made for the sake of man (*Natural History*, 7.1; French 1994: 207).

In addition to this interest in the hegemony of man, the natural histories are also keen to establish a friendly world. One result is that while humans and animals are seen as categorically different, the natural histories also present some animals as rather similar to humans. Thus the natural histories reflect an important characteristic of human–animal relations, namely a sort of double view or internal ambiguity in the relationship. There is both a categorical division between humans and animals based on reason/lack of reason and a web of correspondences between them that criss-cross the natural world. Aelian, for instance, attributes wisdom (*sophia*) and intelligence (*synesis*), and even justice (*dikaiosyne*), to animals (Kindstrand 1998: 2966). Pliny says of the elephant that it is nearest to man in intelligence and "possesses virtues rare even in man, honesty, wisdom, justice, also respect for the stars and reverence for the sun and moon" (*Natural History*, 8.11). The cleverness of horses Pliny finds beyond description (*Natural History*, 8.65).

There are several examples of how the division between animals and humans is ignored in radical ways, for instance in the many stories of reincarnation across species and, not least, in the stories of love and friendship between a human and an animal. Pliny, as well as Oppian and Aelianus, passed on many classical stories in which animal intelligence and goodness were praised.

Oppian writes of dolphins that they had earlier been men and had "lived in cities along with mortals" (1.649–50). He regards the hunting of dolphins as immoral (5.416ff). Aelian (*c.* 170–230 CE), an Italian Sophist and priest who lived in Praeneste, never left Italy but nevertheless wrote in Greek and only quoted Greek authors, describes peculiarities of animal behaviour, their names, habits and characteristics. In *On the Characteristics of Animals*, a work in seventeen books, ethnographic reports are combined with myths and fables in an odd mixture. Aelian writes of storks that when they reach old age, they are transformed into human shape (he insists that it is no fairytale! (3. 23)). He also reports that on the island of Diomeda, there are birds that were originally Greeks and contemporaries of Diomedes (1.1). Pliny is more sceptical; for instance, he does not believe that humans can turn into werewolves (*Natural History*, 8.34). But stories about friendship between humans and dolphins, as well as about dolphins that are helpful to humans, which are commonplaces in natural histories, are also told by Pliny (*Natural History*, 9.8–10).

In Aelian's work, several anecdotes about cross-species love relationships appear (Kindstrand 1998: 2964; cf. Salisbury 1994: 84–101). Humans are paired with a dog, a horse, a dolphin and a serpent, but also with a ram and a goose. Usually, the animal makes the first move (1.6, 2.6, 5.29, 6.15, 6.17; cf. *Natural History*, 7.13–14), signalling, perhaps, that it is the human form that is the object of the love and lust of the animal because the human form is the highest of animate beings and therefore the most attractive. Aelian has only one example of a human being who takes the initiative (4.8). It is a groom falling in love with a mare. But when the groom consummated his union with the mare, he was immediately killed by the mare's foal. Thus, in this case, the overstepping of this limit was promptly punished. All the same, in these stories about love and friendship between animals and humans, the dividing line between the categories is transcended in an important way.

In the natural histories, animals are both modelled on humans and in their turn used as models for humans. Pliny calls special attention to the elephant, the dolphin, the eagle and the bee, species that he regards as especially outstanding in their respective animal categories. The strong moralizing tendency in Pliny and Aelian conveys the message that animals are sometimes and on some points better than humans, and that humans can learn lessons from animals about how to live and behave towards each other. Several of the authors stress how some animals have a meagre diet and only copulate when the female wishes to conceive – characteristics that they found highly admirable and ideal.

In pseudo-Oppian's work the *Chase*, Artemis urges the poet to "tell me of the hates of wild beasts, sing their friendships, and their bridal chambers of tearless love upon the hills, and the births which among wild beasts need no midwife" (1.38–40). According to this description, the life of beasts has a certain similarity to the life and passions of humans as described in ancient novels (Klingender 1971: 91–2; Bartley 2003). With his voluminous work *On the Characteristics of Animals*, Aelian wanted to inform, entertain and teach his readers morals, therefore he constructed the animal world as a reflection of the world of humans, a mirror in which Aelian's contemporaries were invited to see themselves. Jan Fredrik Kindstrand characterizes Aelian's manner of thinking about animals as typical of a general moral/philosophical attitude based on Stoic-Cynic ideas, an attitude that was common in these centuries (Kindstrand 1998: 2965, 2990).

There is a strong tendency to model animals on humans. Pliny, for instance, draws a picture of elephants that makes them close to humans (*Natural History*, 8.1–13). According to him, elephants are near to man in intelligence. They understand human language, show reverence towards heaven, form close friendships with each other and are reported to fall in love with humans. It is also possible to teach elephants to do tricks, a token of their capacity for intelligent learning.

But the ability of animals to learn tricks is a two-edged sword, because it also makes them subordinate to humans and makes them recognize humans as their masters. Pliny writes about an elephant that was scolded because of its mediocre performance and because of that kept rehearsing during the night to get its performance right (*Natural History*, 8.3). Is the dog cleverer than the cat because it can learn tricks, or is the cat cleverer because it refuses to do as humans tell it? When the "cleverness" of animals is measured against a human ideal, it tends to turn animals into abortive humans. In contrast to the way that, for instance, Alexander, Philo's nephew, mentioned the ability of animals to learn tricks as proof of their intelligence, Augustine used performing animals as examples of animals' subordination to humans (*Questions on Various Topics*, 83).

While elephants resemble humans and may be taught tricks, other animals are unaffected by humans and in some cases develop societies that may appear as models for human societies. This perspective is most systematically exploited with regard to insects. Insects, especially bees and ants, are frequently referred to and treated as models for humans. Pliny gives pride of place to bees because they alone among insects "have been made for the sake of man" (*Natural History*, 11.4). But an important reason why he admires them is that bees work together, are intelligent and have natural abilities (*ingenium*) (*Natural History*, 11.4ff). Pliny also marvels at the society of ants (*Natural History*, 11.36). This admiration for bees and ants is found in earlier authors too, such as Plato and Virgil (Plato, *Phaedo*, 82b; Virgil, *Georgics*, 4), as well as in Celsus (*Against Celsus*, 4.81–5). These small creatures had a special significance with regard to human life.

A similar admiration also shines through with regard to fish (cf. Chapter 1). Fish – except for those kept in fish ponds – are not domesticated. Land animals were controlled by domestication in quite another way and, in the empire, also by the technology of the arena. Fish belong to a strange world and interact only to a small degree with humans (Plutarch, *On the Cleverness of Animals*, 975E–976A; see also Purcell 1995). They live in mysterious societies in the depths of the sea, societies that are not accessible to humans. Fish were not usually sacrificed: they were not "contract animals" (see Chapter 1). That these creatures evaded human control and seemed to live independently of humans and in their own societies was probably a characteristic that made them useful as archetypal animals.

Because insects and fish interact with humans to only a small degree, they could be described as intelligent and industrious without challenging the fundamental division between humans and other species. Seldom did humans have a real relationship with these animals, which continued to lead their lives independently of men. Their independence was apparently seen as admirable in a society where the general rule was that most known animals and nations were sooner or later placed under the rule of Rome.

As time went by, the genre of natural histories changed into pious histories. The development of the genre from Pliny to Aelian is a series of stages along a road that also leads to the immensely popular Christian *Physiologus* ("The Natural Scientist"), composed some time between the second and fourth century CE. In *Physiologus*, animals, as well as stones and plants, received a Christian interpretation and became marvellous moral examples for human life (Miller 2001: 61–73).

It is the wavering between different views of animals that is so fascinating in the natural histories composed during the empire. They are constantly moving back and forth between a conception of animals as merely beasts and a conception of them as human, only with tails and fur, hooves or claws.

⌈Physiognomics⌉

A more systematic combination of similarities and differences between animals and humans is found in the physiognomic tradition. Physiognomics (*physiognomonia*) is the study of the relationship between the external form of animals and humans and their inner characteristics. Animals are used as examples and symbols. In ancient times, animals were believed to inherit specific characteristics, and a species of animals could therefore appear as a symbol of these characteristics. Thus animals could be seen as representing a human passion, a virtue or a vice. Physiognomics presupposed parallels in the nature of animals and of humans and was built on a schematic and one-dimensional view of animals.

According to a treatise assigned to Aristotle (but probably not written by him but by one of his pupils), "no animal has ever existed such that it has the form of one animal and the disposition of another, but the body and soul of the same creature are always such that a given disposition must necessarily follow a given form" (*Physiognomics*, 805a12–15). The principle of the connection between bodily and mental characteristics was transferred to humans. Pseudo-Aristotle says about one branch of physiognomists that "they have supposed one type of body for the animal and then have concluded that the man who has a body similar to this will have a similar soul" (*ibid.*, 805a22–4). Although the author of this treatise voices his scepticism concerning partial and simplistic ways of using physiognomic methods, cultural stereotypes of animals were created and frequently used by Graeco-Roman authors to describe human types (Malina 1996: 125). Thus these ideal animal types served as psychological categories.

One example is the lion. The lion had the most perfect image as a male type and was brave in a manly way, which meant that "in character he is generous and liberal, magnanimous and with a will to win; he is gentle, just, and affectionate towards his associates" (*Physiognomics*, 809b34–37). The lion was a symbol of the ideal hero. The panther, in contrast, was more female, and although it was brave, its character was "petty, thieving and, generally speaking, deceitful" (*ibid.*, 810a7–9). The use of the lion and the panther as ideal types for good males and bad females was repeated by later authors, for instance Polemo from Laodicea, who was an illustrious rhetorician in Smyrna and who wrote an influential treatise on physiognomics at the beginning of the second century CE in which he followed Aristotle by showing close parallels between animals and humans (Evans 1969: 11ff). According to Polemo, the lion is "brave, a bold hero, angry when hurt, long suffering, modest, generous, great-hearted and ready to spring" (Barton 1994: 127). Polemo also made a list of the characteristics of ninety-four species of animal. He claimed that it is not possible to find a human who does not resemble an animal or has not a single animal characteristic (Dagron 1987: 72). Physiognomic thinking, built on comparisons between humans and animals, clearly flourished in the following centuries. One example is an anonymous Latin handbook from the fourth century CE (Evans 1969: 15ff).[4]

Why was the parallelism between humans and animals developed, and how was it understood? A "science" of physiognomics can be traced to Aristotle's time, and comparisons between humans and animals had been common in literature from classical times – in Homer, this type of comparison is quite common. In later times, however, and especially in Galen, the parallels between animals and humans in nature and physique were explained with recourse to the doctrine of humours and the relationship between the different principles in the human body. This doctrine had become a basic principle encompassing both animals and humans (Evans 1969: 17ff).

In spite of the fact that physiognomics was based on experience of a close relationship between animals and humans, the way it was used in practice in the Roman Empire was mainly as a means of demonstrating difference. To achieve this goal, antitheses as well as homologies were employed. Humans were opposed to beasts as men were to women and Greeks to barbarians. For even if a man were to be compared to a lion in a laudatory way, animal parallels were used most frequently to blame and abuse people. When male Romans were described with animal characteristics, or for that matter described as feminine or barbarian, this was not intended to boost these men's self-image or to heighten their standing in the eyes of their fellows. Tamson S. Barton illustrates this point well by saying about Polemo that rather "than actually making wax images of his opponents to burn, with physiognomica he constructed their bodies so as to destroy their characters" (Barton 1994: 97). Collective designations for animals were used in a derogatory way in descriptions of humans. To be labelled a *therion* in Greek or a *belua* or *bestia* in Latin was normally an insult.[5]

It seems as if physiognomic thinking was rooted in experience of the similarities between humans and animals, but it was to an increasing degree being used to show up their differences. In the end, the last remainder of any lingering similarity between animals and humans, which had been the original basis for physiognomic thinking, was no longer tolerated. Christians were much more reluctant than their pagan contemporaries to make physiognomic comparisons between animals and humans in a way that presupposed that animals and humans were on the same existential level (Dagron 1987). For the Christians, the case was simple. Humans were made in God's image; animals were not.

Conclusion

During the empire, animals were the subject of cultural concern. As we have seen, in philosophy animals were seen either as categorically different from humans or as different from humans only in degree. These views are exemplified by the Stoics and the Academics, respectively.

In addition to their role in philosophy, animals were also the subject of vegetarian and physiognomic discourses and natural history. The characteristic of these discourses is ambiguity when it comes to the evaluation of animals. Vegetarian practices sometimes reflected solidarity with animals and compassion towards them, but more often they reflected a fear of pollution and a desire to separate humans and animals. Natural histories took as their point of departure the differences between animals and humans but often ended by showing their similarities and using examples in which the categorical boundaries were transcended. Physiognomic thinking, which was based on fundamental similarities between animals and humans, was used to show differences between man and beast. In this way, a shimmering tapestry of similarities and differences characterizes the relationship between animals and humans in these centuries. When differences were revealed, similarities also appeared. Similarities bred differences, and differences bred similarities.

It is interesting to note that some of the authors who wrote so eloquently in defence of animals and/or a vegetarian lifestyle, in later life gave up at least some of their earlier views on animals. This was probably the case with Seneca as well as with Plutarch and Porphyry. Furthermore, Porphyry may in his youth have defended the position that animals had reason, a position he later abandoned. These changes in the attitudes of the authors who had earlier written in defence of animals perhaps illustrate that such views were contested and were somewhat marginal.

When the categorical boundaries between animals and humans were debated in the first centuries CE, it is reasonable to think that it had something to do with actual experience of animals. Animals were by some experienced more than before as being different from humans. The institution of the arena could also have contributed to brutalizing people's attitudes towards animals.

Philosophy, vegetarianism, natural history and physiognomics contributed to the general conception of animals. But while these fields show that animals, with some significant exceptions, were predominantly viewed as different from humans and at the lower end of the ontological hierarchy, there were areas where thoughts and conceptions of animals took more subtle directions. How were the beasts of the imagination cultivated in these centuries of flourishing paganism and growing Christianity when such imagined beasts really thrived in literature and art as well as in religion?

4

IMAGINATION AND TRANSFORMATIONS

Metamorphoses I

In this chapter, we will discuss two types of animal–human transformation that were especially pondered upon by the Graeco-Roman imagination. These were imagined relationships – expressions of myth and fantasy – in which animals were drawn into the human sphere. Here they were internalized and recreated as aspects of human nature and sometimes mixed with human qualities in other ways. The first of these relationships is a human–animal transformation during a single life (*metamorphosis*), while the second is a human–animal transformation during several lives (*metensomatosis*).

Fantasies about animals and humans had their outlet in art, as well as in narratives and literature. One prominent theme is transformation between animals and humans. A transformation could be a *metamorphosis*, a change of bodily form or species, taking place within one life-time. Alternatively the change takes place in a progression from one life to another in the form of a *metensomatosis*, a change of body. Such tales of transformation do not describe animals as external antagonists, as was the case with the animals that were confronted by Hercules and Orpheus, but they are more directly a reflection of the inherent bestial aspects of the human situation. The theme of transformation between humans and animals is often an elaboration of how the bestial aspect of humans represents a degradation of human qualities. Ovid's tales of transformation focus in singular ways on similarities and differences between animals and humans, on essences and changes, on permanence and flux.

Gods changing into animal shapes had been a popular theme in Greek mythology, especially with regard to Zeus. Disguised as an animal, the father of the gods visited girls on earth: Leda as a swan and Europa as a bull. In Latin also, the topic of metamorphosis was popular. In these metamorphoses, the boundaries between mortals and immortals, as well as those between humans and animals, were crossed and thus made less categorical. Human-to-animal changes were especially loved. Metamorphoses were a popular theme that had been taken up and developed by Roman authors, the most famous being Ovid and Apuleius.[1]

Playfulness is a vital ingredient in Ovid's disparate stories, although serious and moving passages are also found. Human bodies are changed into animals, as well as into trees and plants, always into new and different forms of flora and fauna. In a few cases, humans experience an apotheosis (Hercules, 9.262–70; Aeneas, 14.600–7; Romulus, 14. 823–8; Hersilia (wife of Romulus), 14.829–34).

It has often been emphasized how varied Ovid's metamorphoses are. A marble statue is made into the living woman, Pygmalion (10.247–97), and the nymph Arethusa is made into a well (5.572–641). With few exceptions, Ovid's humans do not usually themselves have the power to turn into animal shapes; they are transformed by a god. This transformation is either a punishment inflicted by the god on the human being – Actaeon was turned into a stag by Diana because he saw her in the nude and was mercilessly torn to pieces by his own dogs (3.177–252) – or a means of salvation from external dangers when the animal body becomes a hiding place for the human personality or soul (Riddehough 1959: 203). When Juno became aware that her husband was having an adventure with the young girl Io, Io was transformed into a heifer by Jove to avoid the fury of Juno (1.610–12). But whether the animal form is an instrument of rescue or a means of punishment and damnation, it is never a preferred form.

Sometimes the animal form may be an accentuation of characteristics inherent in the person who was turned into a beast, as when the girl Arachne, an expert weaver, was turned into a spider by Athena. In this way, Arachne was punished because she outdid the goddess in a weaving contest. In her new shape, Arachne continues her weaving, for ever preserved in the form of a spider (6.144–5). For those whom the gods wanted to punish, a transformation into animals usually stresses their evil characteristics. King Lycaon, who tried to kill Jove and served a dish of human flesh to the god, who had taken on mortal form, was turned into a wolf, a shape that accentuated his "beastly savagery" (1.230–40). In this new shape, he applied his bloodthirsty nature to slaughtering sheep.

In general, the animal shape is never an improvement on the human condition. In the case of Lycaon, who transgressed both the boundaries between god and man (trying to kill a god) and between man and man (cannibalism), he was "rewarded" by being transformed into a beast. His name "Lycaon", derived from the Greek for wolf, *lykos*, suggests that the wolfish essence was inherent in him from the very beginning and that he had now become in external form what he essentially had always been: a bloodthirsty beast. In her recent book *Metamorphosis and Identity*, Caroline Walker Bynum stresses that Lycaon's vices are boundary crossings, that he really changes but yet that he "is what he was before" (Bynum 2001: 169). The wolfish form fits his nature or essence better than his human form, which means that there is a continuity of personality between man and beast. As L. Barkan puts it, we have been witnessing "a complex combination of change and continuity" (Barkan 1986: 25).

A metamorphosis presupposes a process where the distinctions between an animal body and a human body collapse, and it gives rise to a moment when the two forms meet and fuse. This moment is described, for instance, by Ovid when Arachne is made into a spider, or by Apuleius when Lucius is finally transformed from an ass into his former human shape.

> And as she turned to go, she sprinkled her with drugs of Hecate, and in a trice, touched by the bitter lotion, all her hair falls off and with it go her nose and her ears. Her head shrinks tiny; her whole body's small; instead of legs slim fingers line her sides. The rest is belly, yet from that she sends a fine-spun thread and, as a spider, still weaving her webs, pursues her former skill.
>
> (*Metamorphoses*, 6.143–52)

> My bestial features faded away, the rough hair fell from my body, my sagging paunch tightened, my hooves separated into feet and toes, my fore hooves now no longer served only for walking upon, but were restored, as hands, to human uses. My neck shrank, my face and head rounded, my great stony teeth shrank to their proper size, my long ears receded to their former shortness, and my tail, which had been my worst shame, vanished altogether.
>
> (*The Golden Ass*, 11.13)

In these descriptions, there is a continuum between the external elements and bodily structures of animals and humans. A metamorphosis is usually described as flux and movement and sometimes as a large-scale process (as in Ovid's poem). In each individual case, however, the result is not seldom that the transformed individual is stuck – frozen for ever in its new shape, as when Arachne is made into a spider or Lycaon into a wolf.

Usually the transformed human retains some of his or her former human characteristics in the new animal shape. In this way, the transformation is never complete, and the boundaries between the categories of human and animal remain in flux. Hardly ever is the transformed human only temporarily turned into a beast and afterwards turned back into a human shape, as Io eventually was (1.738–46).

Especially striking in Ovid's descriptions of how humans turn into animals is how typical human characteristics, such as hands, an erect posture on two legs and especially the human voice, are changed so that the victim is finally unable to communicate. This is always the outcome when a human is turned into an animal. Because the former human being loses the faculty of speech, he or she is thereby effectively shut out of human society. One of the most moving narratives in the poem is when Actaeon flees from his own hounds and desperately tries to cry out to them, "I am Actaeon! Recognize your own master!" (3.230), to stop them attacking him, but in vain. And when they finally bury their fangs in his body, "till there is no place left for further wounds, he groans and makes a sound, which, though not human, is still one no deer could utter, and fills the heights he knows so well with mournful cries" (3.236–9). Actaeon has lost his human voice but kept his human mind. Thus the human–animal border has been dislocated. Formerly it was found outside Actaeon, but now it reappears as a border between his internal mind and his voice and body. Actaeon thinks but is no longer able to communicate, not even with animals.

What do the metamorphoses of Ovid imply? What is changed, and what remains the same? Most striking in many of these transformations is the way that being an animal is described as being in a foreign place. It is as if the human soul is peeping out from an animal body, and the human consciousness is trapped within the beast. Classicist Penelope Murray has stressed that the continuity in human consciousness from a human to an animal incarnation is the distinctive feature of Ovid's poem: "the retention of human consciousness within a bestial or other kind of form enables Ovid to explore questions about human identity in a peculiarly disturbing way" (Murray 1998: 89). Murray argues convincingly that according to Ovid it is not primarily the human soul or a moral superiority in relation to other creatures that differentiates human beings from other creatures, but the human body. Humanity is firmly tied to the human shape. So when humans are changed into animal forms, they lose not only their human shape but also their humanity.

It could be added that the continuity in human consciousness also means a narrowing of it. Even if human qualities survive in the altered bodily shape – Cadmus and Harmonia, who were changed into serpents, are still in love with each other (4.575–603) – the new bodily forms also determine the soul's expression and often seem to narrow the spectrum of feelings and understanding in a way that makes the soul into a single-layered entity. Only the essential qualities of the person remain. There are exceptions – Actaeon and Io, for instance, are clearly humans trapped in the bodies of beasts. But when humans are transformed into beasts, they are normally simultaneously moving away from individuality into typicality, not only on the level of body but also psychologically. In this way, these tales also reveal a reductionist view of animals in relation to humans, a view that conforms to allegorical and metaphorical thinking: humans have individual traits; animals are stereotypes. The individual animal is similar to other animals of the same species.

It is possible by means of a metamorphosis to be transferred from one layer of the universe – divine, human or animal – to another. But the transition takes place more easily in some directions than in others. This is in accordance with the concept of a great chain of being that orders the different species and spiritual beings in a hierarchy. There is a fluctuation between the layers, but after being transformed, the victim is usually stuck in their new shape and state of being for ever. However, gods may cross the different layers at will. In the story about Arachne, the girl depicts animal forms that the gods used to deceive mundane girls (6.1–145). Gods may turn into beasts when it suits them and back into their original form.

However, most important for human–animal relations and for the boundaries between the two categories in these tales is the fact that the boundaries are held firm in one direction but not in the other. In the case of Io, she was transformed into a heifer and back again. This example shows that animals that in reality are transformed humans can be turned back into human form. But animals that have never been humans are never transformed into a man or a woman. This is in accordance with the view voiced by Plato, who pointed out in the *Phaedrus* that only a soul that had once been human could pass from an animal into a human; a soul that had never been human could not pass into a human.

That mere animals do not become humans is also in accordance with the type of metaphorical system that is expressed through Ovid's metamorphoses. Humans are characterized as animals, not the other way around.

The fact that mere animals do not turn into humans is also consonant with Ovid's concern, which is with human beings. However, one of the things that this work also does is to give etymologies and aetiologies for phenomena in the natural world. Animals come in along with plants and other objects that humans are transformed into. Ovid is not writing about animals as such, but all the same his representations of animals reveal something about how the different species of animal are perceived and how the different layers of the universe work in relation to each other.

That a "real" animal does not change into a human being is a limitation on the possibilities of transformation that is important because it reveals that there are impassable boundaries in the hierarchy of being that reflect differences between gods, humans and animals, differences that it is impossible to eliminate. It has been argued that changes from man to god or into an animal do not imply a movement up or down the existential ladder (for example, Solodow 1988: 190–2). But animals are never transformed into humans precisely because gods, humans and animals in Ovid's *Metamorphoses* are also locked into a system that in several ways functions hierarchically.

In this system, it is possible to be transformed into lower categories and back again, and in some rare cases, a human being may be transformed into a god. But while it is possible for humans and gods to turn into animals, it is never possible for an animal to turn into a human being or to change into a god. These limitations of the transformation process are not in accordance with what is suggested in Book 15, that the spirit passes "from beast into human bodies" (15.167–8). They imply a more fundamental division between animals and humans than between humans and gods, which is in accordance with a general tendency in people's thinking concerning animals in these centuries.

Metamorphoses II

Another *Metamorphoses* was written by Apuleius, a writer and orator who was born in 125 CE in Madaurus in Africa. This *Metamorphoses* is not, like Ovid's work, a poem but a novel. The transformations in this novel are also different from those in Ovid's poem. In Apuleius' work, people are not so much transformed: they transform themselves into animals, seen as convenient vehicles for their activities. No god is initiating these original transformations; the hero and the minor characters change from man or woman into beast by acts of magic. At the same time, there is a clear direction in the novel: its hero, Lucius, goes from man to animal and back to man before he is finally saved by the goddess Isis. This is clearly different from the way in which metamorphoses are described by Ovid. With a few exceptions, in Ovid's poem, the humans who have been transformed into beasts are stuck in their new animal shapes and remain for ever what they have become. Charles Segal pointed out an essential element when he characterized the movement in Ovid's *Metamorphoses* as "a downward movement" (Segal 1969: 285–6). If the movement in Ovid's work is downwards, the movement in Apuleius' work, written nearly two centuries later, is definitely upwards. Paradoxically, however, the upward movement takes place within the body of an ass, an animal that was regarded as low in the hierarchy of animals.

This novel, which was written in Latin in the second part of the second century, is built on an older Greek text. A comparison with the narrative *Onos* (Ass) or *Lucius*, written by Lucian, which is based on the same Greek precursor as *Metamorphoses*, helps to reveal Apuleius' special changes in relation to the older novel. It has been exhaustively discussed whether Apuleius had religious aims and motives in writing the book or whether his intention was only to entertain his audience. Is it a religious document or only a novel? The problem is created especially by Book 11, because in this book the transformed ass is finally made into an Isiac, an adherent of the goddess Isis. Because of this "religious" ending, a special light is also thrown on other parts of the novel, and it is tempting to detect a religious meaning in these parts too (see Winkler 1985: 8). Obviously, the novel can be read in both ways; as a collection of entertaining episodes in which the transformed ass explores the social life and network in its contemporary Mediterranean world (Millar 1981), or as a conversion story. John J. Winkler in particular opened up new avenues by arguing for the open-ended character of the novel as a whole (Winkler 1985). At least it cannot be denied that the novel is rather complex. It includes a string of different narratives within the larger narrative and a conversion story at the end. This conversion story has often been interpreted as being built on Apuleius' own experiences with the Isis cult.

The hero of the novel is Lucius, an educated, upper-class man from Corinth. His lover is a slave-girl who served in the house of the witch Pamphile. Lucius watches Pamphile transform herself into an owl and wants to change in the same manner, assisted by the slave-girl. Alas, the magical procedure goes wrong, and Lucius changes instead into an ass. From the upper reaches of human society, he is trapped by fate in a being belonging to the lower reaches of animal society. Just as in Ovid's *Metamorphoses*, a human soul is trapped within an animal form when Lucius is turned into an ass. As an ass, he trots around the ancient world and experiences dangers as well as comic episodes – painfully aware of his obtrusive bestiality. In the end, he is redeemed from his animal form by receiving a garland of roses from a priest of Isis.

However, not only is a human soul trapped within an ass, but many of the human protagonists in the book clearly reveal animal traits. These traits contribute to revealing the underlying conceptual metaphors and the conception of animals that these metaphors are based on. Nancy Shumate has especially pointed out how terms for animal activities are employed to denote human activity, so that humans are characterized as animals in all but form (Shumate 1996: 107–8). A vocabulary usually used of animals is repeatedly used to characterize human mentality and actions. In Books 7 through 10, the characters routinely behave like wild animals (*ibid.*: 117). As mused upon by Shumate, it is a paradox that "this ass with human sensibilities, serves as a kind of foil to all the *homines sapientes* raging with animal passions through the penultimate books of the *Metamorphoses*" (*ibid.*: 123). This trait of the *Metamorphoses* is clearly a response to a certain "*zoomorphisme des passions*" in these centuries (Dagron 1987: 71). In contrast to all those humans with animal traits who appear in the novel, its hero, Lucius, has the form of an ass but is a man – although not quite. According to Shumate, "it is not simply a case of a man becoming an animal. Lucius is stuck somewhere between the two; he does not belong unambiguously to one category or the other" (Shumate 1996: 65).

Against this view, one could argue that the hybrid nature of Lucius consists mainly of his being a man within an ass's body. Lucius' "ass-like nature" consists of his bodily shape and of nothing else. But as for being "nothing else", it is really quite a lot: Lucius meets trials and obstacles throughout because of the paradox of being a man within an animal body, and precisely because the expression of Lucius' human soul is determined by his new type of body.

The animal form of Lucius has been seen as an instrument by means of which he develops his true humanity and in the end, through Isis, is turned into a saved human being. Thus the novel may be read as a narrative of conversion. Shumate places it interestingly in a discourse on conversion, but as a type of conversion that works within a cognitive framework rather than a moral framework (Shumate 1996: 14). When Lucius is in the body of the ass, his world is slowly going to pieces, and all the usual categories on which his world had been built are falling apart.

Both Ovid's and Apuleius' *Metamorphoses* presuppose fluctuation between the human and animal categories. They also presuppose a hierarchy of being in which to be a beast is a disadvantage. For a human being to be turned into a beast is in most cases also a disgrace. At the same time, to become painfully aware of one's animal nature at the same time as one realizes one's human nature – to know oneself as one really is – as Lucius does, means to be on the road to recovery of one's full humanity.

What does it really mean to be a beast? Modern commentators have pointed out that a description of how a human being is turned into an animal and how it feels to be an animal can also be a way of describing what it felt like to be what Greeks and Romans vehemently did not want to be: a barbarian, an exile, or a slave. "To Ovid, thought is what separates the human from the animal as it separates the Greek and Roman from the barbarian", wrote classicist G.B. Riddehough (1959: 201). Riddehough also compared Ovid's last years in exile from Rome with the way he described the humans that were transformed into animals: "We imagine him asking whether after all there is so very much difference between the *transformati* of legend and the *relegati* of bitter actuality" (*ibid.*: 209).

Classicist Keith Bradley has recently made an interesting interpretation of Apuleius' narrative as a description of slavery (Bradley 2000; cf. Millar 1981: 65). According to Bradley, *Metamorphoses* describes a process of animalization. He has isolated three recurring traits that link the animal to the slave: Lucius/the ass is a beast of burden, almost always at work; he suffers physical maltreatment; and he is sold several times (Bradley 2000: 115–16). These are traits that characterize human slaves as well as animals. Thus Apuleius' *Metamorphoses* becomes a description of what it is to be a slave and of the process by means of which the human being is made into an object and a commodity, in short, into an animal.

Riddehough's interpretation of Ovid and Bradley's of Apuleius support more generally the view that texts about humans turned into animals have much to say about human categories. The texts are not primarily commenting on the state of being an animal but on what the Greeks and Romans conceived of as homologous states: being a barbarian or a slave, or, simply, being the other, the one who has been expelled from human society or has put himself outside it. At the same time, however, these texts use descriptions of animals as metaphors for human beings and thus also make more general comments on "the otherness" of animals in relation to humans.

Christian authors opposed the idea that humans could transform themselves or be transformed into animals. Augustine had heard stories about wicked landladies who turned men into beasts of burden and used these beasts as long as they needed them. He did not believe such stories. According to Augustine, if these things happened, it was because demons changed the appearance of things, so that transformations *seemed* to happen. Because substances cannot be changed, these transformations do not happen in reality. Bodies and minds do not really change into bestial forms and characteristics; only a sort of semblance is created, a semblance that can also be perceived by others. Phantasms, which do not really exist, may appear. In this way, people may experience themselves, and be experienced by others, as animals (*The City of God*, 18.18). Augustine also suggests that metamorphoses, as in the classical examples of Iphigenia's transformation into a hind or Odysseus' men turned into pigs, may be juggleries and substitutions. He suggests that animals were presented on the scene simultaneously with the humans being whisked away. According to Christian thinking, each creature and thing has their specific place in God's creation. For living creatures, this place is among other things determined by type of species and cannot be overruled.

It is interesting how seriously Augustine tries to explain away what are apparently very common stories. For these theological polemics do not rule out, but rather support, the impression that people often believed that human–animal transformations really were possible. Palladius, for instance, describes how a woman is turned into a horse by means of magic but is returned to her previous form by the monk Makarios (Palladius, *The Lausiac History*, 17.6–9).

Metensomatosis

In Ovid's poem and Apuleius' novel, living beings are changed into new and different forms. But death may also lead to a transformation into other types of living being. Through a *metensomatosis*, a human may also turn into a beast. In the last book of *Metamorphoses*, Ovid, through his mouthpiece Pythagoras, introduces the subject of transmigration of souls into new bodies, human or animal, with these much-quoted words:

> All things are changing; nothing dies [*omnia mutantur, nihil interit*]. The spirit wanders, comes now here, now there, and occupies whatever frame it pleases. From beasts it passes into human bodies, and from our bodies into beasts, but never perishes.
>
> (15.165–8)

Like the last book of Apuleius' *Metamorphoses*, the speech by Pythagoras in the last book of Ovid's poem has been interpreted as the key to the whole work. The message of Pythagoras is in this case that through all changes, the soul remains the same. All beings are interrelated, and souls transmigrate from one bodily shape to another. This Pythagorean idea is also referred to by other authors, such as Seneca (*Epistle*, 108.19) and Sextus Empiricus (*Against the Physicists*, 1.127). We will not be discussing whether the last book of Ovid's *Metamorphoses* is the key to the whole work but only look into what the speech by Pythagoras implies for the relationship between animals and humans.

In the passage about Pythagoras, Ovid is not referring to metempsychosis, which means a change in soul and implies that rational souls of human beings pass only into other human beings, while the souls of beasts pass only into other beasts. Ovid refers to a change of body, which means that the transmigration process crosses the boundaries between the species. In this process, it is explicitly said that the soul remains the same (*Metamorphoses*, 15.171–2). Thus the categorical boundary between animals and humans refers in this case only to bodies, not to souls. The changing of forms while souls remain unchanged and may even travel across the boundaries between species presupposes a basic unity of animate life, encompassing humans as well as animals. Porphyry interprets the theme of transformation from man to beast, often found in fables, as a proof that animals have souls similar to humans (*On Abstinence*, 3.16). This natural philosophical and biological understanding of reincarnation presupposes eternal continuity of life (Dierauer 1977: 1–24).

When Ovid, through Pythagoras, describes the transmigration of souls between humans and animals as a natural and perpetual process, not a moral process with a final salvation, this does not mean that the process is without its moral. The moral lies in this case in the insistence on an alleged community between animals and humans and in the vegetarian point of view, which is forcefully defended. Conceptual borders are closely connected with ethics, and vegetarianism frequently becomes a moral claim when the borders between the species are disregarded from a reincarnation perspective.

The idea that souls are incorporated into new bodies that correspond to the practices of their former life is an idea that was introduced by Plato in *Phaedo* (81d–82b; cf. *Phaedrus*, 249b; *Timaeus*, 91d–92b; *Republic*, 620a–620d). According to Plato, it is the soul's desire for the corporeal that leads it back into a new body. How one leads one's life determines the soul's destiny in a future life. The souls of those who had been gluttonous, wanton and drunken pass into asses and similar animals, while those who had been unjust and tyrannical pass into wolves, hawks and kites. The best destinations for those that pass into new bodies are "some such social and gentle species as that of bees and wasps and ants, or into the human race again" (*Phaedo*, 82b; cf. Chapter 1). In the *Republic*, the souls have a choice of where to go after death, but "the choice was determined for the most part by the habits of their former lives" (*Republic*, 620a). Orpheus chose a swan because he did not want to be born of a woman again. Out of hatred towards the human race, Agamemnon chose to be an eagle, while the soul of the buffoon Thersites went into the body of an ape (*Republic*, 620b–620c).

Plato's conception of reincarnation is based on a hierarchical view of the species. In the *Timaeus*, two-legged creatures are at the top of the hierarchy of being. As for four-footed and many-footed beings, Plato says that "God set more supports under the more foolish ones, so that they may be dragged down still more to the earth" (92a). The most foolish are those who are "footless and wriggling upon the earth" (*ibid.*), with fish and the creatures of the waters as the fourth kind, at the bottom of the hierarchy of being.[2]

Most Christian authors denied that transformation between humans and beasts was possible. Tertullian has an interesting polemic in *A Treatise on the*

Soul, where he argues against the possibility of human–animal transformation. For Tertullian, the doctrine of reincarnation competes with the belief in the resurrection of the body. The doctrine of resurrection implies that each human being has only one life on earth, that the body will rise again, and that the individual soul is raised in its own human body. Tertullian pays special attention to what interests us most, the radical form of the doctrine of reincarnation, that a human soul may pass into the body of an animal, and discusses this doctrine's trustworthiness, function and consequences (*A Treatise on the Soul*, 32). He puts forward weighty arguments to show why rebirth in an animal body is impossible.

One argument is that certain animals may have an aversion to some of the substances from which a human is formed. For that reason, a combination of a human soul and an animal that is composed of contrary substances would lead to "interminable strife". Because cold-blooded animals such as water snakes, lizards and salamanders are produced out of water, they will have an aversion to fire, which is one of the elements of the human soul. A second argument is that a soul that is used to the delicate food of humans will have problems adapting itself to a diet composed of bitter leaves or poisonous worms, not to mention human corpses.

There is also a problem of size. In Tertullian's view, a view he shared with many of his contemporaries, the soul had both a sort of physicality and a certain size. A human soul fits a human body as a hand fits a glove. Therefore, it would cause great problems if a human soul were to fill an animal body of a different size: "How, therefore, shall a man's soul fill [*complebit*] an elephant? How, likewise, shall it be contracted [*obducetur*] within a gnat? If it be so enormously extended or contracted, it will no doubt be exposed to peril" (*ibid.*, 32).

These arguments lead to the question of whether the human soul would undergo changes to fit into an animal. If the soul is changed, we are no longer talking only about a *metensomatosis*, a change in body, but of a full-scale change in the qualities of the human soul. This is Tertullian's main point, to which his other arguments were leading. To put it bluntly, human souls cannot pass into animal bodies because, if they did, they would no longer be human. Tertullian also maintains that comparing humans and beasts is not the same as saying that they have a common identity. Tertullian also opposes the idea that reincarnation would be a fitting retribution for human wrongdoings.

The Cappadocian father Gregory of Nazianzus made a contribution to a similar debate in the fourth century, when the transmigration of souls still seems to have been a live issue. In the poem *On the Soul*, Gregory argues against the idea of the soul's changing bodies as if bodies were only garments for the soul (*On the Soul*, in Moreschini and Sykes 1997). One of his points is that a rational soul never inhabits the irrational body of a beast or a plant. Beasts do not talk. Gregory says: "I have never heard the discourse of a wise beast nor listened to a bush talking. Forever the crow does nothing but caw and always in silence the fish swims through the flowing sea" (450A). Further support for this point of view, that a rational soul never inhabits the body of a beast, is drawn from the fact that the mind does not recall its former bodies.

Gregory of Nazianzus had apparently become acquainted with a belief in the transmigration of souls combined with a belief in a final judgement. According to him, a belief in a final punishment of human beings is incompatible with a concept of a soul that in the course of time is united with different bodies. According to Gregory, a final judgement presupposes the belief in a single soul united with flesh, which is then punished. Plato introduced the possibility of reward and punishment between different incarnations (*Phaedrus*, 294A), but it is probably not this Platonic idea but a Christian variant of a belief in *metensomatosis* that Gregory is arguing against.

Christian versions of a belief in reincarnation did exist (see Schoeps 1957; Sykes 1997: 234–5). Origen, for instance, thought that living beings were reincarnated in different worlds. But he was probably thinking about spiritual states of the soul and not reincarnations in the material world (*First Principles*, 3.4.1, 1.8.4). However, when Jerome commented on Origen's *First Principles*, he understood Origen to have said that angels, human souls or demons can be transformed into beasts because of great negligence or folly. Rather than suffering the agony of punishments and the burning flame, they may prefer to be animals and take their shapes "so that we have reason to fear a metamorphosis not only into four-footed things but even into fishes" (*Letter to Avitus*, 4; cf. Miller 2001: 35–59). However, Jerome adds that Origen did not want to be associated with Pythagoras and that he said he mentioned the idea of transmigration only as a conjecture and did not hold it as dogma.

A more traditional belief in reincarnation is presupposed in the *Apocryphon of John*, a Christian text that has been found at Nag Hammadi in Egypt (see Chapter 10). Here the souls become smaller and smaller in the process of reincarnation as they are continually reborn in new bodies and thus multiply. Like Tertullian's musings over how human souls could be expanded to fill elephants or compressed into gnats, the belief in the diminution of the souls as a result of their multiplication reflects a material and quantitative view of souls and the stuff they are made of. However, human souls in the *Apocryphon of John* are not reborn in animals.

Not only Christian but also pagan authors were reluctant to let the transmigration of souls go beyond the boundaries of the species. The Neoplatonists especially did not support the idea of a psychic continuity between humans and animals. Porphyry, for instance, does *not* argue in *On Abstinence* for a transmigration of souls between animal and human bodies. According to him, the transmigration of souls takes place as a *metempsychosis* within the boundaries of the human species. Against this view, a fragment from Stobaios indicates that Porphyry had at one time thought that the transmigration of souls crossed the boundaries between the species and thus also included *metensomatosis* (see Chapter 2). It could be that Porphyry combined a metaphorical and a literal interpretation of reincarnation, and consequently that his and his fellow Neoplatonists' thoughts on this point are more subtle than has usually been allowed (Smith 1984). A position halfway between thinking that souls actually are reincarnated in new bodies and thinking that references to reincarnation were a way of characterizing humans as being similar to animals was the view that even if a human soul does not enter an animal body, it may be bound in a sympathetic way to that body (see Chapter 6).

If these things are unclear, they at least bear witness to the fact that Neoplatonists did not allow a rational soul to become an irrational one. According to Iamblichus, animals were reborn as animals, humans as humans (Iamblichus, *On the Egyptian Mysteries*, 1.8). The Neoplatonist Sallustius, who lived in the late fourth century, claimed that rational souls seek rational creatures and do not enter into irrational creatures. In the case of Sallustius, these souls remained outside the animal in question, accompanying it from the outside, more like a guardian spirit (*daimon*). Consequently, these Neoplatonist authors eventually ended up interpreting Plato's ideas about reincarnation into animal bodies allegorically, or at least in a severely modified way.[3]

Such interpretations found favour with Christians. In his *On the Nature of Man*, Nemesius of Emesa in Syria discusses Plato and the Platonists' view on the soul. He describes Iamblichus as the one who really understood Plato's meaning. According to Nemesius, when Plato was writing about humans having animal bodies, he did not mean it literally but was speaking in parables, and when Plato was naming animals, he was really alluding to manners and behaviour (*On the Nature of Man*, in Telfer 1955: 286–9). Nemesius thought it absurd to speak of reason in connection with irrational animals. As God had made no superfluous creature, he had not put a rational soul into cattle or wild beasts, "seeing that it would never have the opportunity to exercise its proper function" (*ibid.*, 290). Thus Nemesius wanted to prove that reincarnation between species was impossible. His approach also illustrates the growing tendency in these centuries to view animals metaphorically and as symbols of something else.

Conclusion

Fundamental to the Graeco-Roman world was a great interest in animals that was visible in several areas at the same time. In the cultural imagination, different relationships between humans and animals developed. One idea was that animals were creatures into which man could be transformed, either in this life or in the next.

When authors indulged in fantasies about being an animal, they revealed a mixture of fear and fascination. Thoughts about interchanges between animal and human bodies in a *metamorphosis*, or a transmigration of souls in a *metensomatosis*, engaged the cultural imagination. But one thing remained clear: it was seen as a disadvantage for a human being to be turned into a beast. The idea existed on the level of human imagination but sometimes seems to have also been intended quite literally.

The concept of transmigration of souls presupposes a belief in the separation of mind and body, a view of the soul as being different from the body, and an idea that identity pertains to the soul, not to the body. Souls choose bodies that suit them, which means that bodies are replaceable. A body has some qualities by means of which the soul expresses itself, but the soul is not fully dependent on the body and will leave the body at death. Animals may function as symbols for specific human characteristics, and an animal body may in fact be a better and clearer expression of a certain human personality. It implies that each species of animal is seen as less complex and with fewer but more specialized characteristics than a human being. At the same time, however, as animals are seen as less complex than humans, the transmigration of souls across human and animal species reduces the distance between human and animalian souls and minds.

A metamorphosis of a human into a beast sometimes has something in common with a caricature, because certain characteristics of a person are exaggerated and magnified by means of the animal shape. In a way, these people continue to be what they were before; they are even more the same than they ever were before they were transformed into animals.

When a human being is changed into an animal, it is a move downwards in the hierarchy of being. It also seems to be the case that when animals are described in connection with a metamorphosis or a transmigration of souls, they are seen as creatures that are less complex than humans. In a metamorphosis, the distance between human and animal bodies is reduced, as is the distance between human and animal souls in a transmigration of souls.

The animal expresses only one or a few of the characteristics of the original human being. It is a selective projection of characteristics from an animal to a human, which is typical of metaphors. For the animals in question, the metaphors may backfire in the way that the animal in its turn is reduced to the metaphor that it gave rise to.

A third possible type of transformation is the Christian idea of the resurrection of the body, which means that the body continues in a state of salvation. This idea presupposes that human souls and bodies are interconnected, and it normally excludes the possibility of a transmigration of souls between human and animal species. Tertullian explains this lack of possibility by the human soul being especially adapted to a human body because of both its material and its size. Consequently, the idea of the resurrection of the body implies that animal and human bodies are as different from each other as are human and animal souls. However, the human soul and body may include bestial aspects, aspects that are usually seen as unwanted and better suppressed or transformed into humanity.

A question underlying the different fields of culture, be it in philosophy, natural history, physiognomic thinking or ideas of metamorphosis and the transmigration of souls, was how to identify the borderlines that separate the animal realm from the human one. Where were the categorical boundaries that divided humans and animals? Differences as well as similarities between animals and humans were elaborated on. Part of the process of creating new boundaries was allowing humans to distance themselves from animals in order to approach closer to the divine. As part of this process, a refurbishing of the natural as well as the supernatural world was taking place in the first centuries of the common era.

Art and literature reflect a mental universe, a universe of the imagination. The religious outlook has recourse to the same universe. In these centuries, animals were caught up by the religious imagination and elaborated on by the different religions of the empire. The religious concept of animals is the theme of the next chapter.

5

THE RELIGIOUS VALUE OF ANIMALS

Animals on the religious scene

Religions flourished during the imperial age: as traditional religions thrived, foreign religions were imported and new cults invented. Although the Romans did not worship any gods in animal shapes, in the first centuries CE, animals swarmed on to the religious scene of the Graeco-Roman world (Kötting 1964; Isager 1992).

Sacred animals were kept in the vicinity of temples and used as a source of income, for sacrifices or as symbols for a god. At some temples, there were parks with different species of animal, as Lucian reports from the temple of Atargatis in Hierapolis (*The Syrian Goddess*, 41). Fish with golden ornaments swam in the temple lakes, well fed and marvelled at by onlookers (*ibid.*). Pachomius, who initiated the monastic movement in Egypt, as a child was taken by his parents to the Nile to sacrifice to the creatures in the waters, to the Lates fish, which was held to be sacred in the region where he lived (Frankfurter 1998: 62–3). Dogs and serpents were present in the temple of Asclepius in Epidaurus, and Alexander of Abonouteichos even introduced a living serpent with an artificial human head as "the new Asclepius" in a cult that seems to have been a great success (*c.* 170 CE). In Egypt, sacred crocodiles, cats, ibises and other species were venerated by the natives and visited by tourists. In a depiction of a procession in honour of the goddess Isis in Rome, one of the priestesses has an asp coiled around her arm, while in a wall painting from Pompeii showing ceremonies to Isis that include between thirty and forty people, two ibises are placed in the foreground. What did these non-sacrificial animals signify?

Some of the meanings and hermeneutic mechanisms behind the religious use of animals can be glimpsed in Apuleius' description of a religious procession at Cenchreae in Greece. The procession was held in the spring in honour of Isis (*The Golden Ass*, 11.8–11). Its purpose was the launch of the first ship of the year, which marked the opening of the sailing season. In the Graeco-Roman world, processions were standard when religious festivals were celebrated, and as in Apuleius' novel, they included animals, mostly for sacrifice but sometimes also for festive purposes.

In Apuleius' account, the procession starts in a carnival-like way with people decked out in various costumes. One man is clad in a soldier's outfit, another is dressed as a hunter, and yet another walks by in women's clothing; a gladiator, a magistrate, a philosopher, a fowler and a fisherman also appear. In addition to these, a tame bear is carried on a portable chair, clad as a matron; an ape goes by dressed as Ganymede with a gold cup in his hand; while in an allusion to Pegasus and Bellerophon, an ass with wings glued to its back trots along, accompanied by an old man.[1] After these ludicrous figures comes a special procession of women devotees of the goddess. There are musicians, a choir of youths, and men and women who have been initiated into the cult of Isis. Next to them walk priests, brightly clad in white linen, carrying the special symbols of the goddess. Finally, the gods themselves arrive: Anubis with the head of a jackal is painted partly black, partly gilded, and is followed by the statue of a cow – an image of the goddess Hathor – which is carried on the shoulders of a priest. After these more priests walk by, carrying the symbols of the mysteries of Isis hidden in a basket. The symbol of Isis, which is shown to the spectators, is a gold vessel, the handle of which is an asp with swelling neck and twisting coils (*vipera aspis*).

These animals play different roles. Those in front belong to the carnival part of the procession, and their function is mainly to raise a laugh. The bear, the ape and the ass play the roles of humans or appear as mythological illustrations, but they do so in a comic way. The animals at the rear symbolize gods – the jackal-headed Anubis, Hathor in the form of a cow, and the asp of Isis. These last-mentioned figures are thus not real beasts but images of beasts referring to gods.

The animal nature of these creatures is striking and significant. At one and the same time, it points away from itself and is mingled with humanity and even with divinity. In fact, the animals in the procession either do not behave like animals or are not real animals at all. This characteristic – animality suspended and reinterpreted – is typical rather than peculiar when animals or images of animals appear in religious settings. Thus the religious significance of these animals does not lie primarily in their inherent animal nature but in that to which it gives added meaning. There is a synergetic effect between the actual animal and the being with which the animal is combined or connected – be it a human or a god.

The theme of this chapter is to offer a survey of the role played by animals in some of the religions of the empire. How was their presence experienced? What did it mean? We have already pointed out the great variety of animals and their roles and functions, and the difference between real animals and images of animals. In the following section, various interpretations of the role of animals will be commented upon.

Initially, it is important to stress that the type of connection made between the divine and the bestial varied: animals either partook in the divine, appeared as symbols, were attributes of divinities or were used as instruments. These four types of relationship between animals and gods varied regionally, depending on the different cultures and religions of the empire. Although the instrumental use of animals in sacrifices was generally widespread in Mediterranean cultures, the three other types of relationship were more characteristic of some cultural areas than of others.[2]

I suggest that the direct participation of animals in the divine that was accompanied by a cult of animals and implied veneration of a god in animal form was typical of Egyptian culture, while the symbolic and metaphorical use of animals was typical of the mystery cults, including Christianity, and in Greek and Roman religions, animals were predominantly used to signify the attributes of gods.

Divine animals and their worship – the case of Egypt

The procession described by Apuleius was in honour of Isis, and it is no coincidence that this Egyptian goddess had animals in her entourage. Egypt had a rich and diverse fauna, which for more than four millennia had been abundantly illustrated on wall paintings and depicted in statues and on papyri (see especially Houlihan 1996, 2002). These animals were depicted realistically in their natural habitat or cooperating with humans. In addition, a wide range of animals appear in the hieroglyphs, a holy script that, even if it was less and less understood in the Graeco-Roman period, was prominent on monuments and buildings. Nearly two hundred signs, one in every four or five, refer to animals (te Velde 1977: 76; Houlihan 2002: 132–43). The presence of animals in the Egyptian imagination persisted through the millennia and made this country special in relation to its neighbours. In the last millennium BCE, the religious use of animals became extremely striking. Much of this use may be defined as animal cults,[3] especially when it comes to the worship of specific exemplars of one species or to the worship of whole species. The accompanying ritual practice, and not least its theological interpretation, probably differed from one case to another and over time.

Gods were depicted as humans with animal attributes, as hybrids (usually as a human with an animal head) or as completely theriomorphic.[4] For instance, Horus was depicted either as a man, a falcon or a human with the head of a falcon, while Anubis was depicted as a jackal or with the head of a jackal. In Egypt, the hybrid and theriomorphic forms clearly reflected the divine, that which transcended traditional categories and human limitations (cf. Morenz 1960: 20–1),[5] but even if human and animal elements tended to be fused in the depiction of the Egyptian gods, these gods did not behave like animals but mainly as humans do (Silverman 1991: 13–20). Thus, at the same time as the animal aspect contributed to characterizing the divine, it did not restrict the divine to an animal form or essence. A specific god could be represented by different animal species. The chosen animal of a god was characterized as the *Ba* of the god, which meant that it was a manifestation of the dynamic power of the deity, one aspect of the existence of the god in question (Hornung 1967: 76; Kessler 1986: 572). The ibis, which was the bird of Thoth, is one example of an animal species connected with a specific god.

Sometimes a specific exemplar of a species was singled out for special treatment as a unique representative of the god, such as the Mnevis bull connected to the cult of Re and Atum, and the Apis bull of Memphis, which was conceived of as a living embodiment of the god Ptah. Apis was perhaps the most famous of these divine beings in animal form and was regarded as the king of all sacred animals (Kessler 1986: 571). When an old Apis died, the dead bull became the object of elaborate rituals that finally, through the mouth-opening ceremony, revitalized the mummified beast. A new bull calf was immediately found and installed as the new Apis. Apis bulls, as well as those of Mnevis, were regarded as intermediaries between humans and gods. In the last centuries BCE, the Egyptian religious imagination was, to an increasing degree, preoccupied with animals. The Greek rulers of Egypt, the Ptolemies, went to great lengths to show how they honoured sacred animals. Apis, the bull of Memphis, and Mendes, the ram of Thebes, were even considered to be related to the royal family.

Perhaps even more strange, at least for outsiders, was the veneration of whole species of animals, for instance falcons, ibises, crocodiles and cats. The emotional climate surrounding the divine animals could be very strong, and the killing of sacred animals, intentional or not, sometimes attracted a lynch mob. Most striking were the animal cults that developed in connection with some temples: four million mummified ibises were interred in the necropolis of Saqqarah, but burial grounds for ibises are found in many other places in Egypt. K.A.D. Smelik has described the ibis cult (Smelik 1979). On the basis of data from Greek papyri, he reveals an extensive practice connected with temple cults, breeding and feeding the birds and mummifying dead ones, a procedure that ensured that they continued to exist after death. The ritual of mummification took care of the eternal destiny of the animal in question. But Smelik also remarks that there are few data concerning the Egyptian religious attitude towards the ibis (*ibid.*: 243). It is simply not possible to interpret the meaning of these religious acts directly from the myriads of embalmed birds. Patric F. Houlihan has pointed out that animals that were farmed and mummified were regarded as intermediaries between gods and humans, and that the mummies were finally offered as votive gifts to the temple before they were stored in their underground galleries (Houlihan 1996: 9). At least in the case of mummified cats, some of the animals had been strangled. H. te Velde remarks that this practice "is not killing life to destroy it, but to let it arise from death" (te Velde 1977: 81). It seems likely that these animals acted as intermediaries between humans and gods, but unlike Graeco-Roman sacrificial animals, they were taken care of after death and preserved for ever, which shows that they were regarded as divine.[6]

Why were so many animals considered to be sacred in Egypt? This problem has puzzled ancient commentators as well as modern researchers. Greek and Roman authors regarded what they conceived of as animal worship as a peculiar phenomenon, one of the curiosities of the strange Egyptian culture. Egyptian animal cults clearly offended against the Graeco-Roman world view, which placed animals low in the hierarchy of being. Roman authors in particular described Egyptian "animal worship" with contempt and scorn, while the Greeks were more understanding (Smelik and Hemelrijk 1984: 1999).

The first Greek author to comment on the phenomenon was Herodotus. He was deeply interested in Egypt but refused to give an answer to the question of why animals were held sacred and wrote: "but were I to declare the reason why they are dedicated, I should be brought to speak on matters of divinity, of which I am especially unwilling to treat; I have never touched upon such save when necessity has compelled me" (2.65). Others were not so reluctant. Diodorus of Sicily (59 BCE) gives several explanations, which refer either to mythological or to historical origins, to the animals' function as totemic signs, or to the general usefulness of those animals that were worshipped (1.86–9). Like Diodorus, Cicero also stressed the usefulness of the animals: "Even the Egyptians who are being laughed at, deified a beast solely on the score of some utility which they derived from it" (*The Nature of the Gods*, 1.36). Cicero's example is the ibis, which he describes as a destroyer of serpents.

It seems to have eluded these authors that the Egyptians may also have worshipped animals because they were strange, frightening or generally had qualities not found in humans. They held basically different views of animals from the Egyptians and of why they could possibly have been regarded as sacred (cf. Kristensen 1971: 156). It was obviously very difficult for non-Egyptians to understand that the animal *per se* could be conceived of as sacred and be the object of a cult. And while the usefulness of an animal species may have been a reason for its worship, it must also be added, as a corrective to the argument about usefulness, that in Egypt it was especially undomesticated animals that were given divine attributes (Houlihan 2002: 102).

In addition to the arguments about the usefulness of the animals involved, other explanations had recourse to symbols and allegories, working from the notion that Egyptian animal worship was based on hidden meanings (Plutarch, *On Isis and Osiris*, 71–6; Porphyry, *On Abstinence*, 4.9). Plutarch, who wrote *On Isis and Osiris* at the beginning of the second century CE, is an example of an author who uses symbolic explanations but who also gives a more complex picture of different aspects of animal worship and offers various explanations of the phenomenon, ranging from the aetiological to the symbolic.

Initially, Plutarch claims that the majority of Egyptians who treat animals as gods made not only their sacred offices ridiculous but also their behaviour blameworthy, because it led the weak and innocent into "superstition" (*deisidaimonia*) and the cynical and bold into "atheistic and bestial reasoning" (*atheos kai theriodes logismos*; 71). Plutarch does not believe the traditional explanations of why animals are held to be sacred, for instance that the gods, fearing the evil Typhon (Seth), changed themselves into animals, or that the souls of the dead were reborn in animals. Neither does he set much store by aetiological explanations as background for a subsequent divination: the totemic explanation that animals were originally used on standards for the different squads and companies of Osiris; that later kings used gold and silver masks of wild beasts' heads in battles; or that an unscrupulous king persuaded different peoples to honour different animals, with the result that while they revered their own animal, they sometimes attacked the animals of their neighbours (72). Plutarch had further been told that most animals were sacred to Typhon, and that the priests either venerated these animals to appease him or they tortured and sacrificed the animals to punish the god (73). He also mentions the usefulness of some of the animals that were worshipped, especially stressing their symbolic value. A scarab is an image of the sun god because it rolls its ball of dung with a movement similar to that of the sun in the heavens (74); the crocodile is a living representation of God because it is the only beast that has no tongue and thus illustrates that the divine word does not need a voice (75). Some animals are worshipped for both their usefulness and their symbolism (75). Most interestingly, Plutarch ends his survey with a sort of apology for Egyptian animal worship, because he sees living beings more clearly as mirrors of the divine than lifeless statues: "In view of this the divine is represented no less faithfully in these [animals] than in bronze and stone works of art, which equally take on gradations of colour and tincture, but are by nature devoid of all perception and intelligence. Concerning the animals honoured, then, I approve especially of these views" (76).[7]

While Plutarch does not support animal worship, he at least shows a sympathetic attitude to the phenomenon and attempts to understand what it means. His account is interesting because he mentions a variety of practices and explanations, and he probably reproduces some of the rich mythological reflections and elaborations that in Egypt must have accompanied the cult of animals, although one wonders how many of these reflections were intended for outsiders and what the Egyptian priests themselves really believed. Plutarch obviously filtered the Egyptian conceptions through his Greek perspective and thus Hellenized the idea of animal worship (cf. Froidefond 1988: 317, note 7).

Plutarch's awareness of the symbolic dimension has often been emphasized, although his symbolic interpretations can more fittingly be described as allegories (cf. Froidefond 1988: 67–92; Griffiths 1970: 100–1). Plutarch himself characterizes the connections that the Egyptians made between an animal and its symbolic interpretation as "slight resemblances" (*glischra homoioteta*; 75). It is reasonable to think that Plutarch has underplayed some of the multiple meanings of these animal symbols, and their cross-references within Egyptian myth and ritual, and thus has missed some of the dynamic. Above all, Plutarch did not understand or want to take seriously beliefs in the inherent sacredness of live animals. According to Plutarch, such views belong to the superstitious outlook of common people. As for these ordinary people, modern commentators, as well as ancient ones, have had a tendency to claim that they have misunderstood the real meaning of the cult of animals. However, whether such cults have a "real" meaning, and whether priests are better than others at giving it, is doubtful.

The question of Egyptian animal worship has also vexed modern researchers, and in spite of some interesting attempts, it has perhaps not yet been fully solved. P.F. Houlihan, characterizing these as "inspired attempts at interpreting the complex underlying symbolism of these faunal motifs", concludes that much of the significance of these motifs is still imperfectly understood (Houlihan 2002: 98). One obvious obstacle to giving an adequate explanation of animal worship has been the tendency to see the phenomenon as a sign of decadence and religious perversion (for instance, Brunner-Traut 1986: 557, 567). Animal worship clearly offends the traditional Cartesian notion of a duality between spirit and matter, as well as the Christian notion that the human body is a fit vehicle for divinity, while the animal body is not; and perhaps also a general (although not always conscious) evolutionary attitude to religion according to which totemism and the cult of animals belong to a primitive past. But in spite of these obstacles, there have also been constructive attempts to explain and understand Egyptian animal worship.

Henri Frankfort has stressed that "in Egypt the animal as such, irrespective of its specific nature, seems to possess religious significance" (Frankfort 1961: 9). According to him, the metaphorical relationship between man and beast is not metaphorical but "a strange link" between them (*ibid.*: 9). Animals possessed religious significance precisely because of their unchangeability. By apparently not changing from generation to generation, animal life participated in the static life of the universe, which was an Egyptian ideal. In this way, their unchangeable exterior, which embodied permanence, was interpreted by Frankfort as religiously significant.

Erik Hornung has pointed out that the Egyptians did not establish the kind of division between humans and animals that the Israelites did, for example, and that the distinction between humans and animals was more blurred in Egypt (Hornung 1967: 69). Humans simply did not have the same superior position in relation to the animal world that they had in other parts of the Mediterranean region. Hornung has also stressed that a belief in a partnership between animals and humans existed in Egypt (*ibid.*: 70–2). However, he does not see the animal as a god but characterizes this idea as a popular misunderstanding (*ibid.*: 76). Instead, the animal should be conceived of as a dwelling place, vehicle or living image of the god.

It is easy to subscribe to the view that animals had a much higher status in Egypt than in most other places, and it is probably correct, as Frankfort has pointed out, that the religious relationship between animals and humans in Egypt is not just a metaphorical one. In a similar vein, John Bowman has remarked on the scale of the embalming of animals in the Late Period of Egyptian history that "it would be misleading to see them [i.e. the animals] simply as tokens of the divinity of some higher power. One essentially divine quality was perceived in the animal itself, and this is surely the light in which we should interpret the universal representations of the gods with animal heads, Thoth with the ibis head, Horus the falcon, Hathor the cow, Bastet the cat or lioness, Thoeris the hippopotamus and so on" (Bowman 1986: 173–4). It is natural to agree with Frankfort and Bowman that at least some of the relations between animals and gods and some of the ritual uses of animals must be explained by these animals having an inherently divine quality. In the present context, this view is also consonant with Ragnhild Bjerre Finnestad's understanding that the Egyptian world view regarded the gods as immanent and that the natural world as such expressed ultimate reality (Finnestad 1984).

Consequently, when animals in Egypt were objects of cults, these animals were not only conceived of as symbols of the divine but were themselves essentially seen as divine. They were not only living images of the god but shared in the divine essence of the god, at least in some of the aspects of this essence. This view is also supported by the opposition of Greek and Roman authors: the fact that more than a few animals in Egypt participated directly in the divine seems to have been the single observation that most troubled ancient authors in relation to Egyptian animals. They therefore either derided it or tried to explain it away, for instance by resorting to symbolic and allegorical explanations.

To the question of why the religious use of animals increased in the Late Period of Egyptian history (from 700 BCE) and flourished under Roman rule, a reasonable answer has been suggested by Smelik and Hemelrijk. According to them, this almost limitless use of animals for religious purposes had in the Late Period become a national symbol for the Egyptians: "The choice of animal worship as a new national symbol at a time when the traditional gods no longer served as protectors of Egypt must correspond to the fact that animal worship struck foreigners as the most bizarre note of the entire Egyptian gamut" (Smelik and Hemelrijk 1984: 1863–4). The use of animals as national symbols also implies that they were not only vital elements in the flourishing Egyptian religion of the Late Period but also had important functions to fulfil as markers of cultural and religious boundaries.

Against animals

The general antagonism against Egyptian animal worship is seen, for instance, by Juvenal. He opens his fifteenth satire with the question: "Who knows not, O Bithynian Volusius, what monsters demented Egypt worships?" The jackal-headed god Anubis, clad in a Roman tunica, was sacred to the Egyptians, ridiculous to non-Egyptians. Juvenal mocks people who are duped by a priest wearing a mask in the form of a jackal's head, impersonating Anubis, and he adds, for good measure, that the priest himself cannot resist laughing at the onlookers (*Satire*, 6.532–4). Clement of Alexandria makes fun of "the wallowing animal" one finds in the holiest part of Egyptian temples (*Paedagogus*, 3.2). Even authors who were more positive towards Egyptian religion tried to explain away the animal worship and, as we have seen, to convert the animals into symbols and allegories. The majority of the non-Egyptian inhabitants of the Graeco-Roman world regarded animal worship as an inferior form of religion.

In a thorough article, Smelik and Hemelrijk have investigated "which part Egyptian animal cult played in the general conception of Egypt in Antiquity" (Smelik and Hemelrijk 1984: 1955). Besides pointing out different types of non-Egyptian explanation of animal worship, they also stress as fundamental that the Romans were at the same time fascinated by the exotic character of Egyptian religion and culture but repelled by animal worship (*ibid.*: 1945). Not only was animal worship conceived of as ridiculous, but those who worshipped animals were themselves considered no better than animals. Philo describes what happens when a foreigner sees Egyptians worshipping wild beasts. He thinks them "more miserable than even the objects which they honour, since they in their souls are changed into those very animals, so as to appear to be merely brutes in human form, now returning to their original nature" (*The Decalogue*, 80). A similar point was made by Origen (see Chapter 2). Epiphanius of Salamis describes the Egyptians who worshipped animals "as if they were animals in mind and spirit" (Smelik and Hemelrejk 1984:1983). Christian authors usually explained animal worship as being caused by human degradation since the Fall.

The opposition to animal worship especially hit the Egyptians who really had animal cults – and towards whom the Romans had an ambiguous relationship – but other groups were also affected by the aversion to theriomorphic gods. The Christians made animal worship a test of what counted as inferior religion (cf. 1 Romans 1:23–8). In *Apologeticus* (16) and *Ad Nationes* (I.11, 14), Tertullian twice repeats that the pagans worship animals. Tertullian drips with irony when he says that pagans worship all types of pack animal and even donkeys together with the horse goddess Epona. He jeers at pagans who have accepted gods with the heads of dogs and lions, with ram's horns, bodies of rams, with snakes for legs or with wings on their backs or on their legs.

In *Octavius* (28.4) Minucius Felix mocks the pagans who have horses and donkeys in their stables consecrated to Epona, adorn them in processions to Isis and sacrifice and worship heads of bulls and rams. Minucius Felix derides half-goats, half-humans and gods with lion or jackal heads, and he especially remarks upon the Egyptian cults of the bull Apis and of whole species of animal. There was even the death penalty for harming some of these last-mentioned animals.

Tertullian and Minucius Felix are in fact even more negative than non-Christian authors towards gods in animal form. Their monotheistic and exclusive view of religion gave Christians no openings for regarding either a multiplicity of gods or gods in animal shape in a positive light. Their loathing for such conceptions was connected to the anthropomorphic character of their image of God.

Mystery religions and animal symbolism

Even if Egyptian religion was criticized by foreigners because of its extended use of animals, it was also at the same time a popular export. As early as the sixth century BCE, it had been brought to Greece and its colonies by merchants. One of the attractions of this religion could very well have been its rich display of animal symbolism, which contributed to its mystery. Those who were attracted probably thought that there was more to the animals than met the eye – a point on which they obviously must have been right. However, it was animals interpreted in the symbolic mode, rather than animals conceived of as divine incarnations, that the Graeco-Roman world imported from Egypt.[8]

The presence of animals was prominent in some of the mystery religions, especially in Egyptian cults and Mithraism, but also in Christianity and other religious movements. These were religions that were characterized by personal initiation, transmission of secret knowledge, and the promise of a better lot in this life, and sometimes also in the world to come. In a way similar to Christianity taking part of its identity from Judaism, in several of the mystery cults people took part of their new religious identity from old and foreign traditions – for instance, from Iran, Asia Minor and Egypt, which meant that they created new identities on the basis of a revitalization of these traditions. In the Graeco-Roman world, increasingly varied forms of religious tradition were developed, and in these new forms, old concepts were transformed and redefined.

It was characteristic of the mystery religions that they did not primarily employ living animals but animals that had been reduced to images and symbols. It was also typical of these religions that the symbolic animals were caught in a process of endless *semiosis*, which also characterized these religions in general.

Art historian Jas Elsner has pointed to a transformation in Roman religious art in the late second to the late third century, from the literal to the symbolic mode (Elsner 1995: 190ff). This transformation reflects general religious changes. Elsner compares representations of sacrifices in the state cult, which were read literally, and which referred to real animals, to the ideologies and sacrificial practices of Mithraism and pre-Constantinian Christianity, which have "a symbolic and exegetical relationship with what they represent" (*ibid*.: 190). Civic sacrifices implied that something was given to the gods, while the sacrifices in Mithraism and Christianity involved the god himself in the act, and in addition the worshippers were involved with the god by imitating him. This imitation was part of the process of making the worshippers divine (*ibid*.: 217). Elsner detects a general move from the literal mode of civic Roman religion to "a symbolic and hence polysemic mode of looking at the world" (*ibid*.: 218), and he points out "the enormous possibilities for symbolic accretion and complexity that are open as soon as images enter a symbolic mode which frees them from a direct literal reference" (*ibid*.: 220). What does this general move towards a symbolic mode mean as far as the interpretation of animals is concerned?

Elsner mentions sheep. In a sacrificial procession, a sheep which is going to be sacrificed has a direct and literal meaning. Christianity, on the other hand, is a religion of slaughtering lambs and human sacrifices – but not in any literal sense. The lamb in Christian art has only an indirect reference to live sheep and should be interpreted in the symbolic mode. This observation applies not only to sheep but also to fish, dolphins, doves, peacocks, phoenixes, the sea monster (*ketos*) of Jonah, the beasts that Orpheus enchanted with his play, and the lions of Daniel. Some of these animals may be explained with reference to biblical narratives, but others are not so easy to fit in. Neither the dolphin, the phoenix nor the peacock, which were common symbols for the resurrection, have any connection with biblical passages (Jensen 2000: 159). But whether they fit into a biblical narrative, merely allude to biblical passages or are detached from a biblical context, these are seldom references to real animals but should be interpreted symbolically. Usually, these animals are references to humans, especially to the Christians or to Jesus. Before Constantine, the lamb that appears in the company of the Good Shepherd, but also independently of him, probably symbolizes the members of a Christian community, while after Constantine, the lamb appears as a symbol of Christ and has sacrificial meaning (Snyder 1991: 14–15). Even if a fish in early Christian iconography was sometimes depicted together with bread and wine and referred to a ritual meal, more often the fish appeared as a symbol of the Christians or of Christ. Sometimes the fish had baptismal connotations (*ibid*.: 24–5). These connotations correspond to what Tertullian says about baptism, i.e. that "we, little fishes, after the example of our *ichthys* [Greek for "fish"] Jesus Christ, are born in water, not in any other way than permanently abiding in water, are we safe" (*On Baptism*, 1). It can also be added that Western baptismal fonts were often called "fish ponds" (*piscinae*) (Jensen 2000: 51).

These Christian animal symbols did not have only one implied meaning; they also defined Christians in relation to the Eucharist, baptism, salvation, resurrection and the Christian community. These symbols were characterized by polysemy and cross-references. Robin Margaret Jensen says of the fish symbol: "Christological, eschatological, eucharistic and baptismal symbolism are finally so merged in the fish symbol that it becomes impossible to factor them out" (Jensen 2000: 50–1). The animal symbols referred to biblical passages as well as to the pictorial themes of which they were part – for instance, to sacramental themes on the walls of the catacombs (*ibid.*: 84ff). Pagans used symbols similar to those of Christians, for instance doves, dolphins and phoenixes. Such use of the same animal symbols must also have enriched their Christian meaning. At other times, Christians gave a new symbolic meaning to old forms. While the stag in Graeco-Roman culture was a symbol of Artemis or Diana, it was in the Christian interpretation a symbol of baptism (cf. Psalm 41).

Christian animal symbols are of two kinds. On the one hand, there are the lions and the sea monster of Jonah, which refer to danger and deadly peril. On the other, there are various birds, fish and lambs, mostly small animals and animals that in some way signal peacefulness and community. Taken together, the two types of animal reflect a movement of deliverance from danger to peace and salvation. Lions, which are often rendered peacefully, and the resting Jonah, refer to past trials. Fish sometimes point to the sacramental ritual process, as the lamb also does sometimes, while dolphins and birds are symbols of peace, harmony and resurrection.

Similar use was made of animals in some of the mystery cults. In these cults, animals were also regarded as symbols, although their exact meaning is less known than the meaning of the Christian animal symbols because of the deplorable lack of interpretative texts. In the cult of Mithras, for instance, there was systematic use of animal symbols to mark a hierarchy of grades and priestly functions. Two of the seven initiation grades had animal labels: "raven", which was the first grade; and "lion", which was the fourth. In addition, the stage of *nympheus* alludes to an animal, because this term means not only "male bride" but also the stage before becoming a butterfly. We know that the raven was conceived of as a messenger, the lion was connected with fire, and in the lion grade honey was used in the ritual instead of water, because fire and water are incompatible. Some of the participants wore animal masks in the rituals and were called by such animal names as lions, lionesses and ravens (Porphyry, *On Abstinence*, 4.16). The cult image showed Mithras, who killed the bull, and also a serpent, a scorpion and a dog, which participated together with Mithras in this mythical sacrifice. Porphyry mentions that in the Mithras cult "souls were ox-borne". Does this concept perhaps refer to a symbolic birth through the blood of the ox? Even if the exact meaning of this symbolism of Mithras eludes us, it is clear that its rich imagery referred to several contexts of meaning – to astrological constellations, to a hierarchy of being, to the world above as related to the world below, to grades of initiation, to the transmission of knowledge, to a better lot in this life for those who had been initiated, and probably also to a final salvation. Manfred Clauss says of the bull slaying that it "gives us an insight into the importance of the language of images for the mysteries. Mithraic religious experience was captured in shorthand as it were, a shorthand that, compressed into symbolic format, commuted the whole myth, the entire cult-legend, into a single image" (Clauss 2000: 101).

The different mystery religions used different animals, as for instance the jackal-headed Anubis in Egyptian religion, the bull of Mithras, the lamb of Christ, the serpents in the mysteries of Demeter and Kore at Eleusis, and in the mysteries of Sabazius. These and other animal symbols referred to different rituals and different mythological and social contexts. The important point is not what exactly the animals signified but that they existed as symbols. They had – at least from the believer's point of view – more important functions than remaining beasts and birds: instead, they nourished the social and spiritual development of the believer and took part in a transformative process of initiation into a new religious world-view.[9]

Graeco-Roman religion and animals as divine attributes

Originally, animals were more visible in Greek than in Roman religion, although in Greece animals never had a function similar to that of the Apis or the ibises in the Egyptian cults (Burkert 1985: 64). Semi-divine creatures such as centaurs and satyrs had bestial features: Pan had a goat's head and feet; Python, the oracle god who had preceded Apollo at Delphi, was a serpent; Dionysos sometimes revealed himself as a bull (for instance, Euripides, *Bacchae*, 920–2, 1017; Plutarch, *The Greek Questions*, 36). Gods disguised themselves as animals, as Zeus did when he visited Leda as a swan and Europa as a bull, and when he carried off Ganymede as an eagle; and animals accompanied the gods, such as the owl of Athena, the eagle of Zeus, the ram of Hermes, the dog of Hecate, the doves or sparrows in the retinue of Aphrodite, and the serpent of Apollo. One god could be associated with various animals – Apollo was linked with the serpent, the dolphin, the roe and the stag. The same animal could be an attribute of several gods. The dolphin was associated with the iconography of Apollo, Aphrodite, Dionysus and Poseidon.[10]

More things are possible in myths than in real life; more things are permitted in religious fiction than in reality. One example of the role of animals in myths is the way animals took care of humans: for instance, the Arcadian hero Telephus, whose name – *elaphos* – means "deer" or "hind", was suckled by a hind, as in a painting from Herculaneum (Toynbee 1996: 145), or by a lioness, as represented on the great altar of Zeus at Pergamum. Porphyry remarks that "through these stories the ancients demonstrated honour for animals" (*On Abstinence*, 3.16.5). And, he adds, "every one of the ancients who had the good fortune to be nurtured by animals boasts not so much of his ancestors as of those who reared him" (*ibid.*, 3.17.1).

This point is well taken in relation to Rome. The origin of the city was linked with the she-wolf: Romulus and Remus had been miraculously nourished by her and thus received their strength. This old motif of the wolf suckling the twins acquired a new importance in the propaganda of the emperor, and it was frequently placed on coins, funeral vases, altars and sarcophagi. It appears on the *Ara Pacis*. Statues of emperors, for instance the statue of Hadrian on the Athenian agora, sometimes have the motif of the wolf and the twins on the medallion in the middle of the armour. On coins with the wolf theme, not only Hercules but also Mars, the father of Romulus and Remus, as well as the ruling emperor, are sometimes depicted on the other side (Presicce 2000). Both the mythical origin of the city and the allusions to a golden age of primordial bliss are part of the wolf scenario, according to which the Romans had the most powerful relationship with this wild and crafty animal: that of mother and child. And although the Romans mercilessly scorned Egyptian animal worship, they were proud of their own connection with the she-wolf and of being her descendants. But they did not *believe* in the wolf, and they did not worship it.[11] The wolf was the *attributive* animal of the city of Rome.

The attributive mode was characteristic of the way in which Greeks and Romans in the main regarded the relationship between divinities and animals. When an animal was associated with a divinity as his or her attribute, it was because this animal was specially protected by the god, described the nature of the god or indicated the realm that was specific to the god. Apollo, Hermes and Pan protected sheep, were all working as shepherds, and were shown with sheep.

In contrast to Egyptian religion, where many species of animal were kept permanently in religious focus, fewer species were used as divine attributes in Graeco-Roman religions. The animals associated with the gods were mostly the main domesticated ones such as cattle and equines, or those regarded as the ruling species in the animal hierarchies, such as eagles, lions and dolphins, although the animal attributes were not restricted to these categories. Both domesticated and wild animals were used, depending on the effect to be obtained and on the nature of the god or goddess in question.

When Varro calls the bull "servant of Ceres" (*On Agriculture*, 2.5.3), the goddess appears riding on a bull (Spaeth 1996: 132) and is generally associated with cattle and sheep, it is because Ceres was a protector of farm animals. When Vesta was associated with an ass on coins, reliefs and wall paintings from Pompeii, it was probably because the animal turned the millstone of the goddess and thus supported her in her agricultural functions (Undheim 2001: 40–1).[12] Another goddess, the originally Celtic Epona, is depicted riding or with horses and foals, and in imperial art she is usually seated between horses.[13] The imagery reflects how the goddess protected animals and riders, horse breeding and fertility. She was worshipped by Roman soldiers. The emperor's horse guard and the goddess found each other mostly because of their mutual enthusiasm for horses (Green 1992: 204ff; Davidson 1998: 40–51).

Artemis/Diana, the maiden goddess of the hunt, is usually shown accompanied by a hind. An older Near Eastern goddess type who was a mistress of animals had been assimilated with Artemis. In relation to this archaic goddess, who had been shown naked with an animal dangling from each hand (Marinatos 2000: 10, 97), the attributive animals were more directly linked to the type of space that this goddess inhabited. A similar link to the realm of nature is seen with Cybele (Roller 1999: 49). She may drive a chariot of lions, be seated between lions, be seated on a lion, have a lion on her lap or be accompanied by a lion.[14] The lions reflect the goddess' connections with the wild and above all her power.

Animals were also attributes of male gods, as already noted.[15] For instance, Poseidon was accompanied by creatures of the sea; while Zeus was associated with an eagle, the royal bird of heaven, or with an ox, and Dionysos with a panther. However, it seems as if goddesses were more frequently and more emphatically associated with accompanying animals than the male gods. This may indicate that one aspect of their being, i.e. the female sex, was associated more directly with the beasts. This corresponds with the way classical culture associated women more closely with bestial nature and animal passions (Carson 2002: 85–7; Loraux 1993: 89–110; Thornton 1997: 76ff, 90–1). The association between femininity and animal passions may be connected with the nourishing function of some of these goddesses, with their sexuality; and finally with untamed nature as a source of power – all aspects that were associated with animals, either wild or tame. It might also be thought that the animal connection made goddesses inferior to gods, according to the homological relationship that man is to woman as human to animal. But while this homology is obviously at work in the case of women, with a derogatory effect on them, the same mechanism does not seem to work in relation to goddesses. On the contrary, the animal connection seems to have been a source of natural power for these goddesses without making them less potent than their male colleagues.

Generally, the animal attributes are identity markers for the gods whom they accompany: the owl points to Athena, the eagle to Zeus. At the same time, these animals add something to the gods, because they make them more than human. What these additions are is partly known and shared: the eagle is the king of the birds as Zeus is the king of the gods. Floating effortlessly in the sky, higher in the air than any other bird and with a wider range, it strikes down its prey mercilessly and with precision. Athena's owl is the mysterious bird of wisdom. However, the accompanying attributive animal and the god whom it escorts are not fully interchangeable, and the animal is not an unambiguous sign. The combination of the human and the animal form contributes to the creation of that third entity that is neither man nor beast but a divine being.

The serpent

One animal played a special role in Graeco-Roman culture, in relation to gods as well as goddesses, connected with a wide number of cults, in a wide range of appearances from live beasts to abstract principles, and with positive as well as negative meanings. This was the serpent.

Snakes were guardians of private houses, tombs and sacred places, appeared as symbols of the souls of the dead, were connected to earth and water, were displayed on carved stones and magical papyri, symbolized transformation, and had healing as well as prophetic powers (Turcan 1996: 260–5; Lancellotti 2000: 37–55).[16] In line with the positive use of the serpent is its function as an apotropaic symbol with protective and curative properties. Its positive use is seen, for instance, in jewellery: gold bracelets with snake head terminals were common among the few people who could afford them. Tacitus mentions that a serpent that appeared in the bedchamber of Nero was interpreted as a divine legitimation of his right to rule (*The Annals*, 11.10).

It was not only on earth that snakes appeared. The heavenly serpent *ouroboros* divided the cosmos from the divine space and presided over this world. This snake, with its tail in its mouth, symbolized cyclic eternity and was frequently to be seen, mostly in magical texts. More specialized uses of serpents also appeared. The gnostic sect of the Naasenes, in reality a hybrid between Christianity and paganism, had taken its name from the Hebrew word for serpent, *naas*. The Naasenes taught that *logos* in the shape of a serpent was the divine intermediary principle that animated the world. In a similar way, the Perates taught that the life-giving Word was the serpent, and they identified its image in the starry sky (Hippolytus, *Refutation of all Heresies*, 5.16). Another gnostic sect, the Ophites, had also taken its name from the snake (*ophis*). The religious functions of serpents were not restricted to myths; live serpents were used as well. Epiphanius (315–403 CE) mentions that the Ophites let a live serpent crawl on the bread of the Eucharist to consecrate it (*Panarion*, 37.5).

A common denominator for most of these serpents is that they were mediators. They mediated between life and death, this world and the underworld, between the cosmos and divine space. What is special about this animal is that it can appear in all modes: it appears as an attribute, a symbol, a partaker in the divine and an instrument of divine intervention. This is seen especially in the cult of Asclepius, above all in the way that this cult was recreated by Alexander of Abonouteichos.

In iconography, the divine physician Asclepius was shown with a snake, usually coiled around his staff (Philostratus, *Life of Apollonius of Tyana*, 1.7). The importance of the serpent in the Asclepius cult is also to be seen in the way the cult was transported to new areas by means of the serpent (Victor 1997: 38, note 148). From Epidaurus, the god, in the form of a huge serpent, set sail for Rome and his new abode on an island in the Tiber. In pious narratives, snakes from his temple established new sacred places for Asclepius. For instance, a snake from the sanctuary in Epidaurus had, without anyone noticing, settled in a wagon that brought a patient back to his native town. When the people did not know what to do about the serpent and sent to Delphi for advice, the god proclaimed that they should make a sanctuary for him in the city where it had appeared (B13, *The Epidaurian Miracle Inscriptions*, in LiDonnici 1995: 110–11).

In the temple of Asclepius in Epidaurus, where people came to be healed by the god, serpents and dogs were present and sometimes contributed to effecting a cure. Such cures are described on stelae from the fourth century BCE. They state that one man's toe was healed because a snake came out of the Abaton, the building where the patients slept, and licked it (A17, *ibid.*, 96–7). Another man, Kleimenes of Argos, who was paralysed, was healed when the god wound a large snake around his body in a dream (B17, *ibid.*, 112–13). A mute girl who saw a snake in a sanctuary was filled with fear and cried out for her parents and thus regained her voice (C1, *ibid.*, 116–17). A viper opened the tumour of a certain Melissa (C2, *ibid.*, 118–19). And a woman became pregnant after having dreamed that a serpent lay upon her stomach (B19; *ibid.*, 112–13).

Not only snakes worked as the god's assistants in Epidaurus; dogs are also mentioned: the blind boy, Lyson of Hermione, had his eyes treated "by one of the dogs about the sanctuary" (A20, *ibid.*, 98–9). Another boy, from Aigina, was cured of the growth on his neck when "a dog from the sanctuary took care of him with its tongue while he was awake, and made him well" (B6, *ibid.*, 104–5). Finally, a man from Kios with gout was made well by being bitten by a goose, which made him bleed (B23, *ibid.*, 114–15).

These stories reveal that snakes, dogs and even geese lived in the sanctuary and sometimes were the instruments of Asclepius in the treatment of patients. Twelve out of about seventy such healing stories from the fourth century BCE are about animal cures, which shows that such cures were one of the main healing programmes in Epidaurus. In the late second century CE, Pausanias, who travelled in Greece and wrote about it, saw these stelae (2.27.3). The image of Asclepius, which according to Pausanias was made of ivory and gold and showed the god accompanied by a serpent and a dog (2.27.2), reflected that animals still played their roles. Pausanias also mentions the tame yellow serpents that were peculiar to Epidaurus and considered as sacred to Asclepius (2.28.1).[17]

Most curious is one of the new cults of the empire. This cult not only had a live serpent on show, but the reptile was personalized as the "new Asclepius" and given its own name – Glycon. It is not so easy to put this beast into a fixed category: Glycon was a mixture of a living animal and a hoax, an instrument for prophecies as well as an attribute of a god. Most of our knowledge about this cult comes from a notorious treatise, written by the satirical author Lucian – "Alexander or the False Prophet", in which Lucian derides this Alexander, a man from Abonouteichos in Asia Minor. The name of the serpent is derived from Greek *glukus* and has, like the second part of Asclepius, *epios*, the meaning "friendly, benevolent". Glycon was equipped with an artificial human-like head and acted as an oracle, producing messages in verses of high metric quality.

Alexander conceived of himself as the son of Asclepius and as the grandson of Apollo – both gods to whom serpents were sacred. (These connections also implicitly made Alexander the great grandson of Zeus.) According to Lucian's narrative, the cult became influential in the eastern Mediterranean and was – as many successful religions are – a flourishing religious business enterprise with employees, selling prophecies and souvenirs and with a great turnover of money. Alexander also instituted mysteries with theatrical performances in which he staged a mixture of classical mythology and the new mythology of Alexander and Glycon (39).

Alexander had originally taken the initiative for the new cult when in the temple of Apollo in Chalcedon he buried bronze tablets that predicted the coming of Asclepius in the town of Abonouteichos. Afterwards, Alexander dressed as a god and came into that city. During the night he put a goose egg with a small snake into a muddied pool of water. The next day, he dug out the egg and revealed the serpent, which apparently had been born from the egg, to the assembled crowd (13–14). The onlookers rejoiced greatly!

A few days later, Alexander showed himself in the semi-darkness of a room with the new Asclepius on his breast. The tiny snake had now been exchanged for a huge serpent, which Alexander had bought for a few obols in Pella, where these animals were kept as house pets (*Alexander*, 7). People filed past the couple and were even allowed to touch the beast. Glycon sometimes stated his prophecies with his own mouth (*autophonoi*) – a technical apparatus made it possible to open and shut the mouth of the serpent and by means of a hidden assistant make Glycon speak (15–17). More usually, written and sealed questions were received, and those who asked received written and sealed answers back (*Alexander*, 21). (How this fraud worked is clearly explained by Lucian.) The latest translator and commentator on Lucian's text, Ulrich Victor, stresses that unlike most oracles, people could ask Glycon about anything. No standard formula or questions were required (*Alexander*, 26ff., see Victor 1997: 30–4).

Ulrich Victor characterizes "Alexander – the false prophet" – as "einer der wichtigsten Texte zur Religionsgeschichte der Kaiserzeit [one of the most important textual sources of the religious history of the Roman Empire]" (Victor 1997: VII).[18] Victor clearly has a point: the cult connected with Alexander and Glycon flourished for about two hundred years in the eastern part of the Mediterranean. Its duration is revealed by coins with the image of Glycon (from 161 CE and 251–3 CE), inscriptions, amulets, statues and reliefs. One of the statues of Glycon is 4.67 metres from head to tail.

According to this imagery, the serpent has big ears and long hair. Alexander is known only from Lucian's story.

In the case of Glycon, we are confronted with a real beast, even if it has undergone some changes. Since this beast represents the god directly, we are reminded of Egyptian divine animals such as Apis, Mnevis and Mendes, which in a similar manner have their own names. The physical presence of this reptile also corresponds to the way Ovid describes Asclepius in the form of a huge serpent that set sail for Rome and let the ship feel the superhuman weight of godhead before taking up residence on the Tiber island. In Ovid's description, the physicality of the serpent is obtrusive.

The cult of Glycon was one of the few really new religions in the Roman Empire during these centuries. As such it competed with Christianity. It is probably no coincidence that the Christians were one of two groups with whom Alexander was at war. The other was the Epicureans. This hostility was given a ritual expression during the mysteries that Alexander had instituted when, according to Lucian, he shouted: "Out with the Christians", and the adherents answered: "Out with the Epicureans" (*Alexander*, 38). The reason for this antagonism and ritual expulsion was probably that the Epicureans had debunked Alexander, while the Christians with their miracles and healings were competing in the same market.

Like Christ, Asclepius had become a universal saviour; like Christianity, the cult of Glycon was built on an older cult, but with a new religious concept; like Christianity, this cult had a prominent anthropomorphic side with an incarnate god walking on earth in the form of Alexander; and like Christianity, it was a healing cult. Victor also points out that, like Jesus in the Gospel of John, Glycon is characterized as the light of god (*Alexander*, 18; cf. Victor 1997: 50). But in contrast to Christianity, the cult that was initiated by Alexander had an incarnate serpent. This successful reptile wavered between participating in the divine and being the instrument of Asclepius, being interpreted as a symbol and appearing as an attribute of his master Asclepius. Glycon is one of the most striking examples of the presence of a live animal in a Graeco-Roman cult in late antiquity.

Conclusion

In antiquity, animals were abundantly present, not only in Egyptian religion but in all the religions in the area, traditional as well as new. There were variations in this, depending on whether the animals were seen as participating directly in the divine, as was the case in Egypt, were viewed symbolically, as in the mystery religions, or used as attributes, as they usually were in traditional Greek and Roman religions. In short, it depended on how the relationship between these animals and the divine in each case was conceptualized. These modes of interpretation are ideal types. In real life, there were also transitions between the different modes, as was

111

the case with the serpent Glycon. Obviously, there were also differences within a single tradition as to how various groups conceived of "divine" animals and how they interpreted these animals' relationship with the divine. Because of the limitations of the material, these differences are usually difficult or impossible to reconstruct in any detail.

It is striking that in antiquity most gods were associated with animals as a matter of course. In the Mediterranean area, gods and goddesses were, in the various cultures, represented by, accompanied by or associated with animals. The religious connection between animals and gods has much to do with these societies being agricultural and thus being deeply and directly dependent on animal life, but the human–animal connection is also dependent on a cultural willingness to use animals as symbols of gods.

The gods in question were mostly conceived of in human form, at least outside Egypt. To this human form, animals added something that was not human. Thereby they participated in the creation of an entity that consisted of more than the human or the animal alone but was based on a synergy between the two. Precisely by being taken out of their ordinary habitat and put into a new context, the animals contributed to the conception of the divine. Moreover, it is important to realize that these animals never had only one meaning but were polysemic.

Although some were hybrids or fabled creatures, most of the divine animals had real-life counterparts: the owl is not only the bird of Athena, it also exists as a real animal. These real-life counterparts – the lion or the lamb, for instance – have inherent value that is seen as "natural", i.e. they are conceived of as rooted in nature. At the same time, "natural" descriptions of animals are normally formulated in a human context and according to an anthropomorphic conception of animals, which means that they are not natural at all but are constructions based on human models. The characteristics of these animals are always implicitly, and sometimes also explicitly, based on comparisons with humans, as when the lion is described as strong and powerful and the lamb as mild and innocent. The basic values identified with the animal in question are linked with normative and social values – for instance, with the lion as ruler or the lamb as an archetypal sacrifice.

At the same time as animals are described in human terms, they are also creatures that differ fundamentally from humans. There will always be more to the animal than that which is described in anthropocentric language.

Various explanations have been proposed as to why animals are sacred or are used as symbols for the divine. Frequently, the need to get beyond human limitations is pointed out as the reason why animals are worshipped (Kristensen 1971). As the emblem of a god or goddess, they add new dimensions to the divine or stress certain characteristics. In ancient Palestine and Syria, the dove appears in the wake of a goddess as a symbol of love and tenderness, while the weather god stands on an ox, a symbol of power and fertility (Keel 1992: 154, 179–80). The Greek mistress of animals restrains animals forcibly and is associated with warriors, while the Aegean goddess may be flanked by animals or be handling snakes (Marinatos 2000).

Animals represent a sort of otherness and make the divine more than merely the superhuman, something that clearly surpasses human limitations. Henry Frankfort's explanation of animal worship in Egyptian religion, where it played an unusual role, stresses the otherness of animals. Frankfort says that an animal conforms to the type of species it belongs to in a way that transcends each animal's individuality. Because the continuous succession of generations has brought no change, the animal is seen as a symbol of the eternal quality of reality (Frankfort 1961: 8–14).

Some animals have characteristics that make them able to do things humans cannot do. Some animals are stronger than humans, others run faster; some species live their lives in the sea, while others fly high in the air. Animals may be seen as wiser and more mysterious than humans, with access to secrets hidden to us, and when they are used as symbols, they indicate something that is more meaningful than everyday reality. In the Roman Empire, this "otherness" was exploited for religious purposes. So at the same time as animal symbols refer to living animals, they in fact point away from them. When animals are used in the characterization of gods, the point is not that a divinity is like an animal but that the animal gives added meaning to the divine.

In addition to the mode of direct participation in the divine, the symbolic mode and the attributive mode that have been discussed in this chapter, animals were used instrumentally in sacrifices. The animal sacrifice and its transformation is the theme of the next chapter.

6

ANIMAL SACRIFICE: TRADITIONS AND NEW INVENTIONS

The Graeco-Roman blood sacrifice

After the procession was ended the consuls and the priests whose function it was presently sacrificed oxen; and the manner of performing the sacrifices was the same as with us. For after washing their hands they purified the victims with clear water and sprinkled corn on their heads, after which they prayed and then gave orders to their assistants to sacrifice them. Some of these assistants, while the victim was still standing, struck it on the temple with a club, and others received it upon the sacrificial knives as it fell. After this they flayed it and cut it up, taking off a piece from each of the entrails and also from every limb as a first-offering, which they sprinkled with grits of spelt and carried in baskets to the officiating priests. These placed them on the altars, and making a fire under them, poured wine over them while they were burning.

(Dionysius of Halicarnassus, *Roman Antiquities*, 7.72.15)

Animal sacrifice – killing one or more animals and offering them to the gods – was the central observance of ancient Mediterranean religion, a key symbol of paganism, the pivotal point of the rituals, and a regular feature of Roman life. Greek and Roman alimentary sacrifices were similar to each other in both structure and content. The learned Greek historian Dionysius of Halicarnassus, who wrote his *Roman Antiquities* at the time of Augustus, explicitly stresses the similarities between these rituals (7.72), although differences did exist. These differences had more to do with nuances and shades of shared meaning than with basic dissimilarities, and, besides, during the Augustan age and the early Roman Empire differences were often downplayed as part of the development of an imperial religion.[1]

In the first centuries CE, animal sacrifices flourished and, in comparison with earlier times, sometimes on a grandiose scale indeed. New varieties of sacrifice were invented, and alternative interpretations were made. At the

114

same time, more critical voices were also heard. In this chapter and the next, these developments will be investigated.

The ritual

A traditional sacrifice was made in a ritual setting, which usually consisted of four phases: the preparation with introductory rituals; immolation, transferring the victim from the human sphere to the divine; the slaughter of the animal, which included inspection of the viscera to see if the sacrifice was acceptable to the gods; and, finally, the sacred meal, which was the closing act of the sacrificial process (Ogilvie 1986: 41–52). The sacrifice was always combined with prayers – "without prayers the sacrifice is useless", writes Pliny (*Natural History*, 28.10; cf. Iamblichus, *On the Egyptian Mysteries*, 237.8–240.18). What were the status, value and meaning of the animals that were offered up to the gods and subsequently used in divination?

In archaic and classical Greece, the standard sacrifice (*thysia*), an alimentary blood sacrifice, consisted of domesticated animals.[2] Wild animals were not usually sacrificed, and neither were fish.[3] In Roman religion, the traditional victims of a bloody sacrifice (*immolatio*) were pigs, sheep and cattle, while during the empire the emperor sometimes showed his power by having wild and exotic animals offered to the gods. The number of animals sacrificed at the major festivals was also characteristic of the Roman state cult. Specific animals were sacrificed to specific deities, and the relationship between gods and their chosen animals varied. In Rome, male animals were offered to gods, female ones to goddesses. Sacrifices to Juno and Jupiter were white, while the gods of the underworld got black animals. For Asclepius at Epidaurus, goats were prohibited as victims (Pausanias, 2.26.9–10, 32.12).

In Greece, all meat came in principle from animals that had been sacrificed. The same vocabulary encompassed both sacrifice and butchering, and all consumable meat came from ritually slaughtered animals. In Rome, the consumption of meat was not confined to sacrifices. It was not only meat from public sacrifices that was sold on the market; a secular meat business also thrived (Garnsey 1999: 134; Corbier 1989: 232–3). In the Graeco-Roman world, both gods and humans were nourished with the meat of sacrificial animals, but the gods did not consume the animal flesh in the same way as humans, they did not chew and swallow the roasted meat but were fed by the aroma from those parts of the meat that had been burned at the altar. In this way, gods and humans shared the sacrifice but were also divided by it because of their different ways of consuming the meat of the sacrificed animals (Detienne 1989: 1–20). The gods got those parts of the animal in which its life resided and which were transformed into smoke; humans ate the meat of the animals. But one thing never changed – sacrifices were always made at the expense of the animal victims.

It was not only a hierarchy of gods, humans and animals but also a hierarchy of social relations according to status and sex among humans that was played out in the ritual. The animal sacrifice was an opportunity for humans to share food on a festive occasion, but at the same time distinctions were made between different social groups. The difference in hierarchy and status is to be seen at all stages of the ritual process: in carrying out the sacrifice, in the distribution of the meat, and in the exclusion of certain groups.

People of lower status – freeborn and slaves – led or dragged the animals along and carried out the killing, bleeding and dissecting (*victimarii, popae, cultrarii*). A man with an axe, the *victimarius*, can be glimpsed among them. A flute player did his best to drown the sounds from the animal that was being slaughtered, but except for him and the prayer of the priest, silence ruled. The higher sacrificial personnel consisted of priests and assistants or servants to the priests (*camilli*). In Greece, the *mageiros*, a sort of butcher *cum* cook, was the hired sacrificial specialist who consecrated the animals and led the ritual. On Roman reliefs, the major officiants are always shown fully dressed, clad in togas, while the man who offers the sacrifice has the folds of his toga drawn over his head. Slave assistants are bare-chested. With the probable exception of the Vestal Virgins, women did not participate directly in sacrifices.

The apportionment of meat also confirmed the differences that existed between people, as well as between gods and humans. While the central moment of the sacrifice in Greece was the eating of the internal organs (*splanchna*) and the burning of the bones wrapped in fat on the altar so that the gods would receive the smoke, in Roman religion the internal organs (*exta*) – those parts that are necessary for living (*vitalia*) – and the blood were reserved for the gods, and only the flesh was eaten by the participants.[4] This signifies a stronger segregation between gods and humans in Roman sacrifices than in Greek ones. In Greece, a restricted group ate the *exta*, which were immediately roasted on the altar, while a wider group ate from the boiled meat. In Rome, it was those at the top of the social hierarchy who had the privilege of eating from the sacrificed meat (*ex sacrificio*), although meat from the sacrifice was sometimes served at communal banquets. Other citizens had to purchase meat on the market, some of which originally came from sacrifices (Garnsey 1999: 134).

It was important that nobody should sacrifice in a state of impurity. Otherwise, the gods might be angry and the good relationship between humans and gods might be disturbed. Because the maintenance of that good relationship, the re-establishment of the *pax deorum*, was one of the main reasons for offerings to the gods in the first place, impurity and mistakes had to be avoided. Sacrificial rituals that were regarded as foreign were in principle forbidden. Livius mentions how the magistrates had prohibited sacrificial priests and prophets (*sacrificuli vatesque*) and annulled "every system of sacrifice except that performed in the Roman way" (Livy, 39.16.8).

116

The Romans were preoccupied to a higher degree than the Greeks with doing everything in a strictly correct manner but were nervously aware that things could go wrong all the same.

In a sacrifice, one gave to get, or at least so that one should not lose. As Porphyry put it, quoting Theophrastus (although Porphyry himself preferred bloodless sacrifices), there are three reasons for sacrificing to the gods: "to honour them, to give thanks, or out of need of good things" (*On Abstinence*, 2.24.1). Artemidorus writes that men "sacrifice to the gods when they have received benefits or when they have escaped some evil" (*The Interpretation of Dreams*, 2.33). Thus the sacrifice was part of a prosperous circle of giving and getting and was clearly seen as a promise of fruitfulness and divine blessing.

The sacrificial animal

To contribute to this circle of prosperity, one or more animals had to pay with their lives. The sacrifice was concerned basically with transforming living creatures into food, which means that a Graeco-Roman sacrifice was clearly about life and death. However, whether the death of the sacrificial victim was seen as a drama, or whether the sacrifice was more about life and death as strands in the general fabric of life, is an open question, but one that is pertinent to the interpretation of the status and value of sacrificial animals. Something can be learned from the way these animals are depicted.

In the official iconography of the Roman Empire, we usually see living, healthy animals led to the altar, sometimes an animal that is about to be killed but rarely a dead one in the process of being butchered. Living animals were part of the sacrificial procession that took place before the sacrifice. These animals were led along, decked in ribbons and garlands, and on special occasions their horns were gilded. Sometimes the sacrificial animals were depicted together with the human participants. Such scenes look like a happy coming together of animals and humans, as for instance on the triumphal arch of Marcus Aurelius in Rome (176 CE). Because only an unblemished animal (*purus*) was accepted by the gods, animals always seem to be in good shape. They were, and should have been, beautiful (*pulcher*).

More rarely, the animal is shown dead, for instance on the relief from Trajan's Forum, where the entrails of a dead ox are being examined.[5] On the Ara Pacis in Rome, symbols of life such as garlands with fruit are depicted together with the skulls of dead cattle. As art historian Jas Elsner puts it: "In the Ara Pacis, the cows of fruitfulness, of sacrifice, and the skulls of the precinct wall represent as one thematic continuity the sacrificial transactions by which human social life is ensured and linked to the sacred" (Elsner 1995: 205). But even if a mysterious interconnection of life and death is indicated in the altar friezes, the mystery is spelled out in small letters. The sacrificial images on Ara Pacis, as in Roman sacrificial iconography in general, seem to reveal a matter-of-fact attitude to the business of killing animals in a sacrificial context.

The animals were usually sacrificed on the altar, within the sanctified space but outside the temple. While the moment before the victim was stunned was sometimes shown, as, for instance, on coins, it was unusual to depict the killing itself, and the actual violence done to the sacrificial beast is seldom shown (Durand 1989: 90–1; van Straten 1995: 106, 186ff). One rare example is from the arch of Septimius Severus at Lapcis in North Africa (203 CE). Here a kneeling ox is depicted while the blow is about to fall, at the same time as a kneeling figure plunges the knife into its neck. Thus two separate acts in the process of killing are shown in the same relief.

The reason for not showing the actual killing could be that most sacrifices were occasions for feasting and merriment, with the killing a sort of unpleasant core of the proceedings. It had to be concealed precisely because it was unpleasant. The reluctance to depict the killing could also reflect a wish that sacrifices should appear as stylish and formalized events. Because the killing and bleeding of the animals were not easily controlled and could be messy, they did not contribute so easily to what was expected to appear as a fully ordered and dignified activity. Finally, reluctance to depict the actual killing might imply that even if this act of violence was absolutely necessary, it was not necessarily deeply meaningful.

The last interpretation is attractive. As frequently pointed out, the killing of the animal may have been given such disproportionate significance in modern research partly because the sacrifice of Christ has been used as a model for its interpretation (Durand 1989: 87–8; Stowers 1995: 297–8). It may be that the sacrificial victim has rather undeservedly been given Christ-like qualities. It is also possible that modern academics are prone to exaggerating the significance of the slaughter of animals because of their own lack of direct experience with animal husbandry. But if the killing – the moment when the *popa* stunned the animal with a blow from the axe and the knife-man (*cultrarius*) slit its throat – was not the climax of the ritual, what was its most important moment?

Two moments especially should be noticed. The first was when the living animal was dedicated to the gods by some flour and salt (*mola salsa*) being poured over its head and by a knife being moved over its spine, from the head to the tail. In reality, this act, and not the actual killing, had originally given the sacrifice its name, i.e. *immolatio*. The prayer was probably offered at this moment.

The second, and more tense, moment was when the animal was dead and its carcass was opened up. This was the moment of truth that revealed whether the gods accepted the sacrifice or not. At this point, the animal was changed into a medium of communication between gods and humans. It was transformed into a "natural text" on which meaning was inscribed by the gods, by destiny or by the hidden correspondences of the cosmos and was thus made into an object for the divinator's scrutinizing gaze. The sacrifice could be examined in different ways.

It could for instance be "read" in the traditional Roman way, which meant that the *exta*, consisting of the gall bladder, the liver, the heart and the lungs, were examined inside the animal to see if they were in good condition, implying that the sacrifice was accepted by the gods. Alternatively, the sacrifice was "read" in the Etruscan way. Then the liver, with the gall bladder, was taken out and examined for signs concerning the future. This was a more complicated procedure, undertaken by experts who specialized in interpreting the codes of the liver, i.e. the *haruspices*. These codes can be seen in the famous instruction model of a sheep's liver from Piacenza, which is a map of the zones of heaven, each zone presided over by gods. Some of these gods were benevolent, but others were not. As time went by, the original Etruscan practice merged with the Roman, and it became unusual to let the entrails stay mute (*exta muta*). Emperor Claudius described the *haruspices* as "the oldest Italian art" and contrasted it with "foreign superstitions", thus stressing that this Etruscan speciality should be accepted as a legitimate Roman practice (Tacitus, *The Annals*, 11.15). Not only the Etruscans but also the Stoics thought that the liver was a microcosm of the universe.

If things went wrong during the sacrificial procedure, for instance if the sacerdotal priest tripped over or mispronounced the words of his prayers, it was a bad omen, and the procedure had to be repeated. It was always important to obtain good omens. Therefore, one continued to sacrifice until favourable omens were obtained. Sometimes, however, it was not possible, even if one tried. When Emperor Julian, before his final battle in Persia, had prepared ten fine bulls for a sacrifice to Mars the Avenger, nine of the bulls sank to the ground before they reached the altar, and the tenth escaped; when finally brought back and killed, it showed alarming signs. Then Julian cried out to Jove that he would make no more offerings to Mars. He was wounded in the battle and died shortly afterwards (Ammianus Marcellinus, *The History*, 24.6.17).

What status did sacrifices and divinatory practices based on slaughtered animals bestow on animals? It is safe to say that in sacrifices and divinations based on sacrifices, animals were treated as objects and were more interesting dead than ever they had been alive. All the same, and as already pointed out, just before the killing, a faint notion of the animal as a free-acting agent comes to the fore in the idea that it should give its consent to being killed. The need for the sacrifice to be voluntary was part of Roman cultic prescriptions (Fless 1995: 72, note 21). When water or flour was sprinkled on the head of the animal to make it nod, a pious comedy – in reality a mere formality – was played out. On this point of the sacrificial procedure, it was to a certain degree implied that the animal was free to act. According to Plutarch, people in ancient times "considered it doing some great thing to sacrifice living animals, and even now people are very careful not to kill the animal till a drink-offering is poured over him and he shakes his head in assent. Such precautions they took to avoid any unjust act" (*Table Talk*, 729F).

The idea that animals were always willing to be sacrificed must not be taken at face value. Images from archaic and classical times in Greece show that animals were often restrained by ropes, and an ox could be dragged down on its knees as a sign of voluntary participation (van Straten 1995: 100–2). Also in Rome, the animal was often led by a rope, and the attendants sometimes carried staffs (Fless 1995: 72). In reality, obtaining the animal's formal consent was not seen as particularly interesting or important, even if it was thought to be an unlucky sign if an animal struggled against its keepers, or, even worse, if it broke loose and fled. Such animals had to be caught and killed immediately. It must also be noted that Cato says explicitly about the *suovetaurilia* – the sacrifice of a pig, a lamb and a calf – made at his farm that it was forbidden to call the animals by name during the sacrifice (*On Agriculture*, 141).[6] This scrap of information indicates that the individuality of the animals was denied, at least at the last moment when they were about to be killed. The fact that Cato explicitly warns against personalizing them in the final moment of their lives could imply that there was a risk that they might then turn into demonic entities, which could afterwards afflict humans.

During the sacrificial process, animals were conceived of as intermediaries between humans and gods. But at the same time as the animals were intermediaries, the institution of sacrifice functioned as a justification for killing them. In divinations based on slaughtered animals, it was the dead animal, not the living one, that was inscribed with divine messages and thus was the mediator between gods and humans. When no heart was found in one of Julius Caesar's sacrificial animals, and no lobe in the liver of another, these omens were interpreted as predicting the death of Caesar. Cicero gives a traditional explanation of this phenomenon, although he does not believe the explanation and later jokes mercilessly over people's credulity (*On Divination*, 2.16): "Therefore, when those parts of the entrails without which the victim could not have lived are found to be missing, it must be understood that the parts that are missing disappeared in the moment of sacrifice" (*On Divination*, 1.52). The disappearance of internal organs was due to direct intervention by the gods after the animals were dead. Similar explanations are given by Iamblichus more than three hundred years later. According to him, several factors may contribute to changing the entrails in various ways that may please the gods. Iamblichus mentions such factors as the external souls of the animals, the demon that is set over them, the atmosphere, and the revolution of the surrounding sky (*On the Egyptian Mysteries*, 3.16).

The divination, as well as the apportionment of meat, clearly presupposed that the animal was a lifeless mass and no longer an individual. It also presupposed that external forces took hold of it and inscribed it with the message it transmitted. Consequently, a similar attitude can be observed with regard to dead animals used in divination and to living animals used as oracles. They were media of divine communication, not messengers for the gods.

It must also be stressed that in the Graeco-Roman world animals were sacrificed, not humans.[7] This means that even if the animal in one small sequence of the ritual was treated as a contract partner to the people who sacrificed it, the institution of sacrifice was founded on a basic inequality between animals and humans.

The agricultural view of animals

In contemporary research, there have been several attempts to determine the meaning and function of Greek and Roman sacrifices. One question that has loomed large and has inspired grand theories has been about the *origin* of sacrifice. Walter Burkert (1972) and René Girard (1977) in particular have invested sacrifices with deep meaning and regarded them as those acts *par excellence* that create and maintain culture and reflect the origins of social formation. For Girard, sacrifice is the most fundamental rite and the root of all cultural systems, such as language, civil institutions and religion. In accordance with the significance they have bestowed on animal sacrifices, Burkert and Girard have also stressed the killing of the animal as the most important act during the sacrificial ritual. For Burkert, killing defines human beings as *homo necans*.[8]

However, because our topic is Graeco-Roman animal sacrifices and innovations and criticism of these sacrifices in a period that finally ended with such sacrifices being banned (first–fourth century CE), it is obvious that grand theories about their origin are not as helpful as trying to fathom how sacrifices worked in this period and, not least, why they were eventually terminated. We have already argued against the view that the killing was the most important act during the ritual (see above).

In addition to the question of origin, the discussion on sacrifices has also focused on the question of context. In contemporary research, animal sacrifice has either been traced to hunting customs or has been explained in relation to agriculture as a typical agrarian and pastoral ritual. The main advocate for the hunting hypothesis today is Walter Burkert, who has to some extent been inspired by the theories of Karl Meuli who traced Greek sacrificial ritual to Palaeolithic hunting (Meuli 1946). In consonance with Meuli's theories, Burkert has maintained that the animal sacrifice comes from a ritualization of the hunt.

Jonathan Smith and others, opposed to the views of Walter Burkert, have pointed out that animal sacrifice is universally performed as a ritual killing of a *domesticated* animal by agrarian or pastoral societies (Smith 1987: 197). Smith has also stressed that sacrifice "is, in part, a meditation on domestication" (*ibid*.: 199).

Against the hunting hypothesis and consonant with Smith's view, it must be emphasized that the majority of animals killed in sacrifices in the ancient Mediterranean societies were domesticated animals. In general, the sacrifice of domesticated animals is closely linked with agriculture, and the significance of the sacrificial rite closely corresponds to the importance of animal husbandry (Horden and Purcell 2000: 200; Smith 1987; Jay 1993: 148). Emperor Julian, for instance, comments on the close connection between sacrifices and animal husbandry. He admits that a variety of sacrificial practices with a wide range of animals existed but emphasizes the importance of the traditional alimentary sacrifice:

> it is true that we make offerings of fish in certain mystical sacrifices, just as the Romans sacrifice the horse and many other animals too, both wild and domesticated, and as the Greeks and the Romans too sacrifice dogs to Hecate. And among other nations also many other animals are offered in the mystic cults; and sacrifices of that sort take place publicly in their cities once or twice a year. But that is not the custom in the sacrifices which we honour most highly, in which alone the gods deign to join us and to share our table. In those most honoured sacrifices we do not offer fish, for the reason that we do not tend fish, nor look after the breeding of them, and we do not keep flocks of fish as we do sheep and cattle. For since we foster these animals and they multiply accordingly, it is only right that they should serve for all our uses and above all for the sacrifices that we honour most.
>
> (*Hymn to the Mother of the Gods*, 176d–177a)

A religion that has a sacrificial cult is connected with certain ways of living and with certain types of social organization that are most fruitfully seen as agricultural. In contrast to sacrificial killing of tame animals, in the Graeco-Roman world, ritual killing of *wild* animals took place in the arenas, where such animals (as well as tame ones) were slaughtered in great numbers in an artificial recreation of the hunt.

It is obvious that whether the sacrificial animals are seen in a hunting context or in the context of agriculture is significant in how they are evaluated. For instance, in a hunting situation, as described by Burkert, the prey was conceived of as a worthy antagonist and became the object of anthropomorphization. In contrast to hunting, agricultural life means living with animals in a friendly way. It further implies a type of life that presupposes a certain parallelism between human and animal societies. But, above all, implicit in the agricultural view of animals is a pragmatic attitude to their killing and the ability to make a sudden shift in one's conception of the animal from friend to food. Both the shift of perspective and the pragmatic attitude to killing animals were implicit in the institution of the blood sacrifice in the Roman Empire.

In addition to the questions of origin and context, an important approach in contemporary research on Graeco-Roman sacrifices has been to see these sacrifices as "cultural meditations on differences and relationships" (Smith 1987: 201). This course has been taken in relation to Greek religion by Jean-Pierre Vernant and his colleagues in the so-called "Paris school" (Detienne and Vernant 1989), where, as Einar Thomassen puts it, the animal sacrifice appears more like a dinner party than a ritual murder (cf. Thomassen 2005). Their line of thought, with its stress on how the sacrifices established connections as well as dividing lines between gods, humans and animals, has been refined and developed in the 1990s, especially in relation to the differences between groups in a society.

Stanley Stowers has stressed how the sacrificial cult of the Mediterranean area, with its offerings of grain and animal products, linked its practitioners to land, lineage and the economy (Stowers 1995, 2001). Sacrificial religion was about the productivity of the land, and it presupposed that there was a reciprocity between gods and humans. It was the cult of ethnic communities, people who were organized through kinship, had a common ancestor and connections to a traditional homeland, and who stressed inter-generational continuity. This type of sacrificial culture was common for Greeks, Romans and Jews. According to Stowers, the typical sacrificial religion of the Graeco-Roman world was closely intertwined with economic production and made no sense apart from that production (Stowers 2001: 97ff). Sacrificial religion implied that animals bred on farms were the most natural objects of that religion. It gave power to landowners and made their form of production the one preferred in a religious context.

The cults that were performed usually had a local character, even if they eventually expanded and became the cults of nations. In antiquity, sacrifices were connected with the farm, as in Cato's description of a sacrifice on his own farm (*On Agriculture*, 141); with the local village, as was the case with Saint Felix's shrine at Nola (see below); with the city, as in the rituals performed on the Acropolis in Athens; with the nation, as in the temple in Jerusalem; and with the empire, as in the national temples on the Capitol in Rome. In the cities of the empire, local cults and Roman cults were usually combined. Animal sacrifices were vital ingredients in the cult of the emperor, and multitudes of animals were sometimes slaughtered in his honour and to the honour of Rome in sacrifices that could be orgies of ritual killing. On the accession of Caligula, 16,000 cows were sacrificed in Rome over three months (*Suetonius*, 14.1).

Richard Gordon has pointed out that during the Roman Empire the sacrificial system was closely connected with the imperial system and had become a key link between the emperor and local elites (Gordon 1990). One of Gordon's observations is that in the sacrificial scenes in the official iconography, the main emphasis is no longer on the animal victim but on the sacrificiant, who was the emperor. Extant sacrificial reliefs show the extraordinary dominance of the emperor to the neglect of any others offering sacrifices. Gordon suggests that the institution of sacrifice was one of the key means that helped to create a synthesis between the religion of Rome and a religion of the empire. The imperial sacrifices had moved out of Rome and had become paradigmatic for all parts of the empire.

Participating in sacrifices, at a local shrine or in one of the national temples, was a mark of identity. So even if there is a gap between the sacrifice of one lamb on a local farm and the multitudes of animals that were sacrificed in Rome during the national festivals or in one of the other Graeco-Roman centres, both types of sacrifice contributed to strengthening people's loyalty to land and lineage, be it to the local patrilineal household or to Rome and the emperor. Sociologist Nancy Jay, who sees sacrifice as an activity systematically related to gender, highlights these points: "states depending on sacrifices were what Max Weber called 'patrimonial' states, in which the state is an extension of the ruler's household and political power is inherited within families and lineages" (Jay 1993: 149). The sacrifice was a traditional ritual activity that gave cosmological relevance and legitimacy to the integration and differentiation that it produced. In short, the animal sacrifice gave a divine basis to the social order.

However, it is also important to note how this rite, performed in an urban context, established connections with a past when Romans lived closer to the land. In other words, it is crucial to maintain a fundamental agricultural grounding of this ritual. While the cities were the places where things happened, the urban inhabitants of the empire kept their agricultural past alive through their sacrifices. Agricultural products were used in the sacrifice – not only animals, but also grain and wine – and the knife that killed the animal was hidden in a basket of corn, while a mixture of flour and salt (*mola salsa*) was used to consecrate and dedicate the animal to the god. The Roman calendar was an agricultural calendar with seventy to eighty festivals during the year in which public animal sacrifices were carried out. Mary Beard has argued convincingly against locating ritual meanings in "the primitive community of peasant farmers", because it makes it "hard to understand the practice of those rituals in the complex urban society of the historical period, several centuries later" (Beard 2003: 274). This is obviously correct. Sacrifices spoke to the complex and difficult business of running cities and empire and were key elements in the fabric that kept the cultural, social and political together in the Roman Empire. If it had not been so, sacrifices would not have been performed on the scale they were. However, sacrifices were performed in a world where security and prosperity were based on agriculture, and where the sacrificial animals in the main, but not solely, belonged to the sphere of animal husbandry.

The *taurobolium*

New varieties of animal sacrifice also flourished in the fourth century. These sacrifices were somehow connected with traditional practices, at the same time as they took a new direction in accordance with new religious needs and with the general religious developments in the empire. It is most important in this connection that the sacrificial animals were taken out of their traditional context and reinstalled in new cultic and hermeneutical settings. The most dramatic of these innovations was the *taurobolium*, and the most widespread was the mystery cult of Mithras, while the Neoplatonic creation of theurgy represented a new sacrificial practice as well as a new sacrificial theory.

The *taurobolium* is mentioned in over one hundred inscriptions, mainly from the Western part of the Roman Empire, and in a few literary texts, over a period of 500 years (Duthoy 1969). The bulk of the inscriptions date from 159 CE to 375 CE. The procedure probably changed during this time, but it designated a specific rite at each state of its development. J.B. Rutter (1968) and R. Duthoy (1969) have proposed that the *taurobolium* developed from a public cult on behalf of the emperor into a private cult.

The content of this rite in its earliest phase is not clear. It could have been a sort of bull chasing accompanied by a sacrifice (Rutter 1968). However, most interesting for us is the latest development of the rite, as attested in pagan inscriptions and Christian texts from the last part of the fourth century. The main source of the final phase of the ritual is the Christian author Prudentius. It seems then to have been developed into a dramatic ritual in which an ox was ritually slaughtered. The beast was led out on to some planks that had been laid over a pit. A special weapon was used, probably to make the wound in the animal's body as large as possible. Prudentius mentions that "the vast wound pours forth a stream of steaming blood". The celebrant, who descended into the pit, received the blood that gushed from the ox and poured down through gaps in the planks. This ritual is described by Prudentius as one of the horrors of paganism:

> The priest, hidden in the trench below, catches the shower, holding his filthy head under all the drops, fouling his clothes and his whole body. He even throws back his head and offers his cheeks to the downpour, puts his ears under it, exposes his lips, his nostrils and washes his eyes themselves in the stream. And he does not even spare his mouth, but wets his tongue until his whole body imbibes the dark blood.
>
> (*Crowns of Martyrdom*, 10.1032–40)

In earlier times, a *taurobolium* had often been celebrated in honour of the emperor. We do not know if this public rite ever had such a dramatic character as the late *taurobolium* obviously did, but it is unlikely. According to Duthoy, the dramatic variant of the rite was an invention of the late third or early fourth century. In the fourth century, the emperors were Christians (except for the short reign of Julian), and the *taurobolium* was no longer celebrated on their behalf. Thus the public version of the rite died out, while the private version was continued. Most of the inscriptions from Rome date from after 370 CE. They connect the rite with the Magna Mater, the Syrian mother of the gods, who had been worshipped for several centuries in Rome and who, in the late fourth century, was conceived of as a traditional Roman goddess. Representatives of the pagan aristocracy in Rome were the ones who, at the end of the fourth century, were "taurobolized". The *taurobolium* was now celebrated as a private rite for the benefit of the individual. At the same time, this ritual stood out as a symbol of paganism.

Several traits made the ritual of the *taurobolium* special in comparison with traditional sacrifice. The most obvious of these traits is that, instead of keeping a distance between the one who dedicated the animal to the gods and the sacrificial victim, he/she was now soaked in the blood of the animal.[9] It is not unreasonable to think that the initiation through the blood of the animal bestowed on the celebrant the quality of life that normally belonged to the gods. In any case, the celebrant stepped over the traditional borderline between man and beast through contact with the animal's blood, as well as the borderline between man and god by bathing in a substance that in traditional sacrifices was offered up to the gods.

Two inscriptions from Rome, both made after 375 CE, mention "rebirth" (*renatus*), and one characterizes the person dedicating the sacrifice as *in aeternum renatus*. The late *taurobolium* was thus intimately connected with one person and his/her future religious life and can be interpreted as a ritual and spiritual rebirth (cf. Gasparro 1985: 114f). In some of the inscriptions, it is mentioned that the ritual was celebrated on the birthday of the person on whose behalf the *taurobolium* was held (*natalicium*), which probably means that this day was conceived of as the ritual birthday of the dedicant. Prudentius mentions that the one who was baptized in the blood of the ox afterwards showed himself to those present dripping with blood.

This display is a parallel to the way in which Lucius, in the *Golden Ass*, after he had been initiated into the rites of Isis, showed himself to the worshippers: Lucius was clad in ceremonial robes, which were embroidered with flowers and sacred animals. He held a lighted torch in his right hand and wore on his head a chaplet of palm leaves, resembling the rays of the sun. Lucius calls the day of his initiation "the most happy birthday of my religious life". Parallel to the way Lucius was rigged out, the celebrant of the *taurobolium* was clad in a silk toga as well as in other fineries. However, in contrast to Lucius, he was simultaneously drenched in the blood of the ox.

In both cases, the initiates were spectacular sights, and in both cases the initiation ceremony could be interpreted as a new birth, though the aspect of birth is more explicitly stated in the rite of the taurobolium. It is a striking parallel to the way a baby is born, bathed in blood.

This interpretation of the ritual is dependent on Prudentius. However, Maria Grazia Lancellotti has recently pointed out that the ritual described by Prudentius is suspect because he does not explicitly connect it to the Great Mother and does not mention her priests. In addition, the *fossa sanguines*, which he mentions, has no counterparts in archaeological finds (Lancellotti 2002: 112). Lancellotti proposes instead the hypothesis that the *taurobolium* had a substitute function in respect to the self-emasculation of the Galli, the priests of the Great Mother. Lancellotti refers to Clement and Firmicus Maternus when she emphasizes the importance of the *vires*, the genitalia of the bull, in this ritual.[10] They were used as substitutes for the traditional self-emasculation of the priests. According to her, a permanent self-mutilation restricted the ritual to the masculine world of slaves and freemen, while the use of the *vires* of bulls made it possible for others to participate as well. And, we could add, such a substitution would also have contributed to linking the ritual to a pagan elite, who could afford to buy bulls.

Whether the ritual should be interpreted as a baptism in blood or as a substitute for self-emasculation depends on the evaluation of the value of Prudentius' description and is difficult to decide. However, one must take Prudentius into account for the last phase of the ritual, even if Lancellotti may be right in her hypothesis about the importance of the *vires* for earlier phases. In both cases, the ritual of the *taurobolium* differs from traditional sacrifices either by the use of blood or by the use of *vires*. In both cases, the ritual seems to be an initiation. The initiatory character and context of the late *taurobolium* is also underlined by the fact that those who underwent the ritual commemorated it by listing it together with other initiations they had undergone. The most famous example is the funeral monument of Praetextatus, the prefect of Rome in 367 CE. He, like several of the senators, had undergone the *taurobolium* in the late fourth century (Clauss 2000: 31), which shows that personal religious initiations were attractive options at this time.

A similar focus on the individual celebrant and on the personal and spiritual character of the sacrifice is also found in the mysteries of Mithras (cf. Bjørnebye 2005).

The slain bull of Mithras

In the cult of the originally Persian god Mithras, the central mythical scenario seems to have consisted of Mithras capturing the young bull, carrying it on his shoulders into his cave and killing it by stabbing a dagger into its neck.

Statues and images showing the taurochthony have been found from Syria to Britain. Many have been unearthed, especially in Rome and Ostia, and in the valleys of the Rhine and the Danube. Also present in the picture of Mithras slaying the bull are a serpent, a dog and a scorpion. They are biting the bull or licking its blood. Mithras himself is gazing away from the animal he is killing – either at Sol, who is depicted in the corner of the image, or at us, the spectators.

This fairly standardized image served as a cult icon in the different *mithraea* all over the empire for more than two centuries, comparable to the way in which the crucified Christ appeared on altarpieces in Christian churches at a later time. In contrast to the traditional pagan sacrificial images, which seldom showed the actual killing, the slaying of the animal was the main object of the religious onlooker's gaze in the cult of Mithras (Elsner 1995: 211). A further innovation in comparison with traditional pagan sacrifices is that the god himself kills the animal.

But although the killing of a bull was the focus of this cult, it is doubtful whether a *real* bull was ever killed in the cult of Mithras. The confined space of most *mithraea* hardly allows for a real slaughter to have been carried out. It seems as if in the worship of Mithras, the animal sacrifice was given a symbolic function that was more meaningful than its actual execution (*ibid.*: 210–21).

One function of the symbolism of the taurochthony was astrological (Porphyry, *On Abstinence*, 4.16). The bull and other animals on the cult icon appear as signs, referring to astrological constellations, and in this way the image of Mithras killing the bull serves as a "cosmological code" (Ulansay 1987, 1989: 125). Around the icon of Mithras, who kills the bull, are usually placed minor pictures showing mythological scenes. The different symbols and images point to a cult in which the key signs were shown in different contexts leading to polysemy and symbolic complexity, but because of a complete lack of explanatory texts, we do not know the exact content of this imaginary mythological scene. However, what we do know is that the Graeco-Roman worshippers of Mithras were initiated into a hierarchy of seven grades. In addition to acquiring higher status by means of these initiations, those who were initiated also seem to have been promised a salvatory rebirth.

Mithras' killing of the bull is obviously the crucial act in this cult, figuring as it does on its altarpieces. What is the meaning of the bull-slaying scene? It is reasonable to conclude that we are witnessing a "good" killing, an act that had a pronounced cosmic dimension, functioned primarily in relation to an initiatory religious structure, and most likely had salvatory implications (Hinnells 1975). That the Mithraic cult had an initiatory structure also underlines that there was a personal element to this killing that was not present in traditional animal sacrifices. It was largely the interplay between mythological and astrological references that furnished the participants with a rich and meaningful symbolism by means of which they could relate to a cosmic scenario, participate in profound religious truths and cherish a better hope for the future.

Some further scraps of information can be gained from the images themselves, from references to the cult made by contemporary authors, and from graffiti found in the *mithraea*. In Mithraic iconography, there are also images of the bull, which is grazing peacefully, and of Mithras who captures it and either drags it by its hind legs or carries it on his shoulders into the cave. Sometimes, Mithras is also depicted as riding on the bull. The fact that several other animals are biting at this animal or licking its blood suggests that the bull contains, or stands for, something that is conceived of as attractive. According to Porphyry, with reference to the Mithraic cult, "souls coming into creation are bull-born, and the god who secretly [. . .] creation is called 'ox-stealer'" (*On the Cave of the Nymphs in the Odyssey*, 314). Porphyry's cryptic saying supports the view that the taurochthony represents a greater cosmic scenario, probably of souls descending into bodies and of their ascent into higher realms. Mithras was frequently called *Sol Invictus Mithras* – the invincible Sun Mithras.

As for the bull in the iconography of Mithras, it was not conceived of as a domestic animal but an untamed bull that was actually conquered by the one who finally managed to sacrifice it. Thus the killing of the bull also has connotations of the theme of the hero who subjugates wild beasts, and the animal is in this case a worthy opponent for the victorious god. Like Hercules, Mithras is forcing the bull down, and in the final scene, the bull is depicted as being totally subdued.

The killing of the bull had different meanings from those found in traditional animal sacrifice. A traditional sacrifice was about killing a domesticated animal, giving something to the gods, receiving blessings from them in return, reading the entrails of the animal for signs about the future, and finally eating its meat. In comparison with this sacrifice, the killing of the bull in the Mithraic mysteries seems to be related more to killing in the context of hunting and to the subjugation of animals by a hero, for instance by Hercules, than to sacrificing a tame animal.[11] The bull is not killed in the way that was usual in sacrifices, by being stunned by a blow and having its throat slit, but by Mithras stabbing it in the neck with a knife. In addition, Mithras' killing of the bull was about personal transformation and had a direct relevance to the individuals who were initiated and to their future.

Both in the mysteries of Mithras and in the *taurobolium* we are witnessing developments in Graeco-Roman sacrificial culture, pointing away from the earlier context of the animal sacrifice towards a new personal, spiritual – and not least – cosmological context. In these new cults, the sacrificial animal was seen less as part of a circle of prosperity, encompassing land and lineage, agricultural production and meat, food and festival, and more as a dynamic element in a personal and religious development based on initiation.

As for sacrificial animals in the traditional cults, a vague notion of them as free-acting agents was at work at the moment when they were led to the altar. But even if the bulls in the *taurobolium* and in the mysteries of Mithras had a quality of life that could be transferred to humans and was regarded as beneficial, these animals seem, even less than traditional sacrificial animals, to have been conceived of as "persons". It has been suggested that Mithras is looking away from the bull he is about to kill, either because he really does not wish to kill it or because he is receiving a message or an instruction from Sol. However, the impression is that the bull is no longer a subject but an object, not only for Mithras but also for the snake, the dog and the scorpion, as well as for us, the modern onlookers.

Theurgy as a new justification of the animal sacrifice

Innovations in Graeco-Roman sacrificial culture took place not only in the new cults; the Neoplatonists also adopted a fresh approach to animal sacrifices. One of their aims was to create a theory of sacrifice that effectively countered pagan and Christian criticism (see Chapter 7). This criticism had been concerned with the discrepancy between means and purpose. It was increasingly seen as an internal contradiction in the religious system that bloody sacrifices were being offered to spiritual beings.

In spite of this criticism, in the late third century, several of the Neoplatonists accepted animal sacrifice as an important ingredient of Graeco-Roman culture. The task of these philosophers was to explain why material offerings should be made to spiritual beings, who neither needed nor wanted material things. The construction of a new sacrificial theory was a significant contribution to what has been characterized as "the pagan revival", because it furnished intellectual paganism with a new rationale for animal sacrifice. While Porphyry put forward a rather ambiguous defence of animal sacrifices in *On Abstinence* – as something that was for the masses (*hoi polloi*) and aimed at placating demons (see Chapter 7) – other Neoplatonists, especially Iamblichus, but also Sallustius and Proclus, defended animal sacrifice and gave it a new justification.

Iamblichus (250–325 CE) composed a response to a letter written by Porphyry to the Egyptian priest Anebo. In this letter, Porphyry criticizes a practice called theurgy, which implies that the divine can be influenced by ritual means. Here Porphyry had expressed opinions on animal sacrifice similar to his views in *On Abstinence*. Iamblichus' response, which since the Renaissance has been labelled *On the Egyptian Mysteries* and was written under the pseudonym Abammon (who, like Anebo, was an Egyptian priest), defends a theurgical point of view. Theurgy (*theourgia*) is described by Iamblichus as divine acts (*theia erga*) as well as the work of the gods (*theon erga*). Through theurgical rituals, human beings became fellow workers in creation. In this way, Iamblichus grafted rituals on to the Neoplatonic tradition and saw them as material vehicles by means of which the soul was lifted directly into the divine. When the late Neoplatonic soul actively tried to reach the intelligible world by means of theurgical practices, it used its embodied nature and the world of matter to reach its goal.

Gregory Shaw has made a reassessment of Iamblichus and his contributions and has convincingly stressed that this influential Neoplatonist did not see rituals as inferior to rational contemplation (Shaw 1985, 1995). On the contrary, Iamblichus and his followers held a sacramental world view and stressed that theoretical insights were not sufficient to grasp what was ultimately ineffable. The ritual work of the theurgists aimed at integration of the elements of the world. This world was regarded as being interconnected to the extent that the finite and the infinite participated in each other. Theurgical rituals were the means by which the embodied soul could reach the divine.

Iamblichus approaches the problem of animal sacrifice by posing two sets of questions, both highly relevant. The first pertains to the utility and power of sacrifices in relation to the world at large, in relation to those who perform them and in relation to the gods (5.1.9–12). The content of the first set of questions is, in essence, why are sacrifices performed, and what do the different participants gain from them?

Iamblichus introduces the discussion of this subject by opposing the usual reasons for sacrificing. Sacrifices are not made for the sake of honouring gods, or as thanksgiving, or as first fruits (206.3–9). Iamblichus argues forcefully against the belief that the bodies of demons are nourished by sacrifices (211.19–214.3). Because gods and demons are not material, they have no need of material support. Instead, the sacrifice works because it is part of a movement upwards in which matter is purified. In sacrifices, the higher beings (*hoi kreittones*) never engage in a downward movement. The rising smoke from the victims is enveloped by these beings, it does not envelop them, and while the vapours are absorbed by the higher types of being, they never restrain them (204.4–205.14). The sacrificial process led upwards (*anagogein*). In no way did this process bring anything down (*kato*) to the level of matter (*hyle*) and generated existence (*genesis*). Those who are on a higher level simply cannot be defiled by those who are on a lower one. Gods cannot be contaminated by unclean substances from the burning carcasses of slaughtered animals, as had been suggested by Porphyry (see Chapter 7). Neither the higher types of being nor men who possess intelligence (*nous*) and are undisturbed by passion will be defiled. Defilement (*molusmos, miasma*) is passed on from material things to those who are restricted by a material body (205.8–11). This does not mean that all creatures with material bodies can be defiled. To have a body does not necessarily mean to be restricted by it. For instance, humans who have developed superior qualities are no longer hampered by the negative limitations of their bodies.

To contribute to the upward movement, it was necessary that the sacred rites start with the divinities of matter and work upwards through the different classes of powers and divinities (217.8–11). A crucial point in Iamblichus' argument is that the sacrifice is made through fire (*pyr*). The sacrificial fire consumes matter and brings what is left upwards to the "divine, celestial and immaterial fire" (214.8–9). In this way, matter itself is changed (214.15–16). Analogous to the effect of fire on matter, the divine fire renders humans passionless and makes them like gods (214.17–215.1). By means of the sacrifice and the sacrificial fire, conceived of as a pure and fine substance, humans are led upwards to the fire of the gods.

The slaughter of animals in sacrifice belonged to the realm of matter and pertained to the lower divinities. At the same time, sacrifices were also beneficial on a more general level, because the highest divinities enveloped matter as well – even if they were simultaneously absolutely separated from it (217.17–218.17). Accordingly, from the sacrifice, a common beneficial influence descended into the whole realm of generated existence.

One reason why this could be so was that the same sort of life was distributed throughout the whole of creation. It was as if the cosmos was a single living being. There were sympathies and correspondences between different parts as well as repulsion and opposition between others (207.10ff). In the perfect theurgical sacrifice (teleia thysia), all categories worked together (210.4), and sacred rites, including animal sacrifices, were orchestrated to cater for all types of divinity and to make contact with cosmic and supracosmic hierarchies of beings. Every power and divinity should have its due award, in relation to its cosmic position and order (228.13–230.15), and its mode of being should be imitated through worship (231.9–13). In this way, theurgical rites were made to relate to the totality and harmony of the cosmos. As part of this harmony, numbers also played an important part. In accordance with this thinking, if something was defective or lacking in the way the sacrifice was carried out, the sacrifice simply would not work.

The sacramental view implied that matter could serve as a suitable receptacle for the gods (232.16–233.10) and that a close connection existed between the receptacle that was provided by the person who sacrificed and the divinity it was meant to attract. Such receptacles were made up of diverse things, for instance stones, herbs, animals, aromatics and sacred objects (233.9–12). According to Iamblichus, certain animals, plants and other products of the earth were under the rule of the higher types of being, and thus an inseparable union was formed between the higher beings and the person who sacrificed through especially elected material intermediaries – for instance, through chosen animals (235.5–9). Specific animals and plants were seen as corresponding to different divinities or causes, and these divinities and causes could be moved by means of the sacrifice and by the use of appropriate plants or animals (209.14–19). For instance, according to theurgical thinking, the lion and the cock corresponded to the sun (cf. Proclus, On the Hieratic Art, 4.150.3–4). Iamblichus also mentions some of the animals of Egypt as specially elected (235.12–14). But even if the animal form became an embodied sign and even functioned as an imprint of the divine, this type of symbolic thinking does not seem to have carried with it a heightened status for real animals. On the contrary, one could ask if their new symbolic meanings perhaps made animals less interesting and valuable as real living creatures.

Iamblichus' second question concerning animal sacrifices was about an apparent contradiction: why must interpreters of oracles abstain from contamination by animal substances, while the gods are said to be attracted by the fumes from animal sacrifices (199.12–16)? It was obviously seen as a problem that the person to be initiated should be pure from contact with dead bodies when it was explicitly stated that many of the rites were made effective only through the use of dead animals (241.3–5). Iamblichus solved this problem by saying that while dead human bodies should not be touched because they had been carriers of divine life, it was not unholy to touch "other animals" that were dead, since they did not share the "more divine life" (*he theiotera zoe*) (241.16–242.1). A dramatic and crucial difference in status was in this way established between animals and humans.

In this Neoplatonic world view, animal sacrifices became vehicles for human salvation and transcendence. Through them, the soul participated in an extensive cosmological process aimed at divinification and unification (Shaw 1985: 18). Because animals were part of an interconnected universe, the theurgist was able to use their souls as vital principles to further his own ambitions regarding salvation. According to Sallustius, a contemporary of Emperor Julian who wrote a work called *Concerning the Gods and the Universe*, which has been labelled a Neoplatonic catechism, the life of a slain animal worked as an intermediary (*mesotes*) between gods and humans. Sallustius characterized the animals that were sacrificed as copies (*homoiousios*) or imitations (*mimesis*) of the unreasonable life (*alogos zoe*) in humans (*ibid.*: 15). Through the souls of these animals, or rather by means of their vital principles, the theurgist established a link between humans, demons and divinities.

The reason why the vital principle of the animal was able to function as an intermediary (*mesotes*) was that it was similar (*homoia*) to the two elements that it united, the human life on the one hand and the divine life on the other. In this way, the animal sacrifice functioned as a fuse to make the sacrificial system work: "Prayers with sacrifices are animated words, the word giving power to the life and the life animation to the word", writes Sallustius (*Concerning the Gods and the World*, 6). The importance of the sacrifice for the late Neoplatonists, and the fact that in Sallustius' time it was carried out by a select few, causes him to state that "earlier all men sacrificed, now the blessed ones (*eudaimones*) among men are those that sacrifice" (*ibid.*, 16).

Late Neoplatonism was a monistic system with dualistic consequences. In this system, the great existential dividing line was drawn between animals and humans. While the human soul was the lowest of all divine hypostases, which, in a descending hierarchy consisted of gods, archangels, angels, demons, heroes, sublunary archons, material archons and finally the human soul, animals and plants were not conceived of as divine hypostases. Like the human soul, the animal soul was a vital principle, but unlike the human soul, and in a similar way to plants, the animal soul was not rational. Thus the Neoplatonists were eventually converted to the Stoic view (cf. Sorabji 1993: 187).

Theurgy was a development within the Platonic tradition, but a development that on some points was difficult to harmonize with Platonism. This is to be seen especially in relation to the question of animals, where rather curious solutions were produced to ensure that a balanced system emerged. After Iamblichus, there were for instance attempts both to deny that animals had rational souls and simultaneously – à la Plato – to allow them souls. For even if no rational soul inhabited an animal, the animal might be "accompanied" by a rational soul. What this meant is not easy to understand, but it at least ensured that the soul was not directly involved when the animal was sacrificed. This theory, which Richard Sorabji has fittingly labelled a "remote control theory" (ibid.: 188–94), is associated with Porphyry's pupil Theodore of Asine, and later with Sallustius.

The difficulty of preserving the institution of animal sacrifice, for those who believed that human souls could be reincarnated in animals, was also commented on. Who would be comfortable with the thought of a sacrificial ox that might have been the reincarnation of one's late grandfather? To counter this eventuality and save the theory of reincarnation, a rather curious solution was chosen: Iamblichus cites as the teaching of Pythagoras that a human soul never enters an animal that it is lawful to sacrifice (On the Pythagorean Way of Life, 85), thus implying that Pythagoras thought that wild animals, rather than tame ones, could be inhabited by human souls.

What the new theurgical theories about sacrifice had in common with the taurobolium and the mysteries of Mithras was that sacrificial animals had become instruments of human spiritual progress. Thus the animals had been transplanted from an agricultural context into the sphere of initiation and personal transformation. It does not mean that agricultural symbols and meanings were no longer present in these sacrifices, only that these symbols and meanings were now used in a figurative sense.

The transplantation of the animal sacrifice into a context of personal salvation did not do much for the status of the animals involved. The new theurgical sacrificial theory that the late Neoplatonists developed in fact distanced these philosophers and religious innovators from the more animal-friendly views of their predecessors, such as Plutarch, especially, but also Porphyry. In the works of Iamblichus, Sallustius and Proclus that have survived, there is little concern for animals of flesh and blood.

Although it must be added that even if Proclus regarded animal souls as irrational and inferior to human souls, he claimed that animals too can be evil, that is, when they are not true to their kind: "But if an animal becomes a fox instead of a lion, slackening its virile and haughty nature, or if it becomes cowardly instead of bellicose, or if another assumes any other type of life, abandoning the virtue that is naturally fitting to it, they give evidence that in these [beings] too, there is evil" (*On the Existence of Evil*, 25.24–6).

Conclusion

When animals were sacrificed on a farm, the aim of the sacrifice was prosperity for the land and the people. A farmer who sacrificed a lamb wanted his house to be blessed, his flock to thrive and more lambs to be born. In this case, people and animals had some interests and aims in common. When the Greek rhetorician Libanius, who was a pagan but no Neoplatonist, wrote to Theodosius in defence of pagan shrines, which Christian monks were attacking, he described the temples as places in which "farmers have placed their hopes for themselves and their wives and children, for their oxen and for the ground they have sown and planted" (*For the Temples*, 30.10). That animals and humans had a mutual interest in the long-term outcome of the sacrifice was presupposed in the idea of the existence of a sacrificial contract between animals and humans and in the notion that the sacrificial animals were willing victims. Thus the traditional blood sacrifice was part of a cycle of life and death from which both animals and humans were expected to gain something, even if the short-term effect was that one or more animals lost their lives, while humans and gods received these animals as food.

Human domination over animals is often a matter of course. At other times, it is given some justification. James Serpell stresses how in relation to animals, we construct "a defensive screen of lies, myths, distortions and evasions, the sole purpose of which has been to reconcile or nullify the conflict between economic self-interest, on the one hand, and sympathy and affection on the other" (Serpell 1996: 210). In the Graeco-Roman world, his point is illustrated by the way an animal about to be sacrificed had water or flour sprinkled on its head in order to make it nod and thus seemingly consent to its own slaughter.

Mediterranean societies were agricultural, their prosperity rested on farming, and the sacrificial institution was among other things an important link to rural life, a type of life that had been the origin of Rome. One of the sources of Roman greatness was thought to be the harmonious life on the farm. The traditional aims of the sacrifice were prosperity for the land and for those humans and animals who lived on the land. These aims were continued and reinterpreted in new urban and imperial settings, for instance in relation to the revival of religion and the "new age" of Augustus.

The Roman imperial cult was far removed from the simple life on farms. The animals sacrificed in the national temples were bought on the market, the number of sacrifices was legion, and those who paid for the sacrifices as well as the priests and functionaries who carried them out had not necessarily anything to do with farming or animal husbandry. Animal sacrifices in the Graeco-Roman world had always accompanied a wide range of rituals with various intentions and contexts.[12] This is a fact that is supported by Theophrastus' anthropological work about the origin of Greek sacrifices from the fourth century BCE (partly preserved by Porphyry), as well as by Julian's description of sacrifice from the fourth century CE, quoted above. During the empire, sacrifices functioned in complex urban contexts within a vast empire, contexts that gave them and the animals involved new meanings. Sacrifices were generally seen as remedies against evil. These conceptions were linked with the emperor and his family, and with the empire at large. In this way, the institution of the sacrifice was a symbol of the unity of the empire.

The *taurobolium*, the Mithras cult and the theurgical rites were innovations within traditional sacrificial religion. These innovations were supplements that moved the sacrifice towards a new cosmological and soteriological context in which producing symbolic meaning by means of words and images had become important. In this new context, the animal sacrifice developed a prominent salvatory aspect. The animals that were killed – in myths or in reality – were now used instrumentally to serve the salvatory ambitions of the sacrificers. Thus the sacrificial animals were reinvented as symbols, while their function as food was downplayed. This development also implied that humans and animals no longer had mutual interests in relation to the sacrifice, at least not to the same degree that they had before. The aim of human beings was increasingly to escape from the transient earthly sphere of material being and begetting, in other words from the sphere of animals and animal life.

According to late Neoplatonism, with its theurgical world view, the cosmos was created as part of a decline. The superior principle embraced everything but without itself being sullied by the material and sensual parts of creation. Parallel to the decline, a movement upwards took place simultaneously in the cosmos. The theurgical rites of sacrifice contributed to this upward movement by wiping out the material parts of the sacrifice through cleansing fire. Thus animal sacrifice was seen as a model for the way in which the fetters of the soul would finally be stripped away. The animal sacrifice had become an image of the apotheosis of the soul.

The reinterpretation of the blood sacrifice had some negative consequences for real animals, animals of flesh and blood. They were conceived of as beings that existed on a lower level than humans and were devoid of rational souls. Animals were used to characterize the earthly sphere of becoming and begetting, and especially the lower part of twofold human nature. In *Exhortation to Philosophy*, Iamblichus describes that part of a human that is created by the entrance of the soul into matter as "an alien animal" (*allotrion zoon*) and a "many-headed beast" (*polykephalon therion*) (14.15–16).

In spite of a certain innovative power in traditional religion with regard to animal sacrifice, strong forces had meanwhile been working against offerings of animals to the gods. Christians as well as non-Christians wrote against the ancient blood sacrifices. What were their motives? What views on animals do their critical texts reveal?

7

"GOD IS A MAN-EATER": THE ANIMAL SACRIFICE AND ITS CRITICS

The mythic past

According to Graeco-Roman Utopian views, animal sacrifice had not always taken place. Theophrastus' theory about the origin and development of Greek sacrifice was influential. Theophrastus was the leader of the Peripatetic school after Aristotle (372–328 BCE), but Dirk Obbink stresses that like "many pagan philosophers critical of traditional religion, Theophrastus gained abiding credibility in later antiquity" (Obbink 1988: 273). According to Theophrastus, culture and sacrifice developed from simple to increasingly complex and diverse forms, and at the same time their development was part of a process of degeneration. Following Theophrastus closely, Porphyry argued that animal sacrifices were not as ancient as vegetable sacrifices, and he urged people to return to these original cultic practices (*On Abstinence*, 2.27–32). In accordance with Theophrastus, he lists the evolution of sacrifices from offerings of greenstuff, leaves and roots, via grains to cakes, and finally to animals. Like Theophrastus, Porphyry describes the sacrifice of animals as originally caused by famine or other misfortune (*ibid.*, 2.9.1, 2.12.1). Thus offerings of animals did not constitute the original type of sacrifice (2.5–9, 2.12ff; cf. Pliny, *Natural History*, 18.7) but were the event that ended the Golden Age. In accordance with this view, the first offering of an animal was seen as starting a movement downwards.

However, others saw the first animal sacrifice as a positive development at a time when humans had lived like animals.[1] Athenaeus, who in the 190s wrote his long work in fifteen volumes, *Scholars at Dinner*, mentions that with the introduction of sacrifice, "a bestial and lawless life" of cannibalism and other evils had been changed to civilization, cities and cookery (*Scholars at Dinner*, 660e–661c). In this case, the animal sacrifice had initiated culture and human progress, and, above all, had distinguished humans from animals.

There are also examples of the first sacrifices being described as punishment of animals or, alternatively, as their murder. Ovid describes a mythical past when only Italian herbs were burned on the altar – no foreign spices and no animals were in those days offered to the gods (*Fasti*, 1.337–48). According to Ovid, the first animal sacrifices were instituted by the gods themselves to punish individual animals for having uprooted and destroyed the special plants of the gods. Ceres slaughtered a sow because the sow had pulled up "the milky grain in early spring" with its snout, and Bacchus punished a goat that had nibbled at a vine (*Fasti*, 1.349–61). The sacrifice of the sow is described as "the just slaughter of the guilty beast". Alternatively, the first animal sacrifice took place because a human had unlawfully killed an animal. It was not the animal that was to blame but the human who murdered it. Porphyry tells a story about one Dimos, or Sopatros, who had struck down an ox in anger because the ox had eaten some of the cakes he had intended to sacrifice to the gods (*On Abstinence*, 2.29–30). This act was afterwards repeated by the Athenians in a ritual sacrifice. Part of this ritual was a murder trial in which the sacrificial knife finally got the blame and was found guilty of murder.

When, as in these stories, the animal was conceived of either as a culprit or as a victim, the conception of the animal as a free-acting agent was clearly involved. Thus the first animal sacrifice not only divided humans from beasts but also put an end to a time when animals were conceived of as agents in their own right. However, this conception of animals was mainly relegated to mythology and primeval times and was only to a small degree part of the explicit criticism of the animal sacrifice.[2]

Pagan criticism of animal sacrifice

While giving vent to nostalgic feelings for a mythical time when sacrifices were not yet made, pagan authors also criticized animal sacrifice more explicitly. This criticism had several aspects. We will look at Lucian's satirical diatribe, *On Sacrifices*, which is from the early second century, Porphyry's *On Abstinence* from the third century, and some scattered comments in *The History* of Ammianus Marcellinus from the fourth century. They include pagan criticism of blood sacrifice and will be used as *exempli gratia* to get an impression of the directions of this criticism.

Lucian

Lucian's aim in *On Sacrifices* was to make fun of people's anthropomorphic beliefs about the gods and to mock the use of animals for various religious purposes. One of Lucian's complaints is that sacrifices, feasts and processions reveal a low opinion of the gods: "They sell men their blessings, and from them one can buy health, it may be, for a calf, wealth for four oxen, a royal throne for a hundred, a safe return from Troy to Pylos for nine bulls, and a fair voyage from Aulis to Troy for a king's daughter!" (2). By using everyday examples as well as classical ones from Homer, Lucian illustrates that the *do-ut-des* aspect of the sacrificial business, especially that gods could be bribed, is not according to his taste.

The cruder aspect of the gods' gains is not to Lucian's liking either: "If anybody sacrifices, they [i.e. the gods] all have a feast, opening their mouths for the smoke and drinking the blood that is spilt at the altars, just like flies; but if they dine at home, their meal is nectar and ambrosia" (9; cf. *Icaromenippus*, 27). The comparison between gods and flies is not flattering to the Olympians. A similar image is known from Babylonian literature, where it is used to illustrate how the gods were attracted to the first sacrifice made after the flood. Such an image also has a factual basis. An animal sacrifice, with its butchery, blood and carcasses, must obviously have attracted not only gods but also masses of flies. Flies did not usually behave as Aelian says they did in Olympia at the time of the feast and sacrifices to Zeus: "In spite of the quality of sacrifices, of blood shed, and of meat hung up, the flies voluntarily disappear and cross to the opposite bank of the Alpheus" (Aelian, 5.17; cf. Pausanias, 5.14.1). The fact that Aelian mentions this strange behaviour of the flies underlines that they could be troublesome when a sacrifice was performed.

The bloody and messy parts of the sacrifice, not shown in the official art of the empire, are elaborated upon by Lucian. He is ironic about the fact that those who participate in sacrifices are supposed to be clean at the same time as "the priest himself stands there all bloody, just like the Cyclops of old, cutting up the victim, removing the entrails, plucking out the heart, pouring the blood about the altar, and doing everything possible in the way of piety" (13). This was a common criticism of the sacrificial business – that there was a glaring contrast between means and purpose. How could one expect to reach divinity and elevated spirituality through slaughter and bloody materiality?

Only briefly, in passing, is the animal's own situation commented upon, when Lucian says that it is slaughtered "under the god's eyes, while it bellows plaintively – making, we must suppose, auspicious sounds, and fluting low music to accompany the sacrifice!" (12). Lucian mentions that the Egyptians mourn over the sacrificial victim (15), but this custom he finds equally foolish and as ludicrous as the worship of theriomorphic gods and of the god Apis in the shape of a bull (*ibid.*, 15).

Lucian's criticism of animal sacrifice is made primarily because of the anthropomorphic and rather base view of the gods that it presupposes and secondarily because of the stupidity of the humans who treat gods in this way. The sacrifice is seen as demeaning to the gods as well as for men. The only creature whose role is left almost uncommented on is the sacrificial victim. Lucian makes only an ironic comment on behalf of the sacrificial animals. His intention was to criticize the role that animals played in religion because it was demeaning to gods and men. He shows no remorse for the sacrificial victim. This lack of compassion reflects a common attitude to sacrificial animals during the empire. Compassion for the victims is seldom used as an argument against animal sacrifice.

Porphyry

Another critic of animal sacrifice was Porphyry, who wrote at the end of the third century. *On Abstinence* was written to Firmus Castricius, as already stated a lapsed vegetarian, to get him back on the vegetarian track. The work consists of four books, which cover diet, vegetarianism, animal sacrifice, the general status of animals, men's treatment of them, and finally how they were treated by other nations. Porphyry uses ancient sources extensively and borrows arguments from among others Theophrastus and Plutarch, whom he reproduces verbally or paraphrases. Porphyry's opponents are Epicureans, Stoics and Peripatetics – philosophical schools whose representatives had written in defence of flesh eating – but also individuals, such as a man called Clodius the Neopolitan. Porphyry does not mention Christians.

Book 1 ends with a similar puzzle to that which Iamblichus later presented (see Chapter 6), although Porphyry's solution was different: why, if abstinence from animal food contributes to purity, do people kill sheep and cattle in sacrifices "and reckon this rite to be holy and pleasing to the gods?" (1.57.4).

Porphyry discusses the problem of sacrifices in Book 2. His initial argument is that even if animals are sacrificed, this does not mean that it is necessary to eat them. This argument is obviously crucial for Porphyry, and he returns to it repeatedly. It simply does not follow that because it is proper to sacrifice animals, it is also necessary to feed on them (2.2.1–2; cf. 2.4.1, 2.44.1, 2.53.3, 2.57.3). Another of Porphyry's points is that even if some animals must be destroyed because of their savagery (*agrion*), it does not follow that domesticated animals should also be killed (2.4.2). A third point is that even if some people need to eat meat, such as athletes, soldiers, people who work with their bodies and even rhetors, it does not follow that philosophers too should eat meat (1.27.1, 2.4.3). It is quite clear that Porphyry's opposition to eating meat and sacrifices was not aimed at everyone but at professional philosophers who pondered the deeper questions of life and death and the right way to live and behave (1.27.2, 2.3.1)

Characteristic of Porphyry are the distinctions he makes with regard to his subject: he distinguishes between sacrifice and eating, between a wild animal (*agrios*) and a domestic one (*hemeros*), and between those who need to eat meat and those who do not. In some ways, this is an "animal-friendly" text – Porphyry's views are informed by compassion towards his fellow creatures, at least some of them. For instance, one of his objections to sacrificing animals is that it hurts the animal (2.12.3) and that an injustice is done to it when its soul is taken from it (2.12.4). Another argument, which shows his esteem for animals, is that it is wrong to kill for sacrifice an animal that had done humans no wrong (2.24.2).

However, while Porphyry appears to be "animal-friendly", his views are governed by an urge to make distinctions between types of animal, and even more, between types of human. Porphyry uses animals and people's cultic relationship to them as criteria for creating hierarchies based on the state of people's intellectual, philosophical and religious insights. While this text is "the most comprehensive and subtly reasoned treatment of vegetarianism by an ancient philosopher" (Dombrowski 1987: 777), it is also a perfect illustration of how to make distinctions between oneself and others, using animals to reach this goal. The text reflects a conflict between achieving excellence (*arete*) and humanity (*humanitas*) and is a recipe for becoming the best human being possible. To put it more bluntly, it implies the establishment of a superior elite consisting of philosophers. In Book 4, Porphyry concentrates on different spiritual elites – for instance, Egyptian priests, Jewish Essenes, Indian Brahmins and worshippers of Mithras – and on the way they practised abstinence from eating meat.

Porphyry distinguishes between people in two directions. There is an external division between those who are within Roman law and those who have put themselves outside this law, as well as internal divisions between different groups within this law. Animals are used to illustrate both types of distinction.

The division between those who are inside and those who are outside is described as the difference between domestic animals and wild animals. Porphyry, probably quoting Theophrastus, defends the right "to exterminate those of the irrational animals that are unjust [*adikia*] by nature and evil-doers [*kakopoia*] and impelled by their nature to harm those who come near them" (2.22.2). He compares these animals with human evil-doers, who must also be exterminated and punished. The relationship to justice encompasses animals and humans that do not harm each other. It does not include creatures – either human or animal – that according to Porphyry are harmful and evil by nature (2.23.3; cf. 3.26.2–4).

When Porphyry is talking about wild animals, he recalls an argument that goes back at least as far as Democritus (b. 460–457 BCE). Democritus considered that, like some humans, some animals were capable of injustice and for that reason ought to be conceived of as enemies and treated – like human enemies – in accordance with justice and the law. Apparently, Democritus did not draw a major boundary between men and beasts. In the case of Porphyry, however, he is concerned not only with how wild beasts should be treated but also with the treatment of human enemies. It appears that wild animals are not much like humans, as some humans are like wild animals. Accordingly, Porphyry is "animalizing" some humans rather than "humanizing" all animals.

"Wild animals" is a broad term that could cover all individuals that act outside the law. Among such people were the Christians. They are not mentioned in *On Abstinence*, but they were the target of other works by Porphyry. He even wrote a special work that dealt with them – *Against the Christians*. This work no longer exists, but it is known from refutations of it by Christian authors (Barnes 1994: 53–5). From these references, it seems that Porphyry regarded the Christians as having set themselves outside the law. Christianity was *religio illicita* – an illegal religion. For instance, according to Eusebius' *Ecclesiastical History*, Porphyry characterized Origen's manner of life as "Christian and illegal" (*paranomos*) (6.19.7; see also *Preparation for the Gospel*, 1.2.2–4). Some lines earlier, Eusebius refers to Porphyry as saying that the famous Alexandrian philosopher Ammonius Saccas converted to paganism from being a Christian and in this way changed his way of life in conformity with the laws (6.19.7). With these examples, Porphyry clearly indicated that Christians were lawless creatures and that it was just to punish them for their beliefs (Barnes 1994: 65).

With this in mind, Porphyry's views on "wild animals" in *On Abstinence* must not be read in isolation. They were part of a more comprehensive world view, a world view that he shared with his contemporaries. Part of it was dependent on ideas that went back through the centuries to Plutarch and to Theophrastus before him, and even to Democritus. Wild animals should be prevented from doing harm and ought to be killed. Humans were fighting a just war against them. Because of a general agreement on how to treat wild animals, when people were compared to "wild animals" there was a persuasive power in this label that should not be missed.[3]

Porphyry's sympathy for animals was restricted to domestic animals and excluded their wild cousins, which he regarded as evil by nature. But domestic animals also were part of Porphyry's boundary-making activities. Like other Neoplatonists, Porphyry felt obliged to voice a certain support for animal sacrifice. He tried to promote an ideal spiritual religion while not totally condemning the traditional sacrificial religion, even as he criticized it. By introducing a hierarchy of divine beings, cultic acts and human worshippers, Porphyry attempted to combine the religion of the spiritual elite with the religion of the common people.

At the top of Porphyry's cosmological hierarchy was the highest god, who was pure spirit and had no need of material sacrifices. Porphyry argues that only spiritual sacrifices were appropriate for the highest god – a pure soul, the elevation of the mind (2.34.2–3; also 2.37.1). Below the highest god rank the intelligible gods. They should be worshipped with hymn singing and fine thoughts (2.34.4–5). Then come the other gods, the cosmos, and the fixed and wandering stars – they should be offered sacrifices of inanimate things (2.37.3) – and, finally, the good and evil *daimones* (2.37.4–2.42). In Porphyry's thought, the evil *daimones* "rejoice in the 'drink-offerings and smoking meat' on which their pneumatic part grows fat, for it lives on vapours and exhalations, in a complex fashion and from complex sources, and it draws power from the smoke that rises from blood and flesh" (2.42.3). Porphyry explicitly warns against drawing such beings to oneself (2.43.1) and adds: "If it is necessary for cities to appease even these beings that is nothing to do with us" (2.43.2). These "gods" can only provide things that

Porphyry and his fellow philosophers do not need and that they even despise. Material gods want material sacrifices, while non-material gods want spiritual sacrifices (cf. Iamblichus, *On the Egyptian Mysteries*, 5.14). But even if Porphyry is rather negative about animal sacrifice in *On Abstinence*, Eusebius points out that Porphyry claimed that sacrifices should also be made to the ethereal and heavenly forces (*Preparation for the Gospel*, 4.8). Eusebius agrees that there is an ambivalence in Porphyry's treatment of sacrifices. In *On Abstinence*, Porphyry does his utmost to distance himself and the spiritual elite from that type of sacrifice and from the evil demons that are supported by these sacrifices. All the same, he grants that most people and even cities may have to worship these beings by means of sacrifices. In other words, he reluctantly has to admit that it is sometimes necessary to sacrifice animals (2.44.1).

Since Porphyry is of the opinion that it is sometimes necessary to sacrifice animals but is adamant that it is not necessary to eat them (2.44.1), an ordinary sacrifice becomes similar to a sacrifice performed to drive away evil – an apotropaic sacrifice – in which the victim is never eaten. Traditionally, it was only a small part of the sacrifices that was not eaten. They were made to the gods of the underworld, conceived of as polluting, and accordingly they were called "sacrifices not tasted" (*thysiai ageustoi*) (van Straten 1995: 3). If Porphyry wanted blood sacrifices to be made but did not want the slaughtered animals to be eaten, he really was making all animal sacrifices apotropaic and putting all gods on a par with the gods of the underworld. Porphyry himself explicitly draws a parallel between the traditional alimentary sacrifice and the apotropaic sacrifice (2.44.2), with the result that all eating of meat taken from sacrificial animals was seen as leading to contamination (*miasma*) (2.31.2, 2.50.1). In this way, animal sacrifice was defined as the custom of people who lacked spiritual insight, and it was effectively made into a cultural dividing line between the spiritual elite and the masses (*hoi polloi*) (cf. 1.52.3–4).

How did Porphyry really regard animals? On the one hand, he recognizes that animals are part of the common household of living beings (*oikeiosis*) (1.4.2) and that there is a relationship between animals and humans (2.22.1–2). On the other hand, central to Porphyry's deliberations concerning animals and their status was the question of abstinence from meat, a question that is closely connected to cultural and ritual pollution and purity and that necessarily included a discussion of the traditional animal sacrifice. The title of the work is *peri apokhes empsykhon*, "On abstinence from animates", i.e. from creatures with soul. This title is frequently interpreted as "abstinence from killing animals", which is misleading. The "abstinence" is probably a reference to eating the meat of these animals rather than to killing them. Remember, the treatise was written to turn Castricius away from his meat eating.[4] The question of whether one should eat meat probably has higher priority in this text than the question of whether one should kill animals or not. Porphyry has frequently been depicted as opposed to killing animals. This is incorrect. Porphyry spoke against killing domestic animals, not against killing animals in general. On the contrary, he defended people's right to kill animals that were seen as dangerous.

His preoccupation with eating also implies that Porphyry's motivation for discussing animals was not primarily his regard for animals but his regard for human purity. Also, when he presents wild animals as beings that it is just to kill, it must be noted that he is referring to carnivores. Such animals are not only dangerous to humans, they also subsist on a diet that, in Porphyry's view, would have been polluting.

When Porphyry repeats the Pythagorean argument that friendliness towards animals promotes humanity and pity, while slaughtering them nourishes the murderous and bestial aspects of man (3.20.6–7), he is paraphrasing Plutarch's *On the Cleverness of Animals* (3.20.7–3.24.5 = *Moralia* 959e–963f). Porphyry's reflections reveal both that humans had the highest priority and that their relationship to animals is viewed with regard to its effect on their spiritual progress. Thus the ultimate reason for treating animals in a just and friendly way is that it improves human nature.

In traditional religion, those who were masters of sacrifices, who were able to kill most animals and distribute most meat, had the highest status. The exaggerated sacrifices offered by some of the emperors are cases in point. When Porphyry and his Neoplatonic colleagues made purity their chief symbolic capital, they were introducing an alternative religious value system in which religious power was gained according to rules other than the traditional ones.

Porphyry speaks academically and reasonably about animals, but his passions do not seem to be aroused as, for instance, Plutarch's passions were when he discussed vegetarianism, especially when Plutarch spoke through the snout of Gryllus and made the pig his mouthpiece. Porphyry seems more involved when he is talking about meat, carcasses, entrails and the unhappy souls of slaughtered animals who are roaming about near the place where they were brutally murdered (2.47–50) than when he is bestowing internal and external reason on these creatures. Porphyry uses to a high degree parts of texts from other authors, but his context is not necessarily the same. Dirk Obbink has pointed out that while Theophrastus' purpose in *On Piety* was to find the most appropriate way of honouring the gods, Porphyry used his theory about the origin of culture and sacrifice in a different project, as a theoretical basis in his defence of vegetarianism (Obbink 1988: 273).

What is an animal? Porphyry does not give a clear answer. In some ways, he put animals and humans on a par with each other. He points to the similarities in the physical equipment of humans and animals, he compares the killing of sacrificial animals with the killing of humans, and he likens the eating of animal meat to the eating of human meat. Porphyry does at least grant animals rationality and language. But animals are less rational than humans, reincarnation does not take place across the human–animal barrier, and animals do not seem to be capable of spiritual salvation. Consequently, they are different from humans on the points that really matter.

Individual animals are seldom referred to in the text. The sole animal that is directly connected with Porphyry is a tame partridge, which he mentions in passing that he had once reared in Carthage (3.4.7). In *On Abstinence*, animals are usually described in groups: wild animals, which ought to be killed; tame animals, which should neither be killed nor eaten; polluting bestial bodies, which should not be touched; and unhappy bodiless souls, which are used in divination but otherwise ought to be shunned. The impression is given that pollution and danger are more important in relation to animals than their rationality and friendliness. Accordingly, Porphyry's main incentive seems less to be friendliness towards animals than avoidance of human impurity (4.20).

Ammianus Marcellinus and Julian

Ammianus Marcellinus was a Greek (born in Syria or Phoenicia) who wrote in Latin.[5] He touches on the subject of sacrifice only briefly in his biography of Julian. Although Ammianus comments on animal sacrifices only in passing, his views are interesting because he comments on an emperor who revived sacrificial practices, and is a pagan who is sympathetic to Julian but all the same has a negative attitude towards the sacrificial practices of the emperor.[6] Ammianus contrasts excessive offerings of animals with piety and true religiosity and is critical of sacrificial "overkill".

According to Ammianus, Julian "drenched the altars with the blood of an excessive number of victims, sometimes offering up a hundred oxen at once, together with countless flocks of various other animals, and white birds hunted out by land and sea" (*The History*, 22.12.6). Ammianus adds that the emperor's soldiers "gorged themselves on the abundance of meat" and because of their eating and drinking of wine, almost every day had to be carried to their quarters by passers-by. When Ammianus sums up the qualities and faults of the emperor, he characterizes Julian as superstitious rather than truly religious, because "he sacrificed innumerable victims without regard to cost, so that one might believe that if he had returned from the Parthians, there would soon have been a scarcity of cattle" (25.4.17).

This account leaves us with the impression that ritual butchering was no longer conceived of as a pious religious act – at least not when it was performed on an excessive scale. Ammianus stresses as censurable both the great number of victims and the overeating that was the result of this excessive killing. Pierre Chuvin comments that Julian's pagan restoration and attempt to reintroduce the sacrificial cult suffered from "a secularization of butchering" (Chuvin 1990: 48). In the late fourth century, when Ammianus wrote, excesses in sacrifices were by many simply not regarded as *comme il faut*.

146

However, it should be added that Julian may have based his sacrificial practices on Neoplatonic tradition, as Glen Bowersock (1978) and recently Nicole Belayche (2002) have pointed out. Bowersock points to Sallustius' "little catechism of popular Neo-Platonism" as "the best guide to the religion which Julian sought to establish in his empire" (Bowersock 1978: 86). Julian's restoration of cultic forms, his frequent sacrifices (especially divinatory) and his performing sacrifices in person as a *victimarius* were means to communicate directly with the divine and to partake in the movement upwards. In this way, Julian attached new meanings to civic sacrifices.

Julian is aware of the critical Neoplatonic attitudes towards sacrifice and asks: "Are not fruits pure, whereas meat is full of blood and of much else that offends eye and ear? But most important of all is it not the case that, when one eats fruit nothing is hurt, while the eating of meat involves the sacrifice and slaughter of animals who naturally suffer pain and torment?" (*Hymn to the Mother of the Gods*, 174a–174b). Like Plutarch and Porphyry, Julian is aware of the suffering of animals, but like Iamblichus and Sallustius he regards it as necessary to use their life and blood as a means of lifting the souls of humans towards the sublunar gods (Belayche 2002: 119–24).

It must also be mentioned that in the *Hymn to the Mother of the Gods*, Julian discusses which type of food is appropriate for "he who longs to take flight upwards and to mount aloft above the atmosphere of ours, even to the highest peaks of heaven" (177b). According to Julian, he would "rather pursue and follow after things that tend upwards towards the air, and strive to the utmost height, and, if I may use a poetic phrase, look upward to the skies. Birds, for example, we may eat, except only those few which are commonly held sacred, and ordinary four-footed animals, except the pig" (177b). The reason why the pig is excepted is that "this animal does not look up at the sky, not only because it has no such desire, but because it is so made that it can never look upwards" (177c). Both its internal constitution and external anatomy make the pig a sign of those elements in the world that do not tend upwards, and therefore the pig is useless as a sacrifice.

The case of Julian illustrates conflicting views of sacrifice in the late fourth century. It also illustrates a combination of a civic model of sacrifice and a soteriological model. According to Ammianus Marcellinus, exaggerated sacrifices are improper religious acts, but Julian himself seems to have given traditional sacrifices an added theurgical explanation and thereby a new meaning. According to this explanation, communication with the gods was connected to an upward movement in which many things in the world participated. The pious soul took part in this movement, above all by sacrificing animals.

The Christian polemic

The opposition to animal sacrifice, as exemplified by Lucian, Porphyry and Ammianus Marcellinus, was aimed at several targets, and to a different extent in the different authors: the anthropomorphic view of the gods that this sacrifice presupposed; the false idea that the gods needed sacrifices; the simple *do-ut-des* thinking; the uncleanness that the handling of the dead bodies of animals implied; the excesses in the number of animals offered to the gods; and the overeating that was sometimes involved. This opposition shows greater concern for the negative influence of animal sacrifice on humans than for the animals that were killed.

Christian opposition was similar to that of the authors we have examined. However, unlike the pagan criticism, the Christian polemic against blood sacrifices was presented in an apologetic context and was an ingredient in standard Christian counterattacks against paganism. The apologetic context gave the Christian opposition a few significant additional arguments in relation to those of the pagans. For example, where pagan authors went only part of the way in demonizing the former gods, the Christians went the whole hog. In Christian thinking, pagan gods were systematically reinvented as evil demons, and blood sacrifices were seen as serving the purpose of providing food for these evil beings (Athenagoras, *A Plea for the Christians*, 26–7; Origen, *Exhortation to Martyrdom*, 45). Another difference was that the Christians not only spiritualized the sacrifice, as we have seen that some of the pagan elite had also done, the Christians substituted the human body for the animal body, especially the master body of Christ. In this way, they continued the Graeco-Roman sacrificial discourse, but they also combined it with the spiritualizing and personalizing religious trends that were characteristic of these centuries and thus gave it a special Christian formulation.

Pagans accused Christians for not sacrificing, while Christians on their side used pagan arguments against animal sacrifices. Aryeh Kofsky has described how church historian Eusebius refutes "the two major arguments concerning sacrifices: that Christians did not offer sacrifices, and that they thereby contradicted their claim to follow the patriarchs" (Kofsky 2000: 123). In *The Preparation for the Gospel*, Eusebius based his critiques of sacrifice on Porphyry's view that the development of sacrifice was a symptom of the degeneration of mankind and that spiritual sacrifices were the most worthy. According to Eusebius, Christians offered sacrifice in the form of the sacrament of the Eucharist, which commemorated the sacrifice of the blood and body of Christ and was thus the only true and perfect sacrifice. When the patriarchs offered animal sacrifices, these sacrifices were ransoms for their own lives and prefigurations of the sacrifice of Christ (see *ibid.*: 118–23).

The Christian polemic against animal sacrifice was not aimed against slaughtering animals but against a pagan practice directed to gods in whom the Christians did not believe. With a few exceptions, Christian polemicists were no more interested than pagans in the inherent value of sacrificial animals, and it was not usually sympathy towards animals that motivated them. However, there are exceptions, notably that of Arnobius from Sicca.

In addition to Arnobius' *Against the Gentiles* from the turn of the fourth century, we take as our examples of Christian criticism Tertullian's *Apologeticus* from the turn of the third century and the *Gospel of Philip* from the third century.

Tertullian

In the *Apologeticus*, the work that he wrote in defence of Christianity and also apparently in defence of religious tolerance, Tertullian had few inhibitions in praising the excellence of Christianity in relation to all other religions (Stroumsa 1998). With blunt directness and in his usual ironic way, Tertullian contrasts pagan and Christian worship:

> Let one man worship God, another Jove; let this man raise suppliant hands to heaven, that man to the altar of Fides; let one (if you so suppose) count the clouds as he prays, another the panels of the ceiling; let one dedicate his own soul to his god, another a goat's.
>
> (*Apologeticus*, 24.5)

If sacrifices are about dedication of souls and personal relationships between a human being and the divine, it is easy to see that the soul of a goat ranks low compared with the soul of a man. We must also remember that in his discussion of reincarnation, Tertullian made an absolute distinction between human souls and animal souls. Tertullian neither respected the souls of goats nor found much of interest in an ox about to be sacrificed, describing it as "a worthless ox longing to die" (*ibid.*, 30.6).

The Christian opposition to animal sacrifices often took the form of a polemic of polarities. While Tertullian contrasts the soul of man with that of a goat, Lactantius, for instance, writes that "God does not desire the sacrifice of a dumb animal, nor of death and blood, but of man and life" (*The Divine Institutes*, 6.24), Prudentius contrasts the worship of Christ with "those who offer rotting entrails to carved stones" (*Against Symmachus*, 2.779–80), while John Chrysostom contrasts the spiritual lamb of the Christians with the dumb beast of the pagans (Clark 1999: 210). In this polemic, there is a downgrading of animals in relation to humans, and clear attempts are made to exclude them from the religious discourse as something foreign to the divine world.

The Gospel of Philip

A Christian text that comments more directly on the differences between Christian and pagan sacrifice is the *Gospel of Philip*, which was found at Nag Hammadi in Egypt in 1945. It is a collection of statements about sacraments probably for the benefit of those who were about to undergo the Christian initiation ritual of baptism. It was probably composed in the third century.

In this Coptic text, "animal" (*therion*) is used as a negative designation and appears as a key metaphor. The text's basic view of animals is similar to the view we have met in Origen's *Against Celsus*, and it also has much in common with the Stoic view. Man controls animals and has a hidden superiority to them (60:15–23; 64:12–22). However, the author is less interested in the differences between humans and real animals than he is in using animal metaphors to describe the differences between human beings. For human beings may also appear as animals: for a human to be an animal means that he or she is a pagan and/or lacks spiritual knowledge. The text puts it rather sharply: "there are many animals in the world which are in human form" (81:1–7). To go through baptism and become a Christian implies passing from a bestial state to full humanity.

The *Gospel of Philip* reveals a special interest in animal sacrifices. They are part of the pagan ritual system, which the Christian sacramental system is competing with. Animal sacrifices are seen as having been invented to enslave humans and make them worship powers that are not real gods. The text says explicitly that those to whom animals were sacrificed "were not gods" (63:5; cf. Tertullian, *Apologeticus*, 10.2). On the contrary, these powers are themselves animals. As the text puts it: "Indeed the animals were the ones to whom they sacrificed" (55:1–2).

Animal sacrifices actually prevent humans from being saved, and therefore they ideally suit the powers that originally invented these sacrifices. In contrast, when men have become Christians, they will no longer slaughter animals in honour of these powers (54:32–55:1). The change from animal sacrifice to human symbolic sacrifice is commented upon in a suggestive way:

> God is a man-eater. For this reason men are [sacrificed] to him.
> Before men were sacrificed, animals were being sacrificed, since
> those to whom they were sacrificed were not gods.
>
> (*Gospel of Philip*, 62:35–63:5)

Seldom is the Christian variation and continuity of the Roman sacrificial culture characterized more bluntly: the Christian god is not fed by animals but by humans. In the saying that "God is a man-eater" (Coptic, *pnoute ouamrome pe*), the implications of the Christian discourse on sacrifice are given radical expression when human bodies fully replace animal bodies. This man-eating god is launched as a contrast to the powers that were nourished by animal sacrifices (cf. Tertullian, *Scorpiace*, 7). And in contrast to the animals that were offered up to God alive and then died, man is offered up to God dead and then lives (55:3–5). Behind this antithesis lies the idea that humans are spiritually born through baptism and through baptism will receive true life. The old sacrifice of killing animals is contrasted with baptism, which is described as an offering up to God of the one who is baptized. Through the sacrifice, he/she receives life.

Animals and humans are on a different level, but it is only through the ritual of baptism that humans become "real" humans. Pagans remain animals. To be an animal implies not being fully alive. According to the *Gospel of Philip*, a Gentile does not die, because he has never lived, so that he can die (52:15–17).

To sum up the teaching about animals and humans in the *Gospel of Philip*: There are animals of flesh and blood, animals in human form, gods who are characterized as animals, and finally humans who have no bestial traits. Behind this complex use of the term "animal" lies a conception of animals as standing on a lower existential level than humans and as being fundamentally different from humans, a traditionally Stoic conception. The animal/human opposition is a matrix for polar opposition, which encompasses opposition between contrasting types of human as well as between contrasting types of god. But even if the author of the *Gospel of Philip* uses several images taken from animal husbandry and seems to be familiar with that sort of life, he shows little concern for real animals. As he concentrates on the differences between humans who are living like beasts and those who are fully human, the designation "animal" in this text is mainly used as a metaphor.

Arnobius

A more concerned view of animals is found in Arnobius, the converted Christian and teacher of rhetoric from Sicca in North Africa, who wrote a work in seven volumes titled *Against the Gentiles*. This is a defence of Christianity as well as an attack on paganism. Arnobius is one of the few authors, either pagan or Christian, who bases his opposition to animal sacrifice partly on pity for animals. Influences from Plutarch and Porphyry are clearly visible.

Animals figure prominently in *Against the Gentiles*. Arnobius uses them as examples to illustrate his points and sometimes to ridicule his opponents' views. Arnobius, apparently, sees animals in a positive light. But even if he pities them and seems genuinely concerned about their sufferings, his understanding of animals is similar to that of the *Gospel of Philip*. Certainly, Arnobius stresses that humans are enrolled among the animals, that they have physical features similar to those of animals, and even that the souls of the wicked pass into cattle and other beasts after death (2.16), but Arnobius makes these points to show that the soul of a human being is not created divine and filled with knowledge. In Volume 2, he concentrates on a refutation of such views. It is also important for Arnobius to make clear that even if animals and humans have a similar origin as creatures of nature, the goal of humans is not to remain on the animal level but to acquire knowledge of the Supreme God (2.61) and of Christ, who is the true divinity. If a human being does not learn human ways and become educated, he will always remain similar to a beast (2.19–25).

Volume 7 is especially dedicated to a criticism of animal sacrifice. According to Arnobius, animal sacrifices presuppose gods who are anthropomorphic, and rather on the childish and cruel side at that (cf. Volume 3). Arnobius criticizes the view that gods are nourished (*alere*) on the sacrifices (7.3), that they are given pleasure (*voluptas*) by them (7.4), that they are appeased (*placare*) by them (7.5–8) and that they are honoured (*honorare*) through them (7.13–15). These views imply that gods are human, moody and can be bribed, and that they rejoice in honours that humans confer upon them. Arnobius has nothing but scorn for those who hold such views about the gods.

But Arnobius does not restrict himself to the accusation of anthropomorphism on the part of the gods; he also has something to say on behalf of the animals that are sacrificed and writes against the cruelty and injustice done to them (8.9). His most original move is to bestow a human voice on an ox and let it utter its complaint against the unfairness involved in its killing.[7] In short, the main arguments of the ox are that it is unfair to sacrifice it to placate the gods because of sins committed by humans, that it does not commit sins as humans do, and that there are basic similarities between cattle and human beings. Those similarities include a common breath of life, common senses, common bodily features, for instance the same number of limbs, love for its offspring, and the necessity of carnal union to bring forth human as well as animal offspring. Finally, the ox suggests that it too is a rational being and that the sounds it utters in reality constitute a language. In this way, it claims for itself what the Stoics, and usually also the Christians, restricted to humans, *logos endiathetos* and *logos prophorikos* – internal and external reason. The ox ends its speech with a plea to Jupiter in which it describes the acts of the sacrificers in terms that stress that these acts are bestial and savage – terms that are usually applied to the behaviour of beasts:

> Is not this, then, bestial [*ferus*], monstrous [*immanis*], savage [*saevus*], does it not seem to thee, O Jupiter, unjust [*iniuste*] and barbarous [*barbarus*] for me to be killed, for me to be slain, that thou mightest be appeased and that acquittal rest on the guilty?
>
> (*ibid.*, 7.9)

Michael Bland Simmons has recently shown that Arnobius was partly dependent on Porphyry in his views of animals and in his criticism of the animal sacrifice (Simmons 1995). Simmons points out that Arnobius used inconsistencies in Porphyry's views on the subject of sacrifice to target this anti-Christian Neoplatonist. He has further argued that *Against the Gentiles* was written as a reaction to Diocletian's persecution. The fact that Arnobius devoted thirty-two chapters of Volume 7 to attacking sacrifices is seen by Simmons as evidence that forcing Christians to sacrifice was a contemporary issue in North Africa when Arnobius was writing (*ibid.*: 88).

If this is the case, which seems likely, it gives a new dimension to the way Arnobius uses sacrificial animals. But the argument can be taken further. Is Arnobius' opposition to sacrifices, and also the sympathy he has for the ox, inspired by the fate of the Christian martyrs? It is not unreasonable to presume that Arnobius' pity for the ox may have been given special impetus by being based on an identification between the lot of sacrificial animals and that of Christian martyrs. This means that when he gave a human voice to the beast so that it could air its grievances to its tormentors, we are also listening, through the mouth of the ox, to an argument on behalf of Christian martyrs who like this ox were innocently slain. Arnobius refers to the martyrs several times in his work (1.26; 1.65; 2.5; 2.77ff; 3.36; 4.36; 5.29; 6.27).

In the passage referred to above, the fact that Arnobius wrote on behalf of the sacrificial animal does not mean that he thought animals were on the same level as humans. For besides the passage in which the ox appears as the tragic hero, there is also a passage in Volume 7 where Arnobius clearly uses animals in a *reductio ad absurdum* argument. And while the example of the ox was intended to awaken the pity of his audience, the second example was meant to ridicule pagan religion. In this second example, Arnobius conjures up an assembly of dogs, asses, pigs and small birds. He gives the animals the role of sacrificers, while humans are given the role of gods. Then Arnobius lists what sort of "sacrifices" these "gods" would have received from their "worshippers" (cf. 3.16) and asks his opponents what they would have thought about the beasts' effort to placate them:

> Would you consider it a compliment or rather a plain insult, if the swallows slaughtered and dedicated to you flies, wagtails, ants; if the asses were to place hay on your altars and pour out libations of chaff; if the dogs placed bones there and burned human excrement at your shrines; if, finally, the dear little pigs were to pour out the mire taken from their horrid wallows and from dirty mudholes?
>
> (*ibid.*, 7.17)

Arnobius' point is that the bodies of sacrificed bulls are to gods as the hay of the asses and the bones of the dogs are to humans. In this way, he wants to reveal the absurdity of sacrificing what is pleasing and agreeable to oneself to beings that are far superior. The example also shows that there is a gulf between animals and humans similar to the gulf between humans and God.

But in spite of the existence of this gulf, it is undoubtedly true that Arnobius shows pity for animals. He speaks for instance of sacrificial animals as "harmless creatures" (*innoxia animantia*; 7.14); as bellowing piteously (*miserabilis*) and pitifully giving up their spirit (7.4); and he calls them "the unhappy race of animals" (*infeliccimum animalium genus*). He tentatively characterizes the men who eat them as "half-savage" (*semiferi*) but finally settles for labelling them "savage" (*feri*) (7.4). Arnobius also paints in dark colours the nauseous stench from the sacrificial pyre and the impurity and pollution involved in the whole sacrificial business (7.15–16; cf. 7.12).

His compassionate attitude towards animals may be due to Neoplatonic influence – on this point, Arnobius is a worthy heir of Plutarch and Porphyry. But unlike the Platonists, he did not regard human souls as originally created immortal and with knowledge. On this point, animals and humans were in the same situation. Accordingly, the similarities that this rhetorician from North Africa saw between humans and animals are partly motivated by his opposition to the Platonic doctrine of the pre-existence of the soul and partly related to the situation during the persecution of Diocletian, when Christians were being slaughtered like sacrificial beasts. Consequently, Arnobius pities animals, identifies with them up to a point but feels that the human goal is not to remain with the animals but to realize true humanity, which means becoming Christian.

The end of sacrifice

The non-Christian and Christian critics of the animal sacrifices used similar arguments. Underlying these arguments was a notion of animal sacrifices as being out of place. The agricultural context in which blood sacrifices had originally developed was obviously no longer sufficient to justify convincingly the maintenance of this bloody cult. Arnobius, for instance, rattles off a whole string of wild animals and carnivores as well as birds that could have been sacrificed and asks why these creatures are not just as effective as those that are usually offered to the gods (7.16). The fact that such an argument could be put forward shows that the agricultural context of the sacrifice was no longer taken for granted or thought to be especially important.

At the end of the fourth century, animal sacrifices were banned by Theodosius I – not because he or his Christian subjects were opposed to killing animals but because killing animals in a ritual religious context was regarded from then on as a significant characteristic of pagan religion and for that reason had to be terminated. When animal sacrifice was banned, it was because the religious focus had moved to other types of religious practice that were more in line with the needs of individuals and society, and with the requirements of the state.

Like pagan civic religion, Christianity was an urban religion (Meeks 1983). Urban Christians explicitly labelled any non-Christian a pagan (*paganus*, meaning one who lives in the countryside). In this terminology, there is an opposition between the Christian city-dwellers and pagans, who lived in the countryside and backwaters of the empire.[8] In *Civitate Dei*, "The City of God", Augustine introduced *civitas* as the archetype for the Christian society.

In pagan religion, and through the animal sacrifice, the economy, animal husbandry and the business of the state had been intertwined. When, in the fourth century, the emperor and the state embraced the new Christian religion and its rituals, the religious and secular powers exerted their grip more directly on the identities and minds of human beings as well as on their bodies. Bodies and texts eventually replaced the liver and intestines of domestic animals and became the new objects of interpretation.

Was it Christianity that put an end to the sacrificial cult of the late Roman Empire? In the sense that Theodosius' edict banned and made unlawful animal sacrifice, it did. But the idea that gods looked more favourably on spiritual sacrifices than they did on sacrifices of animals was not new; it was old and widespread, found in Jewish religion as well as in paganism (Ferguson 1980). While the Alexandrian Jew Philo did not reject the temple cult, he nevertheless said that the best sacrifice was to offer the self (*On Special Laws*, 1.272); after the fall of the temple in 70 CE, sacrifices were generally spiritualized and other types of worship were now described as sacrifice (Ferguson 1980: 1156–62).[9] Several of the adherents of religio-philosophical schools, such as Neoplatonists and Pythagoreans, had opposed the animal sacrifice. They intellectualized and spiritualized religion and partly or wholly promoted vegetarianism. Porphyry's books on abstinence are a leading example of this type of opposition to the animal sacrifice.

In this way, cultural processes that opposed animal sacrifices were already at work in the Graeco-Roman world. But this opposition was mainly an elite phenomenon that took the form of a cultural dividing line between a spiritual elite and the common people. The Christian opposition to sacrificial religion was broader and did not aim only at a social elite but encompassed *all* Christians. For them, the animal sacrifice was a significant cultural borderline between themselves and pagans.

Urbanization of the Mediterranean basin had begun before Alexander. This urbanization had accelerated during the Hellenic period and during the empire at its height. The Graeco-Roman cities were places of civilization as well as of change. While the empire was dependent upon the countryside, and agriculture was the basis for its economy, power was now based in the cities (Meeks 1983: 14–16). However, in the third and fourth centuries there was probably a change in the relationship between cities and countryside. These centuries do not seem to have been a period of general agricultural decline or crisis, as was long the common opinion. But from these centuries onward, there was a decline in town building in the north-western part of the empire, and it became more difficult to preserve the great public institutions on the same scale as before. Such factors contributed to making the expensive public cult less attractive to those who had to pay for it (cf. MacMullen 1981: 129ff). Scott Bradbury has pointed out that there was a decline in the ability and willingness to fund the traditional festivals, including sacrifices, and that the financial base of paganism was undermined (Bradbury 1995). Sacred and civic funds as well as private benefaction "were severely reduced in the fourth century" (*ibid.*: 353).

One could further ask if the fact that sacrifices during the empire were sometimes carried out on a gargantuan scale contributed to making the rituals less "religious".[10] It is also a fact that the official sacrificial reliefs no longer stressed mediation between gods and humans but focused instead on the power of the emperor, as Richard Gordon has convincingly argued (Gordon 1990).

It must be mentioned that in the cities, where most sacrifices were made and most animals killed, people did not raise their own animals. Most people in Rome had to buy sacrificial animals in the cattle market (Ogilvie 1986: 44). Porphyry, for instance, points out that "most people who live in cities do not have animals" (*On Abstinence*, 2.14.1) and adds that it was not easy for common people to obtain animals for sacrificial use (*ibid.*, 2.14.2). The combination of the great scale of many sacrifices and the need for most people to buy the sacrificial animals made the whole business of animal sacrifice less attractive, not only for the elite but also for common people.

Influence from the meat-producing areas in the north has been pointed out as a reason for a general increase in the production of animals in the Mediterranean area during the late Roman Empire, when Germanic farming traditions with prominent livestock production were fused with traditional Roman agricultural practices, with the emphasis on crops. Mireille Corbier has stressed how "the Roman diet was in part transformed by the progress of a market that was profitable both to the cities and to the ruling classes" (Corbier 1989: 252). But when meat became a daily item of consumption, it may also have contributed to its secularization. Thus secularization of meat must be seen in connection with that spiritualization of pagan elite religion that has already been referred to. According to Porphyry (and Theophrastus before him), the gods wanted *ethos* rather than *plethos*, quality rather than quantity (2.15.3; cf. Galen, *On the Usefulness of the Parts of the Body*, 3.10).[11]

It can finally be asked if the spiritualization of religion, which involved a turning away from the blood sacrifices, was also a way of establishing cultural and religious distance from surrounding peoples. In Roman stereotypes, barbarians were represented as great meat eaters, and German and Celtic religions incorporated animal sacrifices as an important element (Maier 2000: 162–4; Dinzelbacher 2000: 212–13). It seems that the animal sacrifice was in the process of being reinvented by the Romans as a mark of barbarism, and that the distinction between those who sacrificed animals and those who did not was made into a new cultural border and contributed to establishing a new elite. In line with this, a new religion that did not allow animal sacrifices, Christianity, became the preferred religion of the empire. Among the Christians, pagan barbarians were associated with heathen gods and animal sacrifices (for instance, Prudentius, *A Reply to Address of Symmachus*, 2.449–54).

Since one setting for animal sacrifices during the empire had been the cult of the emperor, it is rather revealing how abruptly Constantine ended the sacrificial aspect of this cult (cf. Drake 2000: 205), It seems as if Christianity was a welcome opportunity for the emperor to get rid of the traditional animal sacrifice with all its costs and commotions.

Edicts included in the *Theodosian Code*, which was published in 438 CE, show that bans on sacrifices were issued over and over again in the fourth century (see especially *Theodosian Code*, Book 16). These edicts reflect not only that the emperors wanted to end this type of cult – except for Julian, who during his short reign reintroduced it – but also that such sacrifices continued to be carried out, and that they were made by some into a key symbol of paganism.

Sacrifice and the human body

In the transition from a pagan to a Christian culture, Christian conceptions of sacrifice were sometimes combined with traditional conceptions. From the Nolan countryside, the Christian monk Paulinus wrote in 406 CE about a pig and a heifer that offered themselves for slaughter at the tomb of Saint Felix (*Carmen*, 20). As Denis Trout has recently shown, when animals were slaughtered at the tomb of Saint Felix, the needs of rural life were thus taken care of, and Christian and pre-Christian religious practices were combined (Trout 1995; cf. Trout 1999: 179–86). It is worth noting that in this Christian amalgamation of traditional sacrificial ritual and Christian piety, the animals were not merely cooperating as they had been expected to do in the traditional sacrificial cults. The pig and the heifer were eagerly and happily hurrying towards their destiny as the Christian martyrs were thought to do. This must be seen as a typical Christian development, even if there are also examples from the pagan tradition of animals that gave themselves up voluntarily for sacrifice and made considerable efforts to be killed for that purpose (Porphyry, *On Abstinence*, 1.25.9).

When the traditional Graeco-Roman sacrificial culture was exchanged for that of the Christians, a symbolic and ritual burden was lifted from sacrificial animals and loaded onto Christian bodies. Traditional religion had been located in the animal body as the most cherished product of agriculture and animal husbandry, and the religious techniques had been aimed at transforming that body from living flesh to tasty meat, to give the gods their due share and to interpret what was inscribed in the intestines of the animal. Christians declined to participate in ritual butchery of animals and on a symbolic level replaced the animal body with the human body: Christians worshipped a god who was himself the sacrifice.

In Christianity, the sacrificial terminology was transferred from animals to humans and used to describe personal salvation. According to Everett Ferguson, sacrifice was the universal language of worship in the ancient

157

world, and therefore "it was natural that the significance of Jesus' death should be interpreted in those terms" (Ferguson 1980: 116). That sacrifice was a sort of religious *lingua franca* is an acute observation. It is also clear that sacrificial language permeated Christian thought. It was applied to the death of Christ and to martyrdom, as well as to different types of worship, including the Eucharist, which was described as a "bloodless sacrifice". At pagan altars, the meat of the sacrificed animal was transformed into food for the gods, while in Christian churches the Eucharist was transformed at the altars, and the relics of the martyrs were in later times placed under or close to these altars.

The high point of sacrificial language in the New Testament is Romans 12.1. Here the Christians are urged to present "your bodies as a living sacrifice, holy, acceptable unto God". The source of this symbolic language was the sacrificial death of Christ. The description of the death of Christ was often based on a ritual slaughter. Melito, bishop of Sardes (before 190 CE), sees the slaughtering of the lamb and the celebration of the Jewish Passover as the model (*typos*) of the suffering, death and resurrection of Christ: "As Son he was born, as lamb led on, as sheep slaughtered, and as man buried; from the dead he rose as God, by nature God and man" (*Homily on the Pasch*, 8; in Markschies 1999: 9). The sacrificial lamb lends its sacrificial role to Christ, who leaves the animal behind in the new unity of man and god. This sort of ritual thinking made Porphyry exclaim that nothing is more beastly than sacrificing human beings. Porphyry is an example of how pagans often associated Christian cultic practice and religious language with human sacrifices and used this comparison to discredit the Christians.[12]

In Christianity, the religious focus was on the soul and the self, new types of kinship and spiritual succession, dead bodies and holy men, miracles and intellectual practices. To be a member of a Christian community presupposed a long period of initiation before baptism and extended explicatory lectures afterwards, aiming at a type of personal transformation that was foreign to traditional Roman religion but part of several of the new religious and philosophical movements of the time. Christianity meant internalizing religion as well as opening up to symbolic thinking on a large scale. At the centre of this thinking was the human body.

This was a body that even if it was material and mortal was destined for resurrection. Accordingly, the material and spiritual qualities of human beings were united in human flesh. This type of bodily reality begged for interpretation – whether the subject of interpretation was the resurrected body of the saviour, his flesh and blood consumed in the Eucharist, the mutilated bodies of the martyrs or the ascetic bodies of the holy men and women of the Church. Sacrificial language was transferred to human beings, primarily to Christ but in principle to all Christians, and especially to the martyrs, and later to virgins and ascetics (Clark 1999: 212–15).

Ignatius, who was martyred in Rome early in the second century CE, wrote a letter to the Roman Christians in which he states: "I am God's wheat, and I am ground by the teeth of wild beasts in order that I may be found pure bread of Christ" (*Romans*, 4.2). Ignatius calls himself "God's sacrifice" (*ibid.*), while Polycarp, who was burned in Smyrna, is described as " a noble ram" and "a burnt offering" (*Mart. Polycarp*, 14.1). In the first complete eucharistic liturgy that has survived and is found in the *Apostolic Constitution* from *c.* 375 CE in Syria, the sacrificial language is striking: "and we beseech you . . . to send down your Holy Spirit upon this sacrifice, the witness of the sufferings of the Lord Jesus, that he may make this bread body of your Christ, and this cup blood of your Christ. . . . " (*Apostolic Constitution*, 8.2.12). In this ritual, the elements of the Eucharist really became the body and blood of Christ. In this way, the transformation from the animal sacrifice to a human sacrifice was completed and continued to be repeated in Christian ritual.

Conclusion

Pagan as well as Christian authors criticized the animal sacrifice. Their criticism mainly concentrated on the effects that animal sacrifices had on humans and on the demonic qualities of gods who wanted such sacrifices. The criticism was not motivated to any significant degree by sympathy towards animals. Among the Neoplatonists, the Platonic idea of reincarnation and souls that were able to migrate between human and animal bodies was now questioned, and the differences between humans and animals were accentuated.

During these centuries and within the variety of ancient religion, two types of religious discourse were competing. In the traditional discourse on sacrifice, power was built on killing animals in a cultic setting and on distributing and eating their meat. In the new soteriological discourse, power was built on the symbolic capital of moral and physical purity and intellectual insight, and the goals were spiritual excellence and salvation.

The situation in the Graeco-Roman world in the first centuries of the common era could be compared to the situation in India several centuries earlier. Like Graeco-Roman religion, Vedic religion and religious discourse had concentrated on animal sacrifices (Jacobsen 1994), but in about 500 BCE, the idea of *ahimsa* (non-injury[13]) towards living beings became popular. The opposition to killing animals in India was not restricted to killing animals in a cultic setting but among many Indians was a universal obligation. It was built on a system of rebirth that presupposed a kinship between animals and humans, a conception of the world in which life was held in common and compassion was shown towards animals.[14] Such ideas were only rudimentarily present in the Graeco-Roman world. And while a significant tendency in India was respect for nature, a significant tendency in the West was the domination of nature.

In the last chapter, we saw that in pagan religion in the third and fourth centuries CE, the sacrificial relationship between gods, humans and animals was continued but reinterpreted in new varieties of the animal sacrifice as the *taurobolium*, the Mithras cult and Neoplatonic theurgy. Christianity represented a different sort of innovation in relation to the sacrificial system – a discourse on sacrifice without bloody offerings of animals. In contrast to adherents of most other religions of the Roman Empire, which accepted sacrifice in one form or another, the Christians declined to perform sacrifices to the gods. For them, the human body became the medium through which truth was revealed – be it the body of Christ, the Eucharist, the ascetic bodies of the desert dwellers, the closed bodies of the virgins, or the bones of the martyrs. The practice of sacrifice fell under an imperial ban issued by Theodosius in 391 CE and reinforced by later emperors.

Changing relations between animals, humans and gods are connected to social, cultural and religious changes. Such changes concern one's place in the natural world and its redefinition. That the sacrifice in honour of the emperor and the state was exchanged for the Christian cult indicated that new relations with animals, new ways of establishing a relationship with the powers and new ways of defining one's place in the social world were being introduced.

In Christianity, a new cultic setting was introduced in which the body of Christ replaced the animal body as a ritual link between God and human beings. Real animals were excluded from Christian rituals, but animal imagery was still used, for instance when Christ was identified with the sacrificial lamb.

Implicit in the Christian polemic against animal sacrifice was the notion that the sacrifice of Christ had replaced the need for animal sacrifices. In the wake of this interpretation, the human body became a key symbol and an intermediary between God and humans. In relation to sacrifice, the human body took the place of the animal body. The *Gospel of Philip* expresses this aspect of the new relationship between God and humans with the poignant phrase: "God is a man-eater." The master body of Christ replaced the animal sacrifice as a religious and cultural key symbol in the Mediterranean area and became a powerful symbol that inspired thought, aroused religious feelings and became a subject of veneration and piety.

Christian sacrificial language developed a special formulation in relation to the Roman arenas, where Christians were treated like animals and killed by animals. The ways in which animals – real as well as metaphorical – were depicted in the Acts of the Martyrs is the theme of Chapter 9. But before turning to this topic, we will return to Christian origins and to the texts of the New Testament.

8

THE NEW TESTAMENT AND THE LAMB OF GOD

Judaism and Christianity

There was no single Christian view of animals in antiquity, and no single view of animals in the New Testament. None of the New Testament texts make animals a special issue, and no systematic theology of animals can be deduced directly from these texts. However, even if none of the New Testament texts treat animals as a specific issue, many of them reflect attitudes towards animals more indirectly. The aim of this chapter is to survey attitudes to animals in the New Testament.

Let us start with the Jewish background. In the earliest form of Christianity, there was some continuation of Jewish tradition at the same time as Christians used animals as cultural and religious markers in the process of separating themselves from Judaism. The different New Testament genres reflect various perspectives on animals. In the Gospels and the Acts of the Apostles, animals are part of the natural environment and frequently used in parables; in the letters of Paul, animals appear only sporadically and are described more negatively, while in the Revelation of John, fantastic animals are included in the rich imagery of apocalypse. These animals are, except for the slaughtered lamb, used mainly to describe destructive forces.

Christianity started out as a Jewish sect and took much of its outlook on the world from Judaism. The close connection between the two religions is to be seen among other things in the fact that the Septuagint was the canonical text for Christians in the first century and that the Jewish Bible was later made part of the Christian canon. It is safe to say that Jewish traditions about animals formed the background to most conceptions of animals in the New Testament. Some of these conceptions continued to be meaningful to Christians, some were rejected, and others were developed in new directions.

Crucial texts about animals are found in Genesis. Here God created animals directly, on the fifth and sixth days of creation, without any intermediaries (Genesis 1:20–5; cf. 2:19), placed the natural world under human dominion (Genesis 1:26–8), and let Adam give names to the

161

animals and thus made him their lord (Genesis 2:19–20). In this way, a distinct hierarchy of being was established between man and animals. None of the animals is Adam's partner, and only man was made in the image of God:

> So out of the ground the Lord God formed every animal of the field and every bird of the air, and brought them to the man to see what he would call them; and whatever the man called every living creature, that was its name. The man gave names to all cattle, and to the birds of the air, and to every animal of the field; but for the man there was not found a helper as his partner.
>
> (Genesis 2:19–20)

After the flood, God strengthened the position of man and weakened that of the beasts by allowing Noah and his sons to eat their meat:

> The fear and dread of you shall rest on every animal of the earth, and on every bird of the air, on everything that creeps on the ground, and on all the fish of the sea; into your hand they are delivered. Every moving thing that lives shall be food for you; and just as I gave you the green plants, I give you everything.

"stewards of God's creations"   (Genesis 9:2–3)

Although it was presupposed that humans bore responsibilities towards animals and that they should be treated well because they were part of God's creation, animals were more like slaves than partners to man.

Normally, animals have neither personality nor human voice in the Old Testament. There are two exceptions: the serpent that talked to Adam and Eve from the Tree of Knowledge (Genesis 3:1–15), and the ass of Balaam (Numbers 22:21–35). Both were taken into Christian tradition, although while the serpent was given a prominent place in the Christian world view, Balaam's ass remains more of a curiosity.[1]

By being characterized as "more crafty than any other wild animal" (Genesis 3:1), the serpent is explicitly labelled as a beast – although admittedly a unique one. But the serpent does not behave like an ordinary animal: it has the power of speech and an agenda of its own. Not until it is cursed by God is it finally reduced to an ordinary snake: "Because you have done this, cursed are you among all animals and among all wild creatures; upon your belly you shall go, and dust you shall eat all the days of your life" (Genesis 3:14). But since the serpent, when it is cursed, is simultaneously characterized as the eternal enemy of man, an evil quality is for ever attached to it: "I will put enmity between you and the woman, and between your offspring and hers; he will strike your head, and you will strike his heel" (Genesis 3:15). The evil nature of the snake was developed in Christian tradition, and this animal became theologically important because it was associated with the Devil. Either this association was viewed literally, which made the snake as such demonic, or the creature was conceived of as a demonic entity that had little or nothing to do with its zoological origin (cf. Grant 1999: 4–5).

The serpent of Genesis also developed a profound "theriological" importance, i.e. an importance for the concept of animals as such, because it sometimes functioned as a prototype for other animals. This is connected to the way the Paradise narrative itself was read as a key scenario in Christianity. According to this narrative, at the beginning of time there were three main types of protagonist, who represented the divine, the human and the animal respectively – God, Adam and Eve, and the serpent. Because the serpent appears as the only powerful representative of the animal world, it became a representative of all animals, which implies that its antagonistic and demonic quality had the potential to infect other animals as well. The evil nature of the archetypal snake rubbed off, as it were, on snakes, often on wild animals, and sometimes even on the animal world in general. In the New Testament, the demonic and antagonistic qualities of beasts were developed especially in the Revelation of John, where satanic forces are described as monstrous animals (see below).

While the serpent was originally an individual in its own right, the second example of a speaking animal in the Bible, Balaam's ass, was an instrument of God that clearly rose to the occasion (Numbers 22:21–35; cf. II Peter 2:15ff). This ass was able to perceive the angel who was sent as a messenger of God, while Balaam was not. The ass refused to proceed further when it saw the angel and was beaten three times by its owner. Then the ass was given human voice by the angel and used its voice to rebuke Balaam. Only then did Balaam see the angel of God. This story has the character of a fable – all the same, this ass bothered Jewish exegetes: what happened to it afterwards? To have a talking animal roaming about at liberty nullified the God-given distinction between animals and humans. *Numbers Rabbah* solves the problem by making the ass die immediately after its appearance so that it should not be made an object of reverence (*Numbers Rabbah*, 20:4; cf. Matthews 1999: 224). Balaam's ass had clearly been no more than an instant device for promoting the will of God, and it was not allowed to function as a prototype for other asses or domestic animals.

A significant form of animal spectacle in the Bible is placed at the end of time. This spectacle is of two kinds: eschatological and apocalyptic. Eschatological peace is characterized by friendly cohabitation between wild and tame animals: "The wolf and the lamb shall feed together, the lion shall eat straw like the ox; but the serpent – its food shall be dust! They shall not hurt or destroy on all my holy mountain, says the Lord" (Isaiah 65:25; cf. Isaiah 11:6–9; Hosea 2:18). In later Jewish and Christian tradition, the animals that appear at the end of time were sometimes even said to regain the power of speech. According to legend, they had lost this ability after the creation because of the sin of man (*The Acts of Philip*, 301, note 2). These eschatological creatures belong to real animal species. Different from them were the fantastic beasts that were intended to symbolize the cataclysmic happenings at the end of time (Daniel 7; I Enoch 85–90). Such monstrous creatures were the stock-in-trade of Jewish and Christian apocalypses and part of a polarized cosmos.

The serpent of Genesis, the ass of Balaam and the eschatological animals in rabbinical tradition that would eventually regain their voices at the end of time demonstrate that ordinary animals are inferior to humans because they do not have the gift of language. But as these creatures also show that animals are not necessarily bound to be without language for ever, their presence reveals a more optimistic attitude to the abilities of animals than that which was expressed by the Stoics and later by Christians. According to rabbinical tradition, animals had an unrealized potential for language and reason.

Apart from eschatological animals, apocalyptic beasts and the rare talking creatures, the most important animals in the biblical world were those that, like most animals in the Graeco-Roman world, served as sacrifice and food. Both small and large cattle were slaughtered in the Jewish sacrificial cult (Borowski 1998: 18–21), which was carried out for a number of reasons: to give thanks, to accompany prayers, and to obtain forgiveness and reconciliation. In Judaism, the attitude to animals was regulated by means of cultic dietary laws (*kasrut*) (Leviticus 11; Deuteronomy 14). These laws were based on how animals were designed and how they behaved, and they not only pertained to which species of animals could legally be eaten but also determined basically how these animals were viewed. Cultic dietary laws are not solely to do with eating – they are part of a total conception of the world. These laws impose structure on the animal world and make it reflect the human conception of the world so that it becomes visible and palpable.

In Judaism, the animals that were allowed as food were those with split hooves that chew the cud. This description effectively excludes the pig, which was the archetype of an unclean animal. If sea creatures were to be eaten, they had to have fins and scales. In addition, the dietary laws included a general prohibition against blood consumption. These laws were an important part of Jewish self-definition. By keeping to them, the Jews preserved their holiness and separated themselves from all other people. The deeper meaning of the dietary laws has been debated since ancient times. Speculations have ranged from medical arguments to allegorical interpretation, and the modern debate has offered symbolic as well as materialistic theories (Garnsey 1999: 91–5). Walter Houston has convincingly argued that the criteria for permitted food in Leviticus 11 should be seen as deriving from the characteristics of known and accepted food: what one already ate determined what should be eaten. It was also a general tendency to restrict people's meat consumption to the types of animal that were sacrificed. Intrinsic to the dietary laws was a separation between wild animals and domestic animals, and while some animals such as deer and gazelles were conceived of as a form of "honorary cattle", domestic animals such as dogs and pigs were associated with wild animals, probably because of their diet, and therefore regarded as unclean (Houston 1998). As our subject is the attitude to animals in the New Testament, the reason *why* the Jews had dietary proscriptions is not as important as *how* Christians reacted to these proscriptions. What is especially interesting about the Christian reaction is that at the same time as the dietary proscriptions are made irrelevant, animals also fade out of focus and are less relevant in Christianity than they had been and continued to be in Judaism. The cultic dietary laws ensured that a cultural and religious focus on animals was continued.

Although the Christians took over general Jewish attitudes towards animals, they split with Judaism over their attitude towards the dietary laws. Dietary laws were clearly an issue in the early relationship between representatives of the two religions and concerned the important question of giving Gentiles access to salvation (Mark 7:19; Acts 15:1–29; Galatians 2:11–14). This subject is most vividly described in Acts. The apostle Peter had been accused of eating with those who were uncircumcised and promptly received a vision to put things right:

> ... he [Peter] fell into a trance. He saw the heaven opened and something like a large sheet coming down, being lowered to the ground by its four corners. In it were all kinds of four-footed creatures and reptiles and birds of the air. Then he heard a voice saying, "Get up, Peter; kill and eat". But Peter said, "By no means, Lord; for I have never eaten any thing that is profane or unclean". The voice said to him again, a second time, "What God has made clean, you must not call profane". This happened three times, and the thing was suddenly taken up to heaven.
>
> (Acts 10:10–16; cf. 11:5–10)

The significance of this vision is revealed by Peter being shown the animals thrice and also by the author of Acts recounting the same episode twice. The main point of the story was to show that the wiping out of differences between the animal species was parallel to the way in which the distinctions between Jews and Gentiles had been wiped out. These words are the converse of God's words in Leviticus 20:24–5: "I have separated you from the peoples. You shall therefore make a distinction between the clean animal and the unclean, and between the unclean bird and the clean; you shall not bring abomination on yourselves by animal or by bird or by anything with which the ground teems, which I have set apart for you to hold unclean" (cf. Houston 1998: 18–19). The vision gave a simple solution to the problem of the admission of Gentiles into the Church and table fellowship with Gentiles.[2] But it is also important to note that when in this graphical description of the animal world the Mosaic food laws disappear, this disappearance has consequences for the conception of animals. When differences are wiped out, sameness abides, and from now on the internal differences between animals were made subordinate to their fundamental difference from man. Whether they were four-footed beasts, reptiles or birds, all animals were united in fulfilling their true destiny as food for humans.

In the narrative of Peter's vision, the verb *thuein* – "to sacrifice" – is used for the killing of animals. But this verb may also have a neutral meaning, "to kill", which is probably the intention here. The permission to kill and eat all animals did not imply that all of them had obtained the highest degree of ritual purity and that they were also fit for sacrifice. Rather, they had become neutral in relation to a ritual continuum of pure/impure. The story of Peter's vision is intended to show that Christians need reject no food (cf. I Corinthians 8:8; I Timothy 4:4; Matthew 15:11–19), and it also implies that butchering of animals is from now on to be secularized.

Not only Jewish dietary prescriptions were debated in the earliest period of Christianity; the eating of sacrificed meat was also questioned. In Paul's first letter to the Corinthians, the topic of sacrificed meat is taken up. In a pragmatic vein, Paul writes that anything sold in the meat market may be eaten, provided that "questions of conscience" are not raised (I Corinthians 10:25). If, on the contrary, one knows that the meat served has been offered in sacrifice to idols, it should not be eaten (I Corinthians 10:28ff). Why does Paul both advise the Corinthians not to eat meat offered to idols and say that it is a matter of moral indifference to do so (*adiaphoron*)? This is a contradiction only if the quality of the meat changed when it was offered to idols. And although there is an impression that some uncleanness is attached to sacrificed meat *per se* (cf. I Corinthians 8),[3] the main idea is that meat as such is neutral. The real problem with sacrifices is related to the demons that receive it; the meat is only problematic indirectly. Later, Christians also had to come to terms with the fact that with the final destruction of the temple in Jerusalem in 70 CE, the Jewish sacrificial cult came to an end.[4]

From what has been said, it is clear that one important way in which the Christians defined their relationship to other people was through their attitude to these people's use of meat and sacrifices. Christians differed from Jews because they ate meat that was prohibited according to Jewish dietary proscriptions and from pagans because they did not sacrifice animals or eat meat that they knew had been taken from animals that had been sacrificed. By eating some types of meat and not eating others, the Christians erected barriers against Judaism and paganism and laid a foundation for their emergence as an independent religion.

It should be noted, and it is essential I think for the Christian conception of animals, that the Christian meat-eating restrictions were not related directly to animals but to other people's meat-eating and sacrificial habits.

Jews, whose diet was determined by the behaviour and design of animals, and pagans, who sacrificed animals, had a more direct relationship with the animal world in this respect than the Christians did. The Christian attitudes to sacrifice and diet may suggest that animals did not have the same immediate significance in *their* world view as they had in the Jewish and pagan conceptions of the world and, consequently, that the Christian attitude was open to making animals of flesh and blood into objects of minor religious significance.

The Gospels

A similar movement to that detected in relation to dietary laws and animal sacrifices may be seen in the use of animals as metaphors. In proverbs, allegories and parables, there is a palpable movement away from the conception of animals as significant in their own right to their being only indirectly significant.

The Gospels and Acts show the busy world of the eastern Mediterranean, where animals were a main source of income. All the same, real-life scenes with animals are seldom described. The exceptions are when we meet "people selling cattle, sheep and doves" in the temple of Jerusalem (John 2:14; cf. Matthew 21:12–13) or when Luke describes "shepherds living in the fields, keeping watch over their flock by night" (Luke 2:8). More often animals are made to illustrate points in parables, appear as the raw material for miracles or as the fulfilment of Old Testament prophecies. This does not mean that animals speak or act in ways that are not consonant with their animal nature; on the contrary, these animals are their natural selves throughout. But it means that the New Testament takes the focus away from the animals and downplays their inherent value as animals. It must also be added that when animals are compared with humans, they are systematically described as inferior to them: "How much more valuable is a human being than a sheep?" (Matthew 12:12; cf. Luke 12:7); "So do not be afraid, you are of more value than many sparrows" (Matthew 10:31).[5] And when humans are compared with birds: "Are you not of more value than they?" (Matthew 6:26).[6] These are examples of an argument *a minori ad maius*, which is also found in rabbinical literature (cf. Bauckham 1998: 44–8). So on this point the Gospels maintain continuity with their Jewish background and reflect a hierarchy within the community of creation, where man is lord over the animals. His dominion also implies that he may use animals for food and sacrifice.

The animals in the Gospels can be grouped according to scenarios that are based on these animals' economic significance and the type of place they normally inhabit. From a point of departure in these real-life scenarios, a hermeneutic movement points away from the literal meaning of animals towards allegorical meanings. This hermeneutic movement is consonant with the way the followers of Jesus left their former occupations as fishermen and craftsmen and became followers of a movement in which one was preoccupied with miracles and salvation. Real animals were no longer a source of income; metaphorical animals obviously were.

There are at least three significant animal contexts in the Gospels, relating to fishing, pastoralism and the desert. Quite a few of the disciples of Jesus were fishermen, and it is not astonishing that fishing appears as one of the key animal scenarios in the Gospels (see, for instance, Luke 5:1; Matthew 4:18). It is not strange, considering that fish, rather than meat, seems to have been the food of the common people in Palestine. All the same, in the New Testament, fish appear primarily as such stuff that miracles are made of or as metaphors: Jesus helps the disciples to catch abnormal amounts of fish (Luke 5:1–7; John 21:6–11), makes seven loaves and a few little fish feed thousands of people (Matthew 15:34–8, cf. Matthew 14:17–21; Mark 6:37–44, 8:1–8; Luke 9:12–17; John 6:9–13) and predicts that money that will pay the temple tax for Peter and himself will be found in a fish that Peter will go down to the sea and catch (Matthew 17:24–7). There is no miraculous power in fish as such; rather, fish appear as symbolically neutral and for that reason apt to make miracles with. The metaphorical value of fish is exploited when Jesus made the fishermen of Galilee into "fishers of men" and thus used fish as images for Christian souls (Matthew 4:19; Mark 1:17; Luke 5:10), or when the kingdom of heaven is likened to "a net that was thrown into the sea and caught fish of every kind" (Matthew 13:47).

Even more important than fish, especially for the later development of Christian metaphors, are sheep. Here the Gospels stand in a rich continuity with rabbinical tradition and its didactic use of sheep. While shepherding was regarded as a low occupation, and shepherds were looked down upon, sheep were important animals in the Palestinian economy, mainly used for their wool, hide and milk, but they were also the preferred animals in the sacrificial cult. However, except for Luke, who describes the circumstances around the birth of Jesus and refers to the flocks of the shepherds, sheep in the Gospels are used as pedagogical instruments and as metaphors. The archetypal sheep scenario is connected to the good shepherd as referred to by John (10:1–18): "I am the good shepherd. The good shepherd lays down his life for the sheep" (John 10:11). We are told about the sheep that had fallen into a pit on the sabbath and was rescued (Matthew 12:11), and we hear the parable about the man who has a hundred sheep and one goes astray, and if he finds it, "he rejoices over it more than over the ninety-nine that never went astray" (Matthew 18:12–13). The hermeneutic movement from real-life creatures to metaphors is further seen when the followers of Jesus are described as sheep (John 10:3ff, 14, 16), and when sheep are used as symbols of humans (John 21:15–17; Matthew 10:6, 16; Matthew 25:32–4; Luke 10:3). In line with a traditional way of describing rulers as well as spiritual leaders in the Middle East, teachers are considered to be shepherds and overseers over their flocks (Acts 20:28; cf. Aune 1997: 369). A special type of sheep scenario is when the sacrificial lamb is adopted as an image of Christ. While Judaism and Christianity in the first century shared the metaphorical use of sheep, the development of the symbolism of the sacrificial lamb is characteristic of Christianity rather than Judaism (see below).[7]

The fishing and the sheep scenarios are based on harmless and domesticated animals.[8] However, the desert scenario is different, because it is based on animals that are not domesticated and sometimes on animals that are harmful to humans. The desert scenario is located in the wilderness (*eremos*) of Judaea. John the Baptist is placed in the wilderness, and his existence on the margins of society is defined by the use of certain animal products for clothes and food. John is dressed in raiment of camel's hair and with a leather girdle about his loins. For food he had grasshoppers and wild honey (Matthew 3:1–4). While the large desert locust was permitted as food and even considered a delicacy (Borowski 1998: 159–60), and honey was commonly used in Palestine, we are in this case talking about foodstuffs that were procured in the wilderness and therefore difficult to obtain. Grasshoppers and wild honey were conceived of as the only ingredients in the diet of John. It was clearly a case of a marginal diet for a person on the margins of society.

Jesus is also associated with the wilderness. According to the evangelists, he lived forty days in the Judaean desert. In the description in Mark's gospel, he is with wild animals: "He was in the wilderness forty days, tempted by Satan; and he was with the wild beasts; and the angels waited on him" (Mark 1:13). The wild beasts are not mentioned by the other evangelists (Matthew 4:1; Luke 4:1). Several types of creature are lumped together in Mark's description – Jesus, wild animals, Satan and angels. Together with angels and demons, wild animals are beings who are not under human control. What do the animals (*therion*) in Mark mean? Which of the protagonists do they support? Are they only the natural inhabitants of the wilderness; are they allies of Satan; or do they prefigure the paradisical state at the end of time, when humans and animals will live together in peace? In modern research, the last solution – which also fits very well with the present Christian attempts to rehabilitate the status of animals – has often been preferred (Bauckham 1994: 5–6). This solution is not quite convincing. On the contrary, the fact that the other evangelists have not bothered to mention any wild animals may suggest that these animals were not regarded as especially important and that in Mark they functioned mainly as indicators of the wildness of the desert. Consequently, the animals in Mark do not have supernatural qualities; nor are they to be closely associated with the other actors in the desert but, because of their inherent nature, are to be interpreted as negative elements and in opposition to the ministering angels. Because wild animals are excluded from the human world, they mark the place where they dwell as uninhabitable by humans and as a place of disorder.

In the New Testament, some animals are associated more directly with evil and even with demons than are Mark's wild animals. When, for instance, uprooting evil is described as "to tread on snakes and scorpions" (Luke 10:19), snakes and scorpions are strongly associated with evil forces. When Jesus scolds the Pharisees and addresses them as "You snakes, you brood of vipers!" (Matthew 23:33), the inherently evil nature of these animals is taken for granted. What man would give his son a snake for food instead of a fish? (Matthew 7:10; Luke 11:11). This saying implies a dualism between good and evil that is cast as a contrast between an animal that is useful because it is nutritious and an animal that is without nutritional value and is also harmful. Harmful creatures ought to be killed. Paul threw a poisonous snake (*eksidna*) that had "fastened itself on his hand" into the fire (Acts 28:3; see Chapter 12). The classification of some of the negative animals in the Gospels and Acts seems to be determined by a mixture of Jewish conceptions of impure animals and more general conceptions of harmful creatures.

Scorpions and serpents are clearly conceived of as evil animals, often representing the demonic world (Luke 10:19),[9] but neither have dogs and swine much to recommend them (Grant 1999: 6–7). Dogs are low in the hierarchy of animals (Matthew 15:26–7; Luke 16:21; Mark 7:27–8). One does not give that which is holy to dogs or cast one's pearls before swine (Matthew 7:6). Dogs are like pigs and will eat anything (Luke 15:16). In later exegesis, pigs and dogs are used to characterize morally depraved individuals, such as pagans, the unbaptized and carnal persons.

Only rarely is Jesus brought into direct contact with animals. One dramatic instance of such an encounter is Jesus' dealings with the Gadarene swine. In this story, which is told by Mark (5:1–20) and Matthew (8:28–34), the impurity of pigs is taken for granted. Mark tells that in Gadarene, a Hellenistic town on the fringes of Palestine, Jesus sent unclean spirits (*ta pneumata ta akatharta*) out of a man and into a herd of about two thousand swine. When the unclean spirits entered them, the swine immediately rushed down a steep bank into the sea and were drowned (Mark 5:1–13). The man who had been possessed by the spirits is characterized as "a demoniac" (*daimonisomenos*; Mark 5:15). Even if we know that swine were sometimes raised in herds (Psalms 80:14; cf. Borowski 1998: 140) and that herds of swine of some size existed, the number of swine in this story is rather overwhelming. Seen from the position of an outsider, this story is disturbing because of its maltreatment of the swine, a point that was also made in antiquity.[10]

In the *Apocriticus* of Macarius Magnes, which probably goes back to some of Porphyry's objections to Christianity, the story of the Gadarene swine was singled out for special treatment.[11] The critic used the versions of both

Matthew and Mark and treated them in a synoptic way. Among other things, he objected to Jesus not sending the unclean spirits directly into the abyss. The critic raised objections to Jesus' divine powers because he only sent the demons into "unclean animals". Jesus relocated evil but made others victim to it. By shifting the demons into swine, Jesus also signalled that swine did not take part in salvation.

This criticism does not mean that the critic had any great interest in swine, let alone their eventual salvation, but rather that he wanted to point to the limitations in the powers of Jesus and to show that Jesus did not want to save everyone. He cared for some, but not for others. In other words, the pagan critic used the story of the Gadarene swine for the purpose of blackening Christians. He also knew that to the Jews swine were the most unclean and hated form of beasts (*Apocriticus*, 64; cf. Cook 2000: 178). But even if the pagan critic does not show any real concern for swine, his opposition was fuelled by what he saw as a maltreatment of animals.

The behaviour of Jesus towards the Gadarene swine is an extreme example. To counter this rather gloomy picture, there are also more compassionate attitudes towards animals in the Gospels. This is to be seen for instance in parables relating to sheep and is not without importance, particularly because the sheep is the Christian metaphorical animal *par excellence*. But in images of speech, as when Jesus compares his gathering of the children of Jerusalem to a hen gathering her chickens under her wings (Matthew 23:37; Luke 13:34), a tenderness towards the animal world is also clearly conveyed. All the same, these instances do not change the basic impression. Even if tenderness towards the animal world is conveyed in some of the images of the Gospels, these texts are not characterized by a concern for animals. When animals are brought into view, they always function as means of furthering human purposes and not as ends in themselves.

As for another preferred animal in earliest Christianity – fish – none of the Gospels shows any concern for their well-being. Fish are never presented as creatures in their own right, and Jesus never saved fish from being caught. This point may sound anachronistic. Who cares about fish? Few do today. But antiquity was not totally devoid of fish lovers, even if they were rare. According to his biographer Iamblichus, Pythagoras once paid fishermen to throw the fish they had caught back into the sea. Iamblichus was a Neoplatonist, and like Pythagoreans, Neoplatonists were known for their interest in animals. Christians were not. It must also be pointed out that the Gospels offer no stories about Jesus giving animals a friendly word or showing kindness towards them. That does not mean that Jesus never did but rather that the bearers of the gospel tradition did not find any good reason to make a Christian point out of it. (Many Christians today would have appreciated it if they had done so.)

Not only the actual description of the animals but also the allegorical style in these texts contributes to the impression that animals as such were of limited value. As metaphors, animals no longer have meanings that are related primarily to their situation as living creatures or to their function as sources of income for humans. These more traditional meanings recede into the background and are suppressed by figurative meanings, often as a form of spiritualization and allegorization. Allegorization implies that sheep and fish are removed from the sphere of shepherds and fishermen and transferred to the sphere of preachers and prophets and used by them as instruments in their teaching. This process was not begun from scratch in the Gospels but is well documented in contemporary Judaism. Many of the parables used by Jesus had roots in rabbinical teaching. The point is that when a sheep becomes the subject of an allegory, it is not solely a tribute to this animal's sheepish nature or to its natural habitat but also a challenge to them. The metaphorical use of sheep presupposes that these animals serve a better purpose as signs pertaining to human moral and salvatory processes than in fulfilling their destinies as sheep. In short, to spiritualize sheep and make them into allegories points away from their inherent value as animals and locks them for ever into human hermeneutical processes.[12]

"Behold the lamb of God"

Even if animals never appear as independent actors in the Gospels and Acts or speak like the serpent and Balaam's ass did in the Old Testament,[13] they sometimes appear as symbols that either point to the divine or are symbols of the divine.

When Jesus rides into Jerusalem on a foal of an ass – a young male animal that none before has sat on (Mark 11:2, 4, 5, 7; cf. Luke 19:30, 33, 35) – or on an ass and its foal (Matthew 21:2, 5, 7; John 12:15), these animals are pointers to Jesus as the expected Messiah. Through their presence, Old Testament prophecies regarding the Messiah were fulfilled (cf. Zechariah 9:9; Genesis 49:11). While the horse was an expensive animal, connected to aristocracy and warfare, the ass is a "prosaic beast of burden", as described by Thomas Mathews (Mathews 1995: 45). Mathews stresses the subversive aspect of the mission of Jesus as expressed through the use of the ass. Jesus does not arrive as an emperor with chariots and horses but rides on this humble beast. Mathews has also pointed to the "surprising prominence" of this animal in early Christian art (*ibid*.: 45–6). All the same, in the Gospels, the ass and its foal were present primarily because they were instrumental in fulfilling Old Testament prophecies. When their mission is accomplished, they fade out of the picture.

The ox and the ass, which according to apocryphal traditions were present at the crib of Jesus, are not mentioned by Luke or by any of the other evangelists. In Christian tradition, however, these two animals were probably there from the very beginning. This is supported by the fact that the ox and the ass worshipping at the crib is a common motif in art, preserved on sarcophagi from the third century. Also, the presence of these animals in the gospel of pseudo-Matthew supports this view.[14] The ox and the ass are closely connected with Jesus as a baby and by their presence they point to the innocence and supernatural nature of the divine child. These animals also fulfil Old Testament prophecies and point to Jesus as saviour (Isaiah 1:3). The ox and the ass have been interpreted as symbolizing the pagans and the Jews, respectively, so these animals do not escape the allegorizing process. But these creatures also had an inherent value in Christian tradition. They invited tenderness and piety and thus managed to slide through the Christian filter, which often sifted out conceptions that were incompatible with the anthropocentric view of this world and the next.

Animals also function in the Gospels as symbols for the divine.[15] One of the animals that refers directly to a divine entity is the dove, which is linked to a rather vague spiritual entity, the Holy Spirit, but makes this entity less vague because by means of the dove it appears as a living creature. The Holy Spirit either descended upon Jesus "in bodily form like a dove" (Luke 3:22) or was "descending from heaven like a dove, and it remained on him" (John 1:32; cf. Mark 1:9–11; Matthew 3:13–17). As pointed out by George Lakoff and Mark Johnson, this symbolic relationship between the Holy Spirit and the dove is not arbitrary: "The dove is conceived of as beautiful, friendly, gentle, and, above all, peaceful. As a bird, its natural habitat is the sky, which metonymically stands for heaven, the natural habitat of the Holy Spirit. The dove is a bird that flies gracefully, glides silently, and is typically seen coming out of the sky and landing among people" (Lakoff and Johnson 1980). However, it must be added that by its physical presence as a bird, the dove transcends its symbolic mode and touches the divine reality more directly. So, in the case of this bird, we are confronted with a Christian divinity appearing in an animal shape. Its animalian presence resembles the way gods appeared in Greek myths and is somewhat odd within a Christian context. But it must be taken into consideration that as a symbol for the divine, the dove had a long history in the Middle East. It was an ancient Palestinian and Syriac goddess symbol that was associated with motherly love and tenderness. It also continued to be developed in Christian tradition. In the Syriac Christian tradition, like the *Odes of Salomon*, the motherly qualities of the Spirit *cum* dove were later expressed in rich symbolic language (Johnson 1999: 201–4). In Roman tradition, the dove is a symbol of faithful love.

More prominent in the New Testament than the symbol of the dove, and with richer connotations, is the symbol of the lamb. This is due to the lamb's being connected to Jesus and his mission. According to Christian tradition, Christ had with his death and by his blood made the only sacrifice that counted. The symbol of the sacrificial lamb became standard for Christ. But when the qualities of the slaughtered lamb were transferred to Christ, the same happened as with other allegorizing processes based on animals:

the qualities that Jesus took from the lamb pointed away from the natural animal. To put it simply, while the lamb furnished Jesus with a web of connotations, Jesus did not give lambs added meaning.[16] The comparison between Jesus and the lamb does not mean that Jesus is like a lamb in all respects. For instance, he is not playful like a lamb or dependent on his mother like a lamb. The intended point of comparison is mainly, but not only, restricted to the sacrificial aspects of the lamb (see below). The comparison uses an animal metaphor (lamb) to express things that are abstract and difficult to grasp in any other way.

The identification between Jesus and the lamb in the Gospels is seen most distinctly in John's gospel, where John says of Jesus: "Here is the Lamb of God who takes away the sin of the world" (John 1:29; cf. John 1:36).[17] For Paul, Christ is the Passover lamb that has been sacrificed (I Corinthians 5:7). In his letter to the Hebrews, there are references to the way the sacrifice of Christ has made the traditional sacrificial cults superfluous (Hebrews 9:12, 13–14ff, 10:4–5). Acts 8:32–5 refers to the sacrificial lamb in Isaiah 53:7ff, and Philip identified this lamb as Jesus. And, finally, in the Revelation of John, we meet the lamb that has been slain, with its seven horns and seven eyes.[18] Even if the lamb symbolism is not identical in the different New Testament texts, the texts stand united in conceiving the lamb as a sacrificial animal and in identifying this animal with Jesus. Walter H. Wagner has pointed out that the merging of messianic and sacrificial language includes not only the Passover lamb but also the oxen slaughtered when the covenant was made between God and Israel at the foot of Mount Sinai, and the two goats sacrificed on the Day of Atonement. Symbolic connotations from these animal sacrifices are all applied to Jesus, together with symbolic meanings taken from the Old Testament figures of Isaac, the righteous sufferer (Psalm 22) and the servant figures of Deutero-Isaiah and the Wisdom of Solomon (Wagner 1994: 100–2).

But even if the sacrificial discourse includes more than the lamb, the lamb is the main symbol within the Christian sacrificial context and the most important link to the Jewish sacrificial cult. The lamb symbol focuses on the Jewish sacrificial discourse and makes it accessible and available for Christianity, while it also represents a total reinterpretation of that discourse. For at the same time as Jesus takes over the function of the lamb, he makes the sacrificial lamb superfluous (cf. Hebrews above). By being taken over by a human being (Jesus), the sacrificial lamb is emptied of its animality and filled with divinity, at the same time as its "lambness" is transferred to Jesus and remains with him. In this way, the sacrifice is spiritualized and made into a one-time happening with an absolute significance for all people. By means of the symbolism of the paschal lamb, Christianity obtains at least three things: this symbolism makes a connection to the traditional sacrificial discourse; it points away from real sacrificial animals to a transcendent reality; and it inscribes itself on the religious and symbolic language of antiquity, especially on the language of the mystery cults in which animals were mainly used in the symbolic mode (cf. Chapter 5).

Does God care for oxen?

Paul obviously did not have the same relationship to sheep and fish as the gospel traditions did. He was not originally a fisherman or a shepherd and was not connected with Palestinian villages as the gospel traditions were, but with Graeco-Roman cities. Paul was, in the words of Wayne A. Meeks, "a city person" (Meeks 1983: 9) who supported himself by making tents. Generally, merchants and craftspeople seem to have been dominant among first-century Christians. In addition, Paul was also a literary person who had received rabbinical education at the feet of the famous Gamaliel. These things taken into consideration, it is not astonishing that Paul uses few metaphors taken from country life.

Paul's intense soteriological drive, which is pointing beyond this world, and also his Stoic outlook, may account for his lack of interest in animals and for his ranking them low in the hierarchy of being.[19] The natural world has simply receded into the background in his letters. This is clearly seen in his comment on Deuteronomy 25:4: "You shall not muzzle an ox while it is treading out the grain", a saying that in Judaism was aimed at decent treatment of animals. Paul asks rhetorically: "Is it for oxen that God is concerned?" (I Corinthians 9:9) and goes on to interpret the saying allegorically, so that it concerns only human spiritual matters and no longer has anything to offer working oxen. Paul seldom refers to animals, and when he does, it is mostly in allegories and not seldom negatively. Paul is not necessarily negative to animals, but he uses them to describe things that are negative. He compares the enemies of Christianity to dogs (Philippians 3:2), mentions the serpent as the one that tempted Eve (II Corinthians 11:3), and when he says " . . . I fought with wild animals [etheriomaksesa] at Ephesus" (I Corinthians 15:32), he identifies those who had opposed him in the city of Artemis with wild animals (cf. Bauckham 1994).[20] Positive animal metaphors appear mainly when Paul characterizes Christians as "sheep to be slaughtered" (Romans 8:36) or Christ as "our paschal lamb" who "has been sacrificed" (I Corinthians 5:7).

The theoretical foundation for Paul's conception of animals is reflected in I Corinthians 15:39. Here Paul points out basic differences between living beings and interprets these differences in accordance with Stoic doctrine. In the above-mentioned text, Paul claims: "Not all flesh is alike, but there is one flesh for human beings, another for animals, another for birds, and another for fish" (I Corinthians 15:39). From these creatures, Paul goes on to speak about differences between the terrestrial bodies and celestial bodies such as the sun, the moon and the stars (I Corinthians 15:40–1). What does Paul mean? He probably means what he says: the quality of flesh depends on which creature we are talking about, a concept that is dependent on Stoicism.

New Testament scholar Dale Martin has pointed out that Paul here uses a Stoic model (Martin 2001; 1995: 123–36). According to this model, different bodies are part of the sphere to which they belong, and different substances constitute their bodies. Lower animals are built of substances from the lower part of the cosmos, higher creatures of substances from higher regions, such as air and pneuma. Pneuma is not immaterial. It is the finest substance in the cosmos and the most refined matter in the human soul. Flesh and blood belong to the lower regions of the cosmos – together with animals. In the resurrection, according to Paul, it is the pneumatic body that will rise. Paul does not discuss whether animals will rise, probably because according to this Stoic model, it is obvious that they will not. Animals belong to the lower parts of the cosmos. The succession of the different elements determines the place of each animal in the hierarchy of being, which means that birds rank higher than beasts and fish. The hierarchy of substances not only determines the place of animals in relation to each other and to humans, it also determines the impossibility of animals attaining salvation. "Does God care for oxen?" This question must be read in accordance with Paul's Stoic perspective on animals and answered in the negative. God does not care for oxen as he cares for Christians. Oxen are mere animals, and accordingly they belong to the perishable part of the cosmos, while the purpose of humans is to attain salvation.[21]

In the non-Pauline letters in the New Testament, commonly shared philosophical notions about animals, and especially Stoic notions, are even more visible. Animals are labelled as "irrational" (Jude 10; II Peter 2:12). There are deprecatory comparisons between evil humans and animals (Titus 1:12; II Peter 2:22; Jude 10), and comparisons that show that some people "are like irrational animals, mere creatures of instinct, born to be caught and killed" (II Peter 2:12). Man's superiority over animals is confirmed, as all animals have been tamed by him (James 3:3, 3:7). Animals exist for the convenience of men, as they generally do according to Stoic doctrine.

The Revelation of John

Nowhere in the New Testament have animals of the imagination been given such free rein as in the Revelation of John. Among the many striking features of this dramatic work is its use of rather peculiar animals. These include "four living creatures, full of eyes in front and behind: the first living creature like a lion, the second living creature like an ox, the third living creature with a face like a human face, and the fourth living creature like a flying eagle" (Revelation 4:6–7), each of which has six wings and is full of eyes (Revelation 4:8); the monstrous locusts that were sent out to torment the race of man: they had shapes like horses, golden crowns, faces of men, hair like women, teeth like lions, breastplates, wings and tails like scorpions (Revelation 9:7–10); and, not least, the archetypal Beast that rose out of the sea with seven heads and ten horns and that looked like a leopard, with the feet of a bear and the mouth of a lion (Revelation 13:1–2).

The theme of Revelation is apocalyptic visions of the future. This enigmatic text is characterized by mythological fantasies, struggles of cosmic proportions, and a basic duality between oppression and despair on the one hand and hope and victory on the other. The seer describes in imaginative language the heavenly world, approaching distress and world catastrophes, the final struggle between God and his enemies, the judgement of this world, the victory of Christ, and the millennium and the new world. The text excels in images and symbols, and researchers as well as laypeople have for centuries been trying to solve its riddles. It has invited a huge amount of secondary literature and ingenious, and not so ingenious, attempts to pin down the beasts and identify their historical settings and whereabouts. What is certain is that these beasts, in addition to being part of a long history, also include contemporary references to the author's own time, indicating specific religious and political issues in the eastern Mediterranean about which the author had strong opinions. The text may either be a reaction to external persecution or reflect inter-Christian strife, or both. Likely candidates for John's wrath were the reign of Rome and the cult of the Roman emperor and also local Church leaders who clashed with John over the right interpretation of Christian myth and practice. In recent research, Pierre Prigent has stressed the relationship of the Christians to the Roman Empire, while Paul B. Duff has pointed to social conflict within the churches of Asia Minor as triggers to the conflict that the text refers to (Duff 2001; Prigent 2001). Originally – and controversially – Bruce J. Malina and John J. Pilch have interpreted John's vision systematically in relation to ancient astrology (Malina and Pilch 2000).[22]

For the present purpose, it is not necessary to identify the references made to the beasts but rather to ask what these beasts say more generally about animals. What sort of creatures are they? What views on animals do they reflect?

These questions may perhaps seem far-fetched. John, the author of Revelation, did not intend to say anything about real animals. Neither were the creatures that sprang from his fertile imagination conceived in his mind from scratch but had roots in Jewish and Middle Eastern mythology. Some obviously had a long pedigree and were part of a flourishing apocalyptic tradition. All the same, like the other New Testament texts, Revelation may also be read with an eye to its views on animals, and even more so, because such a wide range of bestial creatures roam its pages.

First, the animals of Revelation appear as part of a polarized cosmos. At one pole stands the Lamb, which is "as if it had been slaughtered" (Revelation 5:6; cf. Revelation 5:12, 13:8, 14:1). It belongs to the camp of God, the elders and the New Jerusalem, which is the winning team in this text. At the other pole is the Beast, together with Satan, the plagues and Babylon. They are the scoundrels and proponents of evil, and eventually also the losers in the apocalyptic battle. The picture of the Beast is more or less systematically drawn so that this creature appears as a caricature of the Lamb. The contrast between the Beast and the Lamb is also reflected by the other animals in the text, which either belong to the side of God and the Lamb and are employed by them in the battle against the evil forces, or to the side of the Beast as his helpers and instruments.

The Lamb refers to Christ. Two traditional clusters of meaning define this lamb: one is, not astonishingly, the sacrificial lamb; the other is the lamb conceived of as an empowered creature and a ruler or warrior. In accordance with the latter meaning, the lamb is introduced as "the Lion of the tribe of Judah" (Revelation 5:5; cf. Bauckham 1993: 174–98). In other words, its lamb-like qualities have been surpassed and a brand new creature appears. It is characterized as a lamb that had been slaughtered, but unlike other slaughtered lambs it *stands* – this image is interpreted by most commentators as referring to the resurrection of Christ. In striking contrast to real sacrificial lambs, it has seven horns and seven eyes and the capacity to take the book out of God's hands (Revelation 5:6–7), and it is to be married (Revelation 19:7). Finally, the lamb is a warrior.

This lamb strikes the keynote for many of the creatures of the text: they are nearly impossible to visualize, not consistent with only one type of animal, but have traits taken from different creatures and far surpass normal animal behaviour. It is exactly in this lack of realism that there is enormous potential for symbolic interpretation. It must also be noted that the complexity of animals and bestial creatures in Revelation corresponds to the complexity of persons and events in the text.[23]

The Lamb is an example of a positive use of animals in Revelation. The four living creatures (*zoa*) also throw a positive light on the animal world. As they appear in Revelation, they are angelic creatures – cherubim or seraphim – equipped with six wings and full of eyes.[24] They may symbolize the four directions or the four seasons and like other creatures in this text may have some astrological significance. But most important, by being like a lion, a calf, having the face of a man, and being like a flying eagle, respectively, they symbolize the world of living beings (Prigent 2001: 235). *Zoa* is an encompassing term that covers all types of living creature. We have here an archetypal bird (an eagle), an archetypal domesticated animal (a calf) and an archetypal wild animal (the lion), which together with man constitute the living world as a whole. These creatures are finally joined by the creatures on earth in giving praise to God and the Lamb (Revelation 5:14). The four living creatures are examples of a positive symbology of animals in which animals appear together with man in a common living world, a conception of the world that is firmly grounded in the Bible and in Jewish tradition.

The creatures from the evil camp resemble the Lamb in being complex. The chief proponents of evil are the dragon and the two beasts. The dragon (*drakon*) refers to a huge snake or sea monster and is a magnified version of the serpent in Genesis and also an image of Satan (Revelation 12:3, 12:4, 12:7, 12:9, 12:13, 12:16, 12:17, 13:2, 13.4, 16:13, 20:2). The beasts (*therion*) have their origins in two well-known monsters from Jewish mythology, Leviathan and Behemoth, but are set by John in a historical context in which the beast from the sea most probably refers to the Roman Empire and the sea refers to the Mediterranean, while the second creature may be the deified emperor, or more likely, the imperial priesthood (Aune 1998: 780).[25] Accordingly, in this text there is a contrast between two entities, one described as the Lamb, which refers to Christianity, and the dragon/beast, which probably refers to the Roman Empire/paganism/the cult of the emperor, or to one of these rather than to the others. If the emphasis is on the cult of the emperor, which is likely, it is a conflict between worshipping Jesus and worshipping the emperor. Both of these consist of worshipping persons and involve an anthropomorphization of the divine, even if, in Revelation, these anthropomorphic options are masked as Lamb versus Beast.

There is a prominent tendency to cast animals or animal hybrids as demonic beings. The Beast from the sea is described either as having seven heads, ten horns, with ten crowns and with names of blasphemy or "like a leopard, its feet were like a bear's, and its mouth was like a lion's mouth" (Revelation 13:2). Most of the animalian helpers of God are no less monstrous or terrible than the Beast. They are used by God, but in a destructive way. However, these animals fight on the side that John supports, do not act on their own but are directed by God, and appear in flocks, fighting a just war against evil. They are either "normal" animals such as horses used for riding and birds summoned to pick at the flesh of the dead, or supernatural animals such as monstrous grasshoppers. Most of the supranormal animals – but not the slaughtered lamb – are "worse" than ordinary animals and consist, like the Beast, of bits and pieces borrowed from ordinary animals.

There are two main hordes of monstrous animal that are mentioned. They are released by the angels of God, one after the other. The first horde consists of locusts from the Abyss. The locusts are like horses released for battle, have the teeth of lions, human faces, the hair of women, breastplates of iron, wings that sounded like "the noise of many chariots with horses rushing into battle" (Revelation 9:9), and scorpions' tails. They torment those men who do not have the seal of God in their foreheads (Revelation 9:4), but they do not destroy the vegetation, a clear indication that they are not real locusts but demons made up of different animals and animal parts (and the hair of women) to create an impression of utmost terror. Likewise, the second horde of monstrous creatures is an army of horsemen who have heads like lions, tails like serpents with heads on, and out of their mouths issue fire, smoke and brimstone (Revelation 9:16–19).

These chimeras are based among other things on images of horses and riders, horsemen and chariots. Such fantasies obviously have some basis in real-life experiences of horses and men, who together form monstrous creatures with weapons that sting and destroy. They are also conceived of in consonance with the way in the Bible: the horse often symbolizes foreign armies and was an image established for the terrors of war (Michel 1957: 337). In Revelation, this imagery appears in extravagant ways in the fantasies of the monstrous hordes. But creatures that are based more directly on real horses also appear as symbols of terror and battle. Most prominent are the four horses of different colours with their four riders. The fourth horse, which is pale green (*chloros*), symbolizes death and sickness, and the killing that is connected with this horse and its rider is carried out by means of wild animals among other things (Revelation 6:8). The birds that are called in by God to the great supper where they will eat the flesh of the dead are also destructive. This is maltreatment of dead enemies, which represented the utmost degradation of them.

Except for the Lamb and the four creatures of life, the dominant tendency in Revelation is the use of animals and animal hybrids to describe satanic and demonic powers. Carnivores, scorpions and reptiles especially were employed to give faces and bodies to demons. This use of animals further implies that *therion*, "beast", a term that originally referred to wild animals and later to animals in general, was used in a polarized way in opposition to the human as well as to the divine – different from the concept of *zoa*, *theria* never included humans. At the root of this dualism lies the idea that man was made in the image of God, and animals were not. The fact that animals lack divine archetypes was the germ of their later demonization. When the image of God through the figure of Christ is conceived of in anthropomorphic categories, Satan and his creatures, the opposite of the divine, are increasingly thought of in theriomorphic categories. Animal shapes become the natural forms of demons, as when evil spirits appear from the mouth of the dragon like frogs (Revelation 16:13). Revelation can be considered the first Christian example of a systematic use of animal metaphors to illuminate negative things. Social entities are described by means of demonized animals, and some animals appear as evil.

Conclusion

The New Testament has proved to be a rich source for conceptions of animals and has transmitted several models for such conceptions. It reflects different world views and perspectives on animals: the Jewish perspective on the world as a hierarchical community of living beings; the Stoic model of a hierarchy of differences between humans and animals, the most important being that animals are irrational; and finally, a polarized world view according to which at least some animals are demonized. In this complex picture must also be included the Jewish conception of clean and unclean animals.

Sometimes, but not often, animals in the Bible have individual values and appear as creatures with human voices. Examples are the serpent in Genesis and the ass of Balaam, the dove in the Gospels and the eagle in Revelation. Sometimes tenderness towards animals shines through, as in some of the parables. However, it is most important that animals are not present in the New Testament texts for their own sake but because in one way or another – directly or metaphorically – they are being used for human purposes.

An indirect relationship to animals is also characteristic of early Christianity. That Christians neither kept the Jewish dietary laws nor ate meat from animals that had been sacrificed has less to do with their attitudes towards animals than with their need to mark out the distance between themselves and other people who used animals in certain ways.

Another type of indirect relationship with animals is reflected in the hermeneutic movement from literal to figurative meaning that is typical of Christianity. The presentation of animals in the New Testament imposes burdens of human significance on them, which detaches their meaning from the actual way of life of these animals. In the animal world of the Gospels, centre stage is dominated by metaphorical sheep and miraculous fish. It is better to be fishers of men than of fish, and better to be shepherds of men than of sheep. Animals are used as the symbolic capital of teachers and preachers, and just as preachers and teachers are more valuable than shepherds and fishermen, metaphorical sheep and fish are more valuable than their real-life counterparts (cf. I Timothy 5:17). Real animals do not necessarily lose their significance because animals are used as metaphors. On the contrary, animal metaphors presuppose knowledge about animals, and this knowledge contributes to making the metaphors dynamic. All the same, there is a gap in the New Testament texts between the abundant use of animal metaphors and these texts' lack of focus on real animals.

There is a Stoicizing tendency in the letters of Paul and in the non-Pauline letters that works against the view of the world as a hierarchical community of living beings and establishes another type of division between animals and humans based on differences in mental capacity, language, soul and types of flesh. In the Gospels, there is a division between types of animal according to which wild and dangerous creatures are divided from domesticated animals, a division that partly, but not totally, overlaps the division between clean and unclean animals. Pedagogical points are made by the use of duality, for instance by contrasting worms and fish, rams and sheep, goats and sheep, and wolves and sheep (Matthew 10:16; Luke 10:3; John 10:12; Matthew 7:15, 25:32–3), or by employing an ox and a donkey "unevenly yoked" as a symbol of believers and unbelievers (cf. Deuteronomy 22:10).

An even more dramatic polarization between animals and humans is seen in the Revelation of John, where the Beast – *therion* – takes on a demonic quality. This demonization of animals, and especially of carnivores, reptiles and serpents, is dependent on Genesis and on the story of man, who is the sole species made in the image of God. But it is also dependent on the Christian anthropomorphization of the divine, according to which God becomes human in Christ. Because of the dualistic polarity between God and Satan, a logical outcome of the anthropomorphization of the divine is that when God becomes man, Satan becomes a beast.

The biblical texts were rich sources for discourses within Christianity that directly or indirectly related to animals. These discourses evolved over the next centuries and related to the main areas of Christian development. Chief among them were the discourse of the martyrs and the discourse of the ascetics, which both used animals as significant symbols.

9

FIGHTING THE BEASTS

Damnatio ad bestias

In the Roman Empire, the sentencing of humans to the beasts – *damnatio ad bestias* – was a punishment for severe crimes and not open to pardon (Ville 1981: 235–40).[1] It implied being killed by animals in the arena and was a most shameful way to die, a punishment normally not imposed on Roman citizens.[2] It was also a penalty that was expensive and required a considerable amount of planning.

Such killings were staged in the amphitheatres of the great cities at the celebration of feasts and for the general amusement of the spectators. The killing of humans by means of beasts was usually staged in the morning as part of a *venatio*, while ordinary executions were shown in the intermission between the morning programme and that in the evening: "In the morning they throw men to the lions and the bears; at noon, they throw them to the spectators", wrote Seneca (*Epistle*, 7.4). Humans being killed by animals, together with arena performances, such as gladiatorial fights, killing of animals, fights between animals, chariot races, athletic competitions and theatrical performances, were part of the mass entertainment of antiquity, viewed by virtually everyone, even if not everyone appreciated it: Cicero, for instance, asked rhetorically what pleasure it can afford a man of culture "when either a weak human being is mangled by a most powerful beast, or a splendid beast is transfixed with a hunting spear?" (*Letters to his Friends*, 7.1.3).

Classical authors mention the *damnatio ad bestias* sporadically, and scenes in which humans are killed by beasts in the arena are often found in mosaics, especially those from North Africa. Through these mosaics we get a sort of commentary on this type of killing. But even if to be attacked, killed, torn to pieces and sometimes eaten by wild animals is a terrible way to die, depictions of such scenes do not seem to have been thought of as especially revolting by the Romans, who sometimes used them to decorate their dining rooms.[3] We must conclude that the spectators in the Roman world did not usually identify with the victims.

This point of view is convincingly argued by Shelby Brown, who has examined scenes from the arena on Roman domestic mosaics and used them to illuminate these cultural norms that made people want to look at the killings in the arena (Brown 1992). Her conclusion is very clear: the Romans did not see the mosaics in which the victims' wounds and anguish were depicted in the same way as we do with empathy for the victims. On the contrary, the mosaics emphasize the distance of patron and audience from those who were killed. They celebrated a shared social structure according to which this type of punishment had an educational value and was seen as just in relation to the worst crimes. The victims had got what they legitimately deserved. Humiliation and mockery further contributed to alienating the spectator from the offender.

A similar impression is given when one reads Martial's descriptions of the killing of men and animals at the spectacles at the opening of the Flavian Amphitheatre (cf. Coleman 1990). His compassion for the victims is *nil*. This may also imply that in the case of the *damnati ad bestias*, the onlookers, rather than siding with the victims, sided with those who were carrying out the law (*ibid.*: 58) and probably also with the instruments of this justice – which in this case were the beasts.

In contrast to the ordinary Roman attitude, the Christians were a group that did not usually side with the beasts. The Christians were potential victims of such punishment and also had an abhorrence of the arenas, being virtually the only people in the Graeco-Roman world who criticized the entertainment of the arenas (Tertullian, *On the Spectacles*). Since they sometimes became victims of *damnatio ad bestias*, execution by means of animals was a theme upon which the Christian imagination dwelt, and a theme that is treated in the Acts of the Martyrs. But in contrast to pagan art, the Acts of the Martyrs definitely sided with the victims. What is so special about the Christian texts is not only that the story is told from the point of view of the victims but also that the Acts of the Martyrs became one of the main Christian literary genres.

It is also strange that even if Christians were thrown to the beasts, these beasts seldom managed to kill them. Consequently, the theme of this chapter is not only the function and value of animals in the Acts of the Martyrs, i.e. how real animals are described and more fanciful beasts are symbolically invented, but more specific questions are also raised, as to why these sources seldom allow the beasts to kill the martyrs, and why descriptions of beasts killing Christians are almost never given.

A clash of cosmologies

Christians were persecuted sporadically during the first two centuries, but they became subject to empire-wide persecution during the reigns of the emperors Decius (250–1 CE) and Diocletian (303–13 CE).[4,5] There was probably no general law against Christianity, merely a constant suspicion that Christians meant trouble.[6] The test with which they were confronted, when for one reason or another they had been exposed to public scrutiny, was whether they would sacrifice or not, either to the emperor but more often to the gods.[7] Those who refused to sacrifice were potential martyrs. During Emperor Decius' reign, an edict was issued that especially required that everyone should sacrifice to the Roman gods, thus ensuring the loyalty of the emperor's subjects. Those who did obtained an attestation (*libellus*); those who did not risked being confronted by the local authorities.[8]

It is a striking contrast between the pagan and Christian cosmologies that "explained" the events in the arenas. From the Roman point of view, those who were killed were the enemies of Rome, people who by their crimes had cut themselves off from human society. For instance, Tacitus mentions that the Christians who were killed under Nero were dressed as animals and killed by dogs (*The Annals*, 15.44.4). In general, the arena was a stage on which Roman values were re-enacted in the presence of both the common people and the elite (Barton 1996: 33). The proceedings in the arenas were ritualized activities introduced by processions and sacrifices (Tertullian, *On the Spectacles*), where the executions were attended not only by humans but also by the gods, who were present in the form of their statues. The fact that these statues, out of reverence, were veiled when offenders were being executed only underlined the monstrosity of these offenders' crimes. The killing was sometimes even staged within the framework of religious mythology, as in the case of the "fatal charades" described by Martial, when Orpheus was killed by a bear (Coleman 1990; see Chapter 1). Thomas Wiedemann has pointed out that the use of mythological characters and of the framework of Greek myths placed "what went on in the arena into a cosmic universal context" (Wiedemann 1995: 85, cf. Auguet 1994: 100ff). The re-enactment of mythological stories did not take place only in Rome. When the young patrician woman Perpetua and her fellow martyrs were killed in Carthage in 203, they were rigged out in the outfits of Saturnine priests and servants of Ceres.[9] In this way, the enemies of the state were killed within the context of a cosmic drama.

Through Christian narratives about the martyrs, alternative frames of interpretation were established to explain what happened in the amphitheatres (Potter 1993). The amphitheatre was no longer the arena of Roman power and justice; instead, it was described – in Tertullian's words – as "that dreadful [*horrendus*] place". According to Tertullian, the amphitheatre, "is the temple of all demons. There are as many unclean spirits gathered there as it can seat men" (*On the Spectacles*, 97).

In *Scorpiace*, Tertullian introduces a different perspective. He compares the contest of the martyrs to secular contests in which some are winners and others losers, and he describes the arena as being in the service of God. In a way, God himself had staged what happened in the arena, for by means of martyrdom, God tested the steadfastness and endurance of those who believe in him (*Scorpiace*, 6). Tertullian also writes about "the sharp pain of martyrdom" but promises that the suffering of the martyrs will unlock paradise (*A Treatise on the Soul*, 55) and that their ultimate prize is life eternal

(*To the Martyrs*, 3). In his texts, we meet a world turned upside-down where martyrs are better off in jail than in the world. The world is the real prison, because it is filled with sinners, who in Tertullian's perspective appear as the true criminals.

A similar perspective is found in the *Martyrdom of Perpetua and Felicitas*.[10] In one of Perpetua's visions, she is fighting in the arena with an evil Egyptian. In reality, this Egyptian is the Devil, while the person who presides over the games (*lanista*) is to be interpreted as Christ (Bowersock 1995: 51–2).[11] The fight in the arena is also seen in this totally changed perspective. Perpetua and her fellow martyrs returned to prison in high spirits because they had been sentenced to the beasts and later went happily from prison to the amphitheatre as if to heaven (18.1–3). Sometimes the heavenly powers intervened directly in the fate of the martyr, as in the martyrdom of Polycarp, when a voice from heaven encouraged the old bishop to be strong (9.1).

In most of the Acts of the Martyrs, there is a strong appeal to the martyr to sacrifice and an even stronger refusal to do so.[12] The turning-point of the narrative is when the martyr declares that he or she was a Christian. Then those who were not willing to sacrifice were themselves turned into victims.

It varied if beasts were used in the killing of the martyrs. The Acts of the Martyrs mention torture, scourging, beheading and burning as well as *damnatio ad bestias*. In this way, animals that killed Christians became functional equivalents to the stake, the axe and the instruments of torture. This connection is also made when Tertullian lumps together "the merciless sword, and the lofty cross, and the rage of wild beasts, and that punishment of the flames, of all most terrible, and all the skill of the executioners in torture" (*To the Martyrs*, 4), or when Minucius Felix says that Christian boys and women were so inspired to suffer pain that they scorn "crosses and tortures, wild beasts and all frightful torments" (*Octavius*, 37.5; cf. *Hermas*, 2.1; Justin, *Dialogue with Tryphon*, 110). Various sorts of punishment were not seldom measured out to one martyr, with the double purpose of causing as much pain as possible to the victim and presenting varied entertainment for the onlookers. Different animals followed each other, or attacks by animals were combined with other penalties. In Lyons, the slave-girl Blandina was both crucified on a post and at the same time served as bait for the beasts.

Judith Perkins has convincingly argued that characteristic of Christian discourse was a particular understanding of self, the Christian as sufferer. Christian narratives offered "a new literary happy ending for readers – death, in particular, the martyr's death" (Perkins 1995: 24; cf. Shaw 1996).[13] This implies that in the Christian scenario, martyrs were turned into cultural performers who acted out this new plot and rejected a conventional social life. However, when Christians in the Acts of the Martyrs are described as victims, the traditional hierarchy of power is at the same time turned upside-down: through their suffering and death, the martyrs were given power (Perkins 1995: 104–23). In this way, the Christian texts challenged the traditional image of power and gradually created a new one. By embracing martyrdom but denying that they experienced terrible pain or saw death as defeat, the Christians rejected the social order and the power structure that surrounded them (*ibid.*: 117). The Acts of the Martyrs, as texts of subversion, were part of a discourse that eventually contributed to creating a new power structure in the Roman Empire. As pointed out by Jane Cooper, by means of the martyr texts Christians were putting themselves in a new position in relation to pagans by creating a new type of hierarchy and status. They refused to be intimidated by the persecutions and were thus making the Roman system unstable (Cooper 2003).

The new cosmological context into which the Christians had put the *damnatio ad bestias* implied that the drama in the arena was no longer a rightful struggle to maintain law and order, a struggle in which the enemies of the state and of the gods had to pay with their lives through gruesome but well-deserved punishments. Instead, it was conceived of as a struggle between God and Satan in which human and bestial actors also played their parts.

Some of the narratives are fantastic. There has been a continuous discussion as to how far these reports truthfully render what really happened when the martyr was killed. Fantastic and miraculous events are usually not seen as increasing the source value of a text. Sometimes the whole genre of *Acta Martyrum* is described as fictitious, a point of view that undermines the usefulness of an important early Christian genre and does not seem to be very well founded. However, considering that our topic includes imagined animals as well as real ones, that the differences between these categories are blurred (see Chapter 4) and that one goal is to describe the use of animals in cultural processes, the discussion about reality and fiction in the Acts of the Martyrs does not have to bother us too much. In this context, any animal goes. How realistically the beasts are described is less interesting than the use to which they were actually put.

Threatening beasts and cosmological symbols

In the Acts of the Martyrs, animals generally have four functions. In addition to the animals' obvious function as instruments of torture and killing, martyrs were urged to sacrifice animals, and wild animals were used to threaten would-be martyrs. In addition, on a metaphysical level, animals appeared as symbols of a polarized cosmos.

When the animal sacrifice is introduced in the Acts of the Martyrs, it usually appears as a prescribed ritual action in which the animal is presupposed but not present. When Perpetua was brought before the governor, her father urged her: "Perform the sacrifice – have pity on your baby" (6.2), and the governor also bade her "to offer the sacrifice [*fac sacrum*] for the welfare of the emperors" (6.3).[14] No animal is mentioned. Not only is the animal seldom mentioned, but it was not always necessary to sacrifice an animal at all; some incense or wine would suffice (*Of Conon*, 4). Only as an exception is the sacrificial animal really there. When Pionius was executed in Smyrna during the Decian persecution, and he and his companions were dragged off "to offer sacrifice and to taste forbidden meats" (3.1), Pionius is confronted with Euctemon, a Christian who has saved his life by bringing and sacrificing a lamb in the temple of Nemesis. Afterwards, Euctemon is eating of the roasted meat of the little lamb (15.2; 18.13–14) – and is ridiculed for his apostasy.

From the documents, it is clear that animal sacrifices were demanded of the Christians (cf. Price 1986: 227–8). The absence of sacrificial animals in the Acts of the Martyrs is not only due to the fact that the sacrifice was a formality in which the animal was no more than a necessary prop. They are probably also absent because these texts are part of a sacrificial discourse where the martyrs themselves are the real victims. Too much attention to the details of the pagan rites would have taken attention away from the true focus of the narrative, which was the killing of the martyr. The martyrs not only refused to sacrifice, they also usurped the role of the sacrificial animals. In line with this development, it is no longer the sacrificial animals but the Christian martyrs who are described as victims. For instance, in the case of Polycarp, he is characterized as "a noble ram chosen for an oblation from a great flock" (*Martyrdom of Polycarp*, 14.1), "a holocaust" (14.1), and "a rich and acceptable sacrifice" (14.2), while Perpetua describes herself and her fellow martyrs in a revealing phrase normally used of sacrificial animals when she says that they should appear in the arena "in good condition [*pinguiores*]" (*Martyrdom of Perpetua*, 16.3).

The Christians were sometimes threatened with the beasts, and bestial killings were used to deter others from claiming that they were Christians. In the *Martyrdom of Polycarp*, Polycarp was threatened that if he insisted on being a Christian, he would be thrown to the animals (11.1). In the *Letter to Diognetus*, the anonymous second-century Christian apologia, it is said that Christians were thrown to the beasts so that they should deny the Lord, but that they were not defeated (*Letter to Diognetus*, 7.7).

Some were obviously afraid, and some lapsed. Eusebius describes Christians in Alexandria under the Decian persecution who, according to him, were "cowards in everything both in dying and in sacrificing" (*Ecclesiastical History*, 6.41.11). In the *Martyrdom of Polycarp*, a Phrygian named Quintus, who had originally given himself up, turned cowardly when he saw the wild animals, and lapsed (6.41.14).[15]

In addition to real animals, in the Acts of the Martyrs animals are also used as cosmological symbols. The evil powers especially are often made into beasts, a practice that has its roots in Jewish and Christian apocalyptic texts. When Tertullian, in his treatise *To the Martyrs*, addressed Christians who were detained in prison, giving them spiritual sustenance, he describes the prison as the Devil's house and exhorts the Christians to let the Devil "fly from your presence, and skulk away into his own abysses, shrunken and torpid, as though he were an outcharmed or smoked-out snake" (*To the Martyrs*, 1.5). As a symbol for the Devil, the snake is a recurring theme in the martyr texts.

In the *Martyrdom of Perpetua and Felicitas*, Perpetua has a vision and sees a bronze ladder of tremendous height that ascends to heaven. At the foot of the ladder lies an enormous dragon (*draco*), which acts as if it is frightened of Perpetua, and she uses its head as the first step and climbs up (4.3–7).

Afterwards, when Perpetua and her fellow martyrs have been found guilty of the charges against them and sentenced to be thrown to the beasts, Perpetua has a new vision (10.1–15). She is led to the amphitheatre but is astonished that no wild animals are sent in to her. Instead, she is going to fight against an ugly Egyptian. Most remarkably, she is now turned into a man. Perpetua eventually kicks the Egyptian with her heels, is lifted into the air and beats at him from above. Eventually she fights him down and treads on his head. Then Perpetua understands that she is not going to fight against the wild animals (*ad bestias*) but against the Devil (*contra diabolum*). And she knows that she will be victorious.[16]

Both Perpetua's treading upon the head of the dragon and her treading upon the head of the Egyptian, who in reality is the Devil, are described as *calcavi illi caput* (4.7). *Calcare* means deliberately treading something down. The term was used in relation to snakes but also in relation to defeated enemies and, not least, in relation to the Devil (Genesis 3:15; Luke 10:18–19; cf. Dölger 1932; Bremmer 2002: 101).[17]

In this *passio*, the Devil – in addition to the evil Egyptian – is associated with two animals that are closely related, the snake and the dragon. This combination is also found in Revelation, and the image of the dragon in the *Martyrdom of Perpetua and Felicitas* finds a model in this text.[18] Perpetua's fighting against these evil entities most clearly puts her struggle into a cosmological framework. In her visions, their polar opposite is a tall grey-haired man whom she meets when she has climbed the ladder. He sits in an immense garden, milking sheep. This shepherd gives Perpetua a mouthful of cheese or milk as a sort of eucharist, and she is still tasting its sweetness when she awakens after her vision. This shepherd, like the *lanista* – the president of the games in the vision of the Egyptian – is probably to be interpreted as Christ (Bremmer 2002: 103–4; Salisbury 1997: 102). Taken together, he and his sheep constitute an image of the divine world.

The polarization between the divine ruminants and the evil reptile is also found in the *Martyrs of Lyons*. Here the sufferings of Blandina make "irreversible the condemnation of the crooked serpent [*ophis*]" (42; cf. Isaiah 27.1), while one Vettus Epagathus is described as a true disciple of Christ, "following the Lamb wherever he goes" (1.11).[19]

The Acts of the Martyrs are polarized descriptions of human existence in which the actors tend to move to either one or the other of the two poles.

While the lamb or sheep are sometimes used to symbolize the positive pole, the negative pole is more frequently described by beasts or bestial symbols – usually the snake or the dragon.

The human enemies of the Christians are sometimes also described as beasts. Ignatius of Antioch compares the soldiers who accompanied him on his journey from Syria to Rome, where he was to be thrown to the beasts, to ten leopards: "From Syria even unto Rome I fight with beasts [*theriomacho*] both by land and sea, both by night and day, being bound to ten leopards, I mean a band of soldiers, who, even when they receive benefits, show themselves all the worse" (*Letter to the Romans*, 5.1).[20] Lactantius calls Emperor Decius "an accursed wild beast" (*The Death of Persecutors*, 4). The local mob is described as bestial in the Lyonnese letter and characterized as "these wild [*agria*] and barbarous people once stirred up by the wild Beast [*upo agriou theros*]" (1.57), as lacking human comprehension, and as being inflamed with bestial anger (*ten orgen therion*; 1.58).[21] In his *Scorpiace* – antidote for the scorpion's sting – a treatise Tertullian wrote against heretics and in praise of martyrdom, heretics such as gnostics and Valentinians are described as opponents of martyrdom, painted in lively colours as scorpions and referred to as "the little beasts which trouble our sect" (*Scorpiace*, 1).

The beasts of the arena

The most obvious role for animals in the Acts of the Martyrs was as instruments of suffering and death. In the *Martyrdom of Perpetua and Felicitas*, which is the *passio* that contains the most detailed description of a *damnatio ad bestias*, Saturus, who was probably the leader of the catechumens, jailed and killed in Carthage in 203 CE, was first bound beneath a wild boar (*apra*). The boar did not kill him but killed its keeper instead (19.5). Afterwards, Saturus was bound to a bridge, but the bear who should have killed him did not come out of its cage (19.6). Then, as Saturus himself had predicted, he was thrown to a leopard and bitten so that he bled terribly, and he fainted, but he did not die (21.3). According to the text, he is at last killed by an executioner (21.4–8). Two of Perpetua and Saturus' fellow martyrs, Revocatus and Saturius, were first cast to a leopard and then to a bear (19.3). Perpetua herself and the slave-girl Felicitas met a wild cow. They were tossed around and maimed by the cow but were eventually taken back and beheaded by a gladiator (20.1–10; 21.9–10). We will return to this lack of nerve on the part of the animals (see below).

In this *passio*, different animals were used. Most were carnivores, but a wild cow and a wild boar also played roles. None of these animals was hurt, and they could therefore be reused on other occasions, such as in a *venatio*, a hunting game where the animals attacked each other or were attacked by hunters and that could also include a *damnatio*.

The fact that different animals were used is probably also connected to the general demand for novelty and variety. In his letter to a friend, Cicero

190

stressed that there had been nothing new in what he had seen in the arena – meaning that his friend did not miss anything (*Letters to his Friends*, 7.1.3). From the Christian point of view, martyrs meeting various trials and different animals were comparable to athletes competing in different contests (see below). Saturnius, for instance, explicitly wanted "to be exposed to all the different beasts [*omnibus bestiis*]" (19.2).

The animals in the Christian descriptions of the *damnatio ad bestias* are lions, leopards, bears, wild cows and oxen, a wild boar, and dogs. These animals are similar to those we find in pagan texts or depicted on mosaics. From the city of Aphrodisias there are two fragments from panels that may have decorated buildings and that probably show bears attacking people who had been condemned *ad bestias* (Roueché 1993: 39–40). Mosaics with scenes from *venationes*, especially from North Africa, show leopards and other varieties of big cat that have sprung onto men, biting them in the neck or mauling them in the face (from Thysdrus, Zliten, Silin; see Brown 1992; Dunbabin 1999). Big cats gave fatal bites and were usually instant killers. However bears might start to eat their victims while they are still alive. This is reflected in Martial's description of a Scottish bear, which reduced its victim so that its human form was unrecognizable (Martial, *Book of Spectacles*, 7; see below). No wonder Saturus was frightened of bears. In the *Martyrdom of Perpetua and Felicitas*, it is said that he "dreaded nothing more than a bear" (19.4). Bulls with human victims are also depicted on the mosaics. On a mosaic from Silin in North Africa, a huge bull is attacking a man (Dunbabin 1999: 124). Dogs were common in the arenas. They were the animals that, according to Tacitus, were set to attack and kill Christians at the time of Nero. Dogs are also reported to have been used to eat what was left of executed prisoners; for instance those who were strangled in prison in Lyons were later thrown to the dogs (*The Martyrs of Lyons*, 1.59).

Sometimes the nature of the animals is not specified; they appear *en masse* and are collectively designated as "beasts" (Greek, *therioi*; Latin, *bestia*).

God's instrument or the instrument of Satan?

An important point in relation to a *damnatio ad bestias* is that the behaviour of the animals was not always predictable. The behaviour of living creatures seldom is, even if those who arranged the games did their best to get the animals to play their role by chaining them and their victim together, as is sometimes shown on mosaics, or by using some other means of frustrating the animals, such as burning, scourging or stabbing. This unpredictability on the part of the animals opened up the possibility of pious interpretations. The beasts in the Acts of the Martyrs are often described as transcending their bestial ways and revealing a human – or even divine – attitude of mind. At other times, they were seen as the tools of Satan. In both cases, the animals were part of the type of polarized cosmology already described.

The behaviour of the animals can be divided into three different types:

1   The animals behave as predatory animals usually do. Sometimes they go
    in for the kill, while at other times they prowl about, not touching the
    victims. In any case, the description of the animals is realistic.
2   The animals appear as evil by nature and sometimes as the instruments
    of Satan.
3   The animals may decline to kill their victims because they in some way
    or other have been touched by God.

Beasts that are described realistically as well as beasts that are described as
the instruments of either God or Satan may appear together in the same
narrative.In the polarized description of reality of the *Acta Martyrum*, there
is a crucial question: in whose service were the animals? It is true that they
were bought and fed by those in charge of the games and were trained and
tended by specialists (*bestiarii*) with whom they may have had a personal
relation. But, more importantly, these animals sometimes had other lords in
addition to their ordinary paymasters and trainers. In the case of Perpetua
and Felicitas, it is explicitly stated that Satan procured a wild cow and that
he did so because of hostility towards their sex. But, except for this remark,
the animals' behaviour in this *passio* is described realistically.

In the martyrdom of Thecla, as described in the *Acts of Paul and Thecla*,
probably composed in Asia Minor between 185 and 195 CE, the beasts of the
arena are more directly the instruments of both divine and demonic forces.
This hagiographical romance is not canonical. One reason is that too many
fantastic – and, not least, unorthodox – things happen, as for instance when
Paul baptizes a lion, or when Thecla baptizes herself in a pit full of water
with seals (whether the self-baptism of a woman or the baptism of a lion was
conceived of as "worse" with regard to orthodoxy is hard to say).

These Acts include a fight in the arena where Paul is saved from the wild
beasts, and the baptized lion, which has refused to attack Paul, is saved from
archers by an exceedingly heavy hailstorm.

Thecla was also condemned to the beasts (*Acts of Paul and Thecla*, 26–39).
She was attacked by lions and bears in the arena but was protected by a
fierce lioness that lay down at Thecla's feet. Afterwards, the lioness tore a
bear asunder before it perished in a fight against a lion. In this fight, both
felines died. Many beasts were then set on Thecla, and she threw herself into
the pit of water with the seals (*phokai*) to baptize herself. The onlookers
feared that she would be devoured by the seals, but instead the seals saw the
flash of a bolt of lightning and promptly floated dead on the surface. Thecla
was then protected by a cloud of fire, so that she was not touched by the
beasts – neither did the crowd see her naked. More terrible beasts were let
loose, but the female spectators who had earlier mourned the death of the
lioness now threw flower petals and spices on them so that there was an

abundance of perfumes, and the beasts were overwhelmed by sleep. Finally, Thecla was tied to bulls that had had red-hot irons placed beneath their bellies. These devices were meant to enrage the bulls so that they would kill her. However, the flames burned through the ropes. The governor eventually admitted defeat and released Thecla.

Several things are strange in this narrative: the divine repeatedly and actively intervenes on behalf of Thecla; she conquers her adversaries and, in fact, does not become a martyr at all; and, above all, the beasts behave curiously – the heroic lioness on the one hand and the seals, which are conceived of as vicious and likely to attack people, on the other.

The fact that seals are harmless animals and can be trained was known to the Romans (for instance, Pliny, *Natural History*, 9.41, 10.128). Why did these seals behave so strangely? With regard to this question, Horst Schneider has recently pointed to the Greek tradition from Homer onwards in which the seal was described as a *ketos*, a water monster. This monster was conceived of as emitting a hideous stench (Schneider 2001). Schneider also points to Oppian, who mentions that bears had been set against a seal and been vanquished (Oppian, *Halieutica*, 5.38–40). In other words, there were other dimensions to seals than those described by Pliny. In the case of Thecla, the seals had become the subjects of a pious exegesis that was facilitated, not least, as Schneider wryly remarks, by the author probably never having seen a seal.

As for being killed by lightning, it is an explicit tradition in ancient authors that seals were never struck by it and that their hides for this reason were used as protection. Augustus, for instance, protected himself against lightning in that way (Schneider 2001). Therefore, when these seals were finally wiped out, *contra naturam*, by being struck by lightning, it really showed God's miraculous intervention.

The battle of smells must also be mentioned. Generally, evil powers were thought to have a nauseous stench, while beneficial powers smelled sweetly. In the *Acts of Paul and Thecla*, the stench of the evil powers is exemplified by the seals, while the aroma of sanctity is produced by the pious women by means of petals and spices. Because the wild animals represent evil, they cannot stand this sweet smell and are immediately stupefied by it.

Thecla's lioness could perhaps have been associated with the lions and sometimes lionesses in the Mediterranean area that used to accompany goddesses (Marinatos 2000: 124–7). By being protected by a lioness, the invincible Thecla appears as a Christian answer to the pagan goddesses of Asia Minor.

The correspondence between the sex of the lion and the sex of Thecla must also be noted. A similar correspondence is found in the *Martyrdom of Perpetua*, where Perpetua and Felicitas were matched with a wild cow. In this *passio*, it is explicitly said that the Devil had procured the cow and that "it was chosen that their sex might be matched with that of the beast" (20.1;

see Habermehl 1992: 203). In these two cases, there is a structural parallel with animal sacrifice, in which female animals were always sacrificed to goddesses and male animals were offered to male gods. The correspondence between animal and human sex is obviously significant in these two cases, although there is nothing automatic in this type of correspondence. Blandina was tossed around by a bull and, more astonishingly, the lioness of Thecla changed sex over the centuries. In a later version of her ordeal, the lioness was replaced by a lion, when Bishop Ambrose of Milan used the story of Thecla for his own purposes in the late fourth century.[22]

In Ambrose's "rewriting of Thecla" (Burrus 1995: 30–3), the fierce lion that was meant to attack Thecla "was to be seen lying on the ground, licking her feet, showing without a sound that it could not injure the sacred body of the virgin" (*Concerning Virgins*, 2.3.20). In this way, the lion taught men a lesson: "One could see, as it were, by some transfusion of nature, men clothed with savagery, goading the beast to cruelty, and the beast kissing the feet of the virgin, teaching them what was due from men" (*ibid.*). One moral in this story is the admirability of virginity – the lions (which have now multiplied) "kiss the virgin's feet, with their eyes turned to the ground, as though through modesty, fearing that any male, even a beast, should see the virgin naked" (*ibid.*).

The lion's sex-reversal has recently been discussed by Virginia Burrus, who has seen it in relation to the development of ideal Christian gender roles. Burrus has interpreted the lion as representing male sexual violence and has stressed that the animal in this case does not act as a male beast but in fact abandons its attack on Thecla (Burrus 1995; cf. Boyarin 1999: 74–81). Burrus argues that while Perpetua, like Thecla and the lioness in the *Acts of Paul and Thecla*, expressed a virilization of the female, two hundred years later the passive virgin and the feminized lion of Ambrose have rather become an inspiration for the feminized male. These late fourth-century figures have replaced the more virile female expressed in the second-century figures of Perpetua and Thecla. Virginia Burrus and Daniel Boyarin have convincingly argued that the lion and its sex-reversal became embroiled in the development of Christian gender ideals. However, not only the shifting gender of the animal is important; its species must also be commented upon.

The lion was a royal animal, the chief among beasts, and was for that reason used as a symbol for a human ruler. In the Bible, the lions of the Psalms, according to common exegetical traditions, were interpreted as oppressors, either as humans or as demons. Sometimes the lions were explicitly linked with tyrants, like Antiochus IV Epiphanes (see Jackson 1985: 172). Ambrose's narrative was written at the time of Christianity's final breakthrough in the Roman Empire. It is also tempting to see the image of the lion(s) kissing the feet of the Christian virgin as a comment on the new relationship between the secular powers and the Christian faith. The lions acknowledged the virgin's sanctity, but by their kissing of her feet, the virgin was at the same time admired and kept in her place by the lions. Thus the relationship between Thecla and the lions in Ambrose's narrative could also be read as a reflection of the relationship between the Christian Church and the powers of this world, which from this time on held each other in a grip of mutual dependency.

Saintly sacrifices and sacramental language

A puzzling thing in the martyr texts is that the punishment of the *damnatio* is mainly described in the oldest texts and in relation to the martyrs of the second century and beginning of the third, as seen in *Ignatius' Letter to the Romans*, the *Martyrdom of Polycarp*, the *Letter from the Martyrs in Lyons and Vienna*, the *Martyrdom of Perpetua and Felicitas*, and the *Acts of Paul and Thecla*. The reason why the extremely degrading *damnatio* is mostly found in the oldest cases could be that arena punishments in later centuries became rarer. Such punishments may also have become more problematic when Christians increasingly came from the same class as the authorities and because Christians had now multiplied and become widespread in the empire (see Potter 1993: 69ff). However, even more puzzling than the limited number of "damnations" in the Acts of the Martyrs is the fact that even if the martyrs in these texts were sentenced to be killed by the beasts, the beasts did not actually kill them. The killing was finally done by other means. The description of the martyrs of Lyons illustrates this point.

In 177 CE, there was an anti-Christian uprising in Gaul. The trials, torture, sentencing and eventually killing of Christians in the amphitheatre at Lyons are described by the Christian communities in Lyons and Vienna, which wrote a letter to the churches of Asia and Phrygia. This letter is preserved by Eusebius (*Ecclesiastical History*, 5.1.3–2.8). According to the letter from Lyons, the persecution was conceived of as the work of the Devil, who is described as the "serpent" (*ophis*; 1. 42) or the "beast" (*therion*; 1.57 and 2.6).

During the trials, some lapsed, and some even accused their fellow Christians of eating human meat and taking part in incestuous relationships (1.14). They were released, while those who insisted that they were Christians were executed. Maturus, Sanctus, Blandina and Attalus were exposed to the beasts (1.37). They went through different trials, among which they suffered "the mauling by animals" (1.38). Eventually, Maturus and Sanctus were "sacrificed" (*etythesan*; 1.40) and died. This letter states that those who were thought to possess Roman citizenship were beheaded, while the rest were condemned to the beasts (1.47). Therefore, Attalus, who was a Roman citizen, was remanded, but to please the mob he was nevertheless offered to the beasts a second time together with a Christian named Alexander. Attalus and Alexander met different trials but were in the end "sacrificed" (1.51) and not killed by the animals to whom they had been sentenced.

Blandina was hung on a post, and the animals were let loose on her. However, the animals did not touch her. Finally, on the last day of the games, Blandina, together with a young boy, was exposed to "the scourges, the animals, and the hot griddle, she was at last tossed into a net and exposed to a bull" (1.55). In this way, she too was "offered in sacrifice" (*etuthe*; 1.56).

When it is said that these martyrs were "sacrificed", it most probably implies that their throats were cut (cf. Hall 1993: 15). The beasts did not kill them; neither did they kill any of the martyrs in the *passio* of Perpetua and Felicitas.

It is a well-known fact, which cannot be doubted, that Christians were thrown to the beasts. Neither is it to be doubted that the victims were sometimes killed by the beasts, and even eaten – or, at least, partly eaten. Eusebius, in his church history, refers to three persons in Caesarea in Palestine – Priscus, Malchus and Alexander – who "were adorned with divine martyrdom, becoming food for wild beasts" (*The Ecclesiastical History*, 7.12.1), and to Bishop Silvanus in Emesa, who along with others "became food for wild beasts" (8.13.4), thus implying that in these cases the martyrs were not only killed by animals but eaten by them as well. However, Eusebius does not elaborate on this point.

Eating is also referred to by Minucius Felix, who mentions, as one of the horrors committed by the pagans, those who devour wild animals from the arenas – animals that are gorged with the limbs and entrails of men (*Octavius*, 30.6; cf. Tertullian, *Apologeticus*, 9.11).[23] Martial too writes of one criminal who was attacked by a Scottish bear, that "his mangled limbs still lived, though the parts were dripping with blood, and in his whole body there actually was no body" (*Book of Spectacles*, 7). Finally, Artemidorus mentions in his book, the *Interpretation of Dreams*, that "the fighter of beasts nourishes the beasts with his own flesh" and that human flesh is consumed by wild beasts (2.54).

With these descriptions in mind, why do the authors of the Acts of the Martyrs not want to dwell on the gory details of Christians actually being killed by the beasts to whom they were sentenced? David Potter says that "it seems to have been the practice to allow the beast to bite, trample, gore, or – in the case of Apuleius again – to have intercourse with, but not kill, the victim" (Potter 1993: 66). According to Potter, the victim was then, "after a suitable period of abuse" (*ibid.*), taken from the animal and killed outside the arena. This is indeed the impression given by the Acts of the Martyrs. However, it may not be so easy to get a lion or a bull away from a victim they have started to bite, trample or gore. Besides, the evidence from Eusebius, Tertullian, Minucius Felix and Martial contradicts the assertion that the beasts did not kill their victims. Considering their evidence, there are probably other reasons why the beasts in these texts seldom kill and never eat the victims.

These reasons probably are to do with theology, partly with the idea that the Christians were the equivalents of sacrificial animals, partly with the idea of the martyrs as athletes, and partly with sacramental language. In the descriptions of the suffering and death of the martyrs, different images, contexts and interpretations were intertwined and used to enrich each other and to create powerful new images. Some of these images and interpretative contexts were more compatible than others. Some were incompatible. The imagery connected with being attacked, killed and eaten by animals, for instance, was different from imagery based on the martyrs being sacrificial victims; it was different from sacramental language based on either the Eucharist or baptism, and it was different from imagery based on the martyrs as athletes in the service of God. All the same, combinations of some of these scenarios and images could be used.

The identification between Christian martyrs and sacrificial animals has already been mentioned in connection with the sacrificial bull of Arnobius (see Chapter 7). Another example is in Revelation, where the souls of the martyrs are kept beneath the heavenly altar: "And when he had opened the fifth seal, I saw under the altar the souls of them that were slain for the word of God, and for the testimony which they held" (Revelation 6:9). Since the blood of the animals was usually poured at the foot of the altar, the souls of the martyrs gathered under the heavenly altar in this vision replaced the animal blood, as the heavenly altar replaced the earthly altar. In a similar way, Origen compares the forgiveness of sins through the sacrifice of the blood of goats and oxen at the altar of the Jews to the forgiveness of sins at the heavenly altar brought about by the Christian martyrs (Origen, *Exhortation to Martyrdom*, 30). In both these cases, the martyrs had taken the traditional role of sacrificial animals.

When Perpetua demanded better treatment in her prison, she argued that she and her fellow martyrs should be led to the arena "in good condition" (*pinguiores*), the reference being to sacrificial beasts – *pinguis* is used about a sacrificial victim (Habermehl 1992: 193). Similarly, Polycarp was likened to a sacrificial animal, as we have already seen (*Martyrdom of Polycarp*, 14.1–2). Instead of describing the death of the martyrs as being eaten by animals, the killing is characterized as a sacrifice. Ignatius, in his letter to the Romans, prays that he will be "sacrificed to God, while the altar is still prepared" (2); Ambrose presents Thecla as one who teaches others "how to be sacrificed" (*On Virgins*, 2.3); while in the *Martyrs of Lyons*, when Attalus was burning in a brazen seat, "sacrificial savour arose from his body" (52). The comparison that was made between martyrs and sacrificial animals and the description of the martyrs' deaths as sacrifices further implied that their killing had to be made compatible with traditional conceptions of blood sacrifices, for instance, as we have seen, when the victims of *damnatio ad bestias* finally had their throats cut.

The idea of Christians as sacrificial victims dominates the discourse on martyrs and probably prevented a further development of imagery of wild animals killing and eating martyrs. The connection that Ignatius made between himself being "the food of beasts" (*therion bora*) and "the wheat of God" (*sitos theou*) (*Letter to the Romans*, 4–5) remains isolated and slightly strange:

> Suffer me to become food for the wild beasts, through whose instrumentality it will be granted me to attain God. I am the wheat of God, and am ground by the teeth of wild beasts, that I may be found to be the pure bread of God. Rather entice the wild beasts, that they may become my tomb, and may leave nothing of my body; so that when I have fallen asleep, I may not be found troublesome to any one.
>
> (*Letter to the Romans*, 4)

In these lines, Ignatius describes being eaten by animals in sacramental language. However, the explicit sacramental interpretation of martyrs being eaten was rare. Bishop Polycarp, who became a martyr in Smyrna, probably between 155 and 160 CE, when he was eighty-six years old, was not thrown to the beasts because the season for animal hunts was over. Instead he was burned at the stake. In this martyrdom, Polycarp is not only compared to an animal sacrifice, but eucharistic language is also used when the old bishop stands within the flames, not as burning flesh but rather as bread being baked or as costly metals that were purified in a smelting furnace. The flames smelled as delightful fragrance, "as though it were smoking incense or some other costly perfume" (15.2). In contrast to Ignatius' descriptions of his future martyrdom, wild animals are not used in the eucharistic language of the *Martyrdom of Polycarp*.

Andrew McGowan has recently pointed out how in the *Martyrdom of Perpetua and Felicitas* there is a contrast "between blood and killing on the one hand, and milk and peace on the other" (McGowan 1999: 102). The imagery connected with milk and peace is to be seen when Perpetua receives cheese from the hand of the shepherd, in the fact that she is a nursing mother, and in Felicitas' having just given birth. In contrast, the ladder to heaven is framed with all sorts of iron weapons and is guarded by the dragon, and the spectacles in the arena are described as extremely bloody. But even if there is a contrast between milk, peace and paradise on the one hand and killing, blood and arenas on the other, there is also a contrast between two different scenarios of bloody killing, which in reality are two different sacrificial scenarios. The sacrificial animals are killed in honour of the emperor and the gods, while the martyrs are killed in honour of the Christian community and the Christian god.

Baptism and new birth were interconnected in Christian thinking. Martyrdom was drawn into this context too. In the *Martyrdom of Perpetua*, when Saturus was bitten by the leopard, the bite made him bleed terribly, and while the mob mockingly congratulated him on his bath – *salvum lotum, salvum lotum* – the narrator maintains that they were witness to his second baptism and that Saturus was indeed well washed (21:1–3). In this case, the pagan mockery was challenged by an authoritative Christian interpretation. It asserted that this "bath" was a second baptism, a baptism of blood that, according to Tertullian, was a key to paradise, a heroic initiation directly into heaven (Tertullian, *On Baptism*, 16; cf. Origen, *Exhortation to Martyrdom*; cf. Dölger 1930). More generally, Jan Bremmer has pointed out that there was a "profound influence of Christian practices and representations on Perpetua's dream world" (Bremmer 2002: 120).

The similarity as well as the contrast between natural birth and the *damnatio* are also commented upon in this *passio*. When Felicitas was in prison, she bore a baby and "went from blood to blood and to the arena as to the second baptism". Felicitas' fight with the beasts in a similar manner to that of Saturus is described as "a bath after the birth, in a second baptism" (*lotura post partum baptismo secundo*; 15.2). In contrast to Felicitas' giving life to a child through natural birth, by means of the arena she was born into heavenly life. The comparison between birth and martyrdom is also used by Ignatius. He compares the pain and suffering he endured to the experience of a woman in childbirth. But the hope is no longer the birth of a child but "the literal rebirth of one's own body" (Shaw 1996: 290).[24]

Even if the animals and the arena are given a truly life-sustaining meaning as the instruments and birthplace of the new heavenly self, an explicit connection between the actual killing done by wild animals and sacramental language is not, except for Ignatius, really explored in the Acts of the Martyrs. One could, perhaps, have expected a flowering symbolism of martyrs born for paradise by means of wild animals, but such symbolism is not developed. It was obviously felt to be an incongruity that Christians were sacrificed on the one hand and killed by wild animals on the other.

In addition, there is a clash between being physically attacked by animals and fighting against them as an athlete of God. In general, the model of the competitive athlete was central in the Christian interpretation of martyrs. In the *Martyrs of Lyons*, it is said of the martyrs that "Surely it behoved these noble athletes, after sustaining a brilliant contest and a glorious victory, to win the great crown of immortality" (1.36).

It is revealing that according to Perpetua's vision she was not going to fight (*pugnare*) against the wild animals (10.14). The fight against the animals had been supplanted in her vision by the fight with the Egyptian, which in reality was a fight with the Devil. Also in the rare cases of an animal actually killing a martyr, the martyr's courage and heroism were important. In the *Martyrdom of Polycarp*, Germanicus fought manfully with the beast, and even forcefully dragged the beast on top of him, to escape more quickly from "this unjust and lawless life" (3). In these narratives, the victims become heroes and behave as champions.

199

In those Acts of the Martyrs that include a *damnatio ad bestias*, the martyrs' fate in the arena is described either as being thrown to the beasts (*obiecta bestiis*; cf. *Perpetua*, 15.5, 19.2, 21.2) or it is said that the martyrs "fought with the beasts" (Latin, *ad bestias pugnare*; Greek, *theriomachein*; cf. *Perpetua*, 10.14, 18.3). These different concepts reflect either a passive or an active attitude towards wild animals. The contrast is to be seen when, for instance, her keepers told Felicitas that she would be thrown to the wild animals (*facies obiecta bestiia*; 15.5), while Felicitas herself is described as being glad that "she would be fighting with the wild animals" (*ad bestias pugnare*; 18.3). But even if there is a contrast between the passivity of being thrown and the activity of fighting, an active attitude may also be shown in relation to "being thrown", as when Saturnius wanted "to be thrown to all the animals" (19.2). The active attitude is more in consonance with the Christian ideology of the martyr as being a competitive athlete rather than a passive victim.

The lack of descriptions of people really being eaten may also be due more generally to the difficulty of reconciling such descriptions with the Christian idea of martyrs as winners. For a living being to be killed and consumed by an animal is a sort of total destruction and absolute defeat and therefore difficult – perhaps too difficult – to combine with the rhetoric of manly competition and victory. It does not mean that the bodies of the martyrs were not sometimes totally destroyed. For instance, in the letter from Lyons it is said of the bodies of the dead martyrs that "whatever was left of those who had been exposed to the beasts or the fire, some charred and ripped apart as they were, with the heads of the rest and the pieces of their bodies, all this they similarly left unburied and kept under a guard of soldiers for days on end" (1.59). These remains were finally burned and the ashes of the bodies swept into the River Rhône (1.62). It is in this case explicitly stated that the pagans did it to deprive the martyrs of their resurrection (1.63). This suggests more generally that the concept of resurrection played a part in the formulation of the type of suffering and manner of death that was acceptable in the Acts of the Martyrs. According to Caroline Walker Bynum, "the palpable, vulnerable, corruptible body Christ redeems and raises was quintessentially the mutilated cadaver of the martyr" (Bynum 1995: 43). The idea that the experience of martyrdom lay at the heart of the Christian discussion of resurrection is convincing. All the same, in the descriptions of their sufferings and death, it was obviously not seen as desirable to elaborate on the type of destruction brought about by the consumption of the martyrs by animals in the arena.[25]

The horror of digestion and the solution of metaphors

Even if the Acts of the Martyrs avoid descriptions of beasts actually eating martyrs, it does not mean that the question of what happened when animals consumed humans did not appear in Christian texts. On the contrary,

Christian authors found the problem disturbing. It was fear of consumption, not least of chain consumption, which implied that humans might feed on beasts that had eaten humans. Cannibalism, the most acute instance of problematic consumption, also appears in the discussion. The questions of consumption in relation to resurrection became increasingly important in the third century (Bynum 1995: 33ff; Hällström 1988).

Some insisted that there was an incompatibility between human flesh (*sarx*) and animal flesh. Athenagoras claimed that human flesh could not be digested (at least not totally), and Methodius agreed with him, while both Tertullian and Augustine thought that human flesh could be completely digested by animals. However, even those authors who claimed that human flesh was completely digested by animals denied that it meant a final destruction of that flesh. Its scattered elements would finally be reassembled by God. Even if a human body had been eaten by a multitude of animals, as for instance fish, and these animals in their turn had been eaten by other animals, the human parts would in the end be separated from the parts of the animals and brought together by God in the final resurrection (Athenagoras, *The Resurrection of the Dead*, 3–4).

One could ask if fish, beasts and carnivorous birds were to give up the human flesh that they had eaten, would not these animals also have to rise from the dead? Tertullian touches on the problem in passing and rejects it (*On the Resurrection of the Flesh*, 32). "Certainly not!" he snorts. Beasts and fish are mentioned only to show that they have to give up what they had consumed. These animals will not themselves rise from the dead. The accent is on human bodies and only on them. This fleeting moment at the end of time, when Tertullian lets animals who had been eating humans or eaten animals who had eaten humans revive, so that they could vomit up these bits and pieces for the sake of human resurrection and then perish for ever, is scary.

Underlying this argument is a belief in human flesh as qualitatively different from animal flesh because human flesh is combined with an immortal soul. Tertullian leans on Paul, who had said that all flesh (*sarx*) was not the same flesh – humans, birds, animals and fish had different types of flesh (*On the Resurrection*, 52; I Corinthians 15:39). But at the same time Tertullian interprets Paul allegorically. According to Tertullian, when Paul speaks about birds and fish, the birds refer to the martyrs, while the fish refer to those who are baptized. Thus Tertullian also reflects the tendency in these centuries to change real animals into metaphorical ones.

Ironically, considering his rejection of animal resurrection, Tertullian's chief symbol of human resurrection is the phoenix, the fabulous bird of the East (*ibid.*, 13).[26] This phoenix is no ordinary bird, wavering as it does in Graeco-Roman mythology between reality and myth. Besides, Tertullian also hastens to downgrade the bird when he adds: "Our Lord has declared that we are 'better than many sparrows': well, if not better than many a phoenix too, it were no great thing. But must men die once for all, while birds in Arabia are sure of a resurrection?" (*ibid.*). Tertullian both makes use of the phoenix and claims in the same breath that humans are far more valuable than a bird, even if it is a fabulous one. In a similar way to Tertullian, Cyril of Jerusalem lets the phoenix illustrate the resurrection of the body (*Catechetical Lectures*, 18.8). Cyril also downgrades the pagan bird by underlining that it is irrational and does not know its maker.

A more lasting solution to the question of what happens when humans are consumed by beasts was offered not by medical (and imaginative) treatises on digestion. Instead, the problem was transposed into another realm, the realm of allegories and metaphors, on which Christianity thrived. On this level, animals killing and eating martyrs were replaced by martyrs being devoured by God. Tertullian presents God as devouring the martyrs, and the *Gospel of Philip* characterizes God as "a man-eater" (*Scorpiace*, 7; the *Gospel of Philip*). This is a standard Christian technique of reversal and re-evaluation. Things and happenings in the material world are turned upside-down, transported into the divine world and receive new spiritual meanings.

It was not only God but also the Devil that devoured humans. Sometimes, the Devil was explicitly conceived of as a lion. For instance, in the *Mystagogical Catecheses* of Cyril of Jerusalem, the Devil is described as a lion that seeks someone to gobble up (1.10; cf. I Peter 5:8). However, the Devil had to surrender those he had swallowed when they had won salvation. In the conclusion to the letter from Lyons, the Devil appears as a beast that has been forced to spit out those he thought he had digested: "Because of the sincerity of their love this became the greatest of all the contests which they waged against him, to the end that the throttled Beast might be forced to disgorge [*eksemeo*] alive all those whom he at first thought he had devoured" (2.6; cf. 1.25). A reversal has taken place. How real animals kill and eat martyrs is not elaborated upon; instead, the martyrs have been devoured by God or, alternatively, the Devil: "The throttled Beast" has eaten them but has been forced to vomit them up.

To be eaten by the Devil means to be devoured by death, while to be killed as a martyr implies that the Devil has to give up his prey. It is a variant of a common Christian motif, which says that by suffering and death, death is conquered. Thus the image of being eaten by beasts and death has been transposed to the realm of the cosmological battle between God and Satan and turned upside-down.

The theme of problematic eating is also turned back to front in another way. According to the Christian imagination, humans may also eat wild beasts. In the *Gospel of Thomas*, Jesus says that "Blessed is the lion which becomes man when consumed by man; and cursed is the man whom the lion consumes, and the lion becomes man" (CG II, 2, 33:25–9). This saying may either be taken at face value or interpreted in a symbolic way. On the one hand, the author may be talking about types of eating in a hierarchy of being and claim that it is desirable for humans to devour beasts but not for beasts to devour humans. One can even interpret it to mean that the flesh of the animal is transformed in a positive direction by being consumed by man (cf. Valantasis 1997: 64–5). If this is the case, the saying may be read as an early comment in the debate about consumption and digestion. On the other hand, humans do not usually eat lions. It is more likely that the saying should be interpreted in a symbolic way. The author may have thought about animals in a way similar to that of the *Gospel of Philip* (see Chapter 7). If this is the case, the saying is not about real lions but about man, who shall conquer and consume his bestial nature and thus become completely human. If, on the other hand, the bestial nature happened to consume the human nature, man would end up as a beast.[27]

If this last interpretation is correct, there is a great distance in meaning between the roughly contemporary letters of Ignatius and the *Gospel of Thomas*. In both cases, the problem of being eaten by wild beasts is made into a metaphor and reinterpreted. But in the *Gospel of Thomas*, the metaphor has been removed from the context of people actually being eaten by lions and from deliberations on how to meet martyrdom. Instead, it refers to internal self-control. This is yet another way in which it is possible to take control of the uncomfortable subject of Christians being thrown to real animals and eaten by them.

Conclusion

Jan den Boeft and Jan Bremmer have identified recurring themes in the theology of martyrdom in the *Acta et Passiones Martyrum*. According to them, these themes are "the strong belief in God as the Creator of the universe, the conviction that the real battle is not waged against human persecutors but against the devil, the martyrs' joy and gladness, the power of steadfastness, the fear of eternal punishment, and, above all, a strong personal relationship with Christ" (Boeft and Bremmer 1995: 151–2). I would like to add as absolutely crucial another recurring theme: in these *acta et passiones*, human victims took the place that in the Graeco-Roman world had usually been assigned to animal victims. In this way, the traditional Roman institutions of arena and sacrifice were blended and changed and were given a new Christian meaning. According to Christian interpretation, the martyrs became, as it were, the new sacrificial victims of the empire, and sacrificial language permeates the Acts of the Martyrs. According to John Chrysostom, Christ had put an end to the impious and abominable sacrifices of the Israelites, who even sacrificed their sons and daughters to demons (Psalms 106:37). The "sacrifice" of martyrdom served as a replacement for these practices (Clark 1999: 215). In this way, the unique sacrifice of Christ in the New Testament had its successors in the martyrs of the early Church. It was still unique, but not without imitators.

As we have seen, the narratives about martyrs are not without consequences for the conception of animals.

While the Acts of the Martyrs include descriptions of wild animals in the arenas, the textual space devoted to these animals is restricted because the actual killing of the martyrs has to be consonant with the conception of these martyrs' being sacrificed. Sacrificial victims – be they bulls, sheep and pigs *or* the Christian martyrs – were not eaten by wild animals. They were slaughtered, usually by having their throats cut and sometimes by being burned as holocausts.

At the same time as the wild animals in the Acts of the Martyrs fade as real creatures, they rise again in a "supra-bestial" form, for instance as the lion of Paul and the lion(ess) of Thecla, or they appear as metaphorical entities. As metaphorical entities, wild animals gave colour and form to the human and demonic enemies of the Christians. For even if Christians were killed by lions, bears and dogs in the arenas, on the metaphorical level, "the wild animals" were again and again conquered by the martyrs. This use of metaphorical animals had predecessors in Judaism and early Christianity, especially in apocalyptic texts such as the Revelation of St John (see Chapter 8).

As new sacrificial victims of the empire, the Christian martyrs took over cultural space that traditionally had been allotted to sacrificial animals. These animals were removed from the religious role that they had been given in pagan religion and were replaced, not only by human sufferers and sacrificial victims but also by allegorical, metaphorical and symbolic beasts.

When the era of the martyrs was over, a new type of Christian hero emerged. This was the ascetic. Like the martyr, the ascetic was an athlete who fought on God's side in the battle against evil. The ascetic did not fight in the Roman arenas but alone in the desert or wilderness to master the body and its passions. Like the antagonists of the martyrs, some of the ascetics' enemies were also beasts.

10

INTERNAL ANIMALS AND BESTIAL DEMONS

The beasts of Plato

In the *Republic*, Plato describes the essential nature of the soul and the inner workings of the human person, and he does it "by forming in speech an image of the soul" (*Republic*, 588b–589b). According to this image, the human soul has three parts. It is a composite, consisting of a "many-headed and intricate beast, having in a ring the heads of tame and wild beasts, able to metamorphose and make grow from itself all these things". These animals are the desires (*epithymia*). In addition, the soul comprises a lion and a man, which are the spirited and active element, respectively, in man: his emotional side (*thymos*) and his reason (*nous*). Mary Midgley has fittingly characterized Plato as "the first active exponent of the Beast within" (Midgley 1995: 43).

Two alternative attitudes towards these animals are described by Plato. An unjust man feeds the manifold beast but starves the interior man so that he is made weak and is drawn to wherever one of the beasts might lead him. And the beasts bite and devour each other. Unlike the unjust man, a just man is completely in control of the inner man and takes charge so that the many-headed creature nourishes the tame animals and keeps the wild ones from growing: "like a farmer who cherishes and trains the cultivated plants but checks the growth of the wild" (*Republic*, 589b). In this way, he cares for the animals within his soul and makes them friends to each other and to himself. His attitude towards them reflects the ambition to subject body and soul to the controlling power of reason, which was a main project in antiquity. The lion has a special position in relation to the other beasts, because man makes an ally of the lion's nature, thus making use of the spirited part of his soul to control its appetites. Plato's concern is to dominate the bestial within the human soul.

The description of the soul as a collection of beasts and the identification of the human goal as the taming or conquest of these beasts were popular in antiquity. Two of the most beloved heroes of Graeco-Roman culture were Hercules and Orpheus, both of whom conquered animals. Both were also used to describe spiritual life and the subduing of human passions. Hercules is depicted carrying out his labours, in which several animals, some of them fabulous, were killed, while Orpheus charms animals and nature with his music and thus renders them passive. Orpheus charming the beasts is found in several material contexts and works of art, and he appears in several of the religions of the empire. He represented paradisical bliss, awakened the souls of beasts to spiritual life or subdued human passions. For instance, Orpheus figured in the spiritual movement of syncretic Platonism (Murray 1981: 44–6). Like Orpheus, Hercules did not conquer only physical dangers. The wild beasts were eventually interpreted as human pleasures, and the crafty hero became the exemplar of a wise man who struggled successfully against hedonism or against hedonistic opponents (Malherbe 1968). For instance, Hercules was the most important of the Cynic patrons.[1]

The Hercules and the Orpheus themes can be read as two formulations of a key cultural scenario – as metaphorical accounts about the right way to live and act. A cultural "key scenario" is social anthropologist Sherry Ortner's term for a symbol that formulates the culture's basic means–ends relationships in acceptable forms (Ortner 1979: 95). According to Ortner, key scenarios make explicit appropriate goals and suggest effective action for achieving them. The Orpheus and the Hercules themes describe two different strategies, either peaceful subjugation and integration or attack and conquest of external and internal enemies in the form of animals.[2] In Plato's version of the beasts within, the stress is on domination by subjugation and integration.

In the introduction to her book *Theatrical Shows and Ascetic Lives*, Blake Leyerle has analysed a mosaic floor from the suburb of Daphne on the outskirts of fourth-century Antioch (Leyerle 2001: 1–3). In the medallion in the middle of the mosaic, a female figure distributes coins from a large supply. The woman is called *Megalopsychia* – "the great-souled". Close to the medallion are animals attacking their prey, which in their turn are surrounded by hunters fighting against wild animals. Along the outer edge is a topographical border showing the city of Antioch. Leyerle reads the mosaic as an allegory of virtue. The person in the middle distributing largesse has triumphed over her passions, which are depicted as wild animals. Such motifs had a wide distribution.

Philosophers and religious teachers made use of the beasts of Plato. These beasts were easily accepted among the Neoplatonists, but Christians too used them to describe the processes that took place within the human soul. Basilides, a Christian gnostic, is dependent on Plato when he says that passions are appended to the rational soul and foster the growth of impulses and perceptions that he connects with animals like wolves, apes, lions and goats (*Stromateis*, 2:20).[3] Basilides shared the common conception of animals as irrational and base, and he most likely associated specific characteristics with each of the animals he mentioned. Eusebius refers to Plato's text in his

Preparations for the Gospel (12.46.2–6).[4] Evagrius of Pontus (345–399 CE) says that impure demons who trouble the human person as irrational animals "are the passions which we have in common with irrational beings but which remain hidden by our rational thought" (*On Thoughts*, 18). Augustine alludes to the good beasts in the living soul, which "are subservient to reason" (*Confessions*, 13.31).

The wider metaphorical use of animals in antiquity as a means of describing human psychology has been studied by Patricia Cox Miller, who has stressed the variety of these applications and pointed out that "in some texts, animal images were used to explore the very process of figuration of which they were a part, while in other texts, animals were metaphors of the irrational aspects of the human soul whose 'wildness' expressed one aspect of the multiplicity of the self. In still other texts, animals figured as the cunning presence of God in the world" (Miller 2001: 16). Miller further points out how these animals "formed part of an imaginal sign-system in which nature was infused with religious and emotional sensibilities" (*ibid.*). Those who employed them wanted to break the "habituated modes of consciousness". One of Miller's examples is Origen of Alexandria, who filled the interior geography of the human soul with beasts and who investigated the inner life of man and his relationship to God by means of them (*ibid.*: 35–59).[5] Miller shows how Origen sees the beasts as "sportive monsters of the soul" (*ibid.*: 42) and points out that in Origen's thought, corporeal beasts are mute, while "spiritual beasts speak in the heart of soul and text" (*ibid.*: 43). The beasts are the fantasies of the soul and the mind's demons, and it is the monstrous side of the beasts that man is struggling against. These are not "real" animals.

The spiritual beasts that were now made to talk within the soul gave human beings a language to experience the depths of their souls. These beasts were ambiguous creatures that man should make the objects of reflection and gradually draw into consciousness. The aim was that the bestial should be transformed into full humanity and closeness to God. In this way, the Platonic ideal was continued in its new Christian setting.

As these beasts developed in Christian thinking, they were frequently described as frightening, and the soul became an arena for roaring monsters. However, animals were not restricted to human psychology but were used to describe bodily reality and the female sex, as well as forces external to humans – demons and entities of the planetary spheres. How these bestial elements were put together and what these compositions say about animals is the theme of this chapter. We will concentrate on two cases of internal and external beasts, both of them from Egypt: those of the Nag Hammadi texts, and those of the desert father Antony, as described by his biographer Athanasius.

Although these works are closely connected to Christian asceticism, they are not exhaustive for how animals appear in ascetic Christian texts. Both the Nag Hammadi texts and the *Life of Antony* have a strong tendency to use animals for evil forces or obstacles to the ascetic life. However, there are other texts that reveal other ways in which animals can be applied. In the *Apopthegmata Patrorum* and the apocryphal Acts of the Apostles, more positive uses of animals appear. We will consult some of them in Chapter 12.

The Nag Hammadi texts

The Nag Hammadi "library" consists of forty-six different original texts (and some doublets), mostly Christian, most of them unknown before Egyptian farmers dug them out of the earth in 1945. They had probably been buried in the later part of the fourth century because of increasing pressure from Christian bishops against those who owned and read texts that were by then regarded as heretical. The texts are written in Coptic but are believed to be translations from Greek. It is not known when and where they were originally composed; neither do we know their authors. The most likely owners and readers of these texts were monks and ascetics who lived close to where they were found – in late antiquity, there were several Pachomian monasteries in this area. If this "library" had been used by the Christian inhabitants of monasteries and the desert, it was related to a male world and a community in which one did not marry.[6] The general outlook of the texts may confirm this view. It is consonant with an ascetic way of life, not least because many of the texts reflect a negative view of women and procreation.

The ascetic outlook in several of these texts does not mean that they transmit only one view of the world, either of humans or of salvation; on the contrary, variety is allowed. All the same, since these texts were buried together, they are united at least in this regard. The fact that they are concerned with questions about the place of humans in the world and especially questions relating to salvation also makes it legitimate and interesting to view them together. A shared understanding in a large part of the texts in this diverse collection is that the soul has descended into the material world and that its ultimate goal is to transcend this world of reproduction and death. Along with this perspective goes a negative conception not only of the material world but also of animals, which have been made to symbolize the evils of biological life and the depths of human corruption.

These texts are even less concerned with real animals than the New Testament texts and the Acts of the Martyrs, and more with metaphorical and symbolic beasts that are used partly to describe human psychology, partly to characterize demonic entities. In this way, the animalian creatures are either internal to man or appear as his external antagonists. Both categories have mostly negative values and represent the forces that humans should overcome. For a modern reader, this seems to be a sliding scale between psychology and demonology, although one should be careful not to make these beasts match the conceptual apparatus of modern psychology too closely. In the following section, we will consult a selected handful of the Nag Hammadi texts – those in which animality and animal hybrids play significant roles.

Animal passions

In the *Acts of Peter and the Twelve Apostles*, a Christian tractate, a mysterious teacher, Lithargoel, has a pearl hidden in the city with the name "Nine Gates". The road to that city is dangerous:

> No man is able to go on that road, except one who has forsaken everything that he has and has fasted daily from stage to stage. For many are the robbers and wild beasts [*therion*] on that road. The one who carries bread with him on the road, the black dogs kill because of the bread. The one who carries a costly garment of the world with him, the robbers kill [because of] the garment. [The one who carries] water [with him, the wolves kill because] [of the water], since they were thirsty [for] it. [The one who] is anxious about [meat] and green vegetables, the lions eat because of the meat. [If] he evades the lions, the bulls devour him because of the green vegetables.
>
> (*Acts of Peter and the Twelve Apostles*, 5:21–6:8)

Because Peter and the disciples manage not to bring anything with them on the road, they are not attacked by the dangerous beasts and finally reach the city, where they are met by Lithargoel.

Lithargoel is referred to a few times outside this text, but the city is not identified. The journey is an allegorical description of the road leading to an ascetic life. It is not unusual that "city" is used metaphorically – in another of the Nag Hammadi texts, the *Teachings of Silvanus* (see below), "city" is used as a metaphor for the human person. In the case of the *Acts of Peter and the Twelve Apostles*, the fact that the city is called "habitation" and that its inhabitants are described as "those that endure" points in the direction of an allegorization of the ascetic life and the need for renunciation and fasting to gain control over the body and its passions. What is most interesting for our subject is that in the *Acts of Peter and the Twelve Apostles*, the dangers lurking in wait for the seekers are described in four out of five cases as dangerous animals. This fact stresses how natural it is for obstacles to the ascetic life to be identified symbolically with animals. The goal is not to be conquered by these beasts but to escape them, which is in line with Plato's thought.

In the *Teachings of Silvanus* (CG VII, 4) animals and bestiality are used throughout to describe the evils of a carnal life. The *Teachings of Silvanus* is an example of Christian wisdom literature in which a teacher draws upon biblical ideas, Jewish wisdom tradition and Stoic and Middle/Neoplatonic ideas and on the basis of these offers instruction to a pupil. It shows many similarities with Alexandrian theology (Zandee 1991: 1). The text contains admonitions to the soul to wage war on passions and evil thoughts and to follow Christ and thereby receive true knowledge of God. Base passions and evil thoughts are symbolized by animals.

The Teachings of Silvanus starts with the admonition to "put an end to every childish time of life, acquire for yourself strength of mind and soul, and intensify the struggle against every folly of the passions of love and base wickedness, and love of praise, and fondness of contention, and tiresome jealousy and wrath, and anger and the desire of avarice" (84:16–26). The human being is likened to a city and told to guard its gates lest it "become like a city which is desolate since it has been captured. All kinds of beasts have trampled upon it. For your thoughts which are not good are evil wild beasts [hentherion ethoou]. Your city will be filled with robbers, and you will not obtain peace, but only all kinds of savage wild beasts [hentherion therou nagrion]" (85:8–17). Passions are compared to wild beasts (cf. 94:2–4, 7–10; 105:4–7). Opposed to these animalian thoughts are mind (nous) and reason (logos). The battle of man is fought within the human soul and body and is described as a fight against animals. The goal is not to be "an animal [tbne], with men pursuing you; but rather, be a man, with you pursuing the evil wild beasts [ntherion ethoou], lest somehow they become victorious over you and trample you as a dead man, and you perish by their wickedness" (86:1–8). Life is a war, which one has to fight to become victorious over one's enemies (86:24–9). When the battle is won, one will regain one's true humanity: "Do not surrender yourself to barbarians like a prisoner nor to savage beasts which want to trample you. For they are lions which roar very loudly, be not dead lest they trample you. You shall be man!" (108:6–15).

The weapons in this fight are education (paideia) and teaching (techo) (87:4–5). Man is burdened with an animal nature (physis ntbne), which he ought to cast out (87:27–31). In a way, this animalian nature acts on its own. When man desires folly, it is not by his own desire he does these things, "but it is the animal nature [physis ntbne] within you that does them" (89:2–4). Ultimately, every man who is separated from Christ falls into the claws of the wild beasts (110:12–14). Rather amusingly, the pupil is urged not to "become a sausage [made] of many things which are useless" (88:17–19).

Opposed to this animalian nature is the divine nature of man, which the author of the Teachings of Silvanus praises in flourishing terms: "you are exalted above every congregation and every people, prominent in every respect, with divine reason, having become master over every power which kills the soul" (87:1–6). Man's utmost exaltation is stressed when it is said that "you will reign over every place on earth and will be honored by the angels and the archangels. Then you will acquire them as friends and fellow-servants, and you will acquire places in [heaven above]" (91:26–34). The divine nature is realized when you "become self-controlled [enkrates] in your soul and body, then you will become a throne of wisdom and a member of God's household" (92:4–8).

There is a contrast between rational man and irrational animals in this text that is characteristic of Stoic thinking,[7] but the text also makes use of a well-known Platonic model of the three natures of the human soul (Zandee 1991: 530ff). This anthropological model is simultaneously harmonized with a tripartite model of the soul based on an interpretation of the creation of man in Genesis. According to this Platonic/biblical model, the bodily aspect of the soul is from the earth, the soul is formed by the thought of the divine, while the mind is created in conformity with the image of God. The mind is the male part, the soul the female part and the bodily soul, with its passions and desires, is the animalian part of man (92:29–93:15). The soul's choice is either to turn towards the male part or towards the animalian part. If the pupil does not choose the human part, it is claimed that "you have accepted for yourself the animal thought and likeness – you have become fleshly [sarkikos] since you have taken on animal nature [ouphysis ntbne]" (93:15–21). Fleshliness and animality are here conceived of as aspects of the bodily soul.

When the *Teachings of Silvanus* states that "it is better not to live than to acquire an animal's life" (105:6–7), one could ask what an animal's life consisted of? Generally, the meaning of the term *therion* (Coptic, *tbne*) developed from designating wild animals to cover animals in general. Unlike the term *zoa*, which could also include humans, *therion* was the opposite of human and an abstraction that covered an infinite range of species. It was often transferred to humans as a designation of their lower and base parts. In the Nag Hammadi texts, it is normally used with such negative meanings. In the *Teachings of Silvanus*, an animal life is associated with desire (*epithymia*), and although it is said that the devices of desire are many, the sins of lust (*hedone*) are especially mentioned (105:22–6). The pupil is also especially urged to "strip off the old garment of fornication [porneia]" (105:13–15). Accordingly, the special characteristic of animal life, as opposed to the ideal human life, seems to have been sexual activity and lust, even if the animal metaphors also range more widely. A wider range of desires and evil thoughts is obviously referred to when the pupil is urged not to "become a nest of foxes and snakes, nor a hole of serpents and asps, nor a dwelling place of lions, nor a place of refuge of basilisk-snakes" (105:27–32). These "animals" and their accompanying desires are associated directly with the Devil (105:34–106:1).

Animality is further contrasted with rationality, an opposition that goes back at least to Plato: "Entrust yourself to reason and remove yourself from animalism. For the animal which has no reason is made manifest. For many think that they have reason, but if you look at them attentively, their speech is animalistic" (107:19–25). The opposition between bestiality and reason is also commented on in other Nag Hammadi texts. According to the

Authoritative Teaching (CG VI, 3), the soul fell into bestiality (*oumnttbne*) when it left knowledge behind. "For a senseless person [*anoetos*] exists in bestiality [*oumnttbne*], not knowing what it is proper to say and what is proper not to say" (24:20–6). In the last two quotations, reason is directly connected to language in accordance with the way that language was described, especially in Stoic thought, as external reason.

From the short survey of these texts, it becomes clear that the internal animals are associated with negative impulses. Animality is generally connected with irrationality and lack of human language. More specifically, animality is associated with sexual desire and carnal knowledge, seen as the opposite of spiritual knowledge.[8] In the sexual act, humans are imitating savage beasts and taking part in a movement downwards. In the *Origin of the World* (CG II, 5), Adam and Eve are said to be "erring ignorantly like beasts". When the evil powers saw that they behaved as beasts, they rejoiced (118:8–9). This behaviour, which most likely means sexual behaviour, is acclaimed by the evil powers because they want the human race to strengthen their fetters to the material world. Animality is a psychic state, the state of the fallen and not-saved human and a way of experiencing the world. At the same time, animality is a bodily state that is connected directly to the biological facts of life – the cycle of reproduction and death. Metaphorical animals or animals in similes are often said to eat or trample upon people, thus focusing on their destructive qualities.

The bestial body

One significant difference between Christianity and contemporary religions in the Mediterranean area was the new meaning bestowed on the human body (cf. Chapter 7). Christians wanted to tear themselves away from the animal world, but it could not be done merely by tearing the soul away from the body; the human body should also, in one way or another, be saved from its bestial habits and from the sort of life that it shared with the animals. A life characterized by desire and intercourse should be relinquished. One should not merely resist passions; the ideal was not to experience them at all (Clement of Alexandria, *Stromateis*, 3.7.57; cf. Brown 1988: 31ff). Peter Brown has pointed out how sex became the most striking biological fact that humans shared with the animal world (*ibid.*: 31ff). Another biological fact must also be mentioned. Humans and animals do not only share sex, they also share corruptible bodies that are dependent on eating and subject to death. Caroline Walker Bynum has pointed out the terror of change and the desperate effort to reach unchangeability and material continuity as characteristic of Christian thinking about the body (Bynum 1995).

However, whether the accent is on the body's sexuality or on its corruptibility, the human body had obviously become a key symbol in Christianity. It was the medium upon which the battle of salvation was fought, and it could either develop into a temple for the Holy Spirit or a brothel, either be spiritualized or remain a beast. The special position that the body was accorded in Christian tradition not only opened up new opportunities for the metaphysical use of animals – for the animals within – but also laid the foundation for an intertwining of body and beast that acquired great symbolic power in Christianity. How one thought about the body obviously differed in various authors and also within the Nag Hammadi texts, but one prominent tendency was to regard the cycle of intercourse, birth, eating and death as deeply negative. The ambition was to break the cycle, not to remain with the beasts but to be saved from the fallen world of being and begetting.

The problem of the bestial existence of humans and their dependence on the biological cycle as well as their aim to break loose from this cycle are tackled directly in the *Book of Thomas the Contender* (CG II, 7). This text is a dialogue between the resurrected Jesus and his twin brother Judas Thomas and teaches an ascetic doctrine. Here it is said that beasts are begotten, and that "these visible bodies survive by devouring creatures similar to them with the result that the bodies change. Now that which changes will decay and perish, and has no hope of life from then on, since that body is bestial" (139:2–6). In this text, intercourse, death and the devouring of other creatures as well as change are intimately connected. The text ascertains that the body derives from intercourse, and accordingly the author asks rhetorically "how will it beget anything different from beasts?" (139:9–11). In the *Book of Thomas the Contender*, the bestiality of the body, which is its real essence, consists in the manner of its reproduction but also in how it lives, namely by eating other creatures.

However, even if the body was conceived of as negative, it was still the necessary equipment for appearing in the material world. In the *Paraphrase of Shem* (CG VII, 1), Jesus has to take on a body when he descends on his saving mission to earth. The body is called "beast". When Jesus says that he "put on the beast [*therion*]" and that "in no other way could the power of the Spirit be saved from bondage except that I appear to her in animal [*therion*] form" (19:32–5), he is referring to the material body. In the *Interpretation of Knowledge* (CG XI, 1), material existence and bodily reality are throughout described as bestial. Here the world is said to be from the beasts and to be a beast.

The bestial sex and the ambiguous serpent

While animality is so intimately intertwined with the sexual aspect of the body and with worldly existence, one sex is burdened with this animality more than the other. In several of the texts from Nag Hammadi, we find a traditional pattern that is well known in Greek thinking as well as in Christianity. According to this pattern, men are to women as spiritual to material and human to animal. A special connection is made between Eve and the serpent. In some of the Nag Hammadi texts, for instance the

Apocryphon of John (CG II, 1), the *Nature of the Archons* (CG II, 4) and the *Origin of the World* (CG II, 5), the relationship between Eve and the serpent is commented upon.

According to the *Apocryphon of John*, the evil serpent appears on the Tree of Life. Opposite to it is the Tree of Knowledge, upon which Christ sits in the shape of an eagle. Christ teaches human beings spiritual knowledge, while the serpent teaches them carnality and sexuality. The *Apocryphon of John* appears in four different versions, two long and two short. According to one of the short versions, the serpent teaches woman about "sexual desire, about pollution and destruction, because they are useful to him" (BG 58:4–7).[9] In this version, it is Adam who is taught spiritual knowledge. In the long version, it is "her who belongs to Adam into which carnal lust was planted" (II 24:28–9). In the short version, woman, serpent and sex are closely connected, while Christ/eagle and spiritual knowledge are connected with man (Gilhus 1983). In the short version, Eve is described as a weapon made against Adam. She entices him to scatter his seed and thus spread the spiritual elements. The long version is more ambiguous – both Adam and Eve eat from the Tree of Knowledge – but also in the long version, woman is more closely connected with sex than is Adam. Her main purpose is procreation. In both versions, Ialdabaoth fathers sons by Eve. He is called "the ruler of lust", and sexual desire is the chief device made by evil powers to fetter human beings to this world. But what is only suggested in Genesis, that Eve and the serpent were connected, is made explicit in the *Apocryphon of John*, where the cunning reptile is especially related to the sexual and procreative aspects of Eve.[10]

An even closer connection is made between woman and reptile in the *Book of Baruch*, where they are combined in a hybrid being called Eden or Israel (Hippolytus, *Refutation of All Heresies*, 5.26–7).[11] The upper half of Eden is a woman, while the lower half is a serpent. This hybrid is the material and bodily principle of the world, a sort of incarnation of female lust and love. Eden has made the material world together with a divine spiritual being called Elohim and created human beings as a mixture of the spirituality of Elohim and the psychic and material nature of Eden. But when Elohim discovers that a transcendent divine being exists and leaves Eden, Eden is frustrated and angry and wants revenge. Her angel *Naas* (Hebrew for snake) "uses Eve as a whore and Adam as a boy" and becomes the originator of adultery as well as of homosexuality.

Even if the symbolic association between woman and serpent was usually seen as negative in Christianity, some gnostic texts also offer alternatives to this view. In contrast to the *Book of Baruch* and the *Apocryphon of John*, where the combination of woman and serpent symbolizes bestial biological life, consisting of sex, procreation and death, woman and serpent also have positive roles to play. In the *Nature of the Archons*, the spiritual principle appears both in the guise of the serpent and as a woman, and promises Adam and Eve that when they have eaten from the Tree of Life, they will not die, and their eyes will be opened. In the *Origin of the World*, the serpent has a similar function. According to this text, it is "the wisest of all creatures who was called Beast". This creature instructs Eve to eat from the tree and is in reality a saviour.

The different uses of the serpent in these texts confirm what has already been pointed out (see Chapter 5) – that the serpent was a complex animal in antiquity. They also illustrate the special connection that existed between this animal and woman. Two types of serpent are employed in the Nag Hammadi texts. As the first type, the serpent is a promoter of carnal lust and a mouthpiece for evil powers, directing its message especially to Eve. When the serpent was associated with a material woman, it initiated a cycle of carnal desire, sex, procreation and death. Women of flesh and blood were obviously seen as problematic. The other type is not really a snake but a spiritual entity that for a short time uses an animal form as its vehicle. When women and serpents were seen in a positive light, they were not primarily conceived of as creatures of flesh and blood but as spiritual entities who only temporarily inhabited material forms.

These two woman–serpent combinations correspond to two traditional mythological patterns. The first, which connects woman and serpent and sex, is dependent on an interpretation of Genesis that is found in both Judaism and Christianity. The second, which connects serpent, woman and spiritual knowledge, is dependent on another pattern. Even if a positive interpretation of the serpent is attested in the Bible (see Numbers 21:6–9; Mark 16:18; John 3:14), and also later in Christianity when, for instance, Cyril of Jerusalem used it as an image of the newly baptized, a positive combination of serpent, woman and sex is not biblical but rather part of an older Middle Eastern and Mediterranean mythology. In the mystery religions, a combination of woman and serpent as vehicles of knowledge is sometimes present, for instance in the mysteries of Eleusis (Lancellotti 2000: 37–55). As pointed out by historian of religion Lisbeth Mikaelsson, the paradise narrative can in fact be seen as a reinterpretation of this old myth in a negative direction (Mikaelsson 1980). In some of the Nag Hammadi texts, both the biblical pattern and the older Middle Eastern/Mediterranean pattern were elaborated upon. In Christianity at large, it was the negative interpretation of Eve and the serpent – the female sex and the beast – that became predominant.

Planetary animals

So far, we have seen animals and animality that have been used to describe human qualities and as a means of classification, especially related to bodily life, sexual desire and the female sex. In addition, the bestial may also appear in creatures external to man: "But their powers, which are the angels, are in the form of beasts [*therion*] and animals [*zoon*]. Some among them are

215

[polymorphous], and contrary to [nature]" (*Marsanes*, CG X, 1, 25:1–7). These theriomorphous and polymorphous creatures were among other things developed on the basis of the signs of the zodiac.

In the wider world of antiquity, several constellations of the zodiac were habitually depicted as animals (Aries, Taurus, Cancer, Leo, Scorpio and Pisces) or as hybrids (Sagittarius as a centaur with bow and Capricorn, sometimes depicted as a mixture of goat and fish)[12]. The *zodiakos* – the constellations of twelve groups of stars – was applied empire-wide, for instance on mosaics, buildings, statues, paintings, coins and jewellery; thus it was part of people's everyday world of things and commodities (Gundel 1992). Used as decoration, it conveyed astronomical, religious and astrological knowledge. There are extensive material remains of different varieties of zodiac from the ancient world, but the different objects generally show a great similarity in how the zodiac was conceived and depicted (*ibid.*: 161).

The belief in the influence of the stars and the rule of the planets and in the possibility of controlling change by predicting it was part of the geocentric world view and appeared in all religions of the empire: in that of Artemis from Ephesus as well as that of Mithras, in the cult of the emperor as well as in Egyptian graves and, not least, in the figure of the lion-headed god Aion, who had wings and was intertwined with a serpent – a creature that figured widely in late antiquity. The astrological animals were mostly used in these cases as unambiguous signs, although on occasions the beasts of the stars were re-mythologized and appeared with a life of their own. Astral mysticism is seen not only in the mysteries of Mithras, Hermeticism and Neoplatonism but also in some of the Nag Hammadi texts.

In the Nag Hammadi texts, the planetary rulers and the rulers of the stars were re-evaluated and described as monsters with human bodies and animal heads and were given active evil roles to play. Philosopher Hans Jonas labelled the gnostics "the acosmic brotherhood of salvation" (Jonas 1970: 264–5). This characteristic nicely sums up one essential theme in these texts – a triumphant apotheosis of man, which elevates him high above the stars. In some of the texts, the supreme god even bears the name of "Man" (*anthropos*) (cf. Irenaeus, *Against Heresies*, 1.12.4), and the powers and forces of the universe are recast as lower entities, sometimes as outright evil. Their lack of spiritual resources is revealed in their bestial exterior. In the *Apocryphon of John*, the supreme god is called "Man", in consonance Christ is "the Son of Man", while the world creator Ialdabaoth, who is constructed on the basis of the biblical Yahweh, appears as a mixture of man and lion (CG II, 1, 14:13–21:16).

Terrible bestial creatures that are identified with planetary and sidereal powers are present in several of the texts. In the *Apocryphon of John*, there is a list of seven archons that are the rulers of the planets and connected to the days of the week (cf. Welburn 1978). The lists are roughly similar in the different versions of this text, although with small internal differences. According to them, the archons have animal faces or masks. These are the

216

faces of a lion, a donkey, a hyena, a seven-headed dragon/serpent, a dragon and a monkey. The seventh has a face of shining fire.[13] Behind these texts lie more specific ideas concerning the connection between the archons, the animals and the planets. What is obvious is that these animals are not conceived of in a positive light. Sometimes the negative qualities of the animals in question are more important than their actual species, as in the *Nature of the Archons* and the *Origin of the World*. In both these texts, the demiurge Ialdabaoth and his helpers are described as theriomorphic beings with animal heads and human bodies.

In the *Paraphrase of Shem* (CG VII, 1), it is said – with a new interpretation of the Spirit of God who hovered over the waters (Genesis 1:2) – that the likeness of nature "appeared in the water in the form of a frightful beast [*therion*] with many faces, which is crooked below" (Genesis 15:12–16). This is a frightening vision of the terrors of demonic animality, which lie at the very root of the cosmos and nature.

The reason why these hybrids have human bodies and animal heads, not the other way around, could be that it was important to mark them out as similar to humans. The upright position of the body was one special sign that made humans different from animals. When the hybrids were given animal heads, they appeared as bestial humans, not as human beasts.[14] Thus they functioned as negative models for humans as well as being demonic powers that were external to man.

Plato at Nag Hammadi

Plato's metaphor of the complex beast, taken from the *Republic*, has also been exploited in the Nag Hammadi "library", but here the beast has been transformed from internal passions to external enemy. This text, which is the fifth treatise in codex 6, has no title. Not only are the first four–five lines of each page damaged, the text is in fact so changed that it was not recognized by its first publishers as an extract from the *Republic*. The Nag Hammadi version of the metaphor is completely severed from its original context. James Brashler, one of its modern critics, commented bluntly on its state: "As a comparison with the Greek parallel text clearly shows, this attempt on the part of a Coptic translator to translate a summarizing excerpt from Plato's *Republic* is a disastrous failure" (Brashler 2000: 325). The corruption of the original metaphor is obviously the result of a bad translation from Greek to Coptic, as pointed out by Brashler, but some of its modifications are also due to a different mythological background. Unintentional corruptions and intentional modifications offer alternatives to the original text of the Athenian philosopher. One result is that the Plato from Nag Hammadi is much harder on the beast than his Athenian counterpart.

When the Coptic text is studied alongside the original extract from the *Republic*, two things become clear. The original metaphor shines through and is, to a certain degree, the model for the Coptic version. It is equally clear that new elements have worked themselves into the narrative. As Louis Painchaud has pointed out, in the first part of the text, although it is muddled, there are echoes of a traditional gnostic myth about evil powers that created bodily man in their image (Painchaud 1983: 22, 140ff). According to the Coptic version of the metaphor from the *Republic*, hybrid beings descended and created man (49:10–19). What was originally a metaphor of man's predicament in the world is mixed in the Coptic version with echoes from a myth about the creation of man in which evil powers in bestial shapes take part, and man is created in their image as a complex beast.

As for animals, the tame animals of the original myth have gone. The translator has confused *hemeron*, "tame animal", with *hemeron*, "day", or wilfully interpreted the text in that way (49:20, 20:21). Instead of the original Greek text having "Make, then, a single image of a manifold and many-headed beast having heads of tame and wild beasts in a circle and being able to cast off and grow from itself all these things" (588c–588d), the Coptic text has "Certainly it is a single image that became the image of a complex beast with many heads. Some days indeed it is like the image of a wild beast. Then it is able to cast off the first image" (49:16–23). There seems to have been no room for tame animals in this world view. Wild animals figure more prominently, and the bestial has taken on a more sinister existential dimension, being part of the equipment of the demiurgic powers. Man is no longer to tend the animals but to trample upon them, and the lion, which had a more positive role to play in Plato, has turned nasty in the Nag Hammadi version: "But what is profitable for him is this: that he cast down every image of the evil beast [*therion*] and trample upon them along with the images of the lion" (50:24–8). This is clearly a break with the original: in Plato's metaphor, the goal was to tend the animals, tame and wild, so that they lived in harmony with each other, meaning that appetites can be expressed, but in subordination to reason. The Coptic text speaks of "produce" (*gennema*), which designates "products of the earth" instead of tame animals (*hemera*), and ends with the final observation that the wild beasts keep "the produce" from growing (cf. Painchaud 1983: 54, note 46). The agricultural image of farmer and plants, which is used by Plato, is still there, but it has been changed (589b). In Plato's parable, the metaphor of wild and tame animals appears in parallel with a metaphor of wild and cultivated plants. In the Coptic version a mixed metaphor appears, according to which wild animals destroy cultivated plants.

When the meaning is that the animals must be destroyed so that spiritual fruits can grow, the animals in question are reinvented as external evil powers. Howard Jackson, who has worked especially on the gnostic leontomorphic creator and the Platonic tradition, characterizes the changes from Plato to the Nag Hammadi text in this way: "The un-Platonic hostility that the Coptic excerpt breathes towards the lion and the beast is a reflection of the fact that the harsher gnostic mythology has been allowed to override the more strictly anthropological dimensions of the passage in its Platonic context; in CG VI, 5 the lion and the beast are not facets of the soul (only their 'images' are), but autonomous creatures fully independent of man" (Jackson 1985: 211).

Consequently, in the Nag Hammadi version of Plato's metaphor, we are no longer within a model with wild and tame animals – weak passions and ferocious passions – which are dominated by man, but within a model where animal creatures are unambiguously conceived of as negative and accordingly ought to be destroyed. These "animals" are no longer only inside man but also oppose him as external powers. They have taken on the evil aspects of reality to a higher degree and function within a cosmos that is more sharply polarized.

Real animals and the use of positive animal metaphors

In all this exploiting of animals and animalian characteristics to describe aspects of man or external demonic powers, the question arises: what about real animals? The answer is that in the Nag Hammadi "library" real animals are mentioned only in passing. Sometimes, as in the *Apocryphon of John*, they are not mentioned at all. When they are mentioned, they have only peripheral roles to play, as when Adam gives them names, they accompany Noah in the ark, or they are spontaneously generated by nature.[15]

Sporadic instances of positive animal metaphors are found, for instance in the *Teachings of Silvanus*, where noetic man is associated with the shrewdness of the snake and the innocence of the dove (95:4–11), and where the one who is spiritually alert is likened to a gazelle that is saved from snares or to a bird that is rescued from a trap (113:33–114:1). In the *Authoritative Teaching*, the metaphors of the fishing net and the fisherman imply that the ascetic Christians are like fish. They should be alert lest they be lured by the temptations of the evil fisherman and eaten by him or drowned in the dragnet (29:3–17, 30:6–27; cf. Valantasis 2001a: 560–2).

More specific instances of positive animal metaphors are found in the *Origin of the World*. Here the phoenix is referred to (122:16–18, 122:27–33), as well as the two bulls of Egypt, which are connected with the sun and the moon (122:21–6). Most likely, these bulls are the Mnevis ox, associated with Ra/sun, and the Apis ox, associated with Osiris/moon. These creatures are used as baptismal symbols.[16]

However, these instances of positive use of specific animal symbols do not change the fact that "animal" and "animality" are in the main used as negative designations and that comments on real animals are only digressions from the real issue of the Nag Hammadi texts, which is human salvation. These texts are first and foremost salvation manuals. In the battle of salvation, animals are doubly losers, both because they will not be saved and because they are used to describe nature, materiality, desire and sexuality – in other words, the whole inherent fabric of this world – and mark this inherent fabric as deeply negative.[17]

Antony and the demons[18]

One Nag Hammadi text, the *Nature of the Archons*, starts with a quotation from Ephesians 6:12: "the great apostle – referring to the 'authorities of darkness' – told us that 'our contest is not against flesh and blood; rather the authorities of the universe and the spirits of wickedness'" (86:22–6). The same quotation is used by Athanasius (295–373 CE), the to-and-fro bishop of Alexandria, in his influential book about the life of the Christian ascetic, Antony, which incorporated the ideal of monastic life (cf. Brakke 1995; Rubenson 1995). Ephesians 6:12 is quoted once in the *Life of Antony*, and on other occasions it is alluded to (21:3; 51:2). In the gnostic case, the quotation describes the archons – the planetary powers – and the right relationship to them, while in the *Life of Antony*, this quotation is used to justify a fight against demons.

The Nag Hammadi texts and the *Life of Antony* represent different versions of fourth-century Christianity in Egypt. Both promote ascetic values and salvation, and both combine a monotheistic perspective with a dualistic outlook on the world.[19] In both, the fight against destructive powers is central. What is common to the texts in the Nag Hammadi "library" and the *Life of Antony* is that real power belongs to God – the archons/demons only seem to be powerful. They also have in common the idea that animals lend their bodies and characteristics to antagonistic forces – either to the archons or to the demons.

In spite of some similarities, there are important differences between the "library" and the *vita*. Antony appears as a heroic model within mainstream Christianity, while the Nag Hammadi "library" was branded as heretical.[20] Christianity in Egypt in the fourth century was a complex phenomenon (cf. Brakke 1995; Goehring 2001). A difference that is of more relevance to the question of animals is that while the *Life of Antony* is a biography, neither biographical texts nor descriptions of real persons exist in the Nag Hammadi "library". This implies that while no flesh-and-blood animals appear within the covers of this "library", Antony physically encounters both real animals and demons in the shape of animals. Even a centaur appears in this text (*Life of Antony*, 53). This gives one the possibility, not offered by the Nag Hammadi texts, of getting a glimpse of animals of flesh and blood as well as of their demonic cousins. Both animals and demons were conceived of as real within the ancient conception of the world, and both interacted with humans. How does Antony relate to these creatures?

In the *Life of Antony*, the chief demon is the Devil. In accordance with biblical models, he is referred to as the serpent (*drakon*) (6.1; 24.4), is said to roam about as a lion (7:2; cf. I Peter 5:8) and is likened to animals that have to be conquered (24:4–5). More specifically, he is described as a dragon that was drawn out by a hook by the Saviour (cf. Job 41.1), as a beast with a halter around its nostrils, as a runaway slave with nostrils bound by a ring and lips bored with an armlet (cf. Job 41.2), and as a sparrow bound by the Lord to be a plaything for men.

The Devil is usually accompanied by a multitude of demons. In antiquity, demons were part of a spiritual geography and connected to wildernesses and dangerous places and to special times such as the night. They were agents of destruction and illness. Frequently, they appeared as animals or as composite creatures displaying the most frightening part of the animals involved (cf. Chapter 8).[21]

In the *Life of Antony*, demons are mentioned in a large part of the chapters and appear as an integral part of ascetic life. As David Frankfurter remarks: "the *Life of Antony* gives far more attention to Antony's power over demons than to any other subject " (Frankfurter 1998: 273). These creatures are used in external as well as internal modes of attack. Characteristic of them is their ability to transform themselves into different shapes, which is to be seen in their apparitions as women, wild animals, reptiles, giants and soldiers (23:3), sometimes also as monks (25:3). However, their preferred forms are bestial. Characteristic of the *Life of Antony* is that Satan and his demons attack Antony physically in the guise of an army of wild animals. (9.4–10, 39.3, 51.3–5). The main categories of these demonic beasts are wild animals (*therion*; 19:5, 23:3, 39:3, 50:8–9, 51:5, 52:2, 53:2) and reptiles (*herpeton*; 9:5, 12:3–4, 23:3, 39:3, 51:5, 74:5–7). Together, these categories include "lions, bears, leopards, bulls, serpents, vipers, scorpions and wolves" (9:6). Antony's fight with demons creates a huge noise, as the animals are angry indeed. So even if the demons only imitate animals, the fighting is real, and the demons do Antony great bodily harm. Onlookers sometimes observe Antony's fight, although they do not see his adversaries.[22] A metaphorical language focusing on the option of conquering and destroying animals lies at the heart of this conceptualization of the Devil and the demons. Ideally, and with reference to Luke 10:19, Christians should tread on the Devil and the demons, which are depicted as scorpions and serpents (24:5).[23]

A distinction is made in this text between demons masquerading as animals and beasts of flesh and blood. This becomes clear when Antony scolds the demons and rebukes their weakness because they "imitate beings without reason [*aloga*]" (9:9), i.e. animals. But real animals may also run errands for demons. One instance is when the Devil sends almost all the hyenas in the desert against the monk (52:2–3). Another time, the Devil calls together his dogs to attack Antony (9.4; cf. 42.1). In the last case, dogs may refer to demons rather than to real animals, but this could also suggest that there was a sliding scale between demons and certain types of animal.

As flesh-and-blood animals may have their own harmful agendas, it might be preferable to get rid of them. One of the ways in which Antony's power manifests itself is precisely his ability to make animals leave when he wants them to. The monk's power, which is based on a superior ascetic life and on a soul that has taken control of the body and its passions, is revealed when reptiles are made to leave the fortified well in which he dwells (12.3–4), crocodiles let him go unharmed over the Arsino channel (15.1), and wild animals that came to drink water and happened to destroy some of the monk's vegetables are made to move away (50.8–9, 51.5). In the last case, Antony makes the animals leave by talking in a friendly way to them. But Antony is not really friendly towards these creatures. When ordering the animals away, he also prevents them from drinking water in the only place in the desert where water could be found. So even if it is said of Antony that "the wild animals made their peace with him" (51.5; cf. Job 5:23), although he does not kill them, his relationship with animals does not imply a peaceful cohabitation. He has made his Garden of Eden in the desert (cf. Brakke 1995: 226) and made animals obey him as they did Adam, but he does not want them. The message that comes through is that there was no place for animals in the new paradise that Antony had made in the desert.

The attitude to animals in the *vita* could be the result of Athanasius' own preferences. The ideal he created for Antony was a desert made into a city, and cities are definitely more tidy without vermin. Besides, as these desert dwellers were expected to conquer their own bestial nature, sometimes vizualized as aggressive demons in animal shapes, an internal cleaning out of demons and bestial passions could have been seen as a parallel to shooing away destructive animals.

However, not all animals in the *Life of Antony* are evil. Sometimes, chosen specimens may even appear as God's instruments. One example is a camel that God allowed Antony and his friends to regain after it had been let loose because of lack of water (54) Things turned more nasty when the horse belonging to the commander of the Roman military in Egypt, Balacius, tore his master's thigh with its teeth and thereby killed him. The reason given in the *Life of Antony* was that Balacius was a friend of the Arians (86). So even if the animal was in reality the most tranquil of horses, God acted through it. In this case, the potential destructive quality of animals is found even in a horse but is used to promote the right faith and to support Anthony's/Athanasius' side in the Christological quarrels that marred the fourth-century Church (39.3).

Metaphorical use of animals is also included in the *Life of Antony*. Antony refers to monks outside the desert as fish on land (85.3–4). We are here reminded of the metaphor of the evil fisherman in the *Authoritative Teaching* and of the ascetics as fish (cf. above). Antony further designates his opponents, the Arians, as "mules" and thus brands them as spiritually sterile – mules cannot breed.

There is a rich multicultural context to Antony. The biblical references are very visible, not least in the abundance of quotations and allusions. Much of the action takes place in a wilderness that, like the wilderness in the Gospel of Mark (1:13), is characterized by the presence of wild animals and demons. But according to Egyptian conceptions, demons and destructive animals were also connected with the desert. It has further been interpreted as one of the Egyptian traits in this text that the Devil at one point is said to be calling his dogs (9.4, 42.1) (Bartelink 1994: 159). More generally, the intense concern with demons is typical of Egyptian Christianity (Frankfurter 1998: 273).[24]

Extensive use is made of animals in the *Life of Antony*, although most are interpreted negatively. Their common denominator is that they lend their bodily characteristics to demons. There is a clear connection between demons that appear as animals, animals that obey the command of the Devil and animals of flesh and blood, which are evil because of their inherent bestial nature. The evil nature of animals is expressed especially in wild animals and reptiles. Taking into consideration the mainly negative use of animals in the *Life of Antony*, it is hardly astonishing that when Antony criticizes pagan religion, he accuses the Greeks of animal worship (74.5) and of believing in the transmigration of souls between animals and humans (74.7; cf. 76.1). Such accusations were among the stock arguments used to brand religious opponents (see Chapter 11).

The demons fear being trodden on (30). A *topos* that is both alluded to and quoted (24.5, 30.3) is Luke 10:19: "Behold, I have given you authority to tread upon serpents and scorpions, and over all the power of the enemy; and nothing shall hurt you" (cf. Mark 16:17–18). The motif of trampling upon evil in the form of destructive animals, which in Luke was given its archetypal Christian expression, has its roots in the Old Testament. The first time it is mentioned is in connection with the serpent (Genesis 3:15). Here, hostility is established between the family of the woman and the family of the serpent. The descendants of woman shall crush the head of the serpent, while it shall strike at their heels. In Deuteronomy (8:14–16), the dangers of the desert through which Moses led the people are characterized as vipers and serpents, while in Psalms (90:13), it is said that one should tread upon the viper and the basilisk and trample the lion and the dragon under one's feet. Trampling upon evil in the shape of animals is an extremely physical way of illustrating hierarchy and dominance, and it presupposes a polarization between man and beast.

As a final point concerning the relationship between Antony and the animals, it must be mentioned that Antony did not eat meat. Abstinence from meat reflects a concern for keeping a frugal diet with the purpose of making the body holy. Diets including meat were generally seen as fostering sexual drives, and it was felt that they should therefore be abandoned. A sheepskin was one of the few belongings that his fellow monks inherited from the ascetic. It stresses that even if he did not eat meat, Antony was not as concerned about "bothering" sheep as the Neopythagorean Apollonius of Tyana.

Conclusion

According to the tradition stemming from Plato, man should overcome the beasts within. These beasts are the desires and emotions within his soul, which should be kept under the strict control of reason. As we have seen, the beasts that were conquered by Hercules or tamed by the music of Orpheus were sometimes also interpreted as the internal forces in man. Animality became a human quality. From a religious point of view, the battle within the human soul and body was seen as more important than what went on in the external world; internal animals and bestial demons were more interesting than creatures of flesh and blood.

The internalized animals, which had their roots in Platonic thinking, were encountered not only in Christianity but in non-Christian religions as well. It was specific to Christianity that controlling sexual desire and leading it in the right direction was not enough; ideally, it should not get any outlet at all. The passions should not only be mastered but conquered. Taking these things into consideration, it was perhaps not so strange that the forces within manifested themselves as roaring monsters and that Plato's grooming his internal many-headed beast was changed in the Nag Hammadi version to a trampling upon external forces in the shape of animals.

Instead of looking to the countryside and the land as their most cherished mythological landscapes, as the pagan Romans did, urban Christians looked to the desert as their preferred mythical landscape. Seen from the perspective of the desert, the conception of animals also changed. The animals of the desert were not the traditional sacrificial beasts, such as the cow, the sheep and the pig. Instead, they were reptiles and predatory beasts. These wild and dangerous animals behaved in new and amazing ways as instruments of both divine and demonic forces. Sometimes they were seen as helpers of the saints (see Chapter 12), but more frequently they appeared as even more dangerous than any wild animals had ever been, as demonic entities roaming the desert, attacking ascetics and monks.

Hostile animals appeared as external enemies, internal forces and astrological creatures. It was usual to draw the life of the soul by means of animals, and especially the passions, which humans shared with beasts, were described as animals. Complex psychological relations could in this way be referred to by rather simple metaphors, and the obstacles to the ascetic life were understood by means of animals. For instance, animality and animals represented sexuality, desire, lack of reason, stupidity and bodiliness. The body was a beast, women tended towards the bestial, and the sexual drive linked humans to the animal world. Several of the things that the ideal human should avoid simply took on bestial forms.

In a similar way as internal passions were described as animals, external powers – planetary rulers or demons – were conceived of in the shape of animals or animal hybrids. The relationship between the passions within and the demons without is sometimes blurred, and dreams and fantasies obtruded upon reality. Christians were attacked by animals – not real creatures of flesh and blood but demons masquerading as animals. In the texts from Nag Hammadi and in the *Life of Antony*, there was a desperate struggle to leave the beasts and the bestial aspects of reality behind.

The texts that have been consulted have been considered as being directly or indirectly related to asceticism. It is not astonishing either that asceticism was one area in which the Christian fight against animals took place or that animals were interpreted negatively within an ascetic context. The ascetic discourse had the training of the body as its subject. The ascetic was an athlete, the battlefield was the body, and the forces to be conquered were bodily desires. These desires could be conceptualized as animals. Ascetic life and its struggles are made easier to grasp by using concrete examples of animals. The Egyptian context must also be pointed out as an explanation of the abundance of animals in some of these texts. In Egyptian religion, not only gods but also demons were conceived of as animals, and Egyptian magic frequently exploited and alluded to beasts. David Frankfurter has pointed out that there is a continuity with the much older classification of the demonic in Egyptian tradition, generated by environmental realities and a transvaluation of the divinities in the age-old temple cult (Frankfurter 2003: 361ff, 374ff).

In this chapter, with its points of departure in the Nag Hammadi texts and the *Life of Antony*, Christianity – and especially its ascetic variety – has carried the burden of being the religion in late antiquity that largely demonized animals. This is probably true, although it must be added that Judaism too thought about evil spirits in theriomorphic categories. Christianity was dependent on Judaism on this point, as Christian demonology has its most important source in Judaism. The association between demons and animals applied especially to wild animals, but demonization was also found in connection with animals that had been violently killed or were regarded as unclean. The Gadarene swine were close at hand when Jesus wanted to get rid of demons.

Even if the main impression is that Greek demonology did not support animal conceptions of demons and that the literature of the imperial period describes demons in human form (Brenk 1986: 2093), there are non-Christian examples of close connections between animals and demons. However, they may have been influenced by the Judaeo-Christian tradition. Porphyry, the great advocate of abstinence from eating meat, thought that demons were lurking around the sacrificial animals, while Iamblichus lists different orders of divine and demonic entities and mentions that the evil demons are "encompassed by hurtful, bloodsucking and fierce wild beasts". According to the Chaldean oracles, which Iamblichus and his successors included in Neoplatonism, evil demons were described as "beasts of the earth" (*theres chthonos*) or as "beast-like" (*theropolon*) (Lewy 1978: 265, note 19). As referred to above, Apollonius of Tyana claimed that an old beggar who was believed to have caused a plague in Ephesus was really a demon (see Chapter 3). Apollonius urged the people to stone him, which they did. But under the heap of stones, they did not find the beggar but the body of a huge dog. This was the final proof that the beggar really had been a demon.

All this business of designing demons in the shape of animals and making animals into vehicles of demons rebounded on real animals, and especially on wild animals. According to Origen, demons had greater power over wild beasts than over milder animals, because the wild animals "have something about them resembling evil, and although it is not evil, yet it is like it" (*Against Celsus*, 4.92.21–2). Origen makes a further connection between unclean animals and demons: "There seems, therefore, to be some sort of kinship between the form of each species of demon and the form of each species of animal" (*ibid.*, 4.93.14–15). When Athanasius surrounded his hero Antony with destructive animals and demons that took on the shape of animals, his audience, pagans as well as Christians, were familiar with such creatures.

Yet another result of the use of animals to give shapes and bodies to evil powers was to brand other people and their gods as beasts. Sometimes this identification was direct, as some people were described as animals without further ado. In the *Second Treatise of the Great Seth* (CG VII, 2), opponents were characterized as "unreasoning beasts" (59:29–30). However, there were also more intricate ways to use animals to target one's adversaries. We will turn to these in the next chapter.

THE CRUCIFIED DONKEY-MAN, THE *LEONTOCEPHALUS* AND THE CHALLENGE OF BEASTS

Animals as boundary markers

In this chapter, we will look into how animals marked boundaries between different religions and how they were used internally to indicate distance from one's neighbours, from those one lived closest to and shared belief with – those who to external observers looked pretty much the same as oneself. We will focus especially on the ways in which a new Christian identity was created in symbolic and mythological language by the Christians themselves and by their adversaries, and how animals were used as symbolic elements in these identities.

When Artemidorus in his *Oneirocritica*, "The Interpretation of Dreams", comments on customs that are peculiar to some groups (1.8), he mentions six examples. Some groups are characterized by their tattoos; the Mossynes have sexual intercourse with their wives in public just like dogs; all men eat fish except for the Syrians, who worship Astarte; the Egyptians alone venerate animals; Italians do not kill vultures; and, finally, only Ephesians, Athenian youths and the most noble of the inhabitants of Larissa in Thessaly take part in bullfights.

Most striking in this list is the fact that five out of six customs in one way or another refer to animals. It is strange, but also typical. In traditional societies, animals usually describe what is peculiar and thus function as boundary markers. How people treat animals, which animals they do not eat and in what ways they compare other people to animals and liken their way of living to bestial behaviour constitute such boundaries. Sometimes an animal functions as an identity symbol for a group or an area. The fish and the vultures in Artemidorus' examples probably functioned in this way.

Metaphorical animals were used to make and maintain cultural boundaries and to label categories of people and cultural systems. In his recent book, *Racism in Antiquity*, Benjamin Isaac connects the animal comparison with imperialism:

> Comparisons and metaphors identifying people with animals are
> common in ancient literature. There is a rich and varied literary

tradition that uses animals as literary devices. However, not all literary passages that represent people as animals should be interpreted as comparisons or metaphors. Some of them seem to be intended quite literally. Thus Aristotle says that those who yield to unnatural inclinations are not natural, but bestial or diseased. He applies this also to entire peoples. Like the theory of natural slavery and related attitudes towards foreigners, the animal comparison was part of an attitude of mind, a way of thinking about oneself as distinct from a foreigner, which formed the framework in which imperialism could flourish unfettered by moral inhibitions or restraints.

(Isaac 2004: 506)

The animal comparison was one of the imageries that determined ancient ideas about foreigners. When people are called animals, their humanity is denied. Especially faraway peoples were described in this way. However, these descriptions do not necessarily have so much to add to our understanding of the different species. Isaac poignantly observes "that the Greek and Romans often refer to animals and their behaviour without actually looking at them" (*ibid.*: 250).

Wild animals were used to describe barbarians – that which was conceived of as strange, antagonistic and dangerous to civilization. Plutarch, for instance, characterizes barbarians as beastly and savage (Nikolaidis and Rethymnon 1986). Historian Ammianus Marcellinus says in connection with Julian's treatment of the Christian bishops that "no wild beasts are such enemies to mankind as are most Christians in their deadly hatred of one another" (22.4.4). Ammianus Marcellinus took his animal metaphors from the Roman arenas and from the life of wild and dangerous animals such as vipers, birds of prey and lions. T.E.J. Wiedemann has pointed out that "Ammianus chooses parallels taken from his own experience as an official from an urban, curial background, rather than metaphors involving agricultural beasts as was usual in classical literature" (Wiedemann 1986: 198, note 63). According to Wiedemann, all the animals in Ammianus' metaphors illustrate negative qualities (*ibid.*: 201). A similar point is stressed by Timothy D. Barnes who, besides noting that there is "a certain repetitiveness about these comparisons to animals" (Barnes 1998: 108), also points out that "Ammianus' animal comparisons usually have a highly negative connotation" (*ibid.*: 109; cf. Smith 1998: 93).

The Christian Prudentius, who wrote a reply to the pagan Symmachus, likens barbarians to animals. For even if animals drink the same water as humans and breathe the same air: "Yet what is Roman and what is barbarian are as different from each other as the four-footed creature is distinct from the two-footed or the dumb from the speaking; and no less apart are they who loyally obey God's commands from senseless cults and their superstitions" (2.816–19).

An animal comparison may also be used to establish internal hierarchy. The Christian Cassian (*c.* 360–433 CE) comments on a pair of monks who interpreted the saying "take up your cross" (Luke 9:23, 14:27; Matthew 10:38) literally, and staggering under their crosses, became objects of ridicule for their brethren. Cassian characterizes these simple-minded monks as "cattle", although he adds, with reference to Psalm 36:6, that the Lord saves "both man and beast" (*Conlationes*, 8.3; in Clark 1999: 85). In this way, Cassian makes an elitist opposition between himself and his inferiors, because of their stupidity, but he does not make them into barbarians, as he would have done if he had characterized them as some species of wild animal.

Religion was definitively marked out by animals during the Roman Empire. Egypt was unique in its cultic use of huge numbers of animals, in the great variety of species involved and in the fact that some of these animals were considered divine in their own right (see Chapter 5). In Egypt, animal cults were not only used to signal the specifically Egyptian but also to mark boundaries between the different Egyptian regions. Conflicts between towns and regions often started because the sacred animal of one area had been killed by people from another area. Plutarch describes how the Cynopolitans ate the sacred fish of Oxyrhynchus, and the Oxyrhynchites offered the sacred dog of Cynopolis in sacrifice and devoured it. The resulting war was eventually stopped by the Romans (*Isis and Osiris*, 72). Such sacred animals – be they dogs, crocodiles or fish – worked as uniting symbols in one area. They were local symbols, not necessarily seen as sacred in all Egypt (Frankfurter 1998: 66–7).

An overwhelming presence of animals, real or metaphorical, is typical of several of the religions that flourished during the empire. At the same time, one of the most devastating accusations that could be made against a religion and its adherents was that its cult object was an animal. As we have seen, there were different patterns for how animals should be applied in religions, differences in how various groups regarded "sacred" animals and differences in how people thought these animals should be interpreted. Animals were used flexibly and functioned as markers of cultural bound- aries – of what was sacred as well as what was regarded as strange or barbarian.

While the Egyptians stressed their uniqueness by extended use of animals and animal symbols, the Jews and the Christians accentuated their unique- ness exactly by trying as best they could to keep animals out of their religions. Not least the Israelites' dance around the golden calf had made it difficult to embrace anything like sacred animals in these religions. Like the Jews, who no longer sacrificed animals after the temple in Jerusalem had been destroyed in 70 CE, Christians did not sacrifice animals. Like the Egyptians, Jews and Christians used animals as religious and cultural boundary markers, but in a negative way.

Tertium genus

The development of Christian identity in antiquity was among other things a question of redefinition. Christians in the second and third century had a sort of double identity, belonging to pagan culture on the one hand and to Christianity with its strong roots in Judaism on the other, and they had to define those affiliations. In short, they had to define their relationship to Jews and pagans in a language of similarities and differences.

Many of the Christians were converts. In the words of Tertullian from Carthage, who wrote about 200 CE, "Christians are made, not born" (*Apologeticus*, 18.4). Their pagan background and culture were reflected in the philosophical and rhetorical competence of the Christian intellectual elite.

Christianity started as a Jewish sect. The close connection to Judaism can be seen in the way Jewish texts were used in the Christian canon and in the conception of Christianity as a reinterpretation of Jewish religion, in fact as its true interpretation. The two religions used similar exegetical methods, but the Christians saw the Jewish texts in the Bible as a prefiguration of their own texts.

In these centuries, when Christianity was growing, Christians gradually integrated the plural culture of the empire into it. In a way, they sucked it up and swallowed it, and what they could not digest, they spat out. They used something, but not everything, and eventually gave the Roman Empire the only language in which religion could afterwards be expressed. This language is described by the specialist in late antiquity and Byzantine studies, Averil Cameron, as "the rhetoric of empire" (Cameron 1994). In these centuries, a profound change was made in the traditional structures of religion. As we have seen, one of the things that characterized the ideal Christian was that they did not participate in the Roman sacrificial cult. Instead, communication between God and humans took place with the human body as a medium. God took a human form in Christ, the belief in the resurrection of the body was established, the body and blood of Christ were consumed in the Eucharist, and gradually a cult of the martyrs developed. It was a change from the use of animals as key symbols and from interpreting animal intestines to using a human being and his death as a key symbol and interpreting human souls. This change of key symbol also implied a change in the way identity was marked out.

In the Roman Empire during the centuries when Christianity grew from a minority religion to become the religion of the state, there was a process of devaluation of animals and a parallel process working towards an apotheosis of man. The development of human identity in this period took place among other things within the context of these processes.

Christian authors sometimes described the Christians as *tertium genus*, a third race, in relation to Greeks and Romans on the one hand and Jews on the other. This expression is found for instance in Tertullian (*Ad Nationes*,

1.8) and Clement of Alexandria (*Stromateis*, 5.4), as well as in Eusebius (*Preparation to the Gospel*, 2.1).

For the Christians themselves, to be of a third race implied having a heavenly citizenship and belonging to a religious elite. For the Greeks and Romans, as well as the Jews, it implied that the Christians set themselves apart from traditional Roman society and from Jewish traditions. Tertullian asks ironically whether his opponents think that this third race is dog-eyed (*cynopae*) or shadow-footed (*sciapodes*)? In short, do they think Christians are freaks? The designation *tertium genus* catches something significant about Christian identity in the second to fourth century CE, namely that it was established in interplay with and opposition to Graeco-Roman religion on the one hand and Judaism on the other. The designation also shows that the Christian identity was considered as new in relation to traditional identities. And, as is well known, to be conceived of as new and no part of an established cultural and religious tradition was no advantage in the Graeco-Roman world (Warmind 1989). Translated into the language of symbols, the new identity was that of a hybrid between beast and man. Two examples will illustrate how this alleged hybrid identity was elaborated upon.

In the first example, the Christian god was depicted with an ass's head. This caricature seems to have been created by pagans or Jews but was used in Christian apologies for internal Christian purposes when the authors of these apologies wanted to show who the *real* animals were. According to them, the real animals were not the Christians but the pagans. The hybrid ass marks the boundary between Christianity and paganism as well as the boundary between Christianity and Judaism. It is an external boundary between religions.

According to the second example, taken from Christian gnostic texts, the Jewish god is a hybrid monster, partly man, partly lion, partly snake. However, the superior god is truly human and designated Man. This lion-headed god was used as a marker of internal boundaries by groups that challenged the Christian mainstream.

The crucified donkey-man

At the heart of the Roman Empire, in the Paedagogium of the imperial palace on the Palatine, was found a graffito of a crucified man with the head of an ass in 1856. On the left side of the picture stands another man with his arm raised. The drawing has an inscription in Greek: "Alexamenos, pray(s) to god!" The crucified donkey-man is obviously intended as a crude joke referring to Alexamenos, and the unknown joker has put some effort into his joke.

Who was this god? The drawing, now exhibited in the museum on the Palatine, is usually interpreted as a caricature of Christ and one of his worshippers. It was probably made in the second or third century CE and may be an early example of Christianity taken in a broader social context.

However, the equine head is not necessarily that of an ass. It could as well be a horse. If this is the case, the drawing may be a depiction of a man worshipping a "race demon". In tombs on the Via Appia, magical papyri have been found with drawings of hybrids with the head of a horse and a human body. They were part of spells meant to ensure victory for one's own team and mishaps for other competitors. Perhaps Alexamenos was no Christian but a man who was crazy about horse races? Remember, downhill from the Palatine lay the Circus Maximus.

But even if this caricature was not intended to be Christ and one of his worshippers, two Christian apologists mention similar pictures. In this case, the drawings were undoubtedly intended as a mockery of Christianity. The apologists are Tertullian in his two related works, *Apologeticus* and *Ad Nationes,* and Minucius Felix in *Octavius.* All three works were written in the late second or early third century CE (Price 1999).

You have "dreamed", writes Tertullian in *Apologeticus*, "that our God is an ass's head" (16.1). Then Tertullian proceeds to discuss something that had happened "quite recently" and "in this town [*in ista proxime civitate*]", probably Carthage. A criminal who was hired to tease and frustrate the animals in the arena had exhibited a picture with an inscription usually read as "The God of the Christians, ass-begotten [*DEUS CHRISTIANORUM onoikoites*]" (16.12). The figure had the ears of an ass, one foot was a hoof, it carried a book and wore a toga. "We laughed at both the name and the form", writes Tertullian, who continues by using one of his standard techniques, namely to turn the accusers' allegations against themselves and blame the pagans for worshipping animals (16.12–13; cf. 16.5).

In *Ad Nationes*, the criminal is said to be a Jew who earns his money by hiring himself to the arena. In this way, Tertullian blames the Jews for the slander but adds that the rumour has a weak position because it started with a criminal Jew.

In *Octavius* by Minucius Felix, we are in the vicinity of Rome, to be more specific, in Ostia. The Christian Octavius discusses the value of Christianity and paganism, respectively, with the pagan Caecilius. The accusation that the Christians are worshipping the head of an ass is accompanied by accusations that they worship the genitals of their priest and participate in orgies of child murder and incest (9, 28.7). These accusations are also mentioned by Tertullian (*Apologeticus*, 7, 8) and were probably well-known slanders about the Christians, for Minucius Felix writes:

> We too were once in the same case as you, blindly and stupidly sharing your ideas, and supposing that the Christians worshipped monsters, devoured infants, and joined incestuous feasts; we did not understand that the demons were for ever setting fables afloat without either investigation or proof.
>
> (*Octavius*, 28.2)

232

Such severe accusations are not known from non-Christian authors who wrote about the Christians, for instance Pliny, Galen and Celsus. The lack of similar allegations in pagan texts does not mean that Tertullian and Minucius Felix were not repeating actual rumours about Christians, but the fact that such accusations were repeated as standard themes in Christian texts at the turn of the second century, must imply that in addition to their pagan and Jewish use, these rumours also had some internal Christian significance and that the refutation of them served an edifying purpose.

In the texts of Tertullian and Minucius Felix (and perhaps in the graffito from the Palatine), the ass is portrayed as an object of worship. This divine ass has a past, which is evoked by Tertullian, who refers to the well-known idea that it was an ass or the head of the ass that the Jews worshipped in the temple in Jerusalem. Tacitus (*The Annals*, 5.4), Josephus (*Against Appion*, 2.112–14, 80, 9) and Plutarch (*On Isis and Osiris*, 31 363D) mention this idea. Misconceptions about Jewish worship could easily have been transferred to the Christians, probably because Christianity was usually seen as a branch of Judaism, a fact also remarked upon by Tertullian.

Tertullian connects the story about the ass with the Jews in two ways, both because he states that Tacitus located the ass in the temple in Jerusalem and because it was a Jew who created the caricature. Tertullian also blames the Jews in general for making up stories about the Christians (*Ad Nationes*, 1.14). When Tertullian states in this way that the story of the divine ass originally referred to the Jews and in this particular case was also connected with a Jew who had tried to transfer it to the Christians, he manages to place the responsibility for the animal on the Jews.

The image of the crucified ass must be connected to a strong tendency in these centuries to degrade gods in animal form and to mock people who worshipped them. As we have seen, animals – be they serpents, bulls or asses – were used in a negative way in the creation of religious identity. This campaign was specially aimed at the Egyptians, who had animal cults and with whom the Romans had an ambiguous relationship – they both imported Egyptian cults and mocked Egyptian religion. As put by the satirical author Lucian: "All sort of animals are stuffed into heaven from Egypt" (*The Assembly of the Gods*, 10). But other groups were also affected by the aversion to theriomorphic gods. The intellectual elite of the non-Egyptian inhabitants of the Graeco-Roman world regarded animal worship as an inferior form of religion. This general tendency is clearly reflected in our texts and in the caricature from the Palatine.

Why was an ass chosen? It could have been because of the connection with the stories about the Jews and the alleged veneration of the ass in the temple in Jerusalem referred to above. To label the Jews as ass-worshippers was in fact one of the standard ways of slandering them. This slander seems to have originated in Egypt in the third century BCE (Bar-Kochva 1996; van Henten and Abusch 1996; Frankfurter 1998: 206–8, but against

Bickermann 1927). In Egypt, such stories could further have been linked to the mythological fight between the Egyptian god Horus and his evil opponent Seth-Typhon. In this fight, Horus was interpreted as the symbol of the Egyptians, while Seth-Typhon was generally associated with foreigners and with people who threatened Egypt. These enemies of the Egyptians were sometimes identified with the Jews, who were said to be worshipping Seth-Typhon. Standard ways of depicting this god were as an ass, with the head of an ass or connected to an ass (van Henten and Abusch 1996; Bar-Kochva 1996).

However, the use of an ass in such caricatures as those referred to by Tertullian and Minucius Felix could also be connected with more general conceptions of this animal in Mediterranean societies, where it was a beast of burden and a riding animal and was ranked low in the hierarchy of animals. Philo, although he praises the hearing of the ass, writes that it was "thought to be the stupidest of the beasts" (*On the Posterity of Cain*, 161). Plutarch observes that the ass is the most stupid of the tame animals (*On Isis and Osiris*, 50 371C). Minucius Felix describes it as "the meanest of all beasts" (*Octavius*, 9.3). Artemidorus states that if a man dreams that he "has the head of a dog, horse, ass, or any four-legged creature instead of his own, it signifies slavery and misery" (*The Interpretation of Dreams*, 1.37). In the physiognomic tradition, the ass is characterized by its sexual excitement and foolishness (Aristotle, *Physiognomics*, 808b 35, 811a 26), while in the anonymous Latin physiognomic treatise that sums up the catalogue of faults of the ass, the animal is described as lazy (*iners*), dull (*frigidum*), unteachable (*indocile*), slow (*tardum*), insolent (*insolens*) and with an unpleasant voice (*vocis ingratae*) (119).

However, the fact that the ass appears together with an ox at the manger of Jesus in sarcophagi from the third century, referring to Isaiah 1.3 and to the prophecy that the ox and the ass will recognize their master (cf. Justin Martyr, *Apology*, 1.63), shows that the ass sometimes also had a positive meaning in Christian interpretations, although this positive interpretation certainly does not surface in the interpretation of the ass hybrid.[1]

Animals, anthropocentrism and cultural change

Christianity and Judaism share anthropomorphic ideas about God. In these religions, both humans and animals were created by God, but only humans were made in God's image. Adam gives names to the animals and is appointed master over them. God became human in Christ, and Christ's sacrifice on the cross replaced the pagan institution of sacrifice. The ultimate religious goal was the salvation of the human soul. Animals had no part in salvation. In Greek and Roman religions, too, an anthropomorphic conception of the gods is prominent as gods and goddesses were depicted as perfect exemplars of the human form.

As already mentioned, the crucified donkey-man on the Palatine and the texts of Tertullian and Minucius Felix must be interpreted as part of more extensive religious processes. For centuries, something had been happening at the social and symbolic boundaries set between animals, humans and gods. Anthropocentric processes were accompanied by a social redefinition of animals in which they were radically devalued. The devaluation of animals is seen in the ban on sacrifice, in the flourishing of the arenas and in the fact that philosophers usually denied animals mental capacities similar to humans. Animals were driven out of heaven, and man was left alone as the only creature created in God's image.

The caricature of the donkey-man must accordingly be seen as part of a general discourse in which animals were devalued, lost their mystery and were no longer seen as channels to the divine. But the caricature of the crucified donkey-man not only tells us something about animals, it also tells us something more general about the way in which Christian identity was established by the Christians and their opponents. What did the mockers really mean by their slander? And why did the Christians repeat such mockeries and even dwell upon them in their own texts?

The caricature signalled that the Christian attempt to establish a new religion in which anthropocentrism had gone so far that God really became a human being of flesh and blood was rejected by non-Christians. Instead, this divine human was recast as a hybrid. This specific hybrid form could have been created because the product of a union between the Jewish god, who by outsiders was caricatured as an ass, and a human mother logically became a mixture between ass and man, an *asionocephalus*.

The caricature of the donkey-man also has a certain likeness to the Egyptian Anubis, with his human body and jackal's head. This hybrid god was frequently mocked by pagans. In the Vatican museum there is a statue of Anubis, cast as a Roman with a tunic and a chlamys, but instead of the head of a high-nosed Roman male, it has the head of a jackal. It is probably a statue of a priest in the cult of Isis who is wearing the mask of Anubis. We also, who are the heirs to this Graeco-Roman culture and are in fact living in the very latest sequel to antiquity, see clearly what Juvenal and others meant when they mocked those hybrids with heads of jackals, cats or lions. These hybrids have not been easily accepted into Western culture. In the case of the caricatures referred to by Tertullian and Minucius Felix, they appeared even more stupid than the Egyptian *cynocephalus* – the jackal-headed god – because the caricature of the Christian god had taken its bestial characteristics from the most stupid of all animals, the despised ass.

The Christians may have repeated the accusation about worshipping this hybrid because they knew with absolute certainty that it was untrue. Therefore, such allegations said more about those who made them than they did about those they were aimed at. When Tertullian follows traditional rhetorical practice by turning his opponents' own arguments against themselves

235

(*retorsio*) by blaming them for animal worship, he has no further need to exaggerate. The accusations of Tertullian and Minucius Felix are less overstated than the rumours about themselves and their fellow believers. Their own accusations against the pagans are momentarily recognizable as based on facts: Epona *was* worshipped in the empire, horses and mules *were* decorated in her honour, and hybrids appeared in the iconography – especially in Egypt. Consequently, Tertullian and Minucius Felix struck at their adversaries by using the ass and boosted morale in their own ranks. They knew that they did not worship a god with animal characteristics, let alone an ass, while their adversaries apparently worshipped animals. Consequently, the Christians had a fully human identity, while pagans, who created gods in the form of beasts, had not.

The *leontocephalus*

The caricature of a hybrid god was not only restricted to mockery aimed at the Christians and used by them in a sort of rhetorical *retorsio* – turning their adversaries' arguments against themselves. A hybrid was also used by some Christians in an attempt to establish their own identity as superior to other Christian groups and to Jews. This creature is one of the versions of the gnostic demiurge, the world creator, who has already been introduced (see Chapter 10). He is envisaged as a cross between man and beast, a parody of the Jewish god Yahweh.

According to the *Apocryphon of John*, the lowest entity in the spiritual world, Sophia, conceived alone without a male and gave birth to a monstrous son. This son is described as an abortion. His appearance is bestial, with the face of a lion, or both a lion and a snake, and he has fiery eyes. The opening line of this figure is "It is I who am God, there is none apart from me". In this he is totally wrong, because the transcendent world of light exists above him with its host of spiritual powers. The readers of the text know of this spiritual world, not least because they read about it in several pages preceding the birth of the demiurge. Because the demiurge is ignorant of these things, which the readers know very well, he appears to be stupid. This caricature of the Old Testament god is usually called by the enigmatic name Ialdabaoth, but he is also called Saklas ("fool") and Samael ("the blind god"), which stresses his stupidity. He is responsible for the creation of the material world and for human beings. He and his demonic powers invent different devices to keep human beings locked in the material world, the most important being sex. Through the demiurge, bestial appearance and sex are interconnected.

This lion-headed god is associated with man as a biological and psychic being belonging to the material world. Opposed to him is the real god. The fact that the highest god is several times called Man in some gnostic texts also reflects a special formulation of anthropocentrism in this branch of Christianity.

The lion-headed god has several sources, as a leontocephaline god is not only found in gnostic texts. On the contrary, such a god figures prominently in other religions of this period, for instance in Orphism and the mysteries of Mithras (Jackson 1985: 43–4). Part of his wider cultural context is the solar monotheism of the third century as well as general astrological ideas. The astrological connection is seen in the *Apocryphon of John*, where the demiurge is described with many faces, which points to the sun's passage through the different houses of the sky.

However, the past of this lion-headed god is not as interesting as the uses to which such creatures were put. As the mainstream Christian interpretation of Jewish texts had as their point of departure the conception of Jesus as the Messiah, some of the gnostic Christian texts had as their point of departure a conception of Yahweh as an inferior god, a mixture of evil and stupidity. And in contrast to the way in which the Jew Philo interpreted the Old Testament to find the true meaning of Moses, in the *Apocryphon of John* it is explicitly stressed: "It is not as Moses wrote and you heard" (CG II, 1, 22:22–3).

In Tertullian's two apologetic works and in some gnostic texts, the development of Christian identity in relation to Judaism is expressed through the symbol of the hybrid ass and the lion-headed god. A special type of cultural work undertaken by Christians, and also by Jews, was identifying the differences and underplaying the similarities between them. Christian converts who were former Jews or pagans (remember Tertullian's words: "Christians are made, not born"), were people who had started to participate in new narratives and rituals – Christian narratives and Christian rituals – but they had acquired a new type of relationship to Judaism into the bargain. At least in Tertullian the hybrid ass appears explicitly in the context of Jewish/Christian relationships at the same time as the worship of theriomorphic gods, hybrids and animals is placed in a wider pagan cultural context.

In these cultural stereotypes of hybrids of animals and humans are layers of meaning. Underlying them is a binary opposition, which says that Hellenist culture is to barbarian culture as human is to animal, male to female, soul to body. For the two poles one could substitute other meanings. For Hellenist culture one could substitute Christians, and for barbarian culture one could substitute pagan culture: Christians are to pagans as humans are to animals, or in another identification, namely the one made by the Jew to whom Tertullian refers: Jews are to Christians as humans are to hybrids. Celsus made use of similar forms of binary opposition when he compared Christians to worms, ants and frogs (cf. Chapter 2).

Depending on the animal that was used in such binary opposition, different connotations were evoked. We have seen that animals tended to appear as fixed signs in relation to certain characteristics. The ass was a stupid animal, while the lion was often associated with manliness, bravery and kingship. In the case of the gnostic demiurge, the traditional characteristics of the lion were put into a new frame and given a new twist, because the lion-headed hybrid thinks and acts as if he is the superior god, while he is, in reality, an evil fool.[2] This is consonant with the way Artemidorus interpreted animals in dreams. He claimed that even if animals had some basic meanings, their actual meaning varied according to context.

In actual use, different animals referred to different stories. In our case, the ass was connected with common slander about the Jews and with what happened in the temple in Jerusalem. The lion-headed god had specific astrological connotations and appeared in several of the religions of the empire as well as in magical lore. Perhaps he also brought with him connotations from these contexts, from the mysteries of Mithras, from the god of time – Aion – and, not least, from Saturn, the most popular god of North Africa. When some Christian groups marked Yahweh out as a lion-headed god, they not only made him into a beast, they also associated him with these pagan divinities and mocked them.

Heretics and serpents

Animals were also used in a more systematic and "scientific" way to label religious opponents. About 374–7, Bishop Epiphanius of Salamis (on Cyprus) made an impressive attempt in his *Panarion* to describe all philosophical schools, Christian sects and pagan religions that existed or had existed and characterize them as heresies.[3] While "heresy" for Irenaeus covered sectarian Christians, and Hippolytus also included Jews in this category, Epiphanius refers to pagan religious and philosophical systems and views as well, refuting no less than eighty heresies (Vallée 1981: 97ff).[4] The strength of this work is its comprehensiveness and its use of rich and varied source material. Epiphanius made use of written[5] and oral sources, as well as his own experiences and observations concerning persons and sects outside the Christian mainstream. Thus the *Panarion* offers a unique access to the Christian landscape as seen by a late fourth-century bishop. Several points are made about this landscape, not least by means of the metaphorical use of serpents.

Much was at stake for Epiphanius. He wanted to keep the faith pure and the Church one, uncontaminated by all competing creeds and pagan religions. The result is a huge work, a heresiology, the point of which is to enlighten people about the dangers of all religious movements except the orthodox Church. In three volumes and seven tomes, Epiphanius furnishes his medical chest – *Panarion* – with antidotes for all heresies. In the preface to the work, he describes it in this way:

> Since I shall be telling you the names of the sects and exposing their unlawful deeds like poisons and toxic substances, matching their antidotes with them at the same time – cures for those who are

already bitten, and preventives for those who will have this experience – I am drafting this Preface here for the scholarly, to explain
the "Panarion", or chest of remedies for the victims of wild beasts'
bites. It is a work in three Volumes and contains eighty Sects,
which stand symbolically for wild animals or snakes.

(Panarion, Proem, I, 1.1)

Epiphanius describes these heresies so that the different types emerge from
and relate to each other in a huge genealogical system – "a global genealogy
of heresies" (Vallée 1987: 70). This model was not new, having already been
applied to good effect by Irenaeus in his *Against Heresies*.[6] It implies giving
his adversaries a certain unity by revealing their common history and their
dependency upon each other, and using this unity as a weapon against them.
However, Epiphanius introduces an additional model for the way religions
and sects relate to the main Church when he introduces serpents and wild
animals, and especially serpents, as his main model for describing heretics.
The genealogical model and the serpent model could even be combined, as
was the case in the presentation of Satornilius:

> So whether Satornilius obtained venom from the ancients like a
> viper and has imparted it to Basilides, or whether Basilides
> imparted it to Satornilius, let us leave their poison behind us,
> deadly as it is, and coming from such serpents as these – for with
> the Lord's teaching, as with an antidote, we have weakened it and
> deprived it of its strength.

(Panarion, 3/23, 7.3)

The model of the serpent is applied to heresies from Simon Magus onwards
(from heresy 21 to 80). The serpent had been used by earlier refuters of heresies like Irenaeus and Eusebius, but Epiphanius is unique among them in
using the model systematically (Pourkier 1992: 80).[7]

The animals that Epiphanius refers to are not based on fantasy.
Epiphanius mentions as his sources a specialist on serpents (Nicander) and
several authors of natural history (*Preface*, 2.3.1). According to Jürgen
Dummer, Epiphanius has taken these animals from one of the numerous
handbooks that were used in the treatment of people who had been bitten
by poisonous animals. However, this lost handbook is not identical to any of
those that Epiphanius mentions (Dummer 1973: 299).

In addition to a wide range of serpents, other animals are enlisted in the
text, animals that like some serpents sting or bite or in other ways do harm,
for instance scorpions, fish and insects, but also moles and lizards:

> For Heracleon may justly be called a lizard. This is not a snake but
> a hard-skinned beast as they say, something that crawls on four feet,

239

like a gecko. The harm of its bite is negligible, but if a drop of its spittle strikes a food or drink, it causes the immediate death of those who have any. Heracleon's teaching is like that.

(*Panarion*, 16/36, 6.7)

Epiphanius' point is that the animals infect the body of the Church with their poison. His volumes have a double purpose, to have a preventive effect on those who have not yet been bitten and to be an antidote for those who have. The antidote, or *pharmakon*, that Epiphanius eloquently offers is the orthodox creed. It must be mentioned that Epiphanius was not in favour of allegorical interpretation of scripture —we have already seen his scruples over the interpretation of the dove as the Holy Spirit (see Introduction). But even if he intends his model of serpents and wild animals as an analogy, he does not avoid making allegorical interpretations of it as he goes along.

Gérard Vallée has made a survey of the way Epiphanius constructs his description and refutation of each heresy (Vallée 1981: 69, 88–91). Epiphanius uses a recurrent scheme that includes introduction, exposition, first invective, refutation, further invective and finally transition to the next heresy. The serpent metaphor is sometimes referred to in the introduction, sometimes elsewhere, but usually as part of the "further invective", where Epiphanius presents an analogy with a species of serpent (or another harmful animal) injecting the venom of heresy. (It must be added that Epiphanius matches the venom of the serpents by his abusive and insulting language when he describes the heresies.[8])

The categorization by means of serpents and other animals is not the only one that Epiphanius uses. In the introduction and the concluding sections of *Panarion*, "About the faith" (*De fide*), a metaphorical system with roots in the Song of Songs is predominant (2.8, 21.1). When Epiphanius reckons with eighty heresies, he has taken this number from the Song of Songs and the eighty concubines therein (6:8). These concubines are contrasted with the one true bride, who is likened to a dove (6:9): "One is my dove, my perfect one", that is, "the holy bride and catholic Church herself" (*De fide*, 35, 3.5). The two metaphorical systems, the serpent system and the bride system, are combined when the bride – the dove – is once contrasted with the serpents: "But his bride too is a peaceable dove, with no poison, or teeth like mill-stones, or stings – unlike all these people with their snake-like appearance and sprouting of venom, each eager to prepare some poison for the world and harm his converts" (15/35, 3.8).

Epiphanius enlists a lot of serpents in his project and reveals much knowledge of their nature and behaviour. Some of these species of animal are largely harmless, but their archetype is a harmful and poisonous creature. This archetypal serpent is closely related to the serpent of Genesis and connotes to Satan: "And see how far the serpent, the deceiver of the Ophites, has gone in mischief! Just as he deceived Eve and Adam at the beginning so even now, [and he does it] by concealing himself, both now and in the Jewish period until Christ's coming" (*Panarion*, 17/37, 1.3). Epiphanius distinguishes between Satan and the Genesis serpent when he says that "It was the snake who spoke in the snake" (*ibid.*, 1.6). He elaborates upon the serpent-like nature of the Devil, which does not pertain to his exterior but lies in his character: "Indeed, sacred scripture calls the Devil a serpent; not because he looks like one, certainly, but because to man he appears extremely crooked, and because of the treacherous fraud which was originally perpetrated through a snake" (*ibid.*, 2.3).

The use of a serpent to describe heresies could have been suggested by the identification of Satan as the Genesis serpent. In addition, the expression "brood of vipers" characterizes opponents in the New Testament (Matthew 3:7, 23:33; Luke 3:7; cf. Pourkier 1992: 79), and there is an exhortation "to tread on serpents and scorpions" (Luke 10:19; Mark 16:17–18; cf. Psalm 90:13).[9] However, when the comparative system of serpents and wild animals is introduced, it offers endless possibilities for making theological and heresiological points.

Epiphanius creates a rich associative field where these creatures are set to work – they direct thought, give emotional impetus and have been given a scientific basis because they refer to real species of animal. Things are woven together by means of the serpent as, for instance, in his description of the Nicolaitans, he compares the flute, a flute player and Satan to a serpent: The flute is a copy of the serpent through which the Devil spoke and deceived Eve, the flute player "throws his head back as he plays and bends it forward, he leans right and left like the serpent", and the Devil "makes these gestures too, in blasphemy of the heavenly host and to destroy earth's creatures utterly while getting the world into his toils, by wreaking havoc right and left on those who trust the imposture, and are charmed by it as by the notes of an instrument" (*Panarion*, 5/25, 4.11).

We have seen that the model of serpents was associated with the genealogical model, but the serpent model can also be combined with other models or metaphors, as when the Christian life is likened to a journey, for instance in the first part of *De fide*:

> We have discussed the various, multiform, and much divided teachings of the crooked counsels of our opponents, have distinguished them by species and genus, and, by God's power, have exposed them as stale and worthless. We have sailed across the shoreless sea of the blasphemies of each sect, with great difficulty crossed the ocean of their shameful, repulsive mysteries, given the solutions to their hosts of problems, and passed their wickedness by. And we have approached the calm lands of the truth, after negotiating every rough place, enduring every squall, foaming, and tossing of billows, and, as it were, seeing the swell of the sea, and its whirlpools, its

shallows none too small, and its places full of dangerous beasts, and experiencing them through words.

(Panarion, De fide, 1.1–3)

This is a lasting model for Church history according to which the Church is manoeuvring through troubled waters, attacked by dangerous beasts – theologians, sects and movements that challenge its teaching and religious monopoly.

One can learn much about serpents by means of Epiphanius' *Panarion*, but even more about how flexibly these animals are used to characterize the opponents of the Church. The animals that Epiphanius refers to are not big but small, However, they have the means to harm and poison by stinging or biting the "body" of the Church or the believers and thus make fatal wounds. The image of poisonous animals implies that the Church and the believers constitute a pure body and that all those who do not fully agree with the teachings of the Church are estranged from it and are its enemies. They are characterized as evil and as running the errands of Satan. Behind the various serpents and harmful creatures is the archetypal serpent, which is associated with the Devil, who is described by means of this serpent, and serpents and other harmful animals get their true meaning from him. The capacity of these creatures to harm humans by biting, stinging and poisoning them is interpreted as an expression of their inherently evil nature. The characteristics of these animals are then transferred to the Church and to Epiphanius' opponents. Sects are "beast-like" (*Panarion*, 7/27, 8.4). However, the animals that contributed to this model of Church history are left with an aura of metaphysical evil. Sects are beast-like in their evil functions because the beasts that they are compared to are evil.

Conclusion

The caricature of the donkey-man and that of the *leontocephalus* must be seen in relation to processes in which the human form was on the way to becoming the primary symbol for the divine and in which the animal form was correspondingly devalued. Nobody wanted to be stuck with the wrong image, to give the impression that they worshipped a god who was an animal, appeared as an animal or had clearly bestial attributes. Tertullian and Minucius Felix did their best to get rid of the donkey-man by shuffling him over to the Jews and to dismiss the more general accusation of worshipping animals by redirecting it against pagans. Thus they employed the caricature of the donkey-man for all it was worth in their own anti-pagan and, especially, in anti-Jewish propaganda. At the same time, Christians who wanted to be less dependent on Judaism or more selective in their interpretation of Jewish texts than other Christians used the lion hybrid to characterize the Jewish god as inferior.

To be described as worshipping animal gods was to be *labelled* and to be stuck with an inferior human identity. Such labels were invented in a process where different cultural and religious identities existed as options for individuals and groups. Myths about animals were part of the creation of identity and gave those who used them creatively a greater ability to manoeuvre in the complex cultural and religious labyrinths of the time.

In one way, it is a paradox that the cultural stereotype of the animal hybrid was applied to Christians to place them within the view of reality held by society at that time, as Christians did not worship anything remotely resembling this hybrid. On the contrary, they worshipped God in human form and represented the lasting expression of the anthropocentric religious processes of the empire. In another way, the accusation of worshipping animals could be seen as logical, considering the binary cultural polarization that was regarded as normal. In Graeco-Roman thinking, animal was to human as body was to spirit. If one was worshipping a god who had become human and was incarnated in a human body and human flesh, one could in some sense be said to worship something animal. Characteristics from different ends of the negative pole could be transferred to each other. According to such mytho-logic, worshipping a human made of flesh and blood was in reality worshipping an animal.

As for the Jews, they worshipped neither an animal nor a hybrid being. But in relation to Christianity and the anthropocentric processes that had gone further in Christianity than in Judaism, the Jews and their holy texts were regarded by Christians as being on a lower level. Accordingly, in contrast to the god of the Christians, who was revealed in human form in Christ, the god of the Jews was connected with the world of matter and was described as an animal or hybrid being. There is a prominent tendency in these centuries working against the inclusion of animals in religions, or more precisely, against certain modes of such inclusion. While the use of animals in a symbolic mode flourished in Christianity, the instrumental use of animals and the use of live animals were forbidden.

It is natural to connect Christian exclusivity regarding man at the expense of all other species with this religion's lack of tolerance towards other religions, and to see these developments as parallel. When Epiphanius wrote his *Panarion* in a climate of asceticism, opposition against pagan thinking, and a firm belief in the one true Church, it is perhaps not so strange that small and venomous animals were set to illustrate the dangers to the Church and to the Christian life. In *Panarion*, the serpent is firmly established as the archetypal evil beast. The tolerance that had been a necessary part of the religious pluralism of the empire had towards the end of the fourth century been exchanged for Christianity and a religious climate that towards the end of that century had rapidly become less tolerant.

However, to maintain an absolute segregation between the human and the "bestial" in a way that made the one into the positive pole and the other into the negative without any middle ground between them was difficult without making some compromises. There was at least one trait common to certain non-human species that Christians really would have wished to acquire. There was also a more optimistic view of animals in some Christian circles than those that have hitherto been described. We will now turn to them.

1 2

WINGED HUMANS, SPEAKING
ANIMALS

Theios aner – the divine man

In the Acts of the Apostles, there are two stories pertaining to new relations between animals, gods and humans. In Lystra, Paul healed a cripple and made him walk. When people saw what he had done, they shouted that gods had come down to them in the likeness of men (Acts 14:8–11). They "called Barnabas, Zeus; and Paul, Hermes, because he was the chief speaker. Then the priest of Jupiter, which was before their city, brought oxen and garlands unto the gates, and would have done sacrifice with the people" (Acts 14:12–13). However, Paul and Barnabas persuaded the people not to sacrifice to them but to turn to the living God (Acts 14:14–18).

In the second narrative, Paul, who is on his way to Rome, has just suffered a shipwreck off the island of Malta. All aboard the ship saved themselves by swimming to the shore, and the people of Malta helped the survivors by kindling a fire for them (Acts 28:1–2). When Paul had gathered a bundle of sticks for the fire, a venomous viper came out of the heat and fastened on his hand (28:3). The onlookers saw it as a sign that Paul was a murderer, since having escaped from the sea he was immediately attacked by the poisonous reptile (Acts 28:4). But Paul shook the beast off into the fire and felt no harm (Acts 28:5). This made a great impression on the onlookers: "They waited, expecting him to swell up or suddenly fall down dead; but when they had waited a long time and saw no misfortune come to him, they changed their minds and said that he was a god" (Acts 28:6).

What do these stories illustrate? In both, traditional religious practices relating to animals are involved, and the Christian apostle Paul is regarded as divine. The first reflects the immediate connection between a religious event and the killing of a sacrificial victim, and the fact that high-profile communication with the divine presupposed the ritual slaughter of an animal. In Acts 14:8–11, this routine is not criticized as such – the objections of Paul and Barnabas are to their being treated as gods. "The living God" is the only object worthy of worship. In the second case, the snake behaves in an odd way when its poisonous bite is combined with its refusing to let go. It is clearly interpreted as a bad omen and seen as an incarnation of evil. When it is conquered by its superior, a clash of powers – divine and demonic – is involved. When the story ends with the people saying that Paul is a god, no modifications are made and there are no protests. In this case, and unlike Acts 14:8–11, the author apparently accepts that Paul was conceived of as divine.

Common to these New Testament texts is their relation to the old institutions of sacrifice and omens in which animals routinely played their part. At the same time, they introduce the new theme of human apotheosis, although in an ambiguous way when Paul and Barnabas are lent a sort of deputy divinity on behalf of Christ.

The apotheosis of man, which was one of the main characteristics of the religious developments of the first Christian centuries,[1] had its parallel in the tendency to depict gods in human form. Roman influence on religious practice in the western empire was to be seen, for instance, in the way local deities were now depicted as humans (Rives 2000: 269). The apotheosis of humans of flesh and blood, which sometimes included worship of them, took several forms, from a divinization of the select few, as in the case of Jesus of Nazareth and Apollonius of Tyana, to a belief in a continued life after death. The last option implied that physical immortality, which in traditional religion had been a prerogative of the gods, was now in principle available to everyone. While immortality had been available only for those who led a philosophical life in the manner of Plato, and perhaps for those who were initiated into Orphic mysteries and other mystery religions, the possibility of a bodily resurrection available for all those who believed in Christ was new. Paul describes how people at the end of time would be lifted bodily into the sky (I Thessalonians 4:17). It was obviously no longer true that as the Preacher had said: "the fate of humans and the fate of animals is the same; as one dies, so dies the other. They all have the same breath, and humans have no advantage over animals" (Ecclesiastes 3:19).

The cosmological boundaries were remade; some were new, and some traditional ones had been strengthened. In several of the religions and religio-philosophical systems, man's place in the cosmos was rethought. Not only his relationship with animals was renegotiated but also his relations with gods, powers and demons. A general interest in the classification of the cosmos and its inhabitants is striking. Intricate cosmological systems were constructed by Neoplatonists, Stoics, Jews, Christians, and, not least, gnostics and Manichaeans (MacMullen 1981: 79ff), and ever since these cosmological systems have continued to challenge theologians and philosophers. It was characteristic of these systems that they were top-heavy, full of supernatural beings, such as angels and demons, but poorer at representing the diversity of the animal world.

In this final chapter, some of the more peculiar problems that arose in the wake of man's wish to escape from the natural world and animals will be discussed. One problem concerned the trouble that birds created in the neat Christian universe. A different problem arose when animals broke out of the Christian hierarchy and became human.

Birds are a nuisance

The North African rhetorician Lactantius (240–320 CE), a pupil of Arnobius, in a treatise called *On the Workmanship of God*, praises the way the human body is equipped. Lactantius establishes the body's transcendence by pointing to its erectness, its upward thrust, and at the gaze of the eyes, looking towards heaven. In a treatise on the anger of God, in which Lactantius makes anger an essential property of God, he returns to the subject of man's erect posture and elevated countenance (*On the Anger of God*, 7). But he also allows that certain resemblances exist between the ways animals and humans are equipped. Lactantius' examples are speech, the capacity to show joy, intelligence and reflection. In the end, he finds that religion is the only thing of which there is no trace in any animal. Because Lactantius reaches this conclusion, he can make an observation similar to the *Gospel of Philip*: those who do not worship God are far removed from the nature of man, and "will live the life of the brutes under the form of man" (*On the Anger of God*, 7).

The enthusiasm for the way the human body is equipped is also found in other Christian authors, for instance Nemesius of Emesa (cf. Gregory of Nyssa, *On the Making of Man*, 7–9). Nemesius had a scientific, probably medical, training but "pursues scientific matters for their moral and theological bearing" (Wallace-Hadrill 1968: 36). He wrote a work, entitled *On the Nature of Man* (*c.* 400 CE), in which he states that man is the high point of creation – in life and after death – and that the world and its creatures were all made for him, and only for him. Nemesius uses a wide range of philosophical and Christian sources. He is dependent on the anthropology of Genesis, according to which the world and all its creatures are subject to man, (he uses Origen's *Commentary on Genesis*), and he formulates his views in a triumphant praise of man, his abilities, and his bodily superiority, which surpasses all other creatures:

> Who, then, can fully express the pre-eminence of so singular a creature? Man crosses the mighty deep, contemplates the range of the heavens, notes the motion, position, and size of the stars, and reaps a harvest both from land and sea, scorning the rage of wild beasts, and the might of the whales. He learns all kinds of knowledge, gains skill in arts, and pursues scientific enquiry. By writing, he addresses himself to whom he will, however far away, unhindered by bodily location. He foretells the future, rules everything, subdues everything, enjoys everything. He converses with angels and with God himself. He gives orders to creation. Devils are subject to him. He

247

explores the nature of every kind of being. He busies himself with the knowing of God, and is God's house and temple. And all these privileges he is able to purchase at the cost of virtue and godliness.

(*On the Nature of Man*, 2.10)

Nemesius hastens to add that "we must not let ourselves appear to any to be writing, out of place, a panegyric about man instead of a straightforward description of his nature, as we proposed to do". He stresses that man not only "has all the members, but has them perfect, and such that they could not be changed for the better" (*ibid.*, 4.23). Nemesius also makes a point of the fact that not every kind of living creature possesses every kind of corporeal member (*ibid.*). He mentions creatures without feet, such as fish and snakes, and creatures without heads, such as crabs and lobsters, but he says nothing about those that have no wings. It may well be that the human body is perfect, but its lack of wings – this traditional sign of bodily transcendence – is curious and could have been mentioned.

From the time when the Syrio-Palestinian culture of the Bronze Age spread its winged creatures to Mesopotamia, Persia and the Greek world (Caubet 2002: 230), wings had been grafted on to sphinxes, griffins, bulls, horses and anthropomorphic deities to indicate that they represented divinity. Besides, the wise man who flees bodily desire by means of wings is a Platonic motif.[2] In Christianity, too, the divine is sometimes equipped with wings. When the Holy Spirit appeared in the Gospels, it was as a dove. In the Syriac *Odes of Solomon* (Second century CE), the stress is on the motherly wings of this creature: "As the wings of doves over their nestlings, and the mouths of their nestlings towards their mouths, so are the wings of the Spirit over my heart" (*Odes of Solomon*, 28:1–2).[3] Since wings were such obvious marks of transcendence, it might have bothered Nemesius that humans had not been equipped with them.

The lack of wings had troubled Lactantius. In *On the Workmanship of God*, he shows "a striking preoccupation with birds," as the Church historian Virginia Burrus has recently put it (Burrus 2000: 29). Birds take care in raising their young, have highly developed capacities for vocalization and, not least, have wings and are thus not earthbound. Consequently, they challenge the position of humans as the most transcendent beings on earth. As Burrus shows, Lactantius solves the problem by ranking hands far above wings because of their power to act and control (*ibid.*: 29–30).

Birds were a nuisance. Different authors chose different solutions to the "bird problem". Ambrose, the Bishop of Milan (339–97 CE), chose the two-leggedness of man as the characteristic that showed his kinship to the two-legged birds. Like birds, man aims at what is high (*Hexaëmeron*, 6.9.74; in Grant 1999). In this way, Ambrose makes men bird-like, even if they have no wings. Basil of Caesarea (330–79 CE), a younger contemporary of Ambrose and Nemesius, solved the bird problem in his eighth Homily by placing birds firmly at the bottom of the hierarchy of being. His solution was to make birds into pseudo-fish. According to Basil, fish swim through the water by means of their fins, while birds "swim" through the air by means of their wings. The exalted position of birds is thus not original: birds are not really creatures of the air but creatures of the water – in reality, a sort of flying fish (cf. Wallace-Hadrill 1968: 35; Grant 1999: 77, 90). And since, according to Plato, fish and water creatures are at the bottom of the hierarchy of being (*Timaeus*, 92a–92b), making birds into fish really put them in their place.[4] We may note in passing that Basil characterized aquatic animals not only as "mute, but savage and unteachable, incapable of sharing life with man" (8. *Homily*).

In a similar wrestling with the problem of human pedestrian nature, Augustine (354–430 CE) compared birds and demons. Demons dwell in the air, and humans dwell on earth. Why then are demons not superior to men? Augustine points out that it could equally well have been said that birds were superior to humans because they too dwell in the air. But this would have been ridiculous, because birds lack a rational soul (*The City of God*, 8.15). In this way, Augustine breaks the traditional connection between transcendence and being airborne by pointing to rationality as a superior characteristic. Like Lactantius, Augustine does not regard wings as a relevant physiological sign. In relation to demons, Augustine points to men's superior morals and blessed immortality as characteristics that make them better than demons. Man is not only better than birds and demons, he is "a rational being and therefore more excellent and outstanding than any other creature on earth" (*The City of God*, 22.24). Augustine goes on to praise the excellence of man and the ways in which he is endowed with all gifts.

An alternative to all this harping upon real wings was to make wings into metaphors. In one of the Nag Hammadi texts, the *Thomas the Contender*, it is said: "Everyone who seek the truth from true wisdom will make himself wings so as to fly, fleeing the lust that scorches the spirits of men. And he will make himself wings to flee every visible spirit" (140:1–5).

Outsiders were critical of the Christian desire for wings and of what they saw as absurd wishes to be airborne and bird-like. An example of this criticism is found in *Apocriticus*, a text most likely from the early fifth century but which, as has already been mentioned, probably mediates views originally presented by Porphyry. The critic comments on Paul's statement in I Thessalonians 4:15–17, a statement that included comments about the salvation of those on earth: "Then we which are alive and remain shall be caught up together with them in the clouds, to meet the Lord in the air; and so shall we ever be with the Lord" (I Thessalonians 4:17). The critic calls this aspiration a lie and appeals to the common sense of the animals themselves when he makes his protest:

> If this is sung in a stage part to irrational creatures, they will bleat
> and croak with an enormous din when they hear of people in the

flesh flying like birds in the air, or carried on a cloud. For this boast is a mighty piece of quackery, that living things, pressed down by the burden of physical bulk, should receive the nature of winged birds, and cross the wide air like some sea, using the cloud as chariot. Even if such a thing is possible, it is monstrous, and against the sequence [of nature]. For nature which created all things from the beginning, appointed places befitting the things which were brought into being, and ordained that each should have its proper sphere, the sea for the water creatures, the land for those on dry ground, the air for winged creatures, and the ether for the heavenly bodies. If one of these were moved from its proper abode, it would be annihilated on arrival in a strange condition and abode.

(*Apocriticus*, 4.2; in Cook 2000: 229)

The bird theme, here associated with Paul, was obviously embarrassing for Christian authors in the late third and fourth centuries. It could be added that, seen from posterity, it was not made less embarrassing by these authors' own comments. But even if the two-leggedness of humans compensated for their lack of wings in the eyes of Ambrosius, if wings were reduced to fins by Basil, or substituted for by hands and reason in Lactantius and Augustine, respectively, none of these solutions really managed to hide that it really would have been better if humans had been equipped with wings in the first place – or if birds had not existed. Because the human body was so important as a transcendental sign in the Christian project, its lack of wings continued to make trouble.

The lasting solution to the Christian fantasizing about wings was finally found in the figure of the angel. Angels in early Christianity delineated an alternative Christian society, a perfect society directly relating to God. Devoted Christians already belonged to that society, and, at least in the world to come, they would join the company of the angels. Angels were beings who moved through the air. And although they were originally not equipped with wings, they grew them as time passed.[5] Not surprisingly, the main image of an angel in Christianity became precisely that of a winged human.

Apocryphal acts of apostles and animals

In Christianity, animals were part of creation but had no part in salvation. And even if nature and animals were conceived of as good, because they were God's creation and creatures, they were also used, as we have seen, to symbolize evil. Man was made in God's image (and vice versa) to the exclusion of all other creatures. Parallel to this divinization of man, there was a devaluation of animals and sometimes a demonization of them, which implied that animals and demons lent each other characteristics. But difficult as it was to maintain that humans were completely different from animals, it was just as difficult to claim that animals were totally different from humans. Animals resurfaced within the souls and bodies of men and made them bestial, while human faculties such as reasoning and power of speech appeared in animals. Consequently, animals were sometime transformed into human quadrupeds, a development that led to consternation among Church leaders and theologians.

The most important Christian genre in which animals behaved like humans was the apocryphal Acts of the Apostles. The most peculiar of these Acts, when it comes to the subject of animals, is the *Acts of Philip*.[6] These are a mosaic of several texts, specimens of what must have been a flourishing tradition in antiquity. Some are represented by different manuscripts, while others have only a sole witness.[7] Within this corpus, Acts 8–15 form a literary unit with the same ensemble of characters throughout.

The *Acts of Philip* and the "humanization" of animals

In the fourth century, a strange party was thought to have once been travelling through the mountainous areas of Asia Minor. The company included the apostles Philip and Bartholomew (cf. Matthew 10:3), Mariamne dressed as a man, along with a leopard and a kid. The carnivore and the kid were both imitating humans as best they could, conversing in human voices, sometimes walking on their hind legs and often crying. Philip and his menagerie were on their way to Ophiorymos ("the promenade of the snakes") – Heliopolis of Asia, probably today's Pamukkale – where Philip had his mission. Here he reached the place of his martyrdom and was finally buried. What were these animals doing in this august company?

The immediate answer is that they wanted to convert and be baptized. Act 8 is simply called "The conversion of the kid and the leopard in the desert". Let us start with the beginning of Act 8, where we meet a troubled and doubtful Philip and his sister Mariamne. According to the text, Philip has a female mentality, while Mariamne has a brave and virile mentality. Therefore, Mariamne is to accompany Philip on his mission. But Jesus bids her to change her clothes and appearance, all the exterior traits that resemble a female. In this way, she will no longer be like Eve, the archetypal incarnation of the female form. Eve was no ideal. Since the serpent in Genesis had developed a "friendliness" (*philia*) towards her, and *philia* indicates an erotic friendship, it is suggested that there had been a sexual relationship between them, a motif that is also found in Jewish and Christian commentaries (Bovon *et al.* 1999: 244, note 15). The poison of the serpent had then been transmitted from Eve to Adam. While Augustine allowed hereditary sin to be transmitted by the male seed, according to *Acts of Philip* 8 it seems to be transferred by women because of Eve's cohabiting with the serpent.

Philip, Mariamne and Bartholomew set out towards the land of the Ophians – the worshippers of the serpent. As they are walking into the wilderness (*eremos*), a huge leopard comes forth from the forest that covers the mountains. He throws himself down before the party, speaks in a human voice, refers to the only begotten son of God and begs to be given the ability to speak perfectly, which is granted him. And with a human voice, the cat tells how, in the night, he came upon a herd, caught a kid and took it away to eat. But the kid started to cry "like a little child" and rebuked the leopard for its fierce heart and bestial ways. Gradually, the leopard softened and abandoned its intention of eating its prey. At this moment, the leopard saw the apostles and turned to them. In addition to begging for the power of speech, he also asked if the two animals could be allowed to march with the apostles and to shed their animal nature. Philip and Bartholomew marvelled at the leopard that had stopped eating meat, and the leopard and the kid rose on their hind legs, lifted their forelegs and started to pray to God with human voices. Then the company, including the two animals, continued to the land of the Ophians.

Act 10 is missing, while both Acts 9 and 11 tell of the Christian company meeting a dragon and serpents. In these acts, the antagonistic and evil forces are represented by the mother of the serpents, the viper, which had a cult in Asia Minor.[8] In Act 9, the dragon, the serpents and their offspring are blinded and destroyed by means of a divine fire (9.5). In Act 11, the Christian party encounters a group of demons hidden among stones. Philip prays to Jesus and conjures the demons to show themselves, and they appear as reptiles – fifty snakes – and among them a huge dragon, which is black, blazing, poisonous and terrible. The dragon is female (11.3). In fact, the reptile is the incarnation of a persistent evil in human history, first met in the paradise narrative, but from then on it has continued to do its evil work. Now it is forced on to the defensive, made to show its true nature and to promise to build a church. Miraculously and by demonic means the church is built in six days. Philip also bids the reptile to appear in human form, which it does, and it appears as black, "like an Ethiopian". In the end, it admits to being conquered.

In Act 12, the author exposes his views on salvation and the access of animals to communion. This act clearly presupposes the conversion of the animals. Here the human part of the company receives the Eucharist, while the animals are looking on, weeping. When they are asked why they weep, the leopard delivers a passionate plea for the animals' participation in the eucharistic meal. The speech of the leopard (12:2–5), one of the most edifying in the *Acts of Philip*, raises the question of whether animals are worthy to receive the Eucharist or not. Rhetorically apt, the leopard argues on behalf of the kid and itself that they have already abandoned their animal nature and now want to quit their animal forms as well (14.12–14).

Amsler discusses the theme of nature (*physis*) and form (*morphe*) in relation to the animals. Conversion implies change of nature, salvation change of form. In Act 8, 17:19, a human heart replaces a bestial one, and in several of the preceding acts a change of bestial nature is repeatedly mentioned (Amsler 1999: 362). In Act 12, both nature and form are referred to in the speech of the leopard (4:8–14) when the leopard begs that he and the kid may quit their bestial bodies and animal form "so that our beast-like body may be changed by you and we might forsake the animal form". Internal changes take place in Act 8 and external changes in Act 12. Amsler suggests that the logic behind this passage is that the material affects the material and the spiritual the spiritual. Accordingly, a concrete ritual will change the bodies of the animals. In a curious rite, Philip lifts the cup filled with water and sprays it on the leopard and the kid. When their bestial forms are changed, they rise up on their hind legs and glorify God because they have received a human body (12.8.1–6). In the last part of his answer, Philip mentions that God has included not only humans but also beasts and all animal species in his plan. It is unclear whether he means that God has provided for the animals on earth or if he is suggesting that God has included them in salvation as well (cf. Amsler 1999: 361). Finally, in Act 13, it is said that when the animals die they will be buried beneath the portico of the church.

The leopard and the kid are strange bedfellows, but not without biblical prototypes. In Isaiah 11:6–9 there is a millenarian passage in which the leopard and the kid are a pair, and a Christian interpretation of this passage is part of the background of the *Acts of Philip*. Jews and Christians sometimes shared the idea that animals had lost their capacity of speech when Adam sinned but would regain it at the end of time when all things were restored. Seen in this perspective, the kid and the leopard fulfil traditional millenarian expectations.[9]

However, it is also possible to read these animals allegorically and interpret them as stand-ins for humans: wild animals that have been tamed represent repentant sinners and converted pagans (Amsler 1999: 302). In line with this interpretation, the animals not only represent the classes of wild and domesticated animals, respectively, they also represent pagans (the leopard) and Christians (the kid) who wanted to be converted to a special branch of early Christianity, namely encratism (Bovon 2002: 140–1). Christian encratites were groups that were marked out by their abstinence from animal food, their ascetic agenda (Slater 1999: 298–305) and their opposition to procreation and femininity. The apocryphal Acts clearly include such encratist ideas.[10]

Whether the *Acts of Philip* should be interpreted literally or allegorically, the work belongs in both cases within a tradition where animals were regarded positively, at least under certain circumstances. But parallel to the optimistic view of animals reflected in the figures of the kid and the leopard, is the view that some animals are evil. The dragon and its entourage incarnate evil in these texts.[11] Three times when the dragon appears it is killed together with its serpents (Acts 9, 12.3, 13.3), and the fourth time it is forced to build a church. Demons are wavering between invisibility and reptile form, and the dragon goes from reptile to human form as well. But all the same, even if the dualism between humans and animals is present in the *Acts of Philip*, and reptiles are incarnating evil, these conceptions are overruled by a more optimistic view of animals, and the conception of animals as evil is restricted to demonic and diabolic creatures in reptile form.

An objection could be made to the dominant positive view of animals in these acts, that the leopard and the kid were expected to transform their bestial nature and become human before they were conceived of in a more flattering light. It means that animals as such were not necessarily regarded as positive, only animals that had become human. The leopard is the main animal speaker. Its walking on its hind legs and its human voice have already been mentioned, but its speeches are characterized by their rhetorical qualities and by the way in which both it and the kid spice up their speeches with weeping. Like speech and walking on two legs, weeping is a uniquely human act. The leopard also acts "unnaturally" by completely forsaking its feline nature and abstaining from killing the kid and from eating meat.

The presupposition that animals should convert from being bestial and turn human, or at least become more human-like, has its structural parallel in the conception of women. Mariamne is one of the main actors in this text. According to the author, she has a male mentality (8.3). Mariamne wears male clothes, which the Saviour has presented to her as a means of counter-acting the influence of the diabolic serpent and minimizing her similarity to Eve. The masculinization of Mariamne will break the connection between Eve and the serpent. Precisely because she did not procreate, Mariamne was even more than Mary, the mother of Jesus, a heroine to the encratites.

In the *Acts of Philip*, the dragon is associated with the serpent in Genesis and the Devil but is at the same time also regarded as feminine (9.7:11). In this way, there is an opposition between Mariamne, who has masculinized herself, and Eve/serpent/dragon, which are female creatures who partake in sex and procreation. The moral is that women should suppress their biology and imitate men (i.e. men who are not sexually active), while carnivores should stop eating meat (and the kid should stop being eaten) and deny their bestial nature. In this way, parallel stories are told about Mary and the leopard (and the kid): animals that behave like animals and women who behave like women are inferior to humanized animals and masculinized females.

Whether the *Acts of Philip* is read literally or allegorically, the necessity for animals to change their nature is a key point in both interpretations. However, the positive conception of animals in this text is not limited to the converted leopard and the kid. The world of animals and nature is drawn in, too, and the transformed animals take part in a close dialogue with the wider living world. There is no doubt that the natural world is described positively in these texts. The *Acts of Philip*, for instance, has a beautiful image of God bestowing nourishment on all creatures (8.5; cf. 8.10) and it is said that God watched over "even the wild animals on account of his great heart" (*ibid.*, 12.5).[12]

As in the classical tradition, some of the animals in the *Acts of Philip* are held up as ideals because they beget fewer offspring than others (*ibid.*, 8.10). These "low begetters" are regarded as superior among their kind because they show that the noblest creatures are those that engage the least in sex and procreation. Frequently, in Christian literature, the sexuality of humans is connected with irrationality and with their similarity to animals. Here the opposite point is made. Some animals are regarded as ideals in sexual and procreative matters simply because they very seldom take part in that type of activity,[13] a point that had already been made by classical authors. However, at the same time as animals are seen in a positive light, serpents and dragons incarnate all the evils that the apostle and his party encounter, as well as symbolizing those who were opposed to encratite groups (cf. Bovon 2002: 152–3).

Speaking animals and baptized cats

Although animals play a larger part in this text than they do in other acts, *Acta Philippi* is not unique in its treatment of animals. On the contrary, one of the characteristics of all the apocryphal Acts of the Apostles is that they include speaking and acting animals. Christopher R. Matthews considers the talking animals of the apocryphal Acts of the Apostles as constituting a genus (Matthews 1999: 210). It is normally not the animal world at large that is referred to in these texts but a restricted number of species, not more than a handful. These animals are not related directly to the animal world as such but are based on episodes in the Bible, which are enriched by elements from animal fables. A large number of these animals are pious creatures that want to be Christianized. As for the biblical origins of some of these animals, they include Paul's meeting with the beasts of Ephesus, Balaam's speaking ass, and the serpent of Genesis and its mutations.

In the pious Christian tradition, Paul's encounter with the beasts of Ephesus (I Corinthians 15:32) and the reference to his having been "rescued from the mouth of the lion" (II Timothy 4.17) were combined and developed into a story about Paul's encounter with a lion. The New Testament expressions were most likely figures of speech and had nothing to do with real animals. But the tradition about Paul and the lion was associated with the biblical story of Daniel, who was not hurt when he was cast into the lions' den (Daniel 6:22). Hippolytus, for instance, mentions these two traditions in the same breath (*Commentary on Daniel*, 3.29; cf. Adamik 1996: 66). Like the lion to which Androcles had done a favour, Paul had treated the lion well – sometimes even baptized it (*Acts of Paul*, 7; Coptic papyrus in Hennecke and Schneemelcher 1973–5: 387–90).[14] Like the lion that Androcles met in the arena in Rome, Paul's lion was also meant to fight against him but refused to attack and saved his life.[15] Christian heroes continued to meet lions, not necessarily in the arena but in the wilderness as well. Some of the desert fathers had lions as servants. It was obviously seen as natural that the noblest among Christians encountered the noblest among animals, and that these creatures served them.

As the New Testament expressions had given rise to Paul's lion, the story about the ass of Balaam contributed to generating talking asses in apocryphal texts. In the *Acts of Thomas*, a helpful ass's colt explicitly made the connection to its biblical prototype by stressing that he was of the race that had served Balaam (4.39).

Different types of encounter with speaking animals take place in the apocryphal Acts. They range from the apostles' polite conversation with animals, via the implication – but no explicit mention – that the animals had been or were to be baptized, to animals that were fully baptized. While most of the speaking beasts are friendly, some are hostile towards the mission of the apostles. The archetypal evil beast is as usual the serpent (*Acts of John*, 71–6; *Acts of Thomas*, 31–3).

Some of these animals die properly when their mission is completed, for example the lioness that defended Thecla (*Acts of Paul*, 36). In the *Acts of Peter*, a large dog is Peter's messenger to Simon Magus, but when it has delivered its message it dies (Acts 12). In a similar way, the colt that has carried Thomas dies (*Acts of Thomas*, 41). Christopher R. Matthews reads the motive behind the death of these animals as similar to what was said about Balaam's ass in Jewish tradition – it had better die, so that it would not become an object of reverence (*Numbers Rabbah*, 20:4; cf. Matthews 1999: 223–5). Strictly speaking, speaking animals meant trouble.

Even more problematic than speaking animals were baptized ones. This is reflected in the strategies of evasion that are sometimes involved when the subject is touched on. Amsler remarks that the conversion of the quadrupeds in the *Acts of Philip* seems to have been embarrassing to the critics (Amsler 1999: 299). The explicit wish of these animals, which was to receive the sacraments, was clearly against the Christian hierarchy of being and led to a certain consternation within the text. If the leopard and the kid took part in a eucharistic ritual, no details are offered, and it seems that they never received the promised Eucharist. Only a ritual of spraying with water is mentioned, which may have been a ritual of exorcism. However, as pointed out by Christopher Matthews, the sprinkling of water could also indicate the beginning of an animal fast, which would ultimately lead to full baptismal rites (Matthews 1999: 230). All the same, these baptismal rites are not included in the text, and it remains notoriously vague whether the animals were ever baptized or not. At least in the textual witnesses that have survived, they are not. However, as in the case of Paul's lion, there were also texts that were not as reluctant as the *Acts of Philip* to fully include animals in Christian society.

Resurrection of animals sometimes takes place within the genre of the apocryphal Acts of the Apostles. The theme is brought up with reference to the ass in the *Acts of Thomas* (41). When this ass, which had helped the apostle, dies, the people urge Thomas to raise it up. But he says: "I do not raise it up, not because I am not able, but because this is what is useful and helpful for it". We suspect that we have reached the limits of what apostles were allowed to do if the text was to remain within the catholic circles of mainstream Christianity. However, it is reasonable to believe that there had been versions of this story or similar stories in which the animals in question really were raised from the dead. Photius, a patriarch of Constantinople (810–95 CE), claimed that the Manichaeans had such stories. The only intact example in the apocryphal Acts is a fish (*Acts of Peter*, 13). This is a smoked tunny fish that was revived by Peter and made to swim in a pond. It even eats bread thrown to it by the onlookers. The point of this for Peter was to make people believe through this sign. In this case, one suspects that fish do not really count. For one thing, the New Testament is clearly rich in miracles with fish (even if none of them is resurrected); for another, the revived tunny does not speak. It is more like a thing than an animal. Perhaps for those reasons the story slipped through.

Although the apocryphal Acts of the Apostles were open to different types of elaboration on animals and invited various interpretations, they employed animals in a manner that was not orthodox. It is notoriously unclear in several of the texts whether the animals should be taken literally or interpreted as allegories. Often both interpretations are possible.[16] The space opened up to animals in the apocryphal Acts contributed to keeping these texts on the fringes of what was acceptable within mainstream Christianity. All the same, it may be true, as Christopher Matthews has pointed out, that "certain strains of early Christian optimism saw the [animals] awash in human salvation" (Matthews 1999: 205).

The animals in the apocryphal Acts served various purposes. John ordered the bed bugs that troubled his sleep to behave themselves and leave his bed (*Acts of John*, 61). In the morning, he permitted them to return (*ibid.*, 62). In this case, John made a pedagogical point out of their behaviour – the bugs obeyed him, but humans disobey God's commandments. In a similar pedagogical way, some of the animals behave like ascetics. In the Coptic papyrus, the lion that Paul baptized ran away from a lioness in heat and did not give in to its advances. Such stories were intended to draw an edifying moral for human behaviour rather than promoting animal values

Related to the speaking animals of the apocryphal Acts, animals in the narratives of the desert fathers understand humans and behave in a pious and decent way. These were animals that lived in the wilderness but were tamed by the example of the monks. Like the apocryphal Acts of the Apostles, some of the stories about the desert fathers show animals in a positive light. Like the animals in the apocryphal Acts, these animals forsake much of their wildness, appear as tame and often become human-like.

Ludwig Bieler has pointed out as typical characteristics of the *theios aner* that he reveals his power both by killing or driving away harmful animals and by taming or being served by wild animals (Bieler 1935: 104–11). In the stories about the Egyptian holy men, both characteristics are present, as stressed by David Frankfurter (Frankfurter 2003: 372–4). Animals like snakes, scorpions and crocodiles – real or imagined – serve as images of demons and threaten the ascetic (for instance, in the *Life of Antony*). However, the saints may also tame them and make use of them, as illustrated by stories about the desert fathers and by the apocryphal Acts of the Apostles.

These pious pets do not necessarily talk. When Jerome tells the story about the burial of the hermit Paul, he describes two lions that dig the holy man's grave. The animals were "roaring aloud as if to make it known that they were mourning" (16). And when they had made the grave, "pricking up their ears while they lowered their heads, they came to Antony and began to lick his hands and feet" (16). Antony perceives that they wanted his blessing, which he gave them: "Lord, without whose command not a leaf drops from the tree, not a sparrow falls to the ground, grant them what thou knowest to be best". The lions apparently understand human language but do not themselves talk. No breach of theological decorum takes place. And their future fate is decided by God, not by Antony, nor for that matter by Jerome.

In a similar way, the hyena in the *Historia Lausiaca* of Palladius (*c.* 420 CE) talked by means of signs. This hyena brought its blind cub to the monk Paphnute, and he miraculously cured it by spitting in its eyes. Because it was grateful, the hyena brought the fleece of a freshly killed sheep to the monk. But then it had to promise the monk that it would never more eat the sheep of the poor, or kill an animal. The hyena obviously understood what the monk said but communicated only by nodding and kneeling (*Historia Lausiaca*, Coptic version in Robinson 1898: 123–6). The intelligence of the hyena is explained by God's having given understanding "even to the beasts".

Like the apocryphal Acts, these stories also tell miraculous things about animals, but they usually do not cross the borderline between humans and animals by making the animals speak. Nor were they allowed to become part of salvation. Jerome, who wrote so eloquently about Paul's lions, drew a firm line at baptized cats when he said that "therefore the *Acts of Paul and Thecla* and the whole fable about the lion baptized by him we reckon among the apocryphal writings" (*Lives of Illustrious Men*, 7).

Manichaeism

There is some evidence that Manichaeans knew and used a collection of the Acts of the Apostles. Manichaeism was the last great new religious movement that competed with Christianity in the Roman Empire. Its background was partly in Jewish Christian baptismal sects. Augustine refers to speaking animals among the Manichaeans (*Reply to Faustus the*

Manichaean, 21.10),[17] while the aforementioned Photius indicates in the *Library* that a defined corpus of apocryphal Acts was used by the Manichaeans in the fourth century CE (cf. Schneemelcher 1964: 317; Hennecke and Schneemelcher 1975: 178–88). So far, Manichaeans have only been mentioned in passing. A few words need to be said about this religion and its conception of animals, because this conception is slightly different from those of other religions in the Mediterranean area.

Mani was born in Babylon and lived in the second part of the third century CE. He offered a radical dualistic religion with an elaborate mythology including stories about the origin of animals. These stories furnish them with a demonic pedigree. All the same, the Manichaean conception of animals was on several points more positive than that of mainstream Christianity. These conceptions were one of the themes that Augustine repeatedly returned to in his refutation of Manichaeism. Augustine knew what he was talking about. He had in his youth been a member of the Manichaean church for nine years.[18]

Fundamental to the Manichaean system is the duality of light and darkness. Because of evil attacks by the world of darkness upon the world of light, elements of light had been captured by the evil forces. Different strategies were used to save these elements. The Manichaeans taught that animals and plants were created when the Messenger of Life revealed male and female forms to the evil archons as a trick to get them to release the light they had captured. In their enthusiasm for these beautiful forms, the archons started to give up this light in the form of semen and abortions. These emissions were heavily mixed up with darkness. The semen formed the vegetable world, while the abortions of the female archons gave birth to innumerable species of animal, which were descended from the demonic animals in the Kingdom of Darkness (*Kephalaia*, 33ff, 92:19–22, 123:4; cf. Lieu 1985: 10, 15). According to Augustine, the animal species of the earth belong to the different archons of darkness and for that reason those who slaughter animals are harassed and tormented by these archons, who "own" the animals (*On the Morals of the Manichaeans*, 60). Augustine mentions this fact as a reason why Manichaeans do not kill animals.

The idea that the beings of light have beautiful forms while the beings of darkness have hideous and bestial forms serves as a general principle of division in Manichaeism (Klimkeit 1998: 142–72), and shows that bestial forms are ultimately derived from the Land of Darkness.

Animals as well as plants include light substances from the world above, but animal bodies contain light to a smaller degree than plants. Mani seems to have ranked animals as lower than vegetables in the hierarchy of values. Animals do not seem to have been equipped with elements of light from the beginning, while vegetables included the tormented divine substance as part of their original essence. This divine substance was captured in creation, constantly suffering, and virtually crucified in every tree, herb, fruit and vegetable. This so-called Cross of Light seems to have covered only the light in plants and did not include the animal world.[19] Augustine calls this substance *Jesus patibilis* – the suffering Jesus. Animals received light by eating plants (Heuser 1998: 43–4).

The light in plants, animals and humans was brought into new generations by reproduction and remained mixed. Sexual intercourse was clearly regarded as a source of pollution and made flesh fundamentally impure. Augustine chided the Manichaeans because of their dislike of flesh and said that they would be pleased by the flesh of worms, because worms, according to ancient thinking, were not the product of sexual intercourse but were generated spontaneously from fruit, in wood and in the earth (*On the Morals of the Manichaean*, 49, 61). Because the Manichaeans taught that the souls of animals derive from the plants they ate or from water, Augustine rhetorically asks of them what they think about the eagle, which only eats flesh and needs no drink (*ibid.*, 50).

A practical outcome of this mythology was an urge to free the light that was bound up in plants by eating them. Augustine blames the Manichaeans for having "more mercy on a cucumber than on a human being" (*On the Morals of the Manichaeans*, 52). The Manichaeans were not allowed to do the same with animals – free their souls by eating their flesh – as their ethics prescribed that they should avoid hurting light in its sentient form in animals (Lieu 1985: 20). Augustine remarks in his reply to the Manichaean Faustus that Manichaeans are merciful to beasts because they believe them to contain the souls of human beings (65). This suggests that they believed in a transmigration of souls between animals and humans.

The followers – *auditores* – who served the Manichaean elite were not allowed to kill animals or to participate in blood sacrifices, but they were allowed to eat the flesh of animals that had been killed (*Confessions*, 3.10, 2.3, 4; *On the Morals of the Manichaeans*, 53). Similarly, the elect who ate vegetables and fruit were not allowed to pluck and pull them (*ibid.*, 57). Plucking fruit and pulling vegetables were the work of the *auditores*. So, even if the light in plants was purer than the light in animals, and animals had a more sinister origin in the Land of Darkness, it was held as a greater crime to destroy animals than plants. They were sentient beings and probably took part in a cycle of reincarnation.

Although the picture is blurred, it seems reasonable to conclude that Manichaeans saw humans and animals in a dualistic light and regarded the animal and the bestial form as the negative pole, considered animals as having a demonic origin, but all the same, developed a more compassionate ethic towards the animal world than Christians.

Conclusion

The Christian panegyrics about man, who was the creature closest to God and sometimes even divine, had their predecessors in Greek and Roman authors, especially among the Stoics. Part of Stoic tradition from Posidonius had been transmitted by Origen. In this tradition, there was an enthusiasm for man's uniqueness in relation to other creatures, an enthusiasm that also encompassed man's constitution and physiological equipment. Christians and Stoics shared an admiration for man's natural superiority. Cicero's *On the Nature of the Gods* was influential and used by several Christian authors (2.13ff). But despite the fact that the Christian panegyrics were dependent on pagan predecessors, their flavour is Christian. In addition to all the amazing gifts that had been bestowed on man in the pagan tradition, either by the gods or by nature, the Christian God also promised his worshippers bodily resurrection, and for that reason the human body received a unique status as a transcendental sign.

The stress on the human body as the preferred transcendental sign gave rise to some problems. One of these problems related to wings. Was it a flaw in human bodily equipment that humans had no wings? At least this sad fact had to be accounted for. Consequently, wings are a topic mentioned by several of the Christian fathers, especially in the third and fourth centuries.

If the conception of the human body as a transcendental sign created problems for humans, these problems were small in relation to the problems that this conception created for animals. In its resurrection, the human body distanced itself for ever from the bestial body. Consequently, animals were natural-born losers in the plan of salvation, and salvation was restricted to humans only.

However, in some texts, animal bodies became objects of concern too. The negative view of animals in most Christian texts is matched by more optimistic views in others. The apocryphal Acts of the Apostles is one genre in which animals play positive roles. This genre was developed within Christian encratite circles as well as among Manichaeans – groups that had in common the fact that they did not kill animals or eat meat. Even if abstinence from meat had more to do with asceticism and regard for human purity than with concern for the well-being of animals, it should not be overlooked that it is precisely in the genres in which they are not killed for food that animals appear on speaking terms with humans.

CONSEQUENCES

From pagan to Christian conceptions of animals

In the Christian process of transforming and shaping ancient culture, conceptions of animals did not remain unaffected. Conceptions of animals are dependent on acceptance and reinterpretation of traditions and narratives about animals from the past, as well as on cultural interaction, which in turn will inevitably lead to reinterpretation and change. When Christianity gradually took over the religious discourse of the Roman Empire, it incorporated traditional conceptions of animals into its own intellectual and imaginative universe and gave them some new contexts and meanings. Christian conceptions were clearly dependent on processes that had started several centuries before, but Christianization had a cumulative effect on these processes. The Christian focus filtered and shaped the ways in which animals were regarded, not least because of their new contextualization within its religious universe.

From Genesis comes the idea of man being made in the image of God, that the natural world was placed under human dominion and that man's function is to act as steward to the animals. Because man, exclusively among the species, was made in the image of God, the boundary between animals and humans was strengthened. Even comparing humans and animals became problematic after the victory of Christianity. What was most valuable in life belonged to humans only, and the characteristics through which humans approached God were those that really mattered. Such views were not uniquely Christian, but Christian theology went further than contemporary philosophies when it created its view of animals.

From Greek philosophy, and especially the Stoics, stems the idea that animals are without reason, language and soul. The Stoic conception of animals gave a strong legitimation for using them for human purposes. However, there were other components in the Christian view of animals, for instance that the flesh of animals was categorically different from human flesh. The termination of the animal sacrifice further carried with it a secularization of slaughter.

The end of animal sacrifice in the fourth century CE marked a significant change in the religions of the Mediterranean, indicating a new type of religion with a new type of symbolic capital – the Christian faith. No longer based on sacrifice, religious power became centred on bodily discipline and religious knowledge. The end of sacrifice meant that live animals no longer played cultic roles, and sacrificial terminology was transferred from animals to humans. Having become divine through Christ, man in his hunt for salvation had left the animals behind.

Theologian Christopher Manes has pointed out that when Roman citizens looked at animals there would have been something extra in their gaze that they did not share with us, "a recognition that animals were in touch with the gods and could be used to intervene on behalf of humans" (Manes 1997: 104–5). A big change took place when Christians in the first centuries were taught to see animals differently and to realize that animals were in the main cut off from that type of privileged contact with the divine.

The conceptions of animals within Christianity were closely related to this religion's focus upon God incarnated as man, the human body and flesh as pivots of salvation, and human relics as objects of sacralization, symbolization and ritualization. Christ had made the ultimate sacrifice and made all other sacrifices superfluous. The prohibition against animal sacrifice made animals superfluous as cultic objects and excluded them from sacred space. However, there was still ample room for their metaphorical cousins within Christian discourse as allegorical interpretation became an important instrument in Christian thinking. Complex thoughts about soul and body, reason and emotions, salvation and damnation were conveyed by means of animal symbols and metaphors.

As a parallel to animals being described as essentially different from humans, the beast appeared forcefully within the human soul and body. The bodily life expressed above all in bodily desires, chief of which was the sexual drive, was rejected as the least desirable trait in human beings. The body that ate, drank, defecated, reproduced itself and died was banished to irrational animal nature and was to be changed for a body of glory after death. Animals were called upon to illustrate the life of the earthly, material, sexual, fallen and sinful man in all its negative aspects. These ideas had a philosophical basis in Plato's thought, but the combination of an ascetic life with a belief in the resurrection of the human body was typical of Christianity. The resurrected body was conceived of as a contrast to the type of body that humans shared with animals. Animal bodies, archetypes of irrational nature, were incapable of resurrection.

The bestial other

Christianity developed through internal disagreements and opposition to competing religious world views. Its adherents used a subversive movement's strategies and language to define their creed, to establish distance from other religions and to build up the boundaries of their communities. For these purposes, animals were used as relational categories. Oppositions and clashes of interests were made manageable through a polarized language that included a basic opposition between animals and humans.

When animals are used to describe human identity and behaviour, they may describe man's inner (psychic) qualities as well as selected groups of humans (women, foreigners, pagans). In Christianity, the binary opposites of human and animal were used to designate opposites of soul/body, God/Devil, male/female, Christian/pagan, orthodoxy/heresy, and saved/sinner. In other words, this confrontation was used in the cultural and religious processes of inclusion and exclusion through which a new Christian identity was in the end established.

Bestial metaphors have from an early time been used in processes of inclusion and exclusion. The ancient opposition between animals and humans is part of a larger metaphorical system where forms of human behaviour are understood in terms of animal behaviour. One main focus of meaning in animal metaphors is that they describe "objectionability" or "undesirability" (Kövecses 2002: 124–7). These metaphors are part of what is usually called the Great Chain of Being metaphor, where certain things are related to each other in the world in a hierarchy of concepts. The "basic Great Chain" lists a hierarchy of concepts related to humans, animals, plants, complex objects and natural physical things. This is a folk theory model, which Zöltan Kövecses traces to the Judaeo-Christian tradition but indicates that it may be universal. Humans are characterized by higher-order attributes and behaviour, while animals have instinctual attributes and behaviour. The hierarchy is structured from the top to the bottom. When one level of this chain is used to understand another, the system becomes metaphorical. The model is basic and may be activated in different directions. One target area for the metaphorical sphere of animals is to characterize "the other" as a beast.

Urs Dierauer has pointed out that there had been a growing feeling of superiority towards animals in the fifth century BCE in Greece (Dierauer 1977: 25–66). The bestial life (*theriodes bios*) was seen as belonging to a phase in human history that humans had put behind them because of their competence and diligence. Dierauer connects this feeling of human superiority to a new self-esteem on the part of the Greeks in relation to other people. Foreign people were regarded as being closer to beasts. A similar metaphorical use of animals was taken over and developed in Christianity.

The concept of describing passions as animals and labelling outsiders beasts had a long pre-Christian history in the Graeco-Roman world. However, with the development of Christianity, these concepts were placed in a new context that gave them additional meanings, values and functions. Animals were instrumental in describing all types of evil, internal as well as external. Christians branded both pagans and heretics as beasts. It is not new for foreigners and those on the margins of civilization to be characterized as animals, but the systematic use of animals to describe religious dissenters and pagans was new. Underlying these processes was a strong wish to establish the Christian faith as unique and exclude competing creeds. Christians aimed for transcendence and derided rival religions for being stuck with worldly immanence. Animals were not only part of that immanence but also its primary symbols, and they were used as vital elements in a language of exclusion.

Generally, one use of animals in human societies is to make humans stand out clearly. They are the comparative basis without which it would be impossible to understand ourselves as a species (cf. Midgley 1995: 18–19). Such a function continued in the Christian world view, but imaginary creatures, partly built on animal prototypes, were also important. Idealized humans in the form of angels were contrasted with demons in a polarized cosmos. There is a polarization that made God into a human and the Devil into a beast. The fact that demons were often conceptualized as distorted animals may suggest that the human/animal polarization had been taken to a higher level and mythologized in the contrast between angels and demons. One thing that illustrates the close metaphorical connections between animals and demons was the tendency to interpret passages that in the Bible referred to animals as referring to demons. Sometimes there seems to be a continuum between wild animals and demons; at least there is an interaction between them. It is difficult to avoid the impression that the battle against groups and people who were described as "animals" was an important dimension of Christianity and that this battle had some negative implications for how real animals were perceived.

Metaphors and reality

In several of the key Christian scenarios, animals were given metaphysical qualities as enemies of humans. Two important discourses developed the theme of the relations between humans and animals, one related to martyrs, the other to ascetics.

The point of departure for martyrs' being thrown to the beasts was that wild animals were dangerous and killed people. Since the archetypal martyr was killed by wild animals in the arena, the connection between martyrs and destructive animals was direct and close and in its turn gave rise to a rich discourse of metaphors and symbols that involved beasts. In these stories, real animals, symbolic/supernatural animals and metaphorical animals appear together and lend their characteristics to each other.

No less active in generating hostile beasts was the ascetic life. Asceticism became a special sphere for thinking about demons in the form of animals. Also for ascetics, and especially for those living alone and/or away from other people, wild animals were a threat. The risks that harmful and dangerous animals presented in relation to martyrs and ascetics were interpreted in a Christian metaphysical framework. These animals were set in a polarized cosmos that made them evil in a metaphysical sense.

Two main motifs, both with ancient roots, are included in these discourses. One motif presents animals as enemies that ought to be killed or driven away. Another motif presents the religious hero as the master of animals who either subjugates animals or makes them into his/her friends. The apocryphal Acts of the Apostles in particular, but also the tales of the desert fathers, are examples of genres that sometimes demonstrated friendliness towards animals and non-violent subordination of them. The idea of a future state of bliss when the paradisical state is regained, and wild and tame animals will live peacefully together, has most probably enriched the imagery of beasts in these texts.

There was a strong tendency in late antiquity to interpret nature and the inner man by means of animals, especially those found in scripture. Animals in Christian thinking came mainly from the textual universe of the Bible and from exegetical traditions, although sometimes also from natural histories and fables. Far removed from their natural habitat, these animals were vehicles of human meaning and were used as symbols and metaphors. Although authors like Origen, Basil, Epiphanius and Augustine were clearly knowledgeable about natural history, the text-producing Christian elite was not particularly interested in live animals; their attention was directed at animals used as models or in allegories. One important aspect of this imagery was its persuasive power and capacity to speak to human emotions — as in Epiphanius' image of heresy, where serpents and other wild animals were seen as poisoning the pure body of the Church.

Animals were used systematically to reason about human life and salvation. Like the way Origen reads the beasts of the human soul, *Physiologus* reads nature as a poetic text. Nature was a book that not only pointed to God but also referred to Christian doctrines in minute detail. Everything had a secret meaning, tremendously more important than its mundane reality. In this "natural history", which was not based on observation of real animals but on stories about them, animals and animal behaviour are given a spiritual meaning that is their true meaning. Does this type of Christian interpretation have anything to say to the conceptions of real animals?

Origen's and *Physiologus'* use of animals have been evaluated in different ways, and sometimes they have been praised for revealing a positive interest in nature and animals. At least Origen is knowledgeable about animal life. However, it should be pointed out that the animals of Origen and the *Physiologus* are taken out of the rich diversity of animal life and have been reduced to a limited range of meanings. When animals are converted into signs and made to comment on Christian life and salvation, they point away from the animal realm towards transcendent meanings. The animals and their lives are simply not interesting as such. As metaphorical animals point to transcendent realms, animals of flesh and blood are simultaneously downgraded in the same symbolic act. Christ was a lamb, but lambs had no place in salvation.

Only a limited and select set of characteristics is associated with an animal when it is used as a metaphor. Metaphorical animals are created either on the basis of certain species of animal or on the basis of the general category of animal – *therion* – that has negative or evil metaphysical qualities. When animals figure in binary oppositions with humans, they usually, perhaps always, represent the negative term. This implies that the polarized character of the Christian universe has a tendency to draw animals to the negative pole and associate them with evil. This polarization is played out in several of the key scenarios in which Christianity was developed.

Not all animals were seen as evil, however. Like the way some of the narratives about ascetics and martyrs include stories about animals that are friendly to humans, some of the animal metaphors also describe positive metaphysical qualities. Polarizations of metaphorical animals occur in which some animals are associated with the positive pole and some with the negative: dove versus serpent, lamb versus lion.

Why were Christians not vegetarians?

Christian views on animals were also nourished by more mundane needs than those catered for by symbols and metaphors. One of the things that Christians vehemently opposed in paganism was animal sacrifice. Because the traditional justification for killing animals had been built on the divine sanction of sacrificial killing, it was no longer valid. When sacrifices were forbidden, while slaughtering was continued in a secular context, a new justification for killing animals was required.

One justification was the irrationality of animals. Philosopher Richard Sorabji has pointed out that in the Latin West it was above all Augustine who made the Stoic notion of the irrationality of animals decisive for their treatment (Sorabji 1993: 201). Sorabji has also stressed that before Augustine, the link between animals, reason and immortality was not established within Christian thinking (*ibid.*: 202). In Christianity, the Stoic idea of the irrationality of animals was combined with the Genesis tradition of God giving Adam permission to use animals for human purposes. Augustine returns to this subject in his writings, and he does so in relation to slaughtering. According to him, the commandment "Thou shalt not kill" does not "apply to the non-rational animals which fly, swim, walk or crawl, for these do not share the use of reason with us. It is not given to them to have it in common with us, and for that reason, by the most just ordinance of their Creator, both their life and death are subject to our needs" (*The City of God*, 1.20). Augustine realizes that animals die in pain but turns down the argument of compassion: "For we see and appreciate from their cries that animals die with pain. But man discards this in a beast, with which, as having no rational soul, he is linked by no community of law [*societas legis*]" (*The Morals of the Manichaeans*, 2.17.59).

Because meat was strongly associated with sacrifice, the Christian opposition to paganism could theoretically have led Christians to vegetarianism *en bloc*. Some of the philosophical movements as well as the Manichaean elite were vegetarians, which clearly proves that vegetarianism was an option in these centuries. Diet was an important thing in antiquity: people showed whom they resembled and whom they were different from by means of what they chose to eat and drink. Why then were Christians not vegetarians? The question is not so far-fetched as it could seem, considering that vegetarianism was in fact pursued by some Christian groups. A comparative case could also be brought in, namely the link between opposition to animal sacrifice in Indian traditions and opposition to all slaughtering and eating meat, which shows that these things easily go together.

Even if there were no essential changes in diet within the Church, there were Christian groups which were vegetarians. Andrew McGowan has recently pointed out the importance of a bread-and-water tradition in Christian ritual meals and also that all meals of communities who adhered to such rituals seem to deviate from all meals in more accommodating communities (McGowan 1999: 218–50). The more restrictive communities rejected the ordinary sacrificial meal of meat and wine as well as what was conceived of as "normal" eating (*ibid.*: 271). They also rejected the eating and rituals of mainstream Christianity and established themselves as a purer elite. The anti-meat and anti-sacrificial traditions seem to have been widespread in Syria and Asia. These groups were less integrated into the life of wider society and were not regarded as fully orthodox within the Church. The last point is made very clear when Epiphanius, for instance, rejects such groups and their practices.

Epiphanius describes Jewish and Jewish-Christian groups as well as some Christian "heretic" groups in which people did not eat meat. It is clear from Epiphanius' description that some of these groups interpreted the Gospels, and made emendations to them, so that they were brought into consonance with their vegetarian practices. Some of them saw John the Baptist as a vegetarian, and it is mentioned that James the Just (the brother of Jesus) did not eat meat.

If we consult Epiphanius and ask what reasons he thought these groups had for not eating meat, we find several. Some of the Jewish and Jewish-Christian groups thought it was unlawful (18.1.3ff, 19.3.5ff) or that it was made superfluous by the Gospels (30.18.7). Satornilians wanted to attract others by their rigorous discipline (23.2.5–6); the Ebionites abstained from meat because it was produced by means of intercourse (30.15.3–4); and Marcion believed in the reincarnation of souls in animals (42, *Elenchus*, 24).

When Epiphanius criticizes the vegetarianism of these groups, it was probably not vegetarianism as such he was against. In his afterword to *Panarion* (*De Fide*), where Epiphanius describes the variety of the monastic life, he mentions different sorts of diet that monks kept to – some vegetarian – without being in any way critical (23.4–5). It is therefore natural to think that it was the justification that some groups gave for their vegetarian diet, combined with deviating beliefs and practices, that made Epiphanius react negatively to them.

McGowan connects bread-and-water eucharists and vegetarian diets with an anti-sacrificial stand, which seems reasonable. But while he allows that a rejection of sacrifice gives rise to talking and believing animals in the apocryphal Acts and that they represent a sort of restored paradise, he rejects the notion that transmigration of souls is obvious (McGowan 1999: 266, note 24). However, while Epiphanius gives several reasons why some religious groups abstained from meat, he also points out that some groups believed in transmigration of souls between species. Almost in the same breath as Epiphanius says that Marcion thought it was wrong to eat meat and that he saw a connection between flesh and soul, because the same soul was in men as in animals, Epiphanius points out persons and sects who believe in reincarnation – "Valentinus and Colorbasus, and all Gnostics and Manichaeans" (*Panarion*, 42, *Elenchus*, 24d).

Whether Epiphanius is right concerning the vegetarianism of these groups is not the point, but at least he knows of a connection between the belief in transmigration of souls and the practice of not eating meat, which he thinks is present in some Christian groups. This type of reincarnation presupposes a continuum between the souls of humans and those of animals and is, generally speaking, one of the strongest religious justifications for vegetarianism.

However, even if there were Christian groups who abstained from meat, and some of them also held a belief in the transmigration of souls, most Christians were against sacrifice but ate meat, which implies that they were not against the slaughtering of animals. Why was meat eating not a problem? One reason was probably that Christian meat eating was part of its Jewish background. Even if there were Jewish groups that did not eat meat, it was unusual. This is not so strange taking into consideration the fact that in the Bible killing animals and eating meat are closely connected to man's God-given control over nature. There is no reason to think that slaughtering and meat eating did not continue to have this meaning for the Christians too. And besides, as implied in the Gospels, Jesus ate meat.

Practical considerations obviously also played their part. Meat was a natural ingredient of Mediterranean diet, used especially at festive occasions and enjoyed as a tasty food. To exclude meat from the diet would have been a strong signal in the direction of sectarianism. Broad elements within the Church wanted Christianity to be a universal religion, and the inclusive character of the Church was probably one of the factors that worked against vegetarianism. Seen in a broader perspective, eating meat can be interpreted as a symbol of dominance and, accordingly, in line with the Christian wish to convert the world and thus to be a universal creed.

269

In some ways, Christianity combined characteristics from the elite movements of the time with an inclusive attitude towards its adherents. While eating meat as such was not avoided, the Eucharist was a bloodless meal, and part-time abstinence from meat was established for everyone in fixed periods of fasting. By not promoting wholesale vegetarianism, however, Christians distanced themselves effectively from religious groups that cherished such ideas, examples of which are Neoplatonism, Pythagoreanism and Manichaeism.

However, at the same time as the main Church was distancing itself from these groups, dissenters within the Church marked out their distance from the Church among other things by means of their anti-meat diets. It would have been very interesting to know in more detail how these groups really thought about animals and how they related to them. However, the source material does not allow us to do so, except for pointing out the speaking and acting animals that appear in the apocryphal Acts of the Apostles, which were used by some of these groups. These Acts, which were influenced by encratite ideals and were critical of meat eating, allowed animals to be on speaking terms with humans.[1]

In some ways, Christianity established an indirect relationship to animals. Christians were against animal sacrifice, because an animal sacrifice was the main religious act in pagan religion, not because of opposition to slaughtering animals. While sacrificing was condemned, slaughtering and eating of meat were regarded as neutral in mainstream Christianity. In a similar way, most Christians did not follow the Jewish rules of purity and impurity in relation to animals, thus making the more direct relationship between humans and animals that these rules implied irrelevant. Christians in these cases did not relate to animals as such – like the pagans who sacrificed or the Jews whose diet was determined by the behaviour and design of animals – but related to other people's meat-eating and sacrificial habits.

Animals did not have the same immediate significance in the Christian world view as they had in the traditional religions of the Mediterranean. The allegorizing trend, which turned animals into signs, contributed further to taking animals of flesh and blood out of religious focus.

NOTES

Introduction

1 While our predecessors in the field of the history of religions were interested in the roles that animals played in religion, they usually limited animals' religious significance to the earlier evolutionary stages. In these earlier stages of human cultural development, people believed that animals had souls and that mystical links existed between animals and human beings. As anthropologist Edward Burnett Tylor put it in 1871: "Savages talk quite seriously to beasts alive or dead as they would to men alive or dead, offer them homage, ask pardon when it is their painful duty to hurt and kill them" (Tylor 1979). Nearly a hundred years later, in his posthumously published work *The Meaning of Religion*, Brede Kristensen, the historian of religions, pointed out that there are also a large number of sacred animals in Greek, Indian, Persian and Egyptian religion, but nevertheless he emphasized that "Animal worship brings us close to a 'primitive' sphere which is far away from us" (Kristensen 1971: 153).

2 Jean-Pierre Vernant has pointed out, for instance, basic differences between the sacrificial systems in Greece and India (Vernant 1991). While Vedic religion reinvented the creative sacrifice of the original man, Purusha, and saw it as contributing to generating, sustaining and interconnecting the universe as a totality, according to Vernant, the Greek sacrifice, modelled on Prometheus' offering of a bull, divided men from gods and animals by establishing rules as to which parts of the animal the gods should eat and which parts humans were allowed to consume.

3 Important contributions to this field include Beard *et al.* (1998); Brown (1988; 1995); Cameron (1994); Engberg-Pedersen (2000); and Williams (1996).

4 However, Achilles does not furnish lions with new characteristics. The target domain of the metaphor does not in this case change the source domain. About metaphors, see especially Lakoff and Johnson (1980, 1999).

5 A metaphor evokes a network of cultural associations, has a superfluity of meanings and speaks to the senses. The metaphor of the lion presupposes a cultural representation of lions that was shared in classical Greece and that could only work if this was the case. Although the Roman Empire embraced great cultural diversity it is still possible to see a certain coherence in the metaphors and a certain stability in the meaning of animals across the Mediterranean and the Middle East. Mary Douglas has suggested that "coherence of metaphors works very well as an interpretive rule within one culture" (Douglas 1990: 29). At the same time, there are local variations. The concept of the lion as a supreme animal and a manly beast was shared in the ancient world and was stable through the centuries. In the ancient Near East, the male lion was closely related to royal power as a symbol of kingship, but it had networks of local cultural associations, for instance in Egypt, Mesopotamia, Syria/Palestine and Persia.

271

1 Animals in the Roman Empire

1 Dio Cassius says that Caligula would order some of the mob to be thrown to the wild beasts when there was a shortage of condemned criminals (59.10.3).

2 The similes of Oppian and pseudo-Oppian have recently been the subject of A.N. Bartley's book *Stories from the Mountains, Stories from the Sea. The Digressions and Similes of Oppian's Halieutica and the Cynegetica*. Göttingen: Vandenhoeck & Ruprecht, 2003.

3 In this case, Pythagoras also miraculously predicted the number of fish in advance, and not one of the fish died even though they had not been in water for some time while the fishermen counted them (*On the Pythagorean Way of Life*, 36).

4 Barbro Santillo Frizell (2004) "Curing the flock. The use of healing waters in Roman pastoral economy", in Barbro Santillo Frizell (ed), *PECUS. Man and Animal in Antiquity*. Rome: Swedish Institute in Rome, 84–94.

5 The domestication of animals could be regarded in different ways, from human exploitation of animals to a successful evolutionary strategy benefiting humans and animals alike. The last point has been made by Stephen Budiansky, who has stressed that animals gained measurable advantage from flocking together with humans: "being able to scavenge campsites or grainfields and live under a shield that guarded them from other predators" (Budiansky 1992: 60).

6 When the censors ordered the food of the sacred geese before they did anything else in relation to their office, it was in gratitude for these geese having awakened the Romans when barbarians climbed the ramparts of the Capitol in the Gallic wars (Plutarch, *The Roman Questions*, 98, 287B-1; *On the Fortune of the Romans*, 12.325C–325D).

7 For prodigies in Livy and Obsequens, see Peter Weiss Poulsen, "Divination og politisk magt. Transformationer i romersk religion 2. årh. f. Kr. – 1. årh. e. Kr", Copenhagen 2002–3, unpublished paper.

8 Ammianus Marcellinus uses this occasion to comment on the general ambiguity of omens.

9 The domination of humans over nature may more generally be expressed as a domination over animals. The Near Eastern mistress of animals is depicted standing on lions and holding plants and snakes in her hands. This domination over animals may also be a symbol of social domination. In the oriental kingdoms of Egypt, Mesopotamia and Persia, kingship and power were symbolized by royal hunts, especially for lions. Pharaoh's sovereignty over the ordered world was reflected in his magnificent zoo, with exotic animals (Hornung 1999: 68–9).

10 Most probably, animal sacrifices continued in pockets and recesses of the new Christian culture. Paulinus of Nola, for instance, bears witness to a Christianization of sacrificial traditions in the Italian countryside at the beginning of the fifth century (Trout 1995). In the sixth century, according to Evagrius of Pontus and John of Ephesus, sacrifices were still made at the temple of Zeus at Edessa (Bowersock 1996: 36). However, the main point is that although some of its meaning was continued by Christianity, the greater cultural significance of animal sacrifice was suppressed (see Chapter 7).

2 United by soul or divided by reason?

1 Aristotle's scientific approach towards animals had set them on the agenda, and animals had afterwards been thematized in the Academy, especially by Theophrastus. However, it is likely that the Pythagorean revival from the first century BCE, with its focus on vegetarianism and reincarnation, had led to renewal of the interest in animals. We have examples of debates about the status and value of animals from the first and second centuries CE.

2 Urs Dierauer points out that some of the authors who spoke in favour of animal intelligence used an ancient argumental scheme when they first tried to prove that animals had

speech and then that they also had reason (Dierauer 1997: 26–7). One example is found in Sextus Empiricus, *Outlines of Pyrrhonism*, 1.62–78, where he uses the dog as his example to show first that animals have internal reason (1.64–72) and then that they also have external reason (1.73–7).

3 Urs Dierauer has interestingly pointed out that the anti-Stoic polemic does not attack the specific arguments of the Stoics about animal behaviour. Dierauer thinks: "plûtot que la certitude de l'intelligence animal interdit de vouloir comprendre la démonstration stoïcienne, si bien qu'on ne s'est donné la peine ni de l'aborder ni de la réfuter" (Dierauer 1997: 27).

4 Abraham Terian, who has worked on this text, says that there "can be little doubt about Alexander's cherishing the thoughts attributed to him in *Provid* I–II and *Anim*, for in answering him Philo finds himself in a predicament and, in search for answers, he sometimes contradicts himself" (Terian 1981: 29–30). Terian adds that Philo does not even deal with all the questions that Alexander raises.

5 Even if Philo is overwhelmingly influenced by the Stoics in *On Animals*, Terian stresses that "the Mosaic treatment of animals must be considered as the determining factor in moulding his thought" (Terian 1981: 46).

6 In a recent article, "Philo and the kindness towards animals", Katell Berthelot has demonstrated that Philo, in *On the Virtues* (125–47), has used the injunction to humaneness towards animals that is found in Mosaic law in an *a minori ad maius* argument in order to counter pagan accusations of Jewish misanthropy (Berthelot 2002). She also points out that Philo's argument probably derives from a Pythagorean tradition and that similar arguments were used in Stoic circles.

7 Max Schuster, who wrote a dissertation on this dialogue in 1917, pointed out that it was a school exercise, written for didactic and entertaining purposes, and not to be taken seriously (Schuster 1917). However, even if the dialogue is written in a playful mood, it applies traditional arguments that are well worth taking seriously.

8 One might think that there would have been personal experiences with animals in these stories, but almost all the examples are taken from books. Many of the stories are known from Pliny and Aelian, and Plutarch obviously used a variety of sources and refers to several authors whose works are now lost – and also to Stoics, who, in spite of their low opinion of animal intelligence, seem to have delighted in stories about clever animals (cf. Pohlenz 1948: 85). Only two examples are presented as personal experiences, one about a hedgehog (972A) and another about a performing dog (973E–974A; cf. Jones 1971: 21). However, considering that hedgehogs eat insects and do not spear berries on their quills, which is what Plutarch's story is about, it is not personal experience, but one of those fantastic animal stories that are also encountered elsewhere. Plutarch makes one of his characters say that he is "introducing no opinions of philosophers or Egyptian fables or unattested tales of Indians or Libyans" (975D), which suggests that animal stories were often met with the objection that they were too fantastic and therefore hard to believe.

9 This is an *a minori ad maius* argument, as pointed out by K. Berthelot (2002: 56–7).

10 The nuances are between different species of animal and between different humans. In *Gryllus*, Plutarch writes that he does not believe "that there is such a spread between one animal and another as there is between man and man in the matter of judgement and reasoning and memory" (992E).

11 According to the Stoics, fish are the animals that are lowest in the hierarchy of being (cf. 975B–975C; Pohlenz 1948: 83).

12 Not a few of the animal stories reveal several characteristics at the same time (970E). Among ants, for instance, "there exists the delineation of every virtue" (967E).

13 In Philo's work, *On Whether Dumb Animals Possess Reason*, cattle, oxen, sheep and goats are in a similar way mentioned only briefly (41).

14 It has been discussed whether the dialogue argues against hunting, or, as was the view of

Max Schuster, that members of Plutarch's circle were hunters (Schuster 1917: 80–1). It has further been pointed out that discrepancies between the introduction and the rest may suggest that the different parts were by different authors. However, it is more likely that there are discrepancies in this text because the answers to the dilemmas it contains are not easily solved.

15 Plutarch refers only once to the traditional epithet of gods as animal killers (966A).

16 According to Apollonius' biography, he was born in 4 or 3 BCE and died a hundred years later. Modern scholars have suggested that he was born about 40 CE and died about 120 CE. Tomas Hägg has recently made an analysis of two different "constructions" of Apollonius, the historical magician of the first century: (1) the philosopher of the third century; and (2) the counter-Christ of the fourth (Hägg 2004). In this article, Hägg also discusses some of the recent scholarly constructions of Apollonius.

17 The identity of Celsus has been discussed. One possibility is that he is an Epicurean, mentioned by Galen and Lucian, who wrote books against magic (recently, Hoffmann 1987: 30–3). The difficulty with this hypothesis is that even if Origen too sometimes labels Celsus an Epicurean, Celsus does not promote Epicurean views. Another possibility is that Celsus was a philosopher whose identity is otherwise unknown (as pointed out by Henry Chadwick 1980: xxiv–xxix). There is general agreement that Celsus' views are compatible with middle Platonism. The fact that he uses animals in his argumentation and the way he does it also point towards the Platonic tradition. J.A. Francis describes him as a "synthetic thinker" and stresses "the eclectic nature of Middle Platonism" (Francis 1995: 137).

18 According to Guiliana Lanata, who has written a valuable article about Celsus and animals, Celsus directs his arguments against the *interpretatio christiana* of the biblical stories of creation and against the anthropocentric view of creation found in Christian apologetes of the second century (Lanata 1997).

19 In *Table Talk* (8.8.730), Plutarch mentions that because fish did not harm humans the Pythagoreans "used fish least of all foods, or made no use of it".

3 Vegetarianism, natural history and physiognomics

1 Damianos Tsekourakis discusses the reasons for vegetarianism in Plutarch's *Moralia* and divides them into religious and mystical motives, moral motives and motives concerning hygiene and medicine (Tsekourakis 1987). He concludes "that we cannot speak of Pythagorean views in Plutarch's works on abstinence from animal flesh without qualifications" (*ibid.*: 391).

2 There were different principles for the classification of animals in antiquity. Animals could be divided according to their relations with humans – wild and tame, harmful and harmless. They could further be divided according to external criteria as, for instance, their habitat in land, air or water (such as quadrupeds, birds and fish), with different subgroups according to habit or habitat or according to the quality of their flesh.

3 From a modern point of view, it may seem strange that neither of the authors consulted seems to have considered the killing of animals that took place in the arenas to have been important with regard to their polemics. It is especially animals used as food for humans or as objects of sacrifice that evoke their interest and fighting spirit. An answer to the question of why Plutarch and Porphyry did not take up the arenas for discussion, only mention them in passing (Plutarch, *On the Cleverness of Animals*, 965A; Porphyry, *On Abstinence*, 3.20.6), could be that these authors were partly dependent on older traditions in which the arenas were not yet invented and therefore not yet an issue. However, it is more likely that the subject of the arenas was not raised because the authors on vegetarianism are concerned with eating rather than killing and, in addition, that killing of wild animals was considered to be legitimate and necessary.

4 The sophist Adamantius, who wrote in the fourth century CE, did not develop the comparison between animals and humans.

5 It was not always insulting to be called by animal names. Carlin A. Barton has pointed out that in Rome, "loving, nurturing, and cultivating seem to have involved perpetual mild shaming and teasing" (Barton 2001: 235). Accordingly, the lover called the beloved by animal names as "my little dove", "my little veal" or "my little goat" (*ibid.*)

4 Imagination and transformations

1 Cf. the lost work of Nicander of Colophon from the second century BCE, titled *Heteroioumena* (Transformations), and of Boios, *Ornithogonia* (Bird Origins). Metamorphoses are also a theme in Virgil's *Aeneid*.

2 According to the Stoics, fish were creatures at the bottom of the animal hierarchy "die nicht die reine, sondern eine mit Flüssigkeit stark vermischte Luft atmen und kaum den Namen Lebenswesen verdienen" (Pohlenz 1948: 83).

3 Proclus (412–85), a minor Neoplatonist philosopher in Athens, taught that human souls can enter animals, but he rejected that animal souls were ever reincarnated in humans. He stressed that souls may enter into animals that already have an irrational soul (cf. Opsomer and Steel, *Proclus, On the Existence of Evils*: 117, note 183).

5 The religious value of animals

1 The "mocking and ribald nature" of elements in Roman as well as Greek processions is mentioned by Dionysius of Halicarnassus (7.72.10).

2 The Egyptians did not practise the divination by means of the entrails of animals that had been sacrificed, a divinatory practice that was common in the Mediterranean area, and they also had few animal oracles (Teeter 2002: 349).

3 The "cult of animals" is an inclusive expression that encompasses all cases in which animals were the objects of religious rituals. It presupposes that if these animals were finally sacrificed, their spirit or soul or essence was thought to live on in some form or another.

4 For a survey of which animals were associated and identified with which god, see Teeter 2002: 337.

5 In contrast to the Egyptian hybrids, the Graeco-Roman hybrids were mostly used for decorative purposes, even if such creatures also appear in magical papyri. Demons with the head of a horse and the body of a human were connected with horse racing (Gager 1992).

6 In addition to the religious cult of animals, there were also concepts of animals as symbolizing the evil forces in nature, usually connected with the god Seth. Popular in the Graeco-Roman world were the so-called Horus-cippi (Frankfurter 1998: 47–8; Teeter 2002: 353). These were stelae that came in sizes ranging from a few centimetres to over one metre in height, showing the god Horus as a child, trampling on two or more crocodiles and with animals such as snakes, scorpions, lions and gazelles dangling from his hand. Spells are inscribed on the base, back and sides. These stelae were apotropaic and kept demons and hostile animals away as well as warding off or curing illnesses. Roman emperors could also take on the role of Horus; for instance, Hadrian is depicted on coins spearing a crocodile that he tramples beneath his foot (Ritner 1989: 114). The depiction of the Roman emperor as Horus is an Egyptian parallel to the way emperors were depicted in the role of Hercules. Both Horus and Hercules were divine beings who were fighting enemies in the form of animals.

7 Christian Froidefond has rightly drawn attention to the fact that the Egyptians thought that the divine could be incorporated in objects as well as in living beings (Froidefond 1988: 108–9, 318–19, note 1).

8 J.G. Griffiths remarks that "the animal cults were not for export, and in the Osirian rites outside Egypt the depiction of these animals shows little more than an urge to import a Nilotic atmosphere" (Griffiths 1970: 69).

9 Also, when animals appeared in dreams, they existed in the symbolic mode, as seen in the *Interpretation of Dreams* by Artemidorus. Even if there are certain basic meanings associated with a species or a subspecies and these meanings are the point of departure for the interpretation (Artemidorus, 1.50, 4.56), the interpretation is dependent on the sex and class of the dreamer (1.20, 1.24, 2.42, 4.13, 4.67, 4.83). Sometimes, etymological similarities between the name of the animal and a human characteristic are used in the interpretation (*ibid.*, 2.12).

10 The link between specific animals and gods was also typical of the eastern neighbours of the Greeks. In Mesopotamia, the dragon was linked with Marduk, the lion with Ishtar and the bull with Adad.

11 The wolf is frequently mentioned in African and Spanish inscriptions. According to J. Prieur, in two cases at least, such inscriptions point to a cult of the wolf (Prieur 1988: 32).

12 Ovid explains the ass of Vesta by a story of how it awakened the goddess by its braying and thus prevented the horny Priapus from raping her (*Fasti*, 6.319–48).

13 Epona, was, together with her horses, an object of religious cults from Britain to the Balkans, especially in those parts that were occupied by the Roman army, and especially along the northwestern frontier (Speidel 1994: 141).

14 For images of Cybele and lion(s), see Roller 1999, especially figures 42, 50, 53, 58, 59, 60, 61, 69, 71, 72 and 73.

15 Sometimes the divine attributes were expressed through real animals, for example at the funeral of the emperor, one of the most solemn moments in the life of the empire. Then an eagle – the bird of Zeus and the symbol on the standards of the legions – was released from a cage on the top of the funeral pyre and rose towards heaven, carrying, or symbolizing, the emperor's soul and thus his apotheosis.

16 Not surprisingly, the serpents convey a rich plethora of meanings in Artemidorus' dream world (2.13, 4.67, 4.79).

17 The serpents belong to a type that was earlier called *Coluber aesculapii*. They are yellow-brown and between 1.5 and 2 metres long.

18 Ulrich Victor's point of departure is that Lucian's text is a historically reliable source for Alexander and Glycon (Victor 1997: 8–26).

6 Animal sacrifice: traditions and new inventions

1 Hubert Cancik sees Dionysius of Halicarnassus' efforts as an example of the recognition of Greek cults in Rome. It expresses a commonly felt coherence between different religious anthropologies and theologies in the empire and was a precondition of the emergence of an imperial religion (Cancik 1999).

2 A different type of sacrifice was the sacrifice of expiation. Here the animal body was used to get rid of pollution and danger that threatened society. In sacrifices to the deities of the underworld, the victims were burned and the participants did not eat any part of the meat.

3 An exception is Artemis, who sometimes received wild animals. Sometimes, but not often, the tunny fish was sacrificed to Poseidon. But even he, the sea god, mostly delighted in sacrifices of lambs and oxen. As for the tunny, its blood looked like the blood of mammals (Sissa and Detienne 2000: 170–1).

4 Sometimes, small pieces from other parts of the animal were added to the *exta* – usually in the manner of small dishes (*magmenta, augmenta*).

5 Only one surviving relief, now in the Louvre, shows the dead victim while the liver is being cut out (North 1990: 56; Gordon 1990: 204).

6 *Nominare vetat Martem neque agnum vitulumque*: "It is not permitted to call Mars, the lamb or the calf by name". However, *Martem* should probably be corrected to *porcem* ("pig").

7 Human sacrifices were not unknown in the Graeco-Roman world, but they were highly exceptional.

8 Recently, Dag Øistein Endsjø has asked the interesting question of why death outside sacrifice was polluting when sacrifices were not in classical Greece (Endsjø 2003). He has pointed out the aspect of control of death as an important function of Greek sacrifices: "Sacrifice was performed because it was the only way of gaining control of the dangerous and polluting aspects of death first unleashed by an uncontrolled demise" (*ibid.*: 336).

9 As for an earlier phase of the *taurobolium*, the *vires*, probably the genitals of the animal were given to the *Mater deum*. This is in contrast to the traditional sacrifice, in which it was the *exta* that were given to the gods (cf. Duthoy 1969: 117). However, the *vires* are mentioned only in inscriptions dated before 250 CE.

10 See preceding note.

11 There are also examples from Mithraic iconography where Mithras is depicted as a hunter (Vermaseren 1956–60: 52, 1137).

12 Within the Mediterranean area, there were considerable variations in how and why sacrifices were performed. In Carthage, Egypt, Israel, Greece and Rome, sacrifices were staged differently and in different contexts, with different functions and meanings. Sacrifices of animals on the Capitol in Rome differed from offerings of animals and children to Baal-Haman and Tanit in Carthage. The sacrifices in the temple in Jerusalem were different from those on the Acropolis in Athens. The *taurobolium*, where a bull was killed in honour of the Magna Mater and where the blood of the animal bathed the sacrificer, had a function and meaning different from the killing of a dove or a cat to make a magical formula work.

7 "God is a man-eater": the animal sacrifice and its critics

1 Both Democritus and the Cynics claimed that humans had once lived a life similar to animals. For a discussion of ancient *Kulturgeschichte* and of authors who held the view that in the beginning humans lived like animals (Diodorus, Vitruvius, Tzetzes, Lucretius, Posidonius), see Cole 1967.

2 In general, ancient authors liked to speculate on the rise and development of human civilization. There were cultural positivists as well as negativists. Marianne Wifstrand Schiebe has pointed out that in ancient poetry sheep are a more flexible symbol than cattle. Cattle breeding and cattle holding are associated with settled farmers and agriculture. Unlike sheep, which are always used as positive symbols pointing to abundance or wealth or simplicity and poverty, depending on which ideal the author prefers, a positive evaluation of cattle is dependent on a positive evaluation of agriculture (Schiebe 2004, cf. Schiebe 1981).

3 Porphyry has also been associated more directly with Diocletian's great persecution of the Christians in 303 CE. In fact, the emperor may actively have supported the circulation of Porphyry's *Against the Christians*, because this work expressed erudite and well-informed support for the emperor's anti-Christian policy. For a summary of the discussion concerning the dating of *Against the Christians* and the possibility, and the difficulties, of connecting the work with Diocletian and the persecution of the Christians, see Barnes 1994: 57–60; Meredith 1980.

4 The first Latin translation entitled the text *de abstinentia ab esu animalium* and thus stressed the eating aspect (Clark 2000: 25, note 4).

5 Research on Ammianus Marcellinus has concentrated on his cultural belonging (Greek or Roman), his dependence on his sources, the question of degree of fiction and history in

his work, and his religion and relation to Christianity. There is no general agreement over most of these questions, and there is thus a need for balanced views. See especially Matthews (1989); Barnes (1998); Drijvers and Hunt (1998); Sabbah (2003).

6 Guy Sabbah says that Ammianus "allots a minimal part to religion when he cannot avoid talking about it in his account about Julian. Despite the central place it had in the latter's politics, mentions of religion are restricted to occasional legal dispositions, sacrifices, oracles and ceremonies" (Sabbah 2003: 70).

7 With the speech of the ox, Arnobius illustrates vividly what Plutarch refers to in *The Eating of Flesh* I, when he says: "Then we go on to assume that when they utter cries and squeaks their speech is inarticulate, that they do not, begging for mercy, entreating, seeking justice, each one of them say: 'I do not ask to be spared in case of necessity; only spare me your arrogance! Kill me to eat, but not to please your palate'" (994E). (The speech of this ox is a faint reminder of how in Parsee religion, the soul of the ox complained to Ahura Mazda over his fate (Yasna 29)).

8 Pierre Chuvin has challenged the interpretation of *paganus* as "rustic". Instead, he has proposed that *pagani* were those who preferred the faith of the local unit of government (*pagus*); in other words, they preferred the traditional religion (Chuvin 1990: 7–9).

9 The spiritualization of the Jewish cult did not mean that the animal sacrifice, which had been such an important part of the rituals in the temple at Jerusalem, was repudiated.

10 S.R.F. Price discusses the argument that there was a shift in attention "from the heart to the stomach" (Price 1986: 229). However, Price warns against seeing sacrifice as merely an excuse for a good dinner, and he also warns against making a division between the religious and the secular (*ibid.*: 229–30).

11 The literary evidence from the fifth century BCE in Greece and from Roman authors, beginning with Cicero, shows that gods were thought to favour high moral character and small sacrifices above large sacrifices and dubious moral status (see Dickie 2001).

12 Christians did the same with the pagans and blamed them for sacrificing humans (Rives 1995).

13 The doctrine of *ahimsa* became widely known in the twentieth century, when it was used by Mahatma Gandhi as a political strategy.

14 As pointed out by Knut Jacobsen, there are in fact two traditions of non-injury in India. Either non-violence is a universal norm, or there is a distinction between morally approved and disapproved injury. In the latter case, killing animals in sacrifice is characterized by ritual texts as non-injury.

8 The New Testament and the lamb of God

1 Balaam's ass is referred to once in the New Testament (II Peter 2:15ff).

2 Andrew McGowan has pointed out that in real life things may not have been as simple as in this New Testament story, where the dietary prescriptions were simply made irrelevant (McGowan 1999: 52).

3 Meat eating was also an issue in the letter that Pliny, the governor of Bithynia, wrote to Trajan (111 CE). In this letter, Pliny asked the emperor how a group of Christians should be treated. This group had refused to eat sacrificed meat, and the meat business in the area had consequently started to run low.

4 In Hebrews 10:1–22 and 13:10–16, one of the themes is that the sacrifice of Christ had made the Jewish sacrifices superfluous.

5 Luke has ravens (12:24).

6 Cf. also: "Foxes have holes, and birds of the air have nests; but the Son of Man has nowhere to lay his head" (Luke 9:58).

7 According to Aune, there is only one disputed instance of early Jewish literature in which the lamb is used for the Messiah (Aune 1997: 368).

8 Animal parables lived on in Christian tradition, and they were given continually new and

ingenious interpretations. One example is Mark 10.25: "It is easier for a camel to go through the eye of a needle than for someone who is rich to enter the kingdom of God" (cf. Matthew 19:24; Luke 18:25). Another is a saying directed at the Pharisees: "You blind guides! You strain out a gnat but swallow a camel!" (Matthew 23:24) The camel was both spiritualized and allegorized in Christian tradition (cf. Clark 1999: 94–8). However, what these exegetical endeavours on the topic of camels and eyes of needles and swallowing have in common is that the exegetes had little interest in real-life camels.

9 Serpents are not always depicted as evil. In John 3:14, Jesus is compared to the healing serpent of bronze that Moses made and set upon a pole (Numbers 21:9).

10 Alternative Christian interpretations existed. Epiphanius says that Marcion taught that "Christ freed the swine's souls from their bodies to let them make their ascent", implying that Marcion thought that humans and animals had the same soul (*Panarion*, 42; *Elenchus*, 24g).

11 *Apocriticus* was probably written in the third or early fourth century CE (Cook 2000: 173–4). In a discussion about the identity of the anonymous Hellene in *Apocriticus*, Elizabeth Depalma Digeser has recently argued that he is Sossianus Hierokles, not Porphyry or Julian. Hierokles had presented his *Truth-Loving Discourse* orally just before the edicts of persecution in 303 CE. *Apocriticus* may render one-half of this lost work (Digeser 2002).

12 For the use of allegories in early Christianity and the challenge of allegorical meanings to literal meanings, see Dawson 1992: 1–21.

13 In Revelation, a speaking eagle is used as a messenger of God (6:13).

14 The gospel of pseudo-Matthew is from the eighth–ninth century CE but is built on older traditions.

15 In the Old Testament, animal imagery of God likens him to a lion, panther, leopard or bear (Hosea 5:14, 13:7–8; Lamentations 3:10).

16 This is in line with how metaphors work. The formula A is B implies that a target domain (A) is comprehended through a source domain (B). In this case, A is people, here Jesus, and B is animals, here lamb. Only some characteristics of B are mapped onto A. In this case, only characteristics that have to do with sacrificial animals are used (on metaphor theory, see Lakoff and Johnson 1999; Kövecses 2002).

17 For lamb identification, see also I Corinthians 5:7: "For our paschal lamb, Christ, has been sacrificed"; and I Peter 1:19: "but with the precious blood of Christ, like that of a lamb without defect or blemish".

18 In Christian literature, there are frequent allusions to Christ as the lamb, but in iconography this allegory is not witnessed before the fourth century CE.

19 For the general influence of Stoicism on Paul, see Troels Engberg-Pedersen 2000.

20 In the pseudo-pauline letter to Timothy, Paul's trials in a Roman court are described in this way: "So I was rescued from the lion's mouth" (II Timothy 4:17; cf. I Peter 5:8: "Like a roaring lion your adversary the devil prowls around, looking for someone to devour").

21 Paul uses metaphors related to oxen in I Corinthians 9:8–10. He also refers to yoking in relation to oxen (Williams 1999: 32–3). For metaphors connected with sheep and trapping, see *ibid.*: 33–5.

22 This perspective has its predecessors, especially Franz Boll, who wrote: "Der Einfluss, den die gleichzeitige religiöse Kosmologie des Hellenismus, mit ihrem Sternglauben und ihrer dominierenden astrologischen Spekulation, auf die apokalyptische Dichtung ausgeübt hat, ist kaum zu überschätzen" (Boll 1914: 126).

23 I am grateful to Jorunn Økland for pointing out this connection.

24 They are depicted in a slightly different version from Ezekiel 1:5–24.

25 According to apocalyptic literature, Behemoth and Leviathan will become food for the remnant at the end of time (II Baruch, 29.4–8; IV Ezra 6.49–52; I Enoch 60.7–9, 24–25). In Psalm 74.12–14 and 104.26–7, Leviathan is referred to as food. Behemoth is

sometimes identified as cattle and Leviathan as fish. I am grateful to Liv Ingeborg Lied for this information.

9 Fighting the beasts

1 The punishment of being thrown to the beasts (*bestiis obici*) was first used in 167 BCE against army deserters, who were crushed by elephants (Bernstein 1998: 303, note 429; Futrell 1997: 28–9).

2 There are exceptions. Cases of Roman citizens executed in this way are mentioned, for instance by Cicero (*Letters to his Friends*, 10.32.3) and Suetonius (*Caligula*, 28.8).

3 Children had to get used to it: the young Caracalla wept or turned away when he saw criminals pitted against wild beasts (*Scriptores Historiae Augustae*, 3; in Salisbury 1997: 126).

4 The persecution that was started by Diocletian in 303 CE continued after his retirement in 305 CE and was ended by Constantine.

5 Contemporary research on Christian martyrology has focused on its origins. Two opposing points of view are those of W.H.C. Frend, who argues for a Jewish background and origin (for instance, in Frend 2000), and G. W. Bowersock, who argues for a Graeco-Roman background and for western Asia Minor as the original place of Christian martyrdom (Bowersock 1995). Recently, Daniel Boyarin has argued for a more nuanced relationship and stressed the continuum between Judaism and Christianity in these centuries (Boyarin 1999). Another important theme in contemporary research has been the relationship and conflict between the Catholic Church and Montanism concerning voluntary martyrdom (Buschmann 1995). Finally, there have recently been analyses of discourses with the emphasis on the gender roles in the early Church as reflected in the Acts of the Martyrs (for instance Boyarin 1999; Burrus 1995, 2000; Perkins 1995; Shaw 1996).

6 Herbert Musurillo said that "the legal basis of the persecutions remains vague" (In *The Acts of the Christian Martyrs*; Musurillo 1972: lxi).

7 Anthony R. Birley has recently shown that in the sources there are more occurrences of judges who demand that the Christians sacrifice to the gods than those who demand that they sacrifice to the emperors (Birley 2000: 121–3).

8 Jane Cooper has interestingly pointed out that the persecution of the Christians may be more of a literary phenomenon and that martyr texts are an important pillar of the Christian textual production of the fourth century CE (Cooper 2003).

9 Aline Rousselle has interpreted the killing of the Carthaginian martyrs as ritual killing in honour of the superior god of North Africa, i.e. Saturn (Rousselle 1988: 118–19).

10 The *Martyrdom of Perpetua and Felicitas* has in recent years been the subject of much research. A recent article with an updated bibliography is Jan N. Bremmer: "Perpetua and Her Diary: Authenticity, Family and Vision" (2002).

11 *Lanista* is usually an athletic trainer, but Jan den Boeft and Jan Bremmer have pointed out that in this case the Greek *brabeutes* reveals that *agonothetes* is meant (den Boeft and Bremmer 1982: 390–1).

12 Martyrs became increasingly the heroes of the Church, and the Acts of the Martyrs became a popular genre. When Christians were hunted out and punished, they were interrogated and sometimes tortured. The interrogations were not necessarily conducted in an atmosphere of hostility. On the contrary, the persons in charge often tried to get the accused to withdraw their confession and make the necessary sacrifice. In a similar vein, the worldly authorities were also treated with respect by the Christians.

13 Not only in the Acts of the Martyrs and the apocryphal Acts did the Christians present themselves as sufferers, but also in the Apologies, and later in the Lives of the saints. In this way, the Christians were depicted as a community of sufferers (Perkins 1995: 40).

14 According to S.R.F. Price, in the persecution of Christians the cult of the gods was more

important than that of the emperor. Sacrifices might be made on the emperor's behalf, but only exceptionally to him (Price 1986: 221). A.R. Birley has shown that in the sources, sacrifices to the gods were more frequent than to the emperor (see note 7, this chapter).

15 For the question of the anti-Montanism of this episode and the discussion of it being a later interpolation, see Buschmann 1994: 25–32.

16 Finally, when Perpetua is walking in procession to the arena, she is singing a psalm. This psalm could have been Psalm 90, which refers to the animals that are trampled underfoot (90:13; see Balling *et al.* 1997: 47, note 107).

17 Jan Bremmer has pointed out that the phrase *calcavi illi caput* refers to the words of Genesis 3:15 in the African version of the *Vetus Latina*; he shows that the phrase was popular in martyrological contexts. Bremmer connects the enormous serpent, which Perpetua sees in her vision, to Revelation and to Hermas (Bremmer 2002: 101).

18 In Revelation, the Devil is called "the dragon, the old serpent" (20:2). For the dragon in the *Martyrdom of Perpetua and Felicitas*, see Habermehl 1992: 78–88.

19 In the *Martyrdom of Polycarp*, when Polycarp is pierced by a dagger, "there came out a dove [*peristera*] and such a quantity of blood that the flames were extinguished" (16.1). The dove is obviously meant as a symbol of Polycarp's soul and is a witness to how animals were also used positively to characterize Christian qualities. However, the dove is usually interpreted as a later interpolation (Buschmann 1998: 312–15).

20 D.B. Saddington has suggested that the soldiers labelled "leopards" should rather be *Lepidiana*, referring to a Roman cohort (Saddington 1987). He points out that the giving of the name of an animal to Roman soldiers is unparalleled. Alternatively, it has been suggested that "leopards" could have been a play on the name of the cohort (see Saddington 1987: 411, note 4).

21 Seneca, like Tertullian and Augustine, held that the sight of humans being killed influenced the onlookers in a negative direction (Seneca, *Epistle*, 7; Tertullian, *On the Spectacles*, 84; Augustine, *Confessions*, 6.8).

22 Monika Pesthy has written an interesting survey of the way Thecla is treated by the Church fathers (Pesthy 1996).

23 This bit of information is part of Minucius Felix' counterattack on pagans who say that Christians sacrifice babies. He also adds that Christians should neither see nor hear about human slaughter and that because of their shrinking from human blood they do not even eat animal blood.

24 In accordance with this language of birth, those who lapsed may be described as "stillborn" (*Martyrs of Lyons*, 1.11; cf. 45; see also II Peter 1:18).

25 There are also stories about Christian bodies being miraculously rescued from perishing. A story about Carthaginian martyrs tells about the Romans who loaded Christians and other convicts, living and dead, onto a ship, and rowed them out on the Mediterranean and dumped them in the sea. Immediately, dolphins came and rescued the Christian bodies and brought them to the shore. (*Passio Maximiani et Isaac Donatistarum auctore Macrobio*, Migne PL 8.772–3 in Tilley 1993: 94).

26 Tertullian also bases his interpretation of the phoenix on LXX Ps 91:13, which states that "the just man will blossom like a phoenix" (*phoiniks* is here usually thought to mean "palm tree"). Cf. *On the Origin of the World* (CG II, 5:122).

27 Most scholars are in accord that the "spiritual" interpretation of this logion is the correct one (references in Jackson 1985: 175–6, note 1). Howard M. Jackson, who has made the logion the theme of a book – *The Lion becomes Man. The Gnostic Leontomorphic Creator and the Platonic Tradition*, 1985 – connects it in part to the Platonic tradition. He stresses that the lion represents the human passions, which the ascetic may redeem by integrating them into his spiritual nature. However, even if the spiritual man is "devoured" by the lion, he will not be totally absorbed and annihilated, because the human soul is basically unalterable (*ibid.*, 20).

10 Internal animals and bestial demons

1 Seeing Hercules in a dream, writes Artemidorus of Daldis, the expert on dreams, "is auspicious for all those who govern their lives by sound moral principles and who live in accordance with the law, especially if they have been treated unjustly by others" (2.37). Hercules also appeared as a saviour, and in the Via Latina catacomb, he saves the soul of the dead Alcestis and conquers death. His capture of the dog Cerberus was also interpreted as a salvatory work (Elsner 1995: 274–81). In the gnostic *Book of Baruch*, he liberates the world from twelve evil angels who are bent on harming humans (Hippolytus, *Refutation of all Heresies*, 5.26.27).

2 The motif of man ruling over animals is old. It is a standard way of visualizing how human culture and society are invented and maintained in the face of hostile forces and how man controls and rules the world. It is also a topic in Graeco-Roman cultural history that human society arose as a protection against wild animals, a theme that may have originated with Democritus but is found, for instance, in Diodorus of Sicily (1.8).

3 Clement of Alexandria, who is our source, points out that if the soul is hosting such a variety of different spirits, it loses its unity and becomes like a wooden horse (*Stromateis*, 2:20).

4 Eusebius mentions the beasts of Plato in the same breath as he mentions the four creatures of life in Ezekiel 1.3–4.3.

5 Cf. A. Scott, "Zoological marvel and exegetical method in Origen and the Physiologus" (2002); and G. Lanata, "Thèmes animaliers dans le platonisme moyen" (1997), especially p. 317, note 43.

6 Even if there were female monks as well, it feels safe to say that it was in the main a male world.

7 J. Zandee has pointed out this Stoic influence but has especially stressed the Jewish–Christian influence on the *Teachings of Silvanus* (Zandee 1981: 504, 1991).

8 In *Timaeus*, it is said that the gods had made both the male penis and the female uterus as animated creatures (Plato, *Timaeus*, 91a6–91d6). However, this manner of conceiving the sexual organs did not break through into Christian texts.

9 BG refers to one of the short versions of the *Apocryphon of John*. It is found in *Papyrus Berolinensis* 8502.

10 The combination of woman, serpent and sex is not unique in gnostic variants of Christianity. The historian of religions Daniel Boyarin has recently shown that Hellenistic Judaism had a tendency to make a similar connection. Philo of Alexandria refers to the serpent as "Eve's snake" (Boyarin 1995: 81). Rabbinical Judaism, on the other hand, was more positive according to Boyarin in its evaluation of sex and saw it as a gift. But here one also finds misogynistic sayings, as for instance, Rabbi Aha, who connects the name Eve (Hebrew *Hawwah*) with the word for snake in Aramaic, *Hiwiah*. Accordingly, Rabbi Aha has Adam say to Eve: "The snake was your snake, and you were my snake" (*ibid.*, 88–9), which is in line with the view of the *Apocryphon of John*.

11 This text does not belong in the Nag Hammadi library.

12 This conceptualizing by means of animals had roots in the archaic world of Mesopotamia and Egypt. Its present form is Hellenistic and probably derives from the third century BCE, but it flourished during the empire.

13 In Codex II, a sheep is mentioned too.

14 The historian of religions Michael A. Williams has raised the question of how the bodies of humans resembled their beastly creators and has concluded that the similarity lay in their sexuality (Williams 1996: 122–3).

15 In some of these cases, the animals in question may have been used as allegories. B. Bark, who has studied the *Nature of the Archons*, has mentioned that when Adam names the birds and the fish, it may refer to virtues and vices, respectively (Bark 1980).

16 For a discussion of the animals in the *Origin of the World*, see Tardieu 1974. However, when Tardieu is referring to water monsters in Egypt (*nhydria mmoou ethnkeme*; 122:

18–20), it is most likely a misreading. According to L. Painchaud, *hydria* do not refer to animals but to water jars (Painchaud 1995: 473–5).

17 In *Timaeus*, Plato, after having described the origin of the universe and of man, says of "the mode in which the rest of living creatures have been produced", that only a brief statement is needed (90E), and then goes on to speak of women, birds, wild animals, reptiles and fish and to make their existence dependent on a downward movement of reincarnation. Even if the Nag Hammadi texts only partly reckon with reincarnation, they are influenced by the same hierarchy of values according to which animals are of little importance.

18 For demons in antiquity, see Luck 1985:163–75; Smith 1978; Valantasis 1992.

19 As for asceticism in the Nag Hammadi library, Richard Valantasis has pointed out in a recent article that these texts refer less to ascetic practice than should perhaps have been expected (Valantasis 2001b). Among the texts that Valantasis regards as clearly ascetic treatises are the *Acts of Peter and the Twelve Apostles* and *Authoritative Teaching*, but the *Gospel of Philip*, the *Apocryphon of John* and the *Book of Thomas the Contender* also refer more vaguely to ascetic themes. According to Valantasis, less than one-third of the library refers to asceticism in one way or another (*ibid.*: 188). However, it must be noted that animals figure more prominently in those texts that Valantasis counts as ascetic.

20 It must be mentioned that part of a text that is usually ascribed to Antony is included in the *Teachings of Silvanus*.

21 In the *Life of Paulus the First Hermit*, Jerome writes that the desert "is known to abound in monstrous animals" (7).

22 Evagrius of Pontus writes of the anchorites that "in the night time during sleep they fight with winged asps, are encircled by carnivorous wild beasts, entwined by serpents, and cast down from high mountains. It sometimes happens that even after awakening they are again encircled by the same wild beasts and see their cell afire and filled with smoke" (*On Thoughts*, 27).

23 When Evagrius of Pontus writes about foxes that "find shelter in the resentful soul" and the beasts "which make their lairs in a troubled heart", these animals refer to demons (cf. *Eight Thoughts*, 4.13). Origen too frequently interprets passages in the Bible that refer to animals as referring to demons (cf. Crouzel 1956: 197–206).

24 An interesting supplement to the biblical and Egyptian perspectives on Antony's desert has recently been suggested by the historian of religions Dag Øistein Endsjø, who sees wild animals as systematically related to a Greek world view. He interprets the uncultivated geography of the desert as an example of the primordial landscape. According to Endsjø, Antony lived on the periphery and in a landscape that was liminal. Animals are natural inhabitants of this landscape, pointing back to a time when humans and beasts communicated with each other, as Antony did with the animals, even if it was to drive them away. The wild beasts remained for ever in the wilderness and thus reflected the indiscriminate complexity of this primordial landscape (Endsjø 2002: 98).

11 The crucified donkey-man, the *leontocephalus* and the challenge of beasts

1 Thomas Mathews is of a different opinion. He has pointed out the role of the ass in Christian art. He sees it as part of a Christian world view in which the ordinary world has been turned on its head, so that the lowly were exalted and the saviour rode into Jerusalem on an ass. Mathews also thinks that it is possible that the caricature on Palatine may refer to the same symbolic universe and thus not be intended as mockery (Mathews 1995: 45–50).

2 Howard M. Jackson has made an interesting study of the pedigree of the gnostic leontomorphic demiurge. Jackson stresses the Old Testament background, processes within

Judaism in an Egyptian contexts, Mesopotamian astrological influence, and finally the Christian gnostic development of this figure (Jackson 1985: 171–3).

3 From the end of the second century BCE, *hairesis* (from *haireomai*, "choice") is used about schools of philosophy. Catalogues of Christian heresies have their predecessors in catalogues of philosophical schools. Galenos characterizes medical schools as *haireses*, and Josephus and the New Testament authors characterize movements within Judaism in the same way. Later, *hairesis* is used by Christians about deviations from the true faith. Within Christian discourse, the meaning of "heresy" is an opinion contrary to the orthodox doctrine of the Christian Church. Epiphanius uses the concept mainly in this sense, although it may have a more neutral meaning when he applies it to pre-Christian sects and schools (cf. Vallée 1981: 75–7).

4 About *Panarion*, see especially Vallée 1981; Pourkier 1992; Williams 1987: introduction.

5 Among these sources were Irenaeus, *Against Heresies*, and Hippolytus, *Refutation of all Heresies*.

6 Irenaeus introduces a succession of teachers and disciples and traces them back to Simon Magus. Irenaeus seems to be dependent on Justin Martyr's lost *Syntagma*.

7 Robert Grant has pointed out that Irenaeus had compared the different post-Valentinian gnostic doctrines to the Lernaean hydra (*Against Heresies*, 1.30.15); Hippolytus applied the serpent to the Naassenes (*Refutation of all Heresies*, 5.11); while Eusebius compares the successors of Simon Magus and Menander – Saturnius and Basilides – to a hydra with two tongues and a double head (*Church History*, 4.7.3; Grant 1978: 196–7).

8 Gérard Vallée characterizes Epiphanius as "a past master in persiflage, invective, abusive language". And he adds that "Epiphanius has no equal in the history of heresiology for the art of insulting" (Vallée 1981:73).

9 Some of the "heresies" that Epiphanius describes relate themselves to serpents: the designations "Naassenes", "Ophites", and "Ophians" all refer to serpents, and serpents appear in the myths and rituals of these sects/movements.

12 Winged humans, speaking animals

1 Ludwig Bieler first treated the "divine man" in the Roman Empire in a monograph published in 1935. Bieler's ambition was to describe the characteristics of the type of the holy man pertaining to his life, personality, teaching, practice, followers and connections to the divine world – "ein Gesamtbild des Typus" (Bieler 1935: 140). He stresses the outstanding character of the holy man and his aspect of being a mediator between humans and the divine. Since Bieler, there have been several attempts to catch the variety of the holy man. Patricia Cox distinguishes between two paradigms in the biography of the divine philosopher: he is either the son of a god or has a god-like status. Sons of god work miracles, while those who are god-like do not (Cox 1983: 17–44). Mark J. Edwards points to the range of expressions that are used in ancient sources (*theos, daimon, vios theou, theios aner*), and with "less discrimination by the ancients than in modern studies of them" (Edwards 2000: 53). Graham Anderson also points out "the great diversity of holy men throughout our period, and a more or less consistent degree of ambiguity surrounding their motivation" (Anderson 1994: 33). J.A. Francis argues for viewing "the various elements of the *theios aner* as a continuum in Greek culture" and points out that the nature and function of the holy men "changed very little from the archaic period" (Francis 1995: 123). See also the recent book by N. Janowitz (2001: 70–85).

2 In *Phaedrus*, the perfect soul is winged. The wings are nourished by the divine, which makes the soul ascend upwards, but they are destroyed by evil (*Phaedrus*, 247a–252b).

3 For the tradition of bird imagery for the Holy Spirit in the Syriac tradition, see Johnson 1999: 201–4.

4 However, fish could also challenge systems based on bodily signs. Galen criticizes those who think that man has an erect posture for the sake of looking up to heaven and mentions the fish called *uranoscopus*, "heaven-gazer", as an example of a non-human creature that looks perpetually up to the heavens (*On the Usefulness of the Parts*, 3.3).

5 When Tertullian writes that "every spirit [*omnis spiritus*] is winged, angels and demons" (*Apology*, 22.8), he is referring to fallen and destructive creatures. Wings were a characteristic of demons and divine beings in pagan traditions. For that reason, Christian angels did not have them at the start. All the same, by the time of Gregory (590–604 CE), angels in the Christian traditions had been rigged out with wings.

6 For a bibliography on the research on the *Acts of Philip*, see *Acta Philippi. Commentarius* by F. Amsler 1999: ix–xxxvi. In recent years, the text has been investigated by B. Bouvier, F. Amsler and F. Bovon.

7 The *Acts of Philip* 8–15 is represented by two different manuscripts, *Xenophontos* 32 and *Vaticanus graecus* 824. Act 8, in addition to *Vaticanus graecus* 824, is also witnessed to by a manuscript from the Athenian National Library (*Atheniensis* 346). *Xenophontos* 32, which offered several new acts, was discovered on Mount Athos in 1974. It is named after the monastery to which it belongs (Bovon 1999: 12–13; Bovon *et al.* 1999: 16).

8 Amsler argues that the cult of "the mother of the serpent, the viper" (4:4–7) was directed at the Anatolian goddess Cybele, who had huge influence in Asia Minor (Amsler 1999: 304). Panthers, leopards and lions are usually her animals, while the kid belongs to her lover Attis (Amsler 1999: 305ff). Also the oak, which is mentioned in the text, is part of the meteoric cult of Cybele. Amsler further argues that the kid and the leopard are converts from the cult of Cybele (*ibid.*). According to his view, the *Acts of Philip* is a witness to the conflict between Christianity and the traditional religion of Asia Minor, focusing on Cybele.

9 A Phrygian tradition of millenarianism was connected, for instance, with Bishop Papias of Hierapolis in the second century CE but was criticized by the Church fathers (Amsler 1999: 301).

10 Giulia Sfameni Gasparro rightfully warns against viewing encratism as a simple phenomenon. In reality, it was a non-homogenous and complex entity with different ideologies supporting abstinence from sex and procreation (Gasparro 1998: 129).

11 F. Bovon has pointed out that the description of the dragon in the *Acts of Philip* is similar to those made in the *Shepherd of Hermas*, 22.6–24.9; the *Acts of Thomas*, 31; and the *Questions of Bartholomew*, 4.13 (Bovon 2002: 151).

12 Amsler mentions that some of the encratites not only avoided meat, they also kept away from animal products more generally, and he suggests that this procedure has to do not only with purity but also with the way in which encratites conceived of the place of animals in the creation (Amsler 1999: 367).

13 There were different types of encratite. Some preached absolute abstinence, while others allowed sex for the procreation of children.

14 The story of the baptized lion has survived in the Hamburg papyrus in Greek, a Coptic papyrus, and an Ethiopic text based on older sources (for references and research history, see Schneemelcher 1964; Adamik 1996).

15 Comparison between the story of Androcles (*Aulus Gellius*, 5.14.5–30) and the story of the baptized lion of Paul has been made in a systematic way by Tamas Adamik (Adamik 1996), who concludes that the author of the *Acts of Paul* imitated the story of Androcles.

16 H.J.W. Drijvers, for instance, has interpreted the baptized lion of Paul allegorically (Drijvers 1990).

17 However, this may be a reference to the animals in "the Land of Darkness", which preceded the animals on earth.

18 For the source value of Augustine, who wrote about Manichaeans in a handful of treatises, see J. Kevin Coyle: "What did Augustine know about Manichaeism when he wrote

his two treatises *de moribus?*" (Coyle 2001: 43–56). His conclusion is that Augustine knew a lot about them.

19 This point is made by E. Smagina (2001: 243–9).

Consequences

1 It could be added that the friendliness towards beasts that we find in some of the Christian texts seldom implied a free lunch for the animals in question. When enrolled in the Christian salvation project, animals often became human-like and had to stop being beasts.

BIBLIOGRAPHY

Texts

Acta Philippi, textus, F. Bovon, B. Bouvier and F. Amsler (eds), *Corpus Christianorum, Series Apocryphorum*, 11, Turnhout: Brepols, 1999.

Les Actes de Paul et ses lettres apocryphes, introduction, texts, traduction and commentary by Léon Vouaux, Paris: Libraire Letouzey et ané, 1913.

The Acts of the Christian Martyrs, introduction, texts and translation by H. Musurillo, Oxford: Clarendon Press, 1972.

The Apostolic Constitution, translation by W. Whiston, in A. Roberts and J. Donaldson (eds), *The Ante-Nicene Fathers*, vol. 7, Edinburgh: T&T Clark, 1994.

Aelian, *On the Characteristics of Animals*, translation by A.F. Scholfield, *Loeb Classical Library*, 3 vols, London: Heinemann, 1958–59.

Ambrose, *Concerning Virgins*, translation by H. de Romestin, in A. Roberts and J. Donaldson (eds), *A Select Library of Nicene and Post-Nicene Fathers*, second series, vol. 10, Edinburgh: T&T Clark, 1989.

Ammianus Marcellinus, *The History,* translation by John C. Rolfe, *Loeb Classical Library*, 3 vols, London: Heinemann, 1963–64.

Apuleius, *The Golden Ass*, translation by R. Graves, London: Penguin, 1990.

Aristotle, *Generation of Animals*, translation by A.L. Peck, *Loeb Classical Library*, London: Heinemann, 1963.

Aristotle, *History of Animals*, translation by A.L. Peck, *Loeb Classical Library*, 3 vols, London: Heinemann, 1965–70.

Aristotle, *Parts of Animals*, translation by E.S. Forster, *Loeb Classical Library*, London: Heinemann, 1961.

Aristotle, *Physiognomics*, in *Minor Works*, translation by W.S. Hett, *Loeb Classical Library*, London: Heinemann, 1963.

Aristotle, *Politics*, translation by H. Rackham, *Loeb Classical Library*, London: Heinemann, 1967.

Arnobii adversus nationes, Libri 7, rescension and commentary by A. Reifferscheid, *Corpus Scriptorum Ecclesiasticorum Latinorum*, Vindobonae: C. Geroldi filium bibliopolam academiae, 1875.

Arnobius of Sicca, *The Case Against the Pagans*, translation and annotations by G.E. McCracken, 2 vols, Westminster, Maryland/London: Newman Press/Longmans, Green and Co., 1949.

Artemidorus, *The Interpretation of Dreams*, translation and commentary by R.J. White, Park Ridge, New Jersey: Noyes Press, 1992.

Athanase d'Alexandre, *Vie d'Antoine*, introduction, critical text, translation, notes and index by G.J.M. Bartelink, *Sources Chrétiennes*, 400, Paris: Éditions du cerf, 1994.

Athanasios av Alexandria, *Antonios liv*, translation and introduction by T. Hägg and S. Rubenson, Skellefteå: Artos, 1991.

Athenaeus, *Scholars at Dinner. The Deipnosophists*, translation by C.B. Gulick, *Loeb Classical Library*, 7 vols, Cambridge, Mass.: Harvard University Press, 1927.

Athenagoras, *A Plea for the Christians*, translation by B.P. Pratten, in A. Roberts and J. Donaldson (eds), *The Ante-Nicene Fathers*, 2 vols, Edinburgh: T&T Clark, 1994, 129–48.

Athenagoras, *The Resurrection of the Dead*, translation by B.P. Pratten, in A. Roberts and J. Donaldson (eds), *The Ante-Nicene Fathers*, 2 vols, Edinburgh: T&T Clark, 1994, 149–62.

Augustine, *The City of God against the Pagans*, translation by R.W. Dyson, Cambridge: Cambridge University Press, 1998.

Augustine, *Confessiones, Bekenntnisse*, lateinisch und deutsch, J. Bernhart (ed.), Munich: Kössel, 1955.

Augustine, *Writings against the Manichaeans and the Donatists*, translation by H. Newan and R. Stothert, in A. Roberts and J. Donaldson (eds), *The Nicene and Post-Nicene Fathers*, first series, Edinburgh: T&T Clark, 1989.

Cassiodorus, *The Variae of Magnus Aurelius Cassiodorus Senator*, translated with notes and introduction by S.J.B. Barnish, Liverpool: Liverpool University Press, 1992.

Cato, *On Agriculture*, translation by W.D. Hooper, *Loeb Classical Library*, London:Heinemann, 1967.

Cicero, *On Moral Ends*, translation by R. Woolf, Julia Annas (ed.), Cambridge: Cambridge University Press, 2001.

Cicero, *On Divination*, translation by W.A. Falconer, *Loeb Classical Library*, London: Heinemann, 2001.

Cicero, *Letters to his Friends*, translation by W.G. Williams, *Loeb Classical Library*, 3 vols, London: Heinemann, 1965.

Cicero, *On the Nature of the Gods*, translation by H. Rackham, *Loeb Classical Library*, London: Heinemann, 1967.

Clement of Alexandria, *The Exhortation to the Greeks*, translation by G.W. Butterworth, *Loeb Classical Library*, London: Heinemann, 1982.

Clement of Alexandria, *Paedagogus: Christ the Educator*, translation by Simon P. Wood, *The Fathers of the Church*, vol. 23, Washington: Catholic University of America Press, 1954.

Clement of Alexandria, *Stromateis*, translation by J. Ferguson, in *The Fathers of the Church*, vol. 85, Washington: Catholic University of America Press, 1991.

Columella, *On Agriculture*, translation by H.B. Ash, E.S. Forester and E.H. Heffner, *Loeb Classical Library*, 3 vols, London: Heinemann, 1955.

The Coptic Gnostic Library. A Complete Edition of the Nag Hammadi Codices, 5 vols, Leiden: Brill, 2000.

Corpus Inscriptionum et Monumentorum Religionis Mithriacae, M.J. Vermaseren (ed.), The Hague: Martinus Nijhoff, 1956–60.

Cyrille de Jérusalem, *Catéchèses mystagogiques*, translation by P. Paris, *Sources Chrétiennes*, 126, Paris: Éditions du cerf, 1988.

The Digest of Justinian, T. Mommsen and P. Krueger (eds), translation by A. Watson, vols 1–4, Philadelphia: University of Pennsylvania Press, 1985.

Dio Cassius, *Roman History*, translation by E. Cary, *Loeb Classical Library*, 9 vols, London: Heinemann, 1961.

Diodorus Siculus, *The Library of History*, translation by C.H. Oldfather, *Loeb Classical Library*, 12 vols, London: Heinemann, 1960–67.

Dionysius of Halicarnassus, *The Roman Antiquities*, translation by E. Cary, *Loeb Classical Library*, 7 vols, London: Heinemann, 1937.

Epictetus, *The Discourses as reported by Arrian, the Manual, and Fragments*, translation by W.A. Oldfather, *Loeb Classical Library*, 2 vols, London: Heinemann, 1925.

The Epidaurian Miracle Inscriptions, text, translation and commentary by L.R. LiDonnici, Atlanta: Scholars Press, 1995.

Epiphanius, *The Panarion of Epiphanius of Salamis*, translation by F. Williams, Nag Hammadi Studies 35, Leiden: Brill, 1987–94.

Euripides, *Bacchae*, translation by R. Seaford, Warminster: Aris & Phillips, 1996.

Eusèbe de Césarée, *La Préparation Évangélique*, livre 1, *Sources Chrétiennes*, 206. Paris: Éditions du cerf, 1974

Eusebius, *The Ecclesiastical History*, translation by K. Lake and J.E.L. Oulton, *Loeb Classical Library*, 2 vols, London: Heinemann, 1964–65.

Evagrius of Pontus, *The Greek Ascetic Corpus*, translation, introduction and commentary by R.E. Sinkewicz, Oxford: Oxford University Press, 2003.

Galen, *On the Usefulness of the Parts of the Body*, translation from the Greek with an introduction and commentary by Margaret Tallmadge May, 2 vols, Ithaca, New York: Cornell University Press, 1968.

Gregory of Nazianzus, *Poemata Arcana*, edited with a textual introduction by C. Moreschini, introduction, translation and commentary by D.A. Sykes, English translation of textual introduction by L. Holford-Strevens, Oxford: Clarendon Press, 1997.

Herodotus, *The Histories*, translation by A.D. Godley, *Loeb Classical Library*, 4 vols, London: Heinemann, 1966.

Hesiod, *Works and Days*, translation by H.G.E. White, *Loeb Classical Library*, London: Heinemann, 1963.

Hippolytus, *Refutation of all Heresies. Refutatio omnium haeresium*, M. Markovich (ed.) *Patristische Texte und Studien*, Berlin: de Gruyter, 1986.

Hippocrates, *The Hippocratic Collection*, translation by E.T. Withingston and W.H.S. Jones, *Loeb Classical Library*, 8 vols, Cambridge. Mass.: Harvard University Press, 1923–25.

Iamblichos, *(On the Egyptian Mysteries) Theurgia or the Egyptian Mysteries*, translated from the Greek by A. Wilder, William Rider & Son, 1911.

Iamblichus, *On the Pythagorean Way of Life*, text, translation and notes by J. Dillon and J. Hershbell, Atlanta: Scholars Press, 1991.

Iamblichus, *The Exhortation to Philosophy. Including the Letters of Iamblichus and Proclus' Commentary on the Chaldean Oracles*, translated from the Greek by T.M. Johnson, with a foreword by J. Godwin, S. Neuville (ed.), USA: Phanes Press, 1988.

Ignace D'Antioche, *Lettres*, Greek text, introduction, translation and notes by P.T. Camelot, O.P., *Sources Chrétiennes*, 10, Paris: Éditions du cerf, 1945.

Irenaeus, *Against the Heresies*, book 1, translation by D.J. Unger, in W.J. Birghardt, T.C. Lawler and J.J. Dillon (eds), *Ancient Christian Writers*, New York: Paulist Press, 1992.

Jerome, *Letters and Select Works,* translation by W.H. Fremantle, *A Select Library of Nicene and Post-Nicene Fathers*, second series, vol. 6, Edinburgh: T&T Clark, 1989.

Josephus, *Against Apion,* translation by H.St.J. Thackeray, *Loeb Classical Library*, London: Heinemann, 1966.

Julian, *Hymn to the Mother of the Gods*, oration V, in *The Works of the Emperor Julian*, translation by W.C. Wright, *Loeb Classical Library*, London: Heinemann, vol. I, 1962.

Justin, *Dialogue with Tryphon*, revised by A.C. Coxe, in A. Roberts and J. Donaldson (eds), *The Ante-Nicene Fathers*, vol. 1, Edinburgh: T&T Clark, 1993.

Justin, *Apology*, revised by A.C. Coxe, in A. Roberts and J. Donaldson (eds), *The Ante-Nicene Fathers*, vol. 1, Edinburgh: T&T Clark, 1993.

Juvenal, *The Satires*, translation by G.G. Ramsey, *Loeb Classical Library*, London: Heinemann, 1965.

The Kephalaia of the Teacher, I. Gardner (ed), *The edited Coptic Manichaean texts in translation with commentary*, Leiden: Brill, 1995.

Lactantius, *The Divine Institutes*, translation by William Fletcher, in A. Roberts and J. Donaldson (eds), *The Ante-Nicene Fathers*, vol. 7, Edinburgh: T&T Clark, 1994.

Lactantius, *The Death of Persecutors*, translation by William Fletcher, in A. Roberts and J. Donaldson (eds), *The Ante-Nicene Fathers*, vol. 7, Edinburgh: T&T Clark, 1994.

Lactantius, *On the Workmanship of God*, translation by William Fletcher, in A. Roberts and J. Donaldson (eds), *The Ante-Nicene Fathers*, vol. 7, Edinburgh: T&T Clark, 1994.

Lactantius, *A Treatise on the Anger of God*, translation by William Fletcher, in A. Roberts and J. Donaldson (eds), *The Ante-Nicene Fathers*, vol. 7, Edinburgh: T&T Clark, 1994.

Libanius, *For the Temples*, in *Selected Works*, translation by A.F. Norman, *Loeb Classical Library*, 2 vols, Cambridge, Mass.: Harvard University Press, 1969–77.

Livy, *From the Founding of the City*, translation by B.O. Forster *et al.*, *Loeb Classical Library*, 14 vols, London: Heinemann, 1950–67.

Lucian, *Complete Works*, translation by A.M. Harmon, K. Kilburn and M.D. MacLeod, *Loeb Classical Library*, 8 vols, London: Heinemann, 1913–67.

Lucretius, *(On the Nature of Things) De Rerum Natura*, translation by W.H.D. Rouse, *Loeb Classical Library*, London: Heinemann, 1982.

Lukian von Samosata, *Alexandros oder der Lügenprophet*, Eingeleitet, herausgeben, übersetzt und erklärt von Ulrich Victor, Leiden: Brill, 1997.

Macarius Magnes, *Apocriticus*, translation by T.W. Crafer, *The Apocriticus of Macarius Magnes*, New York/London, 1919.

Martial, *On the Spectacles*, in *Epigrams*, translation by W.C.A. Ker, *Loeb Classical Library*, 2 vols, London: Heinemann, 1961.

Minucius Felix, *Octavius*, translation by G.H. Rendall, *Loeb Classical Library*, London: Heinemann, 1984.

Nemesius, *On the Nature of Man,* in Telfer 1955.

New Testament Apocrypha, I–II, E. Hennecke and W. Schneemelcher (eds), London: SCM Press, 1973–75.

Odes of Solomon, edited with translation and notes by J.H. Charlesworth, Oxford: Clarendon Press, 1973.

Oppian, *Halieutica*, translation by A.W. Mair, *Loeb Classical Library*, London: Heinemann, 1963.

Oppian, *The Chase*, translation by A.W. Mair, *Loeb Classical Library*, London: Heinemann, 1963.

Origen, *(Against Celsus) Contra Celsum*, translation with an introduction and notes by Henry Chadwick, Cambridge: Cambridge University Press, 1980.

Origen, *(First Principles) De principiis*, revised by A.C. Coxe, in A. Roberts and J. Donaldson (eds), *The Ante-Nicene Fathers*, vol. 4, Edinburgh: T&T Clark, 1994.

Origen, *Prayer. Exhortation to Martyrdom*, translated and annotated by J.J. O'Meara, Westminster, Maryland/London: Newman Press/Longmans, Green and Co., 1954.

Origène, *Contre Celse:* introduction, critical text, translation and notes by M. Borret, *Sources Chrétiennes*, 132, 136, 147, 150, 227, Paris: Éditions du cerf, 1967–76.

Ovid, *Fasti*, translation by J.G. Frazer, *Loeb Classical Library*, London: Heinemann, 1967.

Ovid, *Halieuticon*, in *The Art of Love and Other Poems*, translation by J.H. Mozley, *Loeb Classical Library*, London: Heinemann, 1962.

Ovid, *Metamorphoses*, translation by A.D. Melville, introduction and notes by E.J. Kenney, Oxford: Oxford University Press, 1986.

Palladius, *The Lausiac History*, a critical discussion with notes on early Egyptian monachism, C. Butler (ed.), Cambridge: Cambridge University Press, 1904.

Passion de Perpétue et de Félicité, suivi des Actes, introduction, critical text, translation, commentary and index by Jacqueline Amat, *Sources Chrétiennes*, 417, Paris: Éditions du cerf, 1996.

Pausanias, *Description of Greece*, translation by W.H.S. Jones, *Loeb Classical Library*, 5 vols, London: Heinemann, 1965–66.

Philo, *The Decalogue*, in *The Works of Philo*, translation by C.D. Yonge, USA: Hendrickson Publishers, 2002, 518–33.

Philo, *On the Contemplative Life*, in *The Works of Philo*, translation by C.D. Yonge, USA: Hendrickson Publishers, 2002, 698–706.

Philo, *On the Posteriority of Cain and His Exile*, in *The Works of Philo*, translation by C.D. Yonge, USA: Hendrickson Publishers, 2002, 132–51.

Philo, *On the Virtues*, in *The Works of Philo*, translation by C.D. Yonge, USA: Hendrickson Publishers, 2002, 640–63.

Philo, *Philonis Alexandrini De Animalibus*, the Armenian text with an introduction, translation and commentary by Abraham Terian, California: Scholars Press, 1981.

Philo, *The Special Laws*, in *The Works of Philo*, translation by C.D. Yonge, USA: Hendrickson Publishers, 2002, 534–639.

Philostratus, *The Life of Apollonius of Tyana*, translation by F.C. Conybeare, *Loeb Classical Library*, 2 vols, London: Heinemann, 1989–2000.

Plato, *Phaedo*, translation by H.N. Fowler, *Loeb Classical Library*, London: Heinemann, 1966.

Plato, *Phaedrus*, translation by H.N. Fowler, *Loeb Classical Library*, London: Heinemann, 1966.

Plato, *Republic*, translation by P. Shorey, *Loeb Classical Library*, 2 vols, London: Heinemann, 1963.

Plato, *The Statesman*, translation by W.R.M. Lamb, *Loeb Classical Library*, London: Heinemann, 1962.

Plato, *Timaeus*, translation by R.G. Bury, *Loeb Classical Library*, London: Heinemann, 1966.

Pliny, *Natural History,* translation by H. Rackham, *Loeb Classical Library*, 10 vols, London: Heinemann, 1962–67.

Plutarch, *Greek Questions*, translation by F.C. Babbitt, *Loeb Classical Library*, London: Heinemann, 1965.

Plutarch, *(Gryllus) Beasts are Rational*, translation by H. Cherniss and W.C. Helmbold, *Loeb Classical Library*, London: Heinemann, 1968.

Plutarch, *The Life of Marcus Cato*, in *Plutarch's Lives*, translation by B. Perrin, *Loeb Classical Library*, London: Heinemann, 1959.

Plutarch, *(On Isis and Osiris) De Iside et Osiride*, edited with an introduction, translation and commentary by J.G. Griffiths, Cambridge: University of Wales Press, 1970.

Plutarch, *On the Cleverness of Animals*, translation by H. Cherniss and W.C. Helmbold, *Loeb Classical Library*, London: Heinemann, 1968.

Plutarch, *On the Eating of Flesh*, translation by H. Cherniss and W.C. Helmbold, *Loeb Classical Library*, London: Heinemann, 1968.

Plutarch, *On the Fortune of the Romans*, translation by F.C. Babbitt, *Loeb Classical Library*, London: Heinemann, 1965.

Plutarch, *Roman Questions*, translation by F.C. Babbitt, *Loeb Classical Library*, London: Heinemann, 1965.

Plutarch, *Table Talk*, translation by P.A. Clement, *Loeb Classical Library*, London: Heinemann, 1969.

Plutarque, *Oeuvres morales. Isis et Osiris*, texte établie et traduit par C. Froidefond, Paris: Société d'Edition "Les Belles Lettres", 1988.

Polybius, *The Histories*, translation by W.R. Paton, *Loeb Classical Library*, 6 vols, London: Heinemann, 1967–69.

Porphyre, *De l'abstinence*, translation by J. Bouffartigue, M. Patillon, A.P. Segonds and L. Brison, *Budí series*, 3 vols, Paris: Société d'Edition "Les Belles Lettres", 1977–95.

Porphyry, *On Abstinence from Killing Animals*, translation by Gillian Clark, London: Duckworth, 2000.

Porphyry, *On the Cave of the Nymphs in the Odyssey,* A revised text with translations by Seminary Classics 609, *Arethusa monographs*, 1, New York: State University of New York at Buffalo, 1969.

Proclus, *On the Existence of Evils*, translation by J. Opsomer and C. Steel, London: Duckworth, 2003.

Prudentius, *Crowns of Martyrdom*, translation by H.J. Thomson, *Loeb Classical Library*, vol. 2, London: Heinemann, 1962, 98–345.

Prudentius, *A Reply to Address of Symmachus*, translation by H.J. Thomson, *Loeb Classical Library*, 2 vols, London: Heinemann, 1961–62, vol. 1, 344–401; vol. 2, 3–97.

Sallustius, *Concerning the Gods and the Universe,* edited and translated by A.D. Nock, Cambridge: Cambridge University Press, 1926.

Scriptores physiognomici graeci et latini, R. Foerster (ed.), Lipsiae: Teubner, 1843.

Seneca, *(Consolation) De consolatione ad Helviam*, in *Moral Essays*, translation by J.W. Basore, *Loeb Classical Library*, London: Heinemann, 1965.

Seneca, *The Epistles of Seneca*, translation by R.M. Gummere, *Loeb Classical Library*, 3 vols, London: Heinemann, 1962–67.

Seneca, *(On Anger) De ira*, in *Moral Essays*, translation by J.W. Basore, *Loeb Classical Library*, 3 vols, London: Heinemann, 1965.

Seneca, *(On the Happy Life) De vita beata*, in *Moral Essays*, translation by J.W. Basore, *Loeb Classical Library*, 3 vols, London: Heinemann, 1965.

Sextus Empiricus, *Against the Phyicists*, trans. R.G. Bury, *Loeb Classical Library*, 4 vols, London: Heinemann, 1933–49.

Suetonius, *The Lives of the Caesars*, translation by J.C. Rolfe, *Loeb Classical Library*, 2 vols, London: Heinemann, 1959.

Suetonius, *Caligula*, edited with introduction and commentary by Hugh Lindsay, Bristol: Bristol Classical Press, 1993.

Tacitus, *The Annals*, translation by C.H. Moore and J. Jackson, *Loeb Classical Library*, 4 vols, London: Heinemann, 1962.

Tatian. *Oratio ad Graecos and fragments*, edited and translated by M. Whittaker, Oxford: Clarendon Press, 1982.

Tertullian, *Ad nationes*, translation by D. Holmes, in A. Roberts and J. Donaldson (eds), *The Ante-Nicene Fathers*, vol. 3, Edinburgh: T&T Clark, 1993.

Tertullian, *Apologeticus*, translation by T.R. Glover, *Loeb Classical Library*, London: Heinemann, 1984.

Tertullian, *A Treatise on the Soul*, translation by P. Holmes, in A. Roberts and J. Donaldson (eds), *The Ante-Nicene Fathers*, vol. 3, Edinburgh: T&T Clark, 1993.

Tertullian, *De spectaculis*, translation by T.R. Glover, *Loeb Classical Library*, London: Heinemann, 1984.

Tertullian, *On Baptism*, translation by S. Thelwall, in A. Roberts and J. Donaldson (eds), *The Ante-Nicene Fathers*, vol. 3, Edinburgh: T&T Clark, 1993.

Tertullian, *On the Resurrection of the Flesh*, translation by D. Holmes, in A. Roberts and J.Donaldson (eds), *The Ante-Nicene Fathers*, vol. 3, Edinburgh: T&T Clark, 1993.

Tertullian, *Scorpiace*, translation by S. Thelwall, in A. Roberts and J. Donaldson (eds), *The Ante-Nicene Fathers*, vol. 3, Edinburgh: T&T Clark, 1993.

Tertullian. *To the Martyrs*, translation by S. Thelwall, in A. Roberts and J. Donaldson (eds), *The Ante-Nicene Fathers*, vol. 3, Edinburgh: T&T Clark, 1993.

Varro, *On Agriculture*, translation by W.D. Hooper, *Loeb Classical Library*, London: Heinemann, 1967.

Virgil, *Georgics*, translation by H.R. Fairclough, *Loeb Classical Library*, 2 vols, London: Heinemann, 1999.

Books and articles

Adamik, T. (1996) "The baptized lion in the Acts of Paul", in J. Bremmer (ed.), *The Apocryphal Acts of Paul and Thecla*, Netherlands: Pharos, 60–74.

Amsler, F. (1999) *Acta Philippi, Commentarius, Corpus Christianorum, Series Apocryphorum*, 12, Turnhout: Brepols.

Anderson, G. (1994) *Sage, Saint and Sophist*, London and New York: Routledge.

Andrews, A.C. (1957) "Classified zoological index", in Plutarch, *Moralia*, vol. 12, *Loeb Classical Library*, London: Heinemann, 482–6.

Auguet, R. (1994) *Cruelty and Civilization*, London and New York: Routledge.

Aune, D.E. (1997–98) *Revelation. World Biblical Commentary* 52–54, 3 vols, Nashville: Thomas Nelson Publishers.

Bagnall, R. (1996) *Egypt in Late Antiquity*, Princeton, NJ: Princeton University Press.

Baker, S. (2001) *Picturing the Beast. Animals, Identity and Representation*, Urbana and Chicago: University of Illinois Press.

Balling, J., U.M. Bidstrup and T. Bromming (1997) *De unge skal se syner. Perpetuamartyriet oversat og kommentert*, Aarhus: Aarhus Universitets Forlag.

Balsdon, J.P.V.D. (1969) *Life and Leisure in Ancient Rome*, London: Bodley Head.

Barasch, M. (1985–86) "Animal metaphors of the messianic age", *Visible Religion* 4–5, Leiden: Brill, 235–49.

Barc, B. (1980) *L'Hypostase des Archontes. Traité gnostique sur l'origine de l'homme du monde et des arhontes. Bibliothèque Copte de Nag Hammadi*, Section "Textes", 5. Québec: Les Presses de l'Université Laval.

Barclay, J.M.G. (1996) *Jews in the Mediterranean Diaspora. From Alexander to Trajan (323 BCE–117 CE)*, Edinburgh: T&T Clark.

Barkan, L. (1986) *The Gods Made Flesh. Metamorphosis & the Pursuit of Paganism*, New Haven, Conn., and London: Yale Univerity Press.

Bar-Kochva, B. (1996): "An ass in the Jerusalem temple – the origins and development of the slander", in L.H. Feldman and J.R. Levison (eds), *Josephus' contra Apionem*, Leiden: Brill, 310–26.

Barnes, T.D. (1994) "Scholarship or propaganda? Porphyry *Against the Christians* and its historical setting", *Bulletin Institute of Classical Studies* 39, 53–65.

——(1998) *Ammianus Marcellinus and the Representation of Historical Reality*, Ithaca, NY, and London: Cornell University Press.

Bartley, A.N. (2003) *Stories from the Mountains, Stories from the Sea. The Digressions and Similes of Oppian's Halieutica and Cynegetica*, Göttingen: Vandenhoeck & Ruprecht.

Barton, C.A. (1996) *The Sorrows of the Ancient Romans: The Gladiator and the Monster*, Princeton, NJ: Princeton University Press.

——(2001) *Roman Honor: The Fire in the Bones*, Berkeley and Los Angeles: University of California Press.

Barton, T.S. (1994) *Power and Knowledge. Astrology, Physiognomics, and Medicine under the Roman Empire*, Ann Arbor: University of Michigan Press.

Bauckham, R. (1993) *The Climax of Prophecy. Studies on the Book of Revelation*, Edinburgh: T&T Clark.

——(1994) "Jesus and the wild animals (Mark 1:13): a Christological image for an ecological age", in J.B. Green and M. Turner (eds), *Jesus of Nazareth: Lord and Christ*, Grand Rapids, Mich.: Eerdmans, 3–21.

Bauckham, R. (1998) "Jesus and animals I: what did he teach?" in A. Linzey and D. Yamamoto (eds), *Animals on the Agenda*, London: SCM Press, 33–48.

Beard, M. (2003) "A complex of times: no more sheep on Romulus' birthday", in C. Ando (ed.), *Roman Religion*, Edinburgh: Edinburgh University Press, 273–88.

Beard, M., J. North and S. Price (1998) *Religions of Rome*, 2 vols, Cambridge: Cambridge University Press.

Belayche, N. (2002) "Sacrifice and theory of sacrifice during the 'pagan reaction': Julian the emperor", in A.I. Baumgarten (ed.), *Sacrifice in Religious Experience*, Leiden: Brill, 101–27.

Bernstein, F. (1998) *Ludi publici. Untersuchungen zur Entstehung und Entwicklung der öffentlichen Spiele im Republikanischen Rom*, Stuttgart: Franz Steiner Verlag.

Berthelot, K. (2002) "Philo and kindness towards animals", *The Studia Philonica Annual* 14, 48–65.

Betz, H.D. (ed.) (1996) *The Greek Magical Papyri in Translation*, Chicago and London: University of Chicago Press.

Bickermann, E. (1927) "Ritualmord und Eselkult", *Monatsschrift für Geschichte und Wissenschaft des Judentums* 74, 255–64.

Bieler, L. (1935–36) *Theios Aner. Das Bild des "göttlichen Menschen" in Spätantike und Frühchristentum* (2 vols), Vienna: Oskar Höfels.

Birley, A.R. (2000) "Die 'freiwilligen' Märtyrer. Zum Problem der Selbst-Auslieferer", in R. von Haehling (ed.), *Rom und das himmlische Jerusalem. Die frühen Christen zwischen Anpassung und Ablehnung*, Darmstadt: Wissenschaftliche Buchgesellschaft, 97–123.

Bjørnebye, J. (2005) "*Pater patrum et pater familia*s: Mithraskult og makt i det kristne Roma", *Chaos* 43, 31–46.

Bloch, M. (1992) *Prey into Hunter: The Politics of Religious Experience*, Cambridge: Cambridge University Press.

den Boeft, J. and J. Bremmer (1982) "Notiunculae martyrologicae II", *Vigilia Christianae* 36, 383–402.

——(1995) "Notiunculae martyrologicae V", *Vigilia Christianae*, 49, 146–64.

Boll, F. (1914) *Aus der Offenbarung Johannis*, Leipzig and Berlin: B.G. Teubner.

Bomgardner, D.L. (2000) *The Story of the Roman Amphitheatre*, London and New York: Routledge.

Borgen, P. (1995) "Man's sovereignty over animals and nature", in T. Fornberg and D. Hellholm (eds), assisted by C.D. Hellholm, *Texts and Contexts: Biblical Texts in Their Textual and Situational Contexts*, Oslo: Scandinavian University Press, 369–89.

Borowski, O. (1998) *Every Living Thing: Daily Use of Animals in Ancient Israel*, Walnut Creek, Calif., London and New Dehli: Altamira Press.

Bouffortigue, J. and M. Patillon (1977) "Introduction", in Porphyre, *De l'abstinence*, vol. I, xi–lxxxv.

Bovon, F. (2002) "Facing the scriptures: mimesis and intertextuality in the *Acts of Philip*", in C.A. Bobertz and D. Brakke (eds), *Reading in Christian Communities*, Paris: Notre Dame.

Bovon, F., A.G. Brock and C.R. Matthews (eds) (1999) *The Apocryphal Acts of the Apostles*, Cambridge, Mass.: Harvard University Press.

Bowersock, G.W. (1978) *Julian the Apostate*, London and Cambridge, Mass.: Harvard University Press.

——(1995) *Martyrdom and Rome*, Cambridge: Cambridge University Press.

——(1996) *Hellenism in Late Antiquity*, Ann Arbor: University of Michigan Press.

Bowman, A.K. (1986) *Egypt after the Pharaohs 332BC–AD 642*, Berkeley and Los Angeles: University of California Press.

Boyarin, D. (1995) *Carnal Israel. Reading Sex in Talmudic Culture*, Berkeley, Los Angeles and London: University of California Press.

——(1999) *Dying for God: Martyrdom and the Making of Christianity and Judaism*, Stanford, Calif.: Stanford University Press.

Bradbury, S. (1995) "Julian's pagan revival and the decline of blood sacrifice", *Phoenix* 49, 331–56.

Bradley, K. (2000) "Animalizing the slave: the truth of fiction", *Journal of Roman Studies* 40, 110–25.

Brakke, D. (1995) *Athanasius and Asceticism*, Baltimore and London: Johns Hopkins University Press.

Brashler, J. (2000) "Plato, Republic 588b–589b VI, 5:48,16–51,23", in *The Coptic Gnostic Library*, vol. 3, Leiden: Brill, 325–6.

Bremmer, J.N. (2002) "Perpetua and her diary: authenticity, family and visions", in W. Ameling (ed.), *Märtyrer und Märtyrakten*, Stuttgart: Franz Steiner Verlag, 77–120.

Brenk, F.E. (1986) "In the light of the moon: demonology in the early imperial period." *ANRW* 16.3, Berlin and New York: Walter de Gruyter, 2068–145.

Brown, P. (1978) *The Making of Late Antiquity*, Cambridge, Mass.: Harvard University Press.

——(1988) *The Body and Society. Men, Women, and Sexual Renunciation in Early Christianity*, New York: Columbia University Press.

——(1995) *Authority and the Sacred: Aspects of the Christianization of the Roman World*, Cambridge. Mass.: Harvard University Press.

Brown, S. (1992) "Death as decoration: scenes from the arena on Roman domestic mosaics", in A. Richlin (ed.), *Pornography and Representation in Greece and Rome*, Oxford: Oxford University Press, 180–211.

Brunner-Traut, E. (1986) "'Tier' und 'Tierdarstellung'", *Lexicon der Ägyptologie*, Band VI, Wiesbaden: Otto Harrassowitz, 557–71.

Budiansky, S. (1992) *The Covenant of the Wild. Why Animals Chose Domestication*, New York: William Morrow.

Burkert, W. (1972) *Homo Necans: Interpretationen altgriechischer Opferriten und Mythen*, Berlin: Walter de Gruyter.

——(1985) *Greek Religion*, Oxford: Basil Blackwell.

Burrus, V. (1995) "Reading Agnes: the rhetoric of gender in Ambrose and Prudentius", *Journal of Early Christian Studies* 3.1, 25–46.

——(2000) *"Begotten not Made". Conceiving Manhood in Late Antiquity*, Stanford, Calif.: Stanford University Press.

Buschmann, G. (1994) *Martyrium Polycarpi – eine Formkritische Studie*, Berlin and New York: Walter de Gruyter.

——(1995) "Martyrium Polycarpi 4 und der Montanismus", *Vigiliae Christianae* 49, 105–45.

——(1998) *Das Martyrium des Polykarp*, Göttingen: Vandenhoeck & Ruprecht.

Bynum, C.W. (1995) *The Resurrection of the Body in Western Christianity, 200–1336*, New York: Columbia University Press.

——(2001) *Metamorphosis and Identity*, New York: Zone Books.

Cameron, A. (1994) *Christianity and the Rhetoric of Empire. The Development of Christian Discourse*, Berkeley, Los Angeles and London: University of California Press.

Cancik, H. (1999) "The reception of Greek cults in Rome. A precondition of the emergence of an 'imperial religion'", *Archiv für Religionsgeschichte* 1, 2, 161–73.

Carson, A. (2002) "Dirt and desire: the phenomenology of female pollution in antiquity", in J.I. Porter (ed.), *Constructions of the Classical Body*, Ann Arbor: University of Michigan Press, 77–100.

Casson, L. (2001) *Libraries in the Ancient World*, New Haven, Conn., and London: Yale University Press.

Caubet, A. (2002) "Animals in Syro-Palestinian art", in B.J. Collins (ed.), *A History of the Animal World in the Ancient Near East*, Leiden: Brill, 211–34.

Chuvin, P. (1990) *A Chronicle of the Last Pagans*, Cambridge, Mass., and London: Harvard University Press.

Clark, E.A. (1999) *Reading Renunciation: Ascetcism and Scripture in Early Christianity*, Princeton, NJ: Princeton University Press.

Clauss, M. (2000) *The Roman Cult of Mithras. The God and his Mysteries*, Edinburgh: Edinburgh University Press.

Cole, T. (1967) *Democritus and the Sources of Greek Anthropology*, Cleveland: Western Reserve University Press.

Coleman, K.M. (1990) "Fatal charades: Roman executions staged as mythological enactments", *Journal of Roman Studies* 80, 44–73.

Cook, J.G. (2000) *The Interpretation of the New Testament in Greco-Roman Paganism*, Tübingen: Mohr Siebeck.

Cooper, K. (2003) "The voice of the victim. Martyrdom and the subversion of Roman power in late antiquity," lecture at the Theological Faculty, University of Oslo, 25 April.

Corbier, M. (1989) "The ambiguous status of meat in ancient Rome", *Food and Foodways* 3.3, 223–64.

Cox, P. (1983) *Biography in Late Antiquity. A Quest for the Holy Man*, Berkeley and Los Angeles: Univeristy of California Press.

Coyle, J.K. (2001) "What did Augustine know about Manichaeism when he wrote his two treatises *de moribus?*" in J. van Oort, O. Wermelinger and G. Wurst (eds), *Augustine and Manichaeism in the Latin West*, Leiden: Brill, 43–56.

Crouzel, H. (1956) *Théologie de l'Image de Dieu chez Origène*, Paris: Aubier.

Dagron, G. (1987) "Image de bête ou image de dieu", in *Poikilia, Études offertes à Jean-Pierre Vernant*, Paris: EHESS, 69–80.

Davidson, H.E. (1998) *Roles of the Northern Goddess*, London and New York: Routledge.

Dawson, D. (1992) *Allegorical Readers and Cultural Revision in Ancient Alexandria*, Berkeley: University of California Press.

Detienne, M. (1989) "Culinary practices and the spirit of sacrifice", in M. Detienne and J.-P. Vernant (eds), *The Cuisine of Sacrifice among the Greeks*, Chicago and London: University of Chicago Press, 1–20.

Detienne, M. and J.-P. Vernant (eds) (1989) *The Cuisine of Sacrifice among the Greeks*, Chicago and London: University of Chicago Press.

Dickie, M.W. (2001) "Exclusions from the catechumenate: continuity or discontinuity with pagan cult", *Numen* 48.4, 417–93.

Dierauer, U. (1977) *Tier und Mensch im Denken der Antike. Studien zur Tierpsychologie, Anthropologie und Ethik*, Amsterdam: B.R. Grüner B.V.

——(1997) "Raison ou instinct? Le développement de la zoopsychologie antique", in B. Cassin and J.-L. Labarrière (eds), *L'animal dans l'antiquité*, Paris; Librarire Philosophique J. Vrin, 3–30.

Digeser, E.D. (2000) *The Making of a Christian Empire*, Ithaca, NY, and London: Cornell University Press.

——(2002) "Porphyry, Julian, or Hierokles? The anonymous Hellene in Makarios Magnes' *Apokritikos*," *Journal of Theological Studies* 53, 466–502.

Dillon, J. (1977) *The Middle Platonists*, London: Duckworth.

Dinzelbacher, P. (2000) "Mittelalter", in P. Dinzelbacher (ed.), *Mensch und Tier in der Geschichte Europas*, Stuttgart: Kröner, 181–292.

Dinzelbacher, P. (ed.) (2000) *Mensch und Tier in der Geschichte Europas*, Stuttgart: Kröner.

Dölger, F.J. (1930) "Tertullian über die Bluttaufe. Tertullian *De baptismo* 16", in *Antike und Christentum. Kultur- und Religionsgeschichtliche Studien*, Band II, Münster in Westfalen: Aschendorffsche Verlagsbuchhandlung, 115–41.

——(1932) "Der Kampf mit dem Ägypter in der Perpetua-Vision", in *Antike und Christentum. Kultur- und Religionsgeschichtlichen Studien*, Band III, Münster in Westfalen: Aschendorffsche Verlagsbuchhandlung, 177–88.

Dombrowski, D.A. (1984) *The Philosophy of Vegetarianism*, Amherst: University of Massachusetts Press.

——(1987) "Porphyry and vegetarianism: a contemporary philosophical approach", in W. Haase (ed.), *ANRW* 36.2, Berlin and New York: Walter de Gruyter, 774–91.

Douglas, M. (1990) "The pangolin revisited: a new approach to animal symbolism", in R. Willis (ed.), *Signifying Animals: Human Meaning in the Natural World*, London and New York: Routledge, 25–36.

——(2001) "The flesh is weak", *Times Literary Supplement*.

Drake, H.A. (2000) *Constantine and the Bishops. The Politics of Intolerance*, Baltimore: Johns Hopkins University Press.

Drijvers, H.J.W. (1990) "Der getaufte Löwe" in P. Nagel (ed), *Carl-Schmidt-Kolloquium an der Martin-Luther-Universität 1988*, 181–9.

Drijvers, J.W. and D. Hunt (eds.) (1998) *The Late Roman World and its Historian. Interpreting Ammianus Marcellinus*, London and New York: Routledge.

Duff, P.B. (2001) *Who Rides the Beast*, Oxford: Oxford University Press.

Düll, R. (1941) "Archaische Sachprozesse und Losverfarhren", in *Saivigny-Stiftung für Rechtsgeschichte* 61, 1–18.

Dummer, J. (1973) "Ein naturwissenschaftliches Handbuch als Quelle für Epiphanius von Constantia", *Klio* 55, 289–99.

Dunbabin, K.M.D. (1999) *Mosaics of the Greek and Roman World*, Cambridge: Cambridge University Press.

Durand, J.-L. (1989) "Greek animals: towards a topology of edible bodies", in M. Detienne and J.-P. Vernant (eds), *The Cuisine of Sacrifice among the Greeks*, Chicago and London: University of Chicago Press, 87–105.

Duthoy, R. (1969) *The Taurobolium: Its Evolution and Terminology*, Leiden: Brill.

Edwards, C. (1996) *Writing Rome. Textual Approaches to the City*, Cambridge: Cambridge University Press.

Edwards, M.J. (2000) "Birth, death, and divinity in Porphyry's *Life of Plotinius*", in T. Hägg and P. Rousseau (eds), *Greek Biography and Panegyric in Late Antiquity*, Berkeley, Los Angeles and London: University of California Press, 52–71.

Elsner, J. (1995) *Art and the Roman Viewer. The Transformation of Art from the Pagan World to Christianity*, Cambridge: Cambridge University Press.

Endsjø, D.Ø. (2002) *The Body in the Periphery. Reading Athanasius' Vita Antonii from the Perspective of a Traditional Greek Worldview*, Oslo: Faculty of Arts, University of Oslo.

——(2003) "To control death: sacrifice and space in classical Greece", *Religion* 33, 323–40.

Engberg-Pedersen, T. (2000) *Paul and the Stoics*, Edinburgh: T&T Clark.

Engels, D. (1999) *Classical Cats. The Rise and Fall of the Sacred Cat*, London and New York: Routledge.

Epplett, C. (2001) "The capture of animals by the Roman military", *Greece and Rome* 48, 2, 210–22.

Evans, B. (1946) *The Natural History of Nonsense*, New York: A.A. Knopf.

Evans, E.C. (1969) *Physiognomics in the Ancient World*, Philadelphia: American Philosophical Society.

Ferguson, E. (1980) "Spiritual sacrifice in early Christianity and its environment", in W. Haase (ed.), *ANRW* 23.2, Berlin and New York: Walter de Gruyter, 1151–89.

Finnestad, R.B. (1984) "Den hellige natur og religionshistorikerens ontologiske paradigmer", *Norsk Teologisk Tidsskrift* 85, 1, 17–37.

Fless, F. (1995) *Opferdiener und Kultmusiker auf stadtrömischen historischen Reliefs*, Mainz: Verlag Philipp van Zabern.

Fowler, B. H. (1989) *The Hellenistic Aesthetic*, Madison: University of Wisconsin Press.

Francis, J.A. (1995) *Subversive Virtue. Asceticism and Authority in the Second-Century Pagan World*, Philadelphia: Pennsylvania State University Press.

Frankfort, H. (1961) *Ancient Egyptian Religion*, New York: Harper & Row.

Frankfurter, D. (1998) *Religion in Roman Egypt: Assimilation and Resistance*, Princeton, NJ: Princeton University Press.

——(2003) "Syncretism and the holy man in late antique Egypt", *Journal of Early Christian Studies* 11.3, 339–85.

Franklin, A. (1999) *Animals and Modern Cultures: A Sociology of Human–Animal Relations in Modernity*, London: Sage.

French, R. (1994) *Ancient Natural History*, London: Routledge.

Frend, W.H.C. (2000) "Martyrdom and political oppression", in P. Esler (ed.), *The Early Christian World*, vol. 2, London and New York: Routledge, 815–39.

Frizell, B.S. (2004) "Curing the flock. The use of healing waters in Roman pastoral economy", in B.S. Frizell (ed.), *PECUS. Man and Animal in Antiquity*, Rome: Swedish Institute in Rome, 84–94.

Froidefond, C. (1988) *Introduction et commentaires á Plutarque. Oeuvres morales*, Paris: Société d'Edition "Les Belles Lettres", 3–177.

Futrell, A. (1997) *Blood in the Arena. The Spectacle of Roman Power*, Austin: University of Texas Press.

Gager, J.G. (ed.) (1992) *Curse Tablets and Binding Spells from the Ancient World*, New York and Oxford: Oxford University Press.

Galinsky, G. K. (1972) *The Herakles Theme*, Oxford: Basil Blackwell.

Garnsey, P. (1999) *Food and Society in Classical Antiquity*, Cambridge: Cambridge University Press.

Gasparro, G.S. (1985) *Soteriology and Mystic Aspects in the Cult of Cybele and Attis*, Leiden: Brill.

——(1998) "Asceticism and anthropology: *encrateia* and 'double creation' in early Christianity", in V.L. Wimbush and R. Valantasis (eds), *Asceticism*, New York: Oxford University Press, 127–46.

Gilhus, I.S. (1983) "Male and female symbolism in the Gnostic *Apocryphon of John*," *Temenos* 19, 33–43.

——(1985) *The Nature of the Archons. A Study in the Soteriology of a Gnostic Treatise from Nag Hammadi (CG II, 4)*, Wiesbaden: Otto Harrassowitz.

——(1997) *Laughing Gods, Weeping Virgins: Laughter in the History of Religion*, London and New York: Routledge.

Girard, R. (1977) *Violence and the Sacred*, Baltimore: Johns Hopkins University Press.

Goehring, J.E. (1993) "The encroaching desert: literary production and ascetic space in early Christian Egypt", *Journal of Early Christian Studies* 1, 281–96.

——(2001) "The provenance of the Nag Hammadi codices once more", *Studia Patristica* 35, Leuven: Peeters, 234–53.

Goldschmidt, V. (1977) *La Doctrine d'épicure et le droit*, Paris: Librairie philosophique J. Vrin.

Gordon, R. (1990) "The veil of power: emperors, sacrificers and benefactors", in M. Beard and J. North (eds), *Pagan Priests*, London: Duckworth, 199–231.

Grant, M. (1996) *The Antonines: The Roman Empire in Transition*, London and New York: Routledge.

Grant, R.M. (1978) "Eusebius and Gnostic origins", in M. Simon (ed.), *Paganisme, Judaisme, Christianisme*, Paris: Éditions E. de Boccard, 195–205.

——(1999) *Early Christians & Animals*, London and New York: Routledge.

Green, M. (1992) *Animals in Celtic Life and Myth*, London: Routledge.

Gundel, H.G. (1992) *Zodiakos. Tierkreisbilder im Altertum*, Mainz am Rhein: Verlag Philip van Zabern.

Habermehl, P. (1992) *Perpetua und der Ägypter*, Berlin: Akademie Verlag.

Hägg. T. (2004) "Apollonios of Tyana – magician, philosopher, counter-Christ. The metamorphoses of a life", in T. Hägg (ed.), *Parthenope. Selected Studies in Ancient Greek Fiction (1969–2004)*, Copenhagen: University of Copenhagen and Museum Tusculanum Press, 379–404.

Hall, S.G. (1993) "Women among the early martyrs", in D. Wood (ed.), *Martyrs and Martyrologies*, Oxford: Basil Blackwell, 1–21.

Hällstöm, G. (1988) *Carnis Resurrectio. The Interpretation of a Credal Formula*, Helsinki: Societas Scientiarum Fennica.

Hammerton-Kelly, R.G. (ed.) (1987) *Violent Origins: Walter Burkert, René Girard and Jonathan Z. Smith on Ritual Killing and Cultural Formation*, Stanford, Calif.: Stanford University Press.

Hanfmann, Georg M.A. (1979) "The crucified donkey man: Achaios and Jesus", in G. Kopcke and M.B. Moore (eds), *Studies in Classical Art and Archaeology*, Locust Valley, NY, J.J Augustine, 205–7.

Hanson, A.E. (1998) "Talking recipes in the gynaecological texts of the Hippocratic corpus", in M. Wyke (ed.), *Parchments of Gender: Deciphering the Body in Antiquity*, Oxford: Clarendon Press, 71–94.

Harris, W.V. (1994) "Child-exposure in the Roman Empire", *Journal of Roman Studies* 84, 1–22.

Haussleiter, J. (1935) *Der Vegetarismus in der Antike*, Berlin: Verlag von Alfred Töpelmann.

Haymann, F. (1921) "Textkritische Studien zum römischen Obligationenrecht", *Savigny-Stiftung für Rechtsgeschichte* 42, 357–93.

Hellemo, G. (1999) *Guds billedbok*, Oslo: Pax.

Hennecke, E. and W. Schneemelcher (eds) (1973–75), *New Testament Apocrypha*, I–II, London: SCM Press.

van Henten, J.W. and R. Abusch (1996) "The depiction of the Jews as Typhonians and Josephus' strategy of refutation in *Contra Apionem*", in L.H. Feldman and J.R. Levison (eds), *Josephus' Contra Apionem*, Leiden: Brill, 271–309.

Hershbell, J.P. (1992) "Plutarch and Stoicism", in W. Haase (ed.), *Aufstieg und Niedergang der Römischer Welt*, 36.5, Berlin and New York: Walter de Gruyter.

Heuser, M. (1998) "The Manichaean myth according to the Coptic sources" in M. Heuser and H.-J. Klimkeit (eds), *Studies in Manichaean Literature and Art*, Leiden: Brill, 3–108.

Hinnells, J. (1975) "Reflections on the bull-slaying scene", in J. Hinnells (ed.), *Mithraic Studies*, 2 vols, Manchester: Manchester University Press, 290–312.

Hoffmann, R.J. (1987) *On the True Doctrine: A Discourse Against the Christians*, translated with a general introduction, New York: Oxford University Press.

Horden, P. and N. Purcell (2000) *The Corrupting Sea. A Study of Mediterranean History*, Oxford: Basil Blackwell.

Hornung, E. (1967): "Die Bedeutung des Tieres im alten Ägypten", *Studium Generale* 20, 69–84.

——(1973) *Der Eine und die Vielen. Ägyptische Gottesvorstellungen*, Darmstadt: Wissenschaftliche Buchgesellschaft.

——(1999) *Akhenaten and the Religion of Light*, Ithaca, NY, and London: Cornell University Press.

van der Horst, P.W. (1998) "Sortes: sacred books as instant oracles in late antiquity", in L.V. Rutgers *et al.* (eds), *The Use of the Sacred Books in the Ancient World*, Leuven: Peeters, 143–73.

Houlihan, P.F. (1996) *The Animal World of the Pharaohs*, London: Thames & Hudson.

——(2002) "Animals in Egyptian art and hieroglyphs", in B.J. Collins (ed.), *A History of the Animal World in the Ancient Near East*, Leiden: Brill, 97–143.

Houston, W. (1998) "What was the meaning of classifying animals as clean or unclean?", in A. Linzey and D. Yamamoto (eds), *Animals on the Agenda*, London: SCM Press, 18–24.

Hughes, J.D. (1996) *Pan's Travail: Environmental Problems of the Ancient Greeks and Romans*, Baltimore and London: Johns Hopkins University Press.

Ingold, T. (ed.) (1988) *What is an Animal?* London: Unwin Hyman.

Isaac B. (2004) *The Invention of Racism in Classical Antiquity*, Princeton and Oxford: Princeton University Press.

Isager, S. (1992) "Sacred animals in classical and Hellenistic Greece", in T. Linders and B. Alroth (eds), *Economics of Cult in the Ancient World*, Boreas, 21, Uppsala: Acta Universitatis Upsaliensis, 15–20.

Jackson, H.M. (1985) *The Lion Becomes Man. The Gnostic Leontomorphic Creator and the Platonic Tradition*, Atlanta: Scholars Press.

Jacobsen, K.A. (1994) "The institutionalization of the ethics of 'non-injury' toward all 'beings' in ancient India", *Environmental Ethics* 16, 287–301.

Jacoby, A. (1927): "Der angebliche Eselkult der Juden und Christen", *Archiv für Religionswissenschaft* 25, 265–82.

Jameson, M.H. (1988) "Sacrifice and animal husbandry in classical Greece", in C.R. Whittaker (ed.), *Pastoral Economies in Classical Antiquity*, Cambridge: Cambridge Philological Society, 87–119.

Janowitz, N. (2001) *Magic in the Roman World: Pagans, Jews and Christians*, London: Routledge.

Jay, N. (1993) *Throughout Your Generation Forever. Sacrifice, Religion, and Paternity*, Chicago and London: University of Chicago Press.

Jensen, R.M. (2000) *Understanding Early Christian Art*, London and New York: Routledge.

Johnson, C. (1999) "Ritual Epicleses in the Greek *Acts of Thomas*", in F. Bovon, A.G. Brock and C.R. Matthews (eds), *The Apocryphal Acts of the Apostles*, Cambridge, Mass.: Harvard University Press, 171–204.

Jonas, H. (1970) *The Gnostic Religion. The Message of the Alien God and the Beginnings of Christianity*, Boston: Beacon Press.

Jones, C.P. (1971) *Plutarch and Rome*, Oxford: Clarendon Press.

Keel, O. (1992) *Das Recht der Bilder gesehen zu werden. Drei Fallstudien zur Methode der Interpretationen altorientalischer Bilder*, Göttingen: Vanderhoeck & Ruprecht.

Keller, O. ({1909/13}) *Die Antike Tierwelt* (Band 1–2), Leipzig: Wilhelm Engelmann.

Kessler, D. (1986) "Tierkult", in *Lexicon der Ägyptologie*, Band VI, Wiesbaden: Otto Harrassowitz, 571–87.

Kindstrand, J. F. (1998) "Claudius Aelianus und sein Werk", in W. Haase and H. Temporini (eds), *ANRW* 34, 4, Berlin and New York: Walter de Gruyter, 2954–96.

Kippenberg, H.G. (1990) "Pseudikonographie: Orpheus auf jüdichen Bildern", *Visible Religion*, vol. 7, Leiden: Brill, 233–49.

Klimkeit, H.-J. (1998) "The fair form, the hideous form and the transformed form: on the form principle in Manichaeism", in M. Heuser and H.-J. Klimkeit (eds), *Studies in Manichaean Literature and Art*, Leiden: Brill, 142–72.

Klingender, F. (1971) *Animals in Art and Thought to the End of the Middle Ages*, London: Routledge.

Kofsky, A. (2000) *Eusebius of Caesarea against Paganism*, Leiden: Brill.

Kötting, B. (1964) "Tier und Heiligtum" in *Mullus. Festschrift Theodor Klauser, Jahrbuch für Antike und Christentum*, 1, Münster in Westfalen: Aschendorffsche Verlagsbuchhandlung, 209–14.

Kövecses, Z. (2002) *Metaphor. A Practical Introduction*. Oxford and New York: Oxford University Press.

Kristensen, W.B. (1971) "The worship of animals", in *The Meaning of Religion: Lectures in the Phenomenology of Religion*, The Hague: Martinus Nijhoff, 152–63.

Kyle, D.G. (1995) "Animal spectacles in ancient Rome", *Nikephoros* 7, 181–205.

Lakoff, G. and M. Johnson (1980) *Metaphors We Live By*, Chicago: University of Chicago Press.

——(1999) *Philosophy in the Flesh. The Embodied Mind and its Challenge to Western Thought*, New York: Basic Books.

Lamberton, R. (2001) *Plutarch*, New Haven, Conn.: Yale University Press.

Lanata, G. (1997) "Thèmes animaliers dans le platonisme moyen: le cas de Celse", in B. Cassin and J.-L. Labarrière (eds), *L'Animal dans l'antiquité*, Paris; Libraire Philosophique J. Vrin, 299–324.

Lancellotti, M.G. (2000) *The Naassenes*, Münster: Ugarit Verlag.

——(2002) *Attis. Between Myth and History: King, Priest and God*, Leiden: Brill.

Lévi-Strauss, C. (1962) *Le Totémism aujourd'hui*, Paris: Presses Universitaires de France.

Lewy, H. and M. Tardeu (1978) *Chaldean Oracles and Theurgy: Mysticism, Magic and Platonism in the Later Roman Empire*, Paris: Études augustiniennes.

Leyerle, B. (2001) *Theatrical Shows and Ascetic Lives*, Berkeley, Los Angeles and London: University of California Press.

Lieu, S.N.C. (1985) *Manichaeism in the Later Roman Empire and Medieval China*, Manchester: Manchester University Press.

Linderski, J. (1982) "Cicero and Roman divination", *La Parola del Passato*, 102, 12–38.

Linzey, A. (1995) *Animal Theology*, Urbana: University of Illinois Press.

Linzey, A. and D. Cohn-Sherbok (1997) *After Noah. Animals and the Liberation of Theology*, London: Mowbray.

Linzey, A. and D. Yamamoto (eds) (1998) *Animals on the Agenda*, London: SCM Press.

Loraux. N. (1993) *The Children of Athena*, Princeton, NJ: Princeton University Press.

Lorblanchet, M. (1989) "From man to animal and sign in Palaeolithic art", in H. Morphy (ed.), *Animals into Art*, London: Unwin Hyman, 109–43.

Lovejoy A.O. and G. Boas (1935) *Primitivism and Related Ideas in Antiquity*, Baltimore: Johns Hopkins University Press.

Luck, G. (1985) *Arcana Mundi: Magic and the Occult in the Greek and Roman Worlds: A Collection of Ancient Texts*, Baltimore: Johns Hopkins University Press.

MacMullen, R. (1981) *Paganism in the Roman Empire*, New Haven, Conn., and London: Yale University Press.

Maguire, H. (1987) *Earth and Ocean. The Terrestrial World in Early Byzantine Art*, University Park and London: Pennsylvania State University Press.

Maier, B. (2000) "Germanisch-keltisches Altertum", in P. Dinzelbacher (ed.), *Mensch und Tier in der Geschichte Europas*, Stuttgart: Alfred Kröner Verlag, 145–80.

Malherbe, A.J. (1968) "The beasts at Ephesus", *Journal of Biblical Literature* 87, 71–80.

Malina, B.J. and J.H. Neyrey (1996) *Portraits of Paul: An Archaeology of Ancient Personality*, Louisville, Ky: Westminster John Knox Press.

Malina, B.J. and J.J. Pilch (2000) *Social-Science Commentary on the Book of Revelation*, Minneapolis: Fortress Press.

Manes, C. (1997) *Other Creations. Rediscovering the Spirituality of Animals*, London and New York: Doubleday.

Marinatos, N. (2000) *The Goddess and the Warrior*, London: Routledge.

Markschies, C. (1999) *Between Two Worlds: Structures of Earliest Christianity*, London: SCM Press.

Martin, D. (1995) *The Corinthian Body*, New Haven, Conn.: Yale University Press.

——(2001) "Oppstandelseslegemets ideologi", in T. Engberg-Pedersen and I.S. Gilhus (eds), *Kropp og oppstandelse*, Oslo: Pax, 24–37.

Mathews, T.F. (1995) *The Clash of Gods. A Reinterpretation of Early Christian Art*, Princeton, NJ: Princeton University Press.

Matthews, C.R. (1999) "Articulated animals: a multivalent motif in the apocryphal Acts of the Apostles", in, F. Bovon, A.G. Brock and C.R. Matthews (eds), *The Apocryphal Acts of the Apostles*, Cambridge, Mass.: Harvard University Press, 205–32.

Matthews, J. (1989) *The Roman Empire of Ammianus*, Baltimore: Johns Hopkins University Press.

McGowan, A. (1999) *Ascetic Eucharist: Food and Drink in Early Christian Ritual Meals*, Oxford and New York: Oxford University Press.

McK. Camp, J., III (1998) *Horses and Horsemanship in the Athenian Agora*, Athen: American School of Classical Studies.

Meeks, W.A. (1983) *The First Urban Christians. The Social World of the Apostle Paul*, New Haven, Conn., London: Yale University Press.

Meredith, A. (1980) "Porphyry and Julian against the Christians", in W. Haase (ed.), *Principat, ANRW*, Berlin and New York: Walter de Gruyter, 1119–49.

Meuli, K. (1946) "Griechische Opferbräuche", in O. Gigon *et al.* (eds), *Phyllobolia*, Basel: Benno Schwabe, 185–288.

Meyboom, P.G.P. (1995) *The Nile Mosaic of Palestrina*, Leiden, New York and Cologne: Brill.

Meyer, J.C. (2002) "Omens, prophecies, and oracles in ancient decision-making formalistic and substantivistic approaches", in V. Gabrielsen (ed.), *Ancient History Matters. Studies*

Presented to Jens Erik Skydsgaard On His Seventieth Birthday (Analecta Romana Instituti Danici Supplementum XXX), Rome: L'Erma di Bretschneider, 173–83..

Meyer, M. and R. Smith (eds) (1994) *Ancient Christian Magic: Coptic Texts of Ritual Power*, San Fransisco: Harper.

Michel, O. (1957) "Hippos" in *Theologisches Wörterbuch zum neuen Testament*, III, Stuttgart: Verlag van W. Kohlhammer, 336–9.

Midgley, M. (1988) "Beasts, brutes and monsters", in T. Ingold (ed.), *What is an Animal?* London: Unwin Hyman, 35–46.

——(1995) *Beast and Man. The Roots of Human Nature*, London and New York: Routledge.

Mikaelsson, L. (1980) "Sexual polarity. An aspect of the ideological structure in the paradise narration, Gen. 2,4–3,24", *Temenos* 16, 84–91.

Millar, F. (1981) "The world of the golden ass", *The Journal of Roman Studies* 71, 63–75.

Miller, P.C. (2001) *The Poetry of Thought in Late Antiquity*, Aldershot, UK: Ashgate.

Morenz, S. (1960) *Ägyptische Religion*, Stuttgart: Kohlhammer Verlag.

Morphy, H. (ed.) (1989) *Animals into Art*, London: Unwin Hyman.

Murray, P. (1998) "Bodies in flux: Ovid's *Metamorphoses*", in D. Monyserrat (ed.), *Changing Bodies, Changing Meanings. Studies in the Human Body in Antiquity*, London: Routledge.

Murray, S.C. (1981) *Rebirth and Afterlife. A Study of the Transmutation of Some Pagan Imagery in Early Christian Funerary Art*, International series 100, Oxford: BAR.

Nikolaidis, A.G. and Rethymnon (1986) "'*Ellenikós – Barbarikós*. Plutarch on Greek and barbarian characteristics", *Wiener Studien*, 20 (Neue Folge), 229–44.

North, J. (1990) "Diviners and divination at Rome", in M. Beard and J. North (eds), *Pagan Priests*, London: Duckworth, 49–71.

Obbink, D. (1988) "The origin of Greek sacrifice: Theophrastus on religion and cultural history", in W.W. Fortenbough and R.W. Shaples (eds), *Theophrastian Studies*, vol. III, New Brunswick, NJ, and Oxford: Transaction Books, 272–95.

Ogilvie, R.M. (1986) *The Romans and their Gods*, London: Hogarth Press.

Ortner, S.B. (1979) "On key symbols", in W.A. Lessa and E.Z. Vogt (eds), *Research in Comparative Religion*, New York and London: Harper & Row, 92–8.

Painchaud, L. (1983) *Fragment de La République de Platon (NH VI,5). Bibliothèque copte de Nag Hammadi*, Québec: Les Presses de l'Université Laval.

——(1995) *L'écrit sans titre: traité sur l'origine du monde. (NH II, 5 et XIII, 2 et Brit. Lib. Or. 4926{1}), avec deux contributions de Wolf-Peter Funk, Bibliothèque copte de Nag Hammadi*, Section Textes, 21, Québec: Les Presses de l'Université Laval.

Perkins, J. (1995) *The Suffering Self. Pain and Narrative Representations in the Early Christian Era*, London and New York: Routledge.

Pesthy, M. (1996) "Thecla among the fathers of the Church", in J. Bremmer (ed.), *The Apocryphal Acts of Paul and Thecla*, Netherlands: Pharos, 164–78.

Pohlenz, M. (1948) *Die Stoa. Geschichte einer geistigen Bewegung*, Göttingen: Vandenhoeck & Ruprecht.

Potter, D.S. (1993) "Martyrdom as spectacle", in R. Scodel (ed.), *Theater and Society in the Classical World*, Ann Arbor: University of Michigan Press, 53–88.

——(2002) "Odor and power in the Roman Empire", in J.I. Porter (ed.), *Constructions of the Classical Body*, Ann Arbor: University of Michigan Press, 169–89.

Potter, D.S. and D.J. Mattingly (1999) *Life, Death, and Entertainment in the Roman Empire*, Ann Arbor: University of Michigan Press.

Poulsen, P.W. (2002–3) "Divination og politisk magt. Transformationer i romersk religion 2. årh. F. Kr. – 1. årh. e. Kr.", unpublished paper, Copenhagen.

Pourkier, A. (1992) *L'Hérésiologie chez Épiphane de Salamine*, Paris: Beauchesne.

Presicce, C.P. (2000) *La Lupa Capitolina*, Rome: Musei Capitolina.

Price, S.R.F. (1999): "Latin Christian apologetics", in M. Edwards, M. Goodman and S. Price (eds), *Apologetics in the Roman Empire: Pagans, Jews, and Christians*, Oxford: Oxford University Press, 105–29.

Price, S.R.F. (1986) *Rituals and Power. The Roman Imperial Cult in Asia Minor*, Cambridge: Cambridge University Press.

Prieur, J. (1988) *Les animaux sacrés dans l'antiquité*, Rennes: Ouest France.

Prigent, P. (2001) *Commentary on the Apocalypse of St. John*, Stuttgart: Mohr Siebeck.

Purcell, N. (1995) "Eating fish: the paradoxes of seafood", in J. Wilking, D. Harvey and M. Dobson (eds), *Food in Antiquity*, Exeter: University of Exeter Press, 132–49.

Regan, T. (1983) *The Case for Animal Rights*, USA: University of California Press.

Riddehough, G.B. (1959) "Man-into-beast changes in Ovid", *The Phoenix* 13, 4, 201–9.

Riedweg, C. (2002) *Pythagoras. Leben-Lehre-Nachwirkung*, Munich: C.H. Beck.

Ritner, R.K. (1989) "Horus on the crocodiles: a juncture of religion and magic in late dynastic Egypt", in *Religion and Philosophy in Ancient Egypt*, Yale Egyptological Studies 3, 103–16.

Rives, J. (1995) "Human sacrifice among pagans and Christians", *Journal of Roman Studies* 85, 65–85.

——(2000) "Religion in the Roman Empire", in J. Huskinson (ed.), *Experiencing Rome*, London: Routledge.

Robinson, O.F. (1994) *Ancient Rome: City Planning and Administration*, London and New York: Routledge.

Roller, L.E. (1999) *In Search of God the Mother: The Cult of Anatolian Cybele*, Berkeley, Calif.: University of California Press.

Roueché, C. (1993) *Performers and Partisans at Aphrodisias in the Roman and Late Roman Periods*, London: Society for the Promotion of Roman Studies.

Rousselle, A. (1988) *Porneia: On Desire and the Body in Antiquity*, Oxford: Basil Blackwell.

Rubenson, S. (1995) *The Letters of St Antony: Monasticism and the Making of a Saint. Studies in Antiquity and Christianity*, Minneapolis: Fortress Press.

Rüpke, J. (2001) *Die Religion der Römer*, Munich: C.H. Beck.

Rutter, J.B. (1968) "The three phases of the taurobolium", *The Phoenix* 22, 3, 226–49.

Sabbah, G. (2003) "Ammianus Marcellinus", in G. Marasco (ed.), *Greek and Roman Historiography in Late Antiquity*, Leiden: Brill, 43–84.

Saddington, D.B. (1987) "St Ignatius, leopards, and the Roman army", *Journal of Theological Studies* 38, 411–12.

Salisbury, J. (1994) *The Beast Within: Animals in the Middle Ages*, New York and London: Routledge.

——(1997) *Perpetua's Passion: The Death and Memory of a Young Roman Woman*, London and New York: Routledge.

Schiebe, M.W. (1981) *Das ideale Dasein bei Tibull und die Goldzeitkonzeption Vergils. Acta Universitas Upsaliensis*, Studia Latina Upsaliensis 13, Stockholm.

——(2004) "Sheep and cattle as ideological markers in Roman poetry", in B.S. Frizell (ed.), *PECUS. Man and Animal in Antiquity*, Rome: Swedish Institute in Rome.

Schneemelcher, W. (1964) "Der getaufte Löwe in den Acta Pauli", in *Mullus. Festschrift Theodor Klauser. Jahrbuch für Antike und Christentum* 1, Münster: Aschendorffsche Verlagsbuchhandlung, 316–26.

Schneider, H. (2001) "Thekla und die Robben", *Vigiliae Christianae* 55, 45–57.

Schoeps, H.J. (1957) "Bemerkungen zu Reinkarnationsvorstellungen der Gnosis", *Numen* 4, 228–32.

Schuster, M. (1917) *Untersuchungen zu Plutarchs Dialog De sollertia animalium mit besonderer Berücksichtigung der Lehrtätigkeit Plutarchs.* Augsburg: Buch und Kunstdruckerei J.P. Himmer.

Scott, A. (2002) "Zoological marvel and exegetical method in Origen and the *Physiologus*", in C.A. Bobertz and D. Brakke (eds), *Reading in the Christian Communities*, Notre Dame, Ind.: University of Notre Dame Press, 80–9.

Scott, B.B. (1990) *Hear then the Parable. A Commentary on the Parables of Jesus*, Minneapolis: Fortress Press.

Segal, C. (1969) "Myth and philosophy in the *Metamorphoses*. Ovid's Augustanism and the Augustan conclusion of Book XV", *American Journal of Philology* 90, 3, 257–92.

Serpell, J. (1996) *In the Company of Animals: A Study of Human–Animal Relationships*, Cambridge: Cambridge University Press.

Shaw, B.D. (1996) "Body/power/identity: passions of the martyrs", *Journal of Early Christian Studies* 4, 3, 269–312.

Shaw, G. (1985) "Theurgy: rituals of unification in the Neoplatonism of Iamblichus", *Traditio* 41, 1–28.

——(1995) *Theurgy and the Soul. The Neoplatonism of Iamblichus*, Philadelphia: Pennsylvania State University Press.

Shelton, J.-A. (1996), "Lucretius on the use and abuse of animals", *Eranos* 94, 48–64.

Shumate, N. (1996) *Crisis and Conversion in Apuleius' Metamorphoses*, Ann Arbor: University of Michigan Press.

Silverman, D.B. (1991) "Divinity and deities in ancient Egypt", in B.E. Shafer (ed.), *Religion in Ancient Egypt. Gods, Myths, and Personal Practice*, London: Routledge, 7–87.

Simmons, M.B. (1995) *Arnobius of Sicca. Religious Conflict and Competition in the Age of Diocletian*, Oxford: Clarendon Press.

Singer, P. (1975) *Animal Liberation. A New Ethics for our Treatment of Animals*, London: Random House.

Sissa, G. and M. Detienne (2000) *The Daily Life of the Greek Gods*, Stanford, Calif.: Stanford University Press.

Slater, R.N. (1999) "An inquiry into the relationship between community and text: the apocryphal *Acts of Philip* 1 and the encratites of Asia Minor", in F. Bovon, A.G. Brock and C.R. Matthews (eds), *The Apocryphal Acts of the Apostles*, Cambridge, Mass.: Harvard University Press, 282–306.

Smagina, E. (2001) "Das Manichäische Kreuz des Lichts und der *Jesus Patibilis*," in J. van Oort, O Wermelinger and G. Wurst (eds), *Augustine and Manichaeism in the Latin West*, Leiden: Brill, 243–9.

Smelik, K.A.D. (1979) "The cult of the ibis in the Graeco-Roman period", in M.J. Vermaseren (ed.), *Studies in Hellenistic Religions*, Leiden: Brill, 225–43.

Smelik, K.A.D. and E.A. Hemelrijk (1984) "'Who knows not what monsters demented Egypt worships?' Opinions on Egyptian animal worship in antiquity as part of the ancient conception of Egypt", *Aufstieg und Niedergang der Römischen Welt* 17, 4, Berlin and New York: Walter de Gruyter, 1852–2357.

Smith, A. (1984) "Did Porphyry reject the transmigration of human souls into animals?" *Rheinisches Museum* 127, 276–84.

Smith, J.Z. (1978) "Towards interpreting demonic powers in Hellenistic and Roman antiquity", *ANRW* II, Berlin and New York: Walter de Gruyter, 425–39.

——(1987) "The domestication of sacrifice", in R.G. Hammerton-Kelly (ed.), *Violent Origins: Walter Burkert, René Girard and Jonathan Z. Smith on Ritual Killing and Cultural Formation*, Stanford, Calif.: Stanford University Press, 191–205.

Smith, R. (1998) "Telling tales: Ammianus' narrative of the Persian expedition of Julian", in J.W. Drijvers and D. Hunt (eds), *The Late Roman World and its Historian. Interpreting Ammianus Marcellinus*, London and New York: Routledge 89–104.

Snyder, G.F. (1991) *Ante Pacem: Archaeological Evidence of Church Life before Constantine*, USA: Mercer University Press.

Solodow, J.B. (1988) *The World of Ovid's Metamorphoses*, Chapel Hill and London: University of North Carolina Press.

Sorabji, R. (1993) *Animal Minds and Human Morals: The Origins of the Western Debate*, London: Duckworth.

Spaeth, B.S. (1996) *The Roman Goddess Ceres*, Austin: University of Texas Press.

Speidel, M.P. (1994) *Riding for Caesar. The Roman Emperor's Horse Guards*, Cambridge, Mass.: Harvard University Press.

Stowers, S.K. (1995) "Greeks who sacrifice and those who do not: towards an anthropology of Greek religion", in L.M. White and O.L. Yarbrough (eds), *The Social World of the First Christians. Essays in Honor of Wayne A. Meeks*, Minneapolis: Fortress Press, 293–333.

Stowers, S.K. (2001) "Does Pauline Christianity resemble a Hellenistic philosophy?", in T. Engberg-Pedersen (ed.), *Paul Beyond the Judaism/Hellenism Divide*, Louisville, Ky: Westminster John Knox Press, 81–102.

van Straten, F.T. (1995) *Hiera Kala: Images of Animal Sacrifice in Archaic and Classical Greece*, Leiden: Brill.

Stroumsa, G.G. (1998) "Tertullian on idolatry and the limits of tolerance", in G.N. Stanton and G.G. Stroumsa (eds), *Tolerance and Intolerance in Early Judaism and Christianity*, Cambridge: Cambridge University Press, 173–84.

Tammisto, A. (1997) *Birds in Mosaics*, Acta Instituti Romani Finlandiae, vol. 18, Rome.

Tardieu, M. (1974) *Trois mythes gnostiques: Adam, Éros et les animaux d'Égypte dans un écrit de Nag Hammadi (II, 5)*, Paris: Études augustiniennes.

Teeter, E. (2002) "Animals in Egyptian religion", in B.J. Collins (ed.), *A History of the Animal World in the Ancient Near East*, Leiden: Brill, 335–60.

Telfer, W. (ed.) (1955) *Cyril of Jerusalem and Nemesius of Emesa*, London: SCM Press.

Terian, A. (1981) *Philonis Alexandrini, De Animalibus. The Armenian Text with an Introduction, Translation and Commentary*, Chico, Calif.: Scholars Press.

te Velde, H. (1977) "A few remarks upon the religious significance of animals in ancient Egypt," *Numen* 27, 1, 76–82.

Thissen, H.J. (2001) *Des Niloten Horapollon Hieroglyphen-Buch*, Band. I. text und Übersetzung, Munich and Leipzig: K.G. Saur, viii–xxii.

Thomas, K. (1984) *Man and the Natural World: Changing Attitudes in England 1500–1800*, London and New York: Penguin.

Thomassen, E. (2005) "Sacrifice: ritual murder or dinner party?" in H. Whittaker (ed.), *Celebrations* (in press).

Thornton, B.S. (1997) *Eros. The Myth of Ancient Greek Sexuality*, Boulder, Col.: Westview Press.

Tiller, P.A. (1993) *A Commentary on the Animal Apocalypse of I Enoch*, Atlanta: Scholars Press.

Tilley, M.A. (1993) "Martyrs, monks, insects, and animals", in J.E. Salisbury (ed.), *The Medieval World of Nature*, New York and London: Garland, 93–107.

Toynbee, J.M.C. (1996) *Animals in Roman Life and Art*, Baltimore and London: Johns Hopkins University Press.

Trout, D.E. (1995) "Christianizing the Nolan countryside: animal sacrifice at the tomb of St. Felix", *Journal of Early Christian Studies* 3, 3, 281–98.

——(1999) *Paulinus of Nola. Life, Letters, and Poems*, Berkeley, Los Angeles and London: University of California Press.

Tsekourakis, D. (1987) "Pythagoreanism or Platonism and ancient medicine? The reasons for vegetarianism in Plutarch's *Moralia*", in *Aufstieg und Niedergang der Römischer Welt*, Teil II: *Principat* 36, 1, Berlin and New York: Walter de Gruyter, 366–93.

Turcan, R. (1996) *The Cults of the Roman Empire*, Oxford: Basil Blackwell.

Tylor, E.B. (1979) *Primitive Culture*, New York: Gordon Press.

Ulansay, D. (1987) "Mithraic studies: a paradigm shift?" *Religious Studies Review* 13, 2, 104–10.

——(1989) *The Origins of the Mithraic Mysteries: Cosmology and Salvation in the Ancient World*, New York and Oxford: Oxford University Press.

Undheim, S. (2001) "Vestalinnenes jomfrudom", masters thesis, University of Oslo.

Valantasis, R. (1992) "Demons and the perfecting of the monk's body: monastic, anthropology, daemonology, and asceticism," *Semeia* 58, 49–79.

——(1997) *The Gospel of Thomas*, London and New York: Routledge.

——(2001a) "Demons, adversaries, devils, fishermen: the asceticism of *Authoritative Teaching* (NHL. VI.3) in the context of Roman asceticism", *Journal of Religion* 81, 549–65.

——(2001b) "Nag Hammadi and asceticism: theory and practice", in *Studia Patristica* 35, Leuven: Peeters, 172–90.

Vallée, G. (1981) *A Study in Anti-Gnostic Polemics*, Canada: Wilfried Laurier University Press.

Vermaseren, M.J. (ed.) (1956–60) *Corpus Inscriptionum et Monumentorum Religionis Mithriacae*, The Hague: Martinus Nijhoff.

Vernant, J.-P. (1991) *Mortals and Immortals: Collected Essays*, Princeton, NJ: Princeton University Press.

Victor, U. (1997) *Lukian von Samosata: Alexandros oder der Lügenprophet*, Leiden: Brill.

Ville, G. (1981) *La Gladiature en occident des origines à la mort de Domitien*, Rome: École française de Rome.

Volkommer, R. (1998) "Herakles als Bezwinger von (Un)Tieren in der römischen Kunst", in C. Bonnet, C. Jourdain-Annequin and V. Pirenne-Delforge (eds), *Le Bestiaire d'Héraclès, Kernos*, Supplement 7, Liege, 87–107.

Vörös, G. (2001) *Taposiris Magna. Port of Isis: Hungarian Excavations at Alexandria (1998–2001)*, Budapest: Egypt Excavation Society of Hungary.

Wagner, W.H. (1994) *After the Apostles: Christianity in the Second Century*, Minneapolis: Fortress Press.

Walker, R.E. (1996) "Roman veterinary medicine", in J.M.C. Toynbee (ed.), *Animals in Roman Life and Art*, Baltimore and London: Johns Hopkins University Press, 303–16.

Wallace-Hadrill, D.S. (1968) *The Greek Patristic View of Nature*, Manchester and New York: Manchester University Press / Barnes & Noble.

Wallis, R.T. (1972) *Neoplatonism*, London: Duckworth.

Warmind, M.L. (1989) "Holdninger til nyreligiøse i fortid og nåtid", *Chaos* 12, 17–23.

Welburn, A.J. (1978) "The identity of the archons in the 'Apocryphon Johannis'", *Vigiliae Christianae* 32, 241–54.

Wiedemann, T.E.J. (1986) "Between men and beasts: barbarians in Ammianus Marcellinus", in I.S. Moxon, J.D. Smart and A.J. Woodman (eds), *Past Perspectives: Studies in Greek and Roman Historical Writing*, Cambridge: Cambridge University Press, 1989–201.

Wiedemann, T.E.J. (1995) *Emperors and Gladiators*, New York and London: Routledge.

Wilken, R.L. (1984): *The Christians as the Romans Saw Them*, New Haven, Conn., and London: Yale University Press.

Wilkins, J. *et al.* (1995) *Food in Antiquity*, Exeter: Exeter University Press.

Williams, D.J. (1999) *Paul's Metaphors. Their Context and Character*, London: Hendrickson Publishers.

Williams, F. (1987/1994) "Epiphanius. The Panarion of Epiphanius of Salamis", *Nag Hammadi Studies* 35, Leiden: Brill.

Williams, M. (1996) *Rethinking "Gnosticism": An Argument for Dismantling a Dubious Category*, Princeton, NJ: Princeton University Press.

Willis, R. (ed.) (1994) *Signifying Animals: Human Meaning in the Natural World*, London and New York: Routledge.

Winkler, J.J. (1985) *Auctor & Actor*, Los Angeles: University of California Press.

Wistrand, M. (1992) *Entertainment and Violence in Ancient Rome*, Gothenburg: Acta Universitatis Gothoburgensis.

Zandee, J. (1981) "'The Teachings of Silvanus' (NHC VII, 4) and Jewish Christianity", in R. van den Broek and M.J. Vermasern (eds), *Studies in Gnosticism and Hellenistic Religions*, Leiden: Brill, 498–584.

——(1991) *The Teachings of Sylvanus (Nag Hammadi Codex VII, 4)*, text, translation and commentary, Leiden: Nederlands Instituut voor het Nabije Oosten.

Zeuner, F.E. (1963) *A History of Domesticated Animals*, London: Hutchinson.

INDEX